A Place Called Belmont

by
Jerry Martin

Publisher
South Tishomingo County Historical Society
P.O. Box 1206
Belmont, MS 38827

Copyright 1978 Jerry Martin
Copyright 2018, Town of Belmont
All rights reserved

40th Anniversary Edition 2018

Library of Congress Catalog Card Number: 78-61091

Printed in the United States of America

CONTENTS

	Page
LIST OF ILLUSTRATIONS AND MAPS	iv
INTRODUCTION	x
FOREWARD	xi
PREFACE	xii
ACKNOWLEDGEMENTS	xiii

Chapter
1. THIS EARTH, THIS PLACE, THIS BELMONT 1
2. INDIANS AND TREATIES 9
3. EARLY SETTLERS AND SETTLEMENTS 17
4. HEYDAYS OF BAY SPRINGS 28
5. CIVIL WAR AND ITS AFTERMATH 37
6. THE TROUBLED 1870'S 49
7. THE EMERGENCE OF BELMONT 57
8. DAWNING OF THE TWENTIETH CENTURY 77
9. THE COMING OF THE RAILROAD 85
10. THE SQUIRE SHOOK ERA 109
11. GROWING UP DESPITE WAR WITH THE HUNS 131
12. PEACETIME ADJUSTMENTS 147
13. NEW HEIGHTS OF PROSPERITY 161
14. DEPRESSION GLOOM 179
15. BOILING WAR CLOUDS 201
16. AN AGE OF ANXIETY AND EXPANSION 213
17. GROWING WITH THE TIMES 219
18. GROWING PAINS 227
19. ON THE VERGE 241

BIBLIOGRAPHY 261
INDEX 264

LIST OF ILLUSTRATIONS AND MAPS

Map of early settlements in present south Tishomingo County 16

James Files Gresham..36

Map of southern Tishomingo County, including land added from
Itawamba County..51

Dr. M. M. (Mid) Davis, the first Belmont postmaster in 1873..................53

The Bay Springs Masonic Lodge...56

Confederate Veterans Reunion at Bay Springs..60

Remains of the factory and dam on Mackey's Creek at Bay Springs
in the late 1800's...61

Singing School at Liberty in the 1890's..65

The M. M. Davis home in what was to become Belmont.........................78

Patterson Chapel School group in the 1901-1902 term.............................84

New Bethel School group in the early 1900's...84

Charlie Flurry, Dennis rural mail carrier for many years.........................88

Stapps Writing School at "Ebenezer School" in Belmont.........................89

Students and teachers at Belmont Public Free School (Ebenezer
School) about 1907..90

M.M. Davis and Son Store..92

M. L. Harris home in Belmont..92

F. L. (Finess) Harris and his wife, Anna Harris..96

Map of the Noel Survey in Belmont in 1907..97

Map of Golden in 1907..99

The store of L. R. Davis in Dennis in 1904..100

Map of Dennis in 1907..101

The early Dennis Depot..102

The memorable "Doodlebug"..103

The Belmont Depot..104

Construction on the W. T. Ferguson home in Belmont
about 1909...105

Downtown Belmont about 1910...106

Squire C. C. Shook, the first mayor of Belmont...................................108

Wright and Winsett store in early Golden..111

View north up the railroad from Golden..112

Charlie Wofford sorghum mill in Golden...112

The new school building of Belmont Separate School
about 1909...114

Belmont school group about 1909 or 1910.......................................114

Belmont Drug Company, reportedly the first drug store in Belmont..........117

A gathering of downtown Belmontians around 1909............................118

Confederate Veterans Reunion at Bay Springs about 1910....................121

Belmont Concert Band in session..122

Early Belmont scene at the junction of Main Street and Front Street
near the depot...124

View of early Belmont from the depot westward up Main Street.............125

Main Street in downtown Belmont facing east...................................126

Several early Belmontians gathered in front of Allen-Wright Hardware
and Furniture Company..130

Mrs. Lucy Fugitt at the switchboard of Union Telephone Company
In Belmont 132

Dr. L. S. Greene, cashier of The Bank of Belmont around 1913.............134

Third Street view of Main Street in downtown Belmont in 1916............139

First Baptist Church baptism scene at Yarber Pond about 1921.............155

Belmont school building construction about 1922..................................157

The H. M. Shook building, home of Shook Brothers Supply Company.....159

Belmont school group in 1925..160

Inside view of the Allen-Wright Hardware and Furniture Company........167

Singing School at the Hartford Musical Institute of Valley School
in the 1920's..167

The shoe shop of A. G. W. Bryam in Belmont 170

Mrs. Luna C. Davis and several elementary school students at Belmont
about 1925-1926..171

The Golden Saw Mill..174

Golden Saw Mill employees around 1926...175

Main Street in downtown Belmont in 1929...177

South Tishomingo School group about 1929-1930..................................178

Belmont school group in the early 1930's..186

Dennis mayor, E. W. Smith, and Hardie Moore in front of the Smith
Store in Dennis in the late 1930's...201

The "rolling store" of Hugh Nichols at Dennis..202

Casual scene at the Dennis depot in the late 1930's............................202

Kirk Crabb, Dennis rural mail carrier..202

John Crabb, Dennis merchant, in front of his store...............................203

O. H. Byram, a long-time Dennis merchant..203

Mrs. Kate Campbell, Dennis postmaster for many years......................203

Thomas Oscar Lindsey, rural mail carrier at Dennis.............................203

Masons at the 100th anniversary of Bay Springs F. & A.M. Lodge No. 167 in 1953...221

Site of the new high school-administration building on the east side of School Drive in Belmont 224

Map of Belmont in the early 1970's..240

The Belmont depot in early Belmont...249

View in 1978 of the restored Belmont depot...249

View in 1978 from Main Street of Highway 25 (2nd Street) In Belmont..250

Eastward view toward the railroad of Main Street in downtown Belmont in 1978..250

1978 view of Main Street in downtown Belmont from Third Street......251

View of Belmont in 1978 eastward from the junction of Highway 25 (2nd Street) and Main Street...251

View of Belmont in 1978 from the corner of Main Street and Highway 25 (2nd Street)..252

Westward view of Belmont Main Street in 1978 from the railroad and the old Belmont depot site..252

The restored Belmont depot in beautiful Belmont Blue Springs
City Park..253

Belmont City Hall in 1978..253

Map of section, township, and range location of land in the southern
part of Tishomingo County..254

Sketch of the southern part of present Tishomingo County........................255

Map of streams of the Belmont area..256

Map of schools of the Belmont area..257

Map of cemeteries located in the Belmont area..258

Map of post offices of the Belmont area...259

Mayors of Belmont, Mississippi..260

To my parents,

Bill Martin and Eura Martin,

and

to

all Belmontians everywhere

INTRODUCTION

Once in a great while, a person of gifted intelligence, and attitude of service and a sense of lasting good come along. Such was Jerry Martin.

I was privileged to know Jerry for many of his all too few years. I did know him well enough to offer my comments on a life, though short, was very well lived. It is indeed a high honor and humbling experience to present an introduction to the reprinting of Jerry Martin's, **A Place Called Belmont.**

Jerry's book was published in 1978. It chronicled the history of "Beautiful Mountain" and the surrounding area from prehistoric times to the date of the publication. It is a time odyssey for all to enjoy.

Jerry's intelligence was off the scale. His determination to be accurate and comprehensive was just as impressive. Regretfully, Jerry did not live to see the magnitude of the monumental favor he has done for his beloved Belmont. Thankfully, the younger generation has discovered this treasure- a rightful tribute well deserved.

Purchasers of this reissue need to be reminded that Jerry did not just write a book. He served the area in many, many ways. He helped organize the first chapter of the Jaycees. He wrote a play that was presented by the Belmont High School Senior Class of 1966. He, perhaps more than anyone else, was responsible for preserving the original railroad depot building and having it reassembled, plank-by-plank at its present location in Blue Springs Park. He served many years as scorekeeper for Belmont High sports. He coached little league baseball. He did substitute teaching, more than capably, on many occasions. He tutored numerous college students. He was selected to the Hall of Fame at Northeast Mississippi Community College.

It has long been a dream of many locals to see Jerry's book reprinted. For us, that dream is a reality you are holding in your hands. Many thanks to Martha Martin Brown for granting rights to reprint her brother's book. Stephanie Holder, Patti Cook, and Becky Paden have contributed countless hours in bringing this historic project to fruition.

As you read the pages and enjoy the photographs, please say a thank you, in memorial, to Jerry Martin for this priceless gift to the place not just on the map but in his heart and ours. Enjoy!

Belmont, Mississippi   Jerry McAnally

May 2018

FOREWARD

A Place Called Belmont is an account of the earliest years of this town through the many years of growth up to the present time. The substance of this book has been taken from old newspapers, records, deeds, snatches of conversation, and memories recalled by many lifetime citizens.

The author, Jerry Martin, has spent untold hours of research and contacting people who could give him factual information. He would be the first to tell you that he does not claim to be a professional writer, but in his own style he has presented these facts, incidents, and history in a very unique way.

Being the granddaughter of the late Mr. and Mrs. C. C. Shook, I have many memories of hearing my mother reminisce about the early days of Belmont; and she was happy to relate to anyone details and facts of this town so dearly loved by its residents.

This book is notable for the remembrance of things past and the hope of better days in the future. It is the desire of the author to present to you an account of this place called Belmont so that you will appreciate it even more – and this I believe he has done.

Ruth S. Fulton

PREFACE

A Place Called Belmont is simply the result of my love for my home town, Belmont, Mississippi, and my appreciation to those who helped make our proud Belmont heritage. In my researching and interviews, I have found that I am several decades late because much valuable information is destroyed forever; and most of our early Belmontians have passed away. Still, I have worked diligently in the available time of the last two years to gather enough information to do justice to the history of Belmont.

The names of many individuals are used to tell the march of events in this book. Others who are not mentioned may have been more important at times. This book was written based on the names and events contained in research material, interviews, letters, and daily chats with many people. If anyone should take exception to any part of the book, an apology will be forthcoming if necessary. If anyone or any company deems that further credit needs to be given, a sincere, positive response will follow. After all, an earnest effort has been made to include as many people, organizations, and events as available information and the scope of this book would reasonably and economically permit.

My sincere hope is that **A Place Called Belmont** will arouse many nostalgic memories of the Belmont heritage and will encourage many of our young people to appreciate their heritage even more. Hopefully, many others who read the book will become interested enough in Belmont, Mississippi, to visit our peaceful, friendly town and enjoy the history that is unfolding daily.

Belmont, Mississippi   Jerry Martin

May 10, 1978

ACKNOWLEDGEMENTS

So many people have done so many things to help me in making this book a reality. The photographic copying and assistance of R.C. Robbins of Golden is certainly appreciated.

First Citizens National Bank and Winfield Manufacturing Company in Belmont courteously helped in making copies of book material for me. The valuable assistance, constructive criticism, and encouragement of Dr. George L. Robson, Jr. of Mississippi State University are sincerely appreciated. To Ruth S. Fulton, my gratitude is extended for every meaningful suggestions, proofreading, and the foreword.

The library staffs at Belmont, Corinth, Iuka, Tupelo, Aberdeen, and Mitchell Memorial Library at Mississippi State University were very helpful in my research efforts. Tishomingo County chancery clerk, Robert Sims, and his staff were friendly and very helpful in my research. Appreciation is also extended to the chancery clerks and their staffs in Itawamba County, Prentiss County, and Alcorn County for their co-operative assistance. The courtesies extended to me during my days of research at City Hall in Belmont enabled me to gain information necessary to making this book become a reality. Furthermore, the information from the Mississippi Department of Archives and History is graciously appreciated. The National Archives furnished important information along with many others listed in the bibliography.

For others valuable information, pictures, old letters, or assistance in many other ways, I express my sincere appreciation to the following: Mrs. Bertie Tayor, Mrs. Ethel Hurd, Mrs. Ruth Fulton, Mrs. Myrtle Shook, Cecil L. Sumners, Luther Jackson, C. W. Baley, Jr., Mrs. Louise Clark, Mr. and Mrs. Floyd T. Shook, Mrs. Claire Griffin, Mr. and Mrs W. Elbridge Epps, Mrs. Maudie Osbirn, Mrs. Eula Long, Mr. and Mrs. W. R. Akers, Mrs. Rachel Epps Winchester, Mr. and Mrs. Herbert Woodruff, Mrs. Olivia Wood, Mrs. Arah Ivy, Mrs. Evie Cleveland, Mrs. Irene Barnes, Mr. and Mrs. John Trollinger, Carroll Yarber, Raymond Yarber, Paul Allen, Mr. and Mrs. Bill Martin, C. W. Stephens, Mrs. Jo Wright, Miss Mary Hunnicutt, N. C. Deaton, Mr. and Mrs. J. T. Lindsey, L. G. Phillips, Mrs. Hallie Yarber, Mr. and Mrs. E. R. Warren, Mr. and Mrs. Irby Shook, Miss Beulah Warren, Will Clark, Mrs. Mary Morgan, Mrs. Viola Hicks, E. C. Clark, Mrs. Rae Yarber, Miss Jewell Shook, Mrs. Forest Wright, Mrs. Helen Yarber, Mrs. Frances Graham, Mrs. Marie Searcy, Mrs. Jeanetter Mann, Turner Harris, H. R. Davis, M. P. Haynes, A. B. Campbell, Tom Thrasher, Donnie Epps, Mrs. Lera Dollar, Mr. And Mrs. O. E. Bostick, Roy P. Allen, Nathan Wigginton, Mrs. Archie Bell Shook, O. T. Eaton,

C. O. Mitchell, Mrs. Ruby Byram, Mrs. Mary Alexander, Dexter Montgomery, Grady White, Mrs. Ora Northington, Mrs. Cary Poche, Kendle Robinson, Howard Johnson, Miss Gertrude Ozbirn, Mrs. Carrie Moore, Mrs. Fannie Johnson, Noel Caveness, John Caveness, Jr., Mr. and Mrs. A. C. Hammett, Mrs. Loris Long, Bob Yarber, Mrs. Mae Bess Yarber, J.B. Strickland, Mrs. Lourie Allen, Mr. and Mrs. Dallas Wigginton, Mrs. Edna Flurry, Mrs. Eva Spradley, Joe K. Vaughn, Lealon Yarber, Freed Lindsey, Billy Martin, J. R. Martin, Mrs. Fae French, Mrs. Flossie Hollingsworth, Mrs. Lalla Allen, Jim Wall, T. J. Cook, Dr. Webster Cleveland, Jr., K. E. Mayhall, C. D. Rogers, Hoyle Payne, Mrs. Clesta Taylor, Mrs. Edna McCormack, Mrs. Sephyr Choate, Mrs. Jean Lambert, Mrs. Ada Dean, Miss Victoria Pharr, Mrs. Effie Northcutt, Mrs. Bonnie Johnson, Mrs. Thelma Allen, Steve Cain, Dexter Mann, Edward Chumbley, Waymon Fancher, Jackie Senter, Mrs. Beatrice Joslin, Mrs. Evie Hallmark, Mrs. Amelia Ginn, Miss Bessie Montgomery, Mrs. Evelyn Cranford, Mrs. Fonza Smith, Mrs. Ila Shewbart, Dr. Gaston Shook, Bill Paden, Mrs. Margaret Rogers, Charles Bostick, Thomas M. Duncan, John L. Hallmark, James Tesseneer, O. M. Cain, J. W. Davis, L. A. Slayton, G. L. Wiltshire, Claude Stacy, L. C. McAnally, Brooks Ables, H. R. Byram, B. F. Moreland, Mrs. Ollie Ables, Williber Hall, Roy Henley, Brooks Holcomb, Mrs. W. O. Smith, Mrs. Maggie Hayes, Mrs. Paul Dobbins, Mrs. R. M. Caruthers, Mrs. Eudora Kemp, Emory Jones, and many, many others too numerous to continue to mention who know, like I do, that their efforts and information on behalf of this book are also sincerely appreciated.

Reprint Notice

For the reader's convenience and to aid in referencing, the content on each page and the total number of pages are the same in both the original print and the reprinted version. Margins on pages have been altered at times to fit the page.

CHAPTER 1

THIS EARTH, THIS PLACE, THIS BELMONT

Yes, good people, there is a place called Belmont. "This place, this Belmont" prospers in Mississippi and is my home town. If you have never been to my home town – Belmont, Mississippi –you have missed a very memorable experience. Belmont is a neat, friendly town of approximately 1,500 basically good, God-fearing people and is located in the southern part of Tishomingo County in the northeastern hill section of Mississippi. The Alabama line is only about 6 miles easterly from Belmont near Red Bay, Alabama.

Our location is approximately 124 miles from Birmingham, Alabama; 129 miles from Memphis, Tennessee; and 216 miles from Nashville, Tennessee. Area distance relationships to Belmont reveal generally that we are about 40 miles south of Pickwick Lake, 43 miles southeast of Corinth, 22 miles south of Iuka, 8 miles south of Tishomingo, 3 ½ miles south of Dennis, 10 miles southeast of Bay Springs, 28 miles southeast of Booneville, 2 miles northwest of downtown Golden, 22 miles northeast of Fulton, and 42 miles northeast of Tupelo. The state capital, Jackson, is about a 225 mile drive from here.

Actually, Belmont involves more than its corporate limits. It is the hub of the Tishomingo County Fifth District and a trade center for surrounding communities like Golden, Dennis, Valley, Old Bethel, New Bethel, and Moore's Mill. In fact, these and earlier area communities have greatly helped Belmont growth with their contributions of citizens, capital, and commerce.

The land relief of the greater Belmont area is prevailing hilly. An Illinois Central Railroad survey has the elevation above sea level at Dennis 599.5 feet, at Belmont 573 feet, and at Golden 549.5 feet. Narrow, winding ridges separate the drainage areas of the creeks and smaller braches of the area. Despite the overall rolling, hilly, relief, a level to undulating "flat" area exists, generally speaking, between Highway 25 and Bear Creek from the Burgess Cemetery south of Belmont through the Pittsburg community northeast of Belmont. Downtown Belmont is located on a hilly ridge that overlooks Bear Creek flats east across the railroad where the baseball field and the football field once were.

Many Belmontians feel this originally gave rise to the source of our town name. Belmont means "beautiful mountain," This legend is debatable when the fact is considered that the first Belmont post office was located north of present Dennis at the Phillips place in 1873. Although the legendary hill forming our "beautiful mountain" is far from steep as mountains go, it has truly been a "beautiful mountain" to many Belmontians returning home from faraway places as they got off the train and looked west up the hill at Belmont.

The two principal streams of the Belmont area are Bear Creek, east of Belmont, and Mackey's Creek, west of Belmont. Bear Creek enters south Tishomingo County from Alabama near the Bullen farm, flows north, takes in Cedar Creek near Mingo, and eventually drains into the Tennessee River at Eastport. Mackey's Creek flows south through our area and merges into the Tombigbee River in Itawamba County. By and large, rain falling on the Belmont ridge will eventually drain into either Mackey's Creek or Bear Creek.

Streams draining into Bear Creek from the Golden area include the following: Wofford Branch, Epps Branch, Long Branch, Mink Branch, Prairie Branch, and Gee Branch. East beyond Belmont and Bear Creek a few miles are the legendary Freedom Hills, noted for their folklore and moonshining in earlier times. Draining the Freedom Hills into Bear Creek near Belmont and Golden in the Prospect area are Brumley Branch, Fowler Branch and Harris Branch. The Bud Harris Pond formed from the waters out of the Freedom Hills is one of the most challenging fishing places around Bear Creek and also one of the "snakiest." Nearby Spring Branch is practically a swamp. Memorable old Dry Creek has given way to the Bear Creek Channel.

The stream draining the east Belmont area near the old depot site down through the flatwoods past the Joe Deaton place through the Aubrey Hicks farm into Bear Creek has had many names down through the times. Among these are Bill Wood Branch, Ab Wood Branch, Moody Branch, and Duncan Branch. However, one thing about this branch is very clear: it has furnished hours upon days of unforgettable fishing experiences for young people beginning to fish. The "hornyheads," chughead catfish, bass, bream, and jacks caught from here in the past have brightened the day for countless youngsters who wagged their cane poles and fishing "regalia," including pork-and-beans cans full of dirt and worms, for two miles or more just to reach this fishing place of happy memories.

On the east side of Bear Creek in the Valley area are the Mann Branch, Bridges Branch, and Holly Branch. From the west side draining into Bear Creek are the Mauldin (Harrison) Branch, McNutt Branch, Campbell Branch, Hallmark (Byram) Branch, and Carr Branch. In the main Bear Creek bottom south of the Pittsburg Ford are the Ten Islands, a perplexing group amid running sloughs and Bear Creek. Many hunters had serious trouble in finding their way out of the Ten Islands before the Bear Creek Channel was dug. Willie Smith had better luck: he killed an unusual mutant raccoon there several years ago.

The principal stream north of Dennis in our area is McDougal Branch that meanders through the Bob Russell place at Neil and drains into Mackey's Creek. The Yoncopin Pond and the Josh Pond are two wilderness areas near Mackey's Creek that are known for swampy undergrowth, good fishing, and snakes galore. Across the Josh Pond at Allen Line is Riddle Creek, named for some of the earlier settlers in the area. Moore Branch is in the vicinity of Lancaster (Trollinger) Cemetery and reportedly drains into Mackey's Creek. Between Belmont and Bay Springs, which is located on the banks of Mackey's Creek, are Burnt Mills Branch, Perry Branch, Jourdan Creek, Fuller Branch, Betty Branch, Lake Branch, and Rock Creek. Rock Creek has a beginning in the new Belmont Park in Blue Springs and Gum Springs, which were important in early developmental days in Belmont. Moreover, Gin Branch at Bay Springs was strategic in the early economy and livelihood.

In the New Bethel-Old Bethel-Moore's Mill area the principal stream is Red Bud Creek, which drains into Mackey's Creek near the Caveness Bridge. Ben Martin Branch heads in the springs behind the home of Dr. Leon Ratliff in Belmont and flows into the North Fork of Red Bud Creek in the New Bethel area. Lynn Branch is located in the New Bethel area, and Ivy Branch is located near the old South Tishomingo School site.

Along the streams of our area there are nearly level flood plains that are rather wide considering the size and length of the streams. In addition, along most of the larger creeks there is nearly level in gently rolling stream terraces lying from 2 to 15 feet above the adjoining bottoms.

Geologically, most of our land surface is underlain with rather loose material composed of sand and gravel with a small mixture of silt and clay. The Eutaw formation, which underlies the land surface of the approximate western two-thirds of Tishomingo County, consists chiefly of sands and clays with the sands greatly predominating. The Tuscaloosa formation, which underlies the approximate eastern one-third of the county, consists chiefly of gravel and sands. In fact, vast gravel beds occur in the Tuscaloosa formation. Probably, the most prominent gravel pits in the Belmont area are those on the property of Arthur Credille on Fuller Branch in the Mineral Springs area; but the old gravel pits near the Bob Timbs place in the Prospect area were very prominent economically in bygone times. Many other gravel pits have furnished excellent road material down through the years. Moreover, the excellent gravel and sand deposits around Tishomingo, north of Belmont about eight miles, have made valuable contributions to the economy of south Tishomingo County.

Tishomingo State Park, approximately eight miles northeasterly from Belmont on Bear Creek, features outstanding rock formations and is one of the most beautiful natural places in the state. At Southward Bridge, the sandstone bluffs are prominent and are quarried commercially. On McDougal Branch at Neil, more rock outcrops are visible; and an interesting cave is located west of Neil down the branch.

At Bay Springs on Mackey's Creek, the rock bluffs, like at Tishomingo State Park, are a sight to behold. These bluffs furnished a site for the dam that powered the Bay Springs industry in the last half of the nineteenth century. Eastward up Rock Creek, more outcrops are encountered. On the Sparks place that John McRae and A. J. Trollinger formerly owned are several rock bluffs and a unique "rock house."

Natural vegetation has played an important role in the development of this land. To the early settlers, trees furnished building material for homes and fuel to warm their cabins. Later, the timber business formed an economy around which the young town of Belmont and its neighboring towns of Golden and Dennis prospered. In recent years our pulpwood industry has thrived from cutting of pines and some hardwood.

The predominant trees in our forests are shortleaf pine, loblolly pine, blackjack oak, and post oak. They are particularly conspicuous on the narrow hills and ridges; whereas hickories, red oak, white oak, and the pines predominate in the covers. Some other common trees are maple, ash, hackberry, beech, black walnut, dogwood, yellow poplar, persimmon, sassafras, black gum, sweet gum, ironwood, water oak, willow oak, birch, swamp white oak, cypress, and willow. The presence of cedar trees usually indicates planting of trees or seeds by previous residents of bygone times.

Logging down through the years has altered many of the forest-soil type associations, but a few are still noticeable. One association gives credence to the significant fact that post oak and blackjack oak are more abundant and other trees less abundant on the erosion-prone Cuthbert soils than on other soils. Pines seem to predominate over oaks and hickories on the Savannah soils. Water-tolerant trees form conspicuous associations with the poorly drained soils. These trees consist chiefly of water oak, willow oak, willow, cypress, and sweet gum; and with the exception of sweet gum, few of these trees grow on the well-drained soils. Beech trees grow well on the intermediately drained soils and are generally absent on the poorly drained soils. In essence, these associations may seem of little importance to some people when actually they have been important factors in the settlement of our area, the utilization of land, the area economy, and the ultimate emergence of Belmont, Mississippi.

The climate of the Belmont vicinity is of the humid continental type with rather hot summers, mild winters, and an annual average rainfall of about 52 inches. The temperature reflects a monthly average in January of 42 degrees and a monthly average in July of 80 degrees; a survey showed that we have an annual snowfall of about one inch.

Generally speaking, the weather has greatly affected this area since farming, one of our principal livelihoods down through the years, depends upon "changes in the elements." Late spring frost often damage fruit crops and early gardens. Spring rains over a prolonged period delay crop planting. Moreover, late winter and spring flooding on Bear Creek, Mackey's Creek, and Red Bud Creek are very memorable to many Belmontians. The efforts of our very capable supervisors in the construction of the Bear Creek Channel under the auspices of the Bear Creek Water Association have greatly alleviated the ill effects of flooding on Bear Creek where damage was probably the greatest.

By contrast, prolonged dry spells in summer cause yields that are, at times, too small for farmers to make a reasonable profit to justify their expenses, efforts, and investments. Thank goodness, the weather adversities are the exception rather than the rule. Consequently, farming has been good too many of our people down through the years. In recent years many small farmers have given up tilling the soil and have gone to work in factories or at other jobs. Thus, fewer farmers with more modern equipment and larger acreages now work the land around here.

Cotton, soy beans and corn are the principal crops. Some wheat, oats, sweet potatoes, sorghum, peanuts, pepper, and cucumbers are grown. Hay and some silage are also grown, but most is for the livestock of the feed growers.

In marketing the farm products and in the functional travels of our people, roads and modes of transportation have been important to our Belmont area. Our "founding fathers" accomplished this task on horseback, wagon, or buggy. The Illinois Central Railroad was strategic in shipping and in travel into and out of Belmont. Then, the automobile appeared on the scene. In the past several decades trucking has replaced much of the railroad shipping around here. The Continental Trailways bus also goes through Belmont daily.

Trucking and travel dictate the need for good paved roads. Highway 25 enters our area from the south at the county line near Burgess Cemetery and extends northward through the heart of Belmont to Dennis, Tishomingo, and Iuka into Tennessee. The Ridge Road begins at Burgess Cemetery and goes easterly into Red Bay, Alabama. A paved road leaves Highway 25 at Horn Grocery and extends east into Golden. Red Bud Road goes from Horn Grocery, which is south of Belmont on Highway 25, in a westerly direction through Old Bethel to the Moore's Mill community. Highway 366 goes from Belmont easterly into our neighboring town, Golden, and into Red Bay. The Moore's Mill Road extends west from Washington Street in Belmont into the rapidly-growing New Bethel community and onward into Moore's Mill.

Furthermore, another good paved road extends eastward from Belmont across Bear Creek into the Freedom Hills and Alabama. Old Highway 25 joins Highway 25 at Blue Bell in Belmont and goes in an east, then north, direction through one of the older sections of Belmont, continuing past New Providence Primitive Baptist Church and rejoining Highway 25 near Dennis at the overhead bridge near Joel Cemetery, where many of our "founding fathers" are buried. Highway 4 starts at Dennis, after 3 ½ miles north of Belmont, and meanders west through historic Bay Springs into Prentiss County.

A Belmont pioneer once said, "Good supervisors make good roads." This relatively simple, but meaningful, remark has been proven many times over in Belmont country. Many of our rural roads are now paved. Others are in process of being paved under the leadership of our present Fifth District supervisor, Leon Cook. In fact, our gravel roads are in good condition, thanks to the availability of our local gravel combined with the very capable efforts of our supervisors and their workers. Our citizens and visitors can travel daily over safe, sound roads.

Although the Belmont area is blessed with a most significant natural surroundings, the outstanding factor still has to be its people. With our Bible Belt heritage, Belmontians continue to place much emphasis on adherence to Christian values. Sunday still means something in Belmont! "Respect" is still a powerful word around here. Consequently, the home, the church, and the school continue to form the vital backbone of our society despite some erosion in recent years.

People around here are basically proud, somewhat suspicious, often soft-hearted deep down, hesitant about change they do not understand, but progressive and co-operative to movements they feel will help their children and community. In fact, Belmontians are willing to go beyond the call of duty in civic and benevolent efforts to help the community and those in need. Belmont people generally make a point to keep themselves informed and usually stand ready to do their part when asked.

Yes, the Belmont "natives" get "restless" at times and have serious squabbles, especially in politics. Nevertheless, forgiveness and objective reasoning usually prevail in the long run. The inhabitants of the "beautiful mountain" forget past differences when sickness, death, or the advancement of our section of the country are concerned. True to the pioneer family structure, they may sputter among themselves; yet they take exception at all others getting involved. After all, the problems at issue usually resolve themselves. There is "something" about Belmont that creates pride, respect, and compassion in those who have lived in, and have objectively understood, our area.

Essentially, Belmont, Mississippi, my home town, is a wonderful place to live and visit. One can still walk in Belmont at night without fear of harm. "Old Glory" waves daily over downtown Belmont. Here the citizens still treasure "old fashion" values, but they are responsive to progressive ideas that will help make Belmont a better place. Belmontians adjust well to changing times and still hold to the unchanging principles of right and wrong. One thing rarely changes – the love of Belmontians for "this Belmont."

"This Belmont" radiates in its people a proud love for homeland. Etha Mann upon returning home to Belmont with his family from a vacation out west was asked what was the prettiest sight he saw on the whole trip. Etha remarked promptly, "The city limits of Belmont on the way back home."

CHAPTER 2

INDIANS AND TREATIES

Long before the first white settlers came to the Belmont area, prehistoric Indians inhabited the forests and streams. Arrowheads, drills, spears, celts, and other prehistoric artifacts attest to Indian occupancy centuries ago. Carbon 14 tests of charcoal, bone, and other remains from campsites or mounds reveal an approximate time when various Indian groups were here. Many of the campsites were on elevated ground near springs or small streams and on the banks of larger streams. Indian artifacts found in our fields, hill sites, bluffs, mounds, and sites near springs indicate the probable presence of the following periods of the long deceased Indians: Paleo, Archaic, Woodland, Mississippian, and historic.

Of interest at Mingo on the Natchez Trace are remains of a temple mound; and on Cedar Creek is the Bruton Mound, where several Indians were buried. The long white spear from this mound is a beautiful work of craftsmanship. The Pharr Mounds at Pleasant Valley (Hazeldell) near Marietta will interest even more people when the Natchez Trace is completed through there.

Early Indians lived under the rock shelters on Bear Creek, Mackey's Creek, and Rock Creek. Artifacts, flint chips, animal bones, shells, and other remains found under the bluff shelters attest this conclusion. Some excellent bannerstones have been found in bygone years under these rock shelters. A finely polished saddleback bannerstone in the Tom Smith collection and a rose quartz butterfly bannerstone in another local collection are truly beautiful. Both are reportedly from the Bear Creek area. A well-polished milk quartz plummet reportedly from the Mingo area is truly a museum piece with its symmetrical perfection. The extensive collection of Atha Wayne Russell is proof positive of Indian life in our area. The Russell collection presents various types of craftsmanship and utilitarian artifacts of the early inhabitants of our area.

Fall plowing and spring plowing unearth many arrowheads in the fields near the streams around here. For example, Conrad Allen has found two very old points: a Quad point and a Colbert Dalton point. Horace Stepp found a long Benton spear on a gravel bar on Red Bud Creek. Both Richard Patterson and Gene Cook have found rare, very ancient fluted points.

A probable mound was once in Fanchertown on Bear Creek, but the Bear Creek Channel project destroyed it. A gorget, many arrowheads, and pottery fragments have come from the White fields near Golden. The Chinquapin Ridge on the east side of Bear Creek near the Belmont Bridge has furnished many interesting projectile points. West across Bear Creek on the bluffs are other interesting sites. The Bolton Site, east of Bear Creek, has always been archaeologically significant. A stone mound in the hills back of the Thorne home in Valley has been ransacked, destroying one of the most unique Indian sites around here. The Bridges Mound existed west of the Hubert Thorn rent house in Valley, but it was destroyed when the Bear Creek Channel was dug.

Across the Pittsburg Ford on the west side of Bear Creek are the Rob Parrish fields where various Indian villages and camps were set up down through the centuries. Many different types of artifacts have come from here down through the years. Early white settlers liked this area too. Old Tishomingo County records mention a settlement at Pittsburg in 1837.

Numerous other Indian sites are to be found near streams. Evidently, prehistoric Indians lived here a very long time before the first white men came to this area. The Indians living here when the first white men appeared were the cunning, fearless Chickasaws. At one time the Chickasaw Nation included that part of Kentucky and Tennessee between the Mississippi and Tennessee Rivers, a large part of south-central Tennessee and northern Alabama, and northern Mississippi. Here the Chickasaw boundary ran from Chickasaw Bluffs (Memphis) to Cotton Gin Port on the Tombigbee near present Amory and then northeast to the Tennessee River near Guntersville, Alabama.

These Chickasaws were a somewhat advanced civilization at the time the first white men encountered them. The first white explorers found them living in log houses roofed with grass, reeds, and cypress boards. The houses were near outhouses and well-tilled fields in addition to being grouped into villages or communities. A Chickasaw village often consisted of several compounds or households. Each household had a summer house, winter house, corn storage building, and a hut for sick women. Many of these towns numbered over 200 households. In addition, each village had a log palisade fort; council, ceremonial, and ball grounds; a ceremonial rotunda for religious events; and a council house for conducting decisions of local government.

These warlike, aggressive Indians are reported to have been a small nation with probably about 6,000 members including about 500 who were warriors. Yet, De Soto, the French, or other warring Indian tribes never conquered them.

As a race the Chickasaws were tall, erect, and graceful. They possessed a near perfect human figure with a countenance that was open, dignified, and placid. The forehead and brow impressed a person instantly of independence, heroism, and bravery. Their small black eyes were full of fire; their complexion was reddish-brown; and their long, lustrous hair was black as a crow.

The Chickasaw women were clean, industrious, and generally good-looking. They were slender and graceful with a rather delicate frame. These women cared for the young, made trinkets and pottery, rendered bear oil, and fashioned clothes which were objects of admiration from fiber and animal skins. In season, they cultivated the fields and gathered wild fruits and nuts. When a Chickasaw brave killed a deer, he told his wife where it was. She then went forth to fetch it, dress it, and serve it to her husband. Women never ate with the men who, indifferent by custom, were in reality loyal and devoted to their wives. In the social dance alone were women allowed to participate.

The Chickasaw man was master of the household, providing meat through hunting and fishing. He made with his own hands the stone implements of peace and war. Moreover, these noble warriors made and administered laws, conducted all religious rites and ceremonies, deliberated in the councils, memorized treaties and tribal records in order to teach the young men, and made war when necessary. By war the Chickasaw won his name and right to recognition in the affairs of his people and place in the "Happy Hunting Ground" beyond with "He Who liveth in the clear sky." An adventurer at heart, the Chickasaw warrior traveled far and near, carrying on tribal trade and commerce. These were the people upon whose lands our white forefathers settled.

After the close of the Revolutionary War, the United States adopted a policy of treatment toward the Indians in which the tribesmen were not allowed sovereignty but were permitted the following powers: the right of absolute ownership of soil upon which they dwelt, the power to give up this right, the power to make peace, the power to regulate the boundaries of their lands, and the power to enter into treaties with the American government. This policy gave rise to a long list of treaties between the Chickasaws and the United States. Some of these treaties opened up the land upon which Belmont is located for white ownership. Some opened up land in other areas and states.

The Chickasaws entered into a treaty with North Carolina or Virginia in1782 or 1783, which was never reported to Congress. By this treaty, the Donelson and Martin Treaty, which was probably signed at the home of James Robertson where Nashville now stands, the Chickasaws gave up their "Cumberland lands."

The first official treaty between the Chickasaws and the United States was the Treaty of Hopewell, which was concluded January 10, 1786, at Hopewell on the Keowee River near Seneca Old Town in the present state of South Carolina. When the American government proposed to put a trading post at the mouth of Bear Creek, the Chickasaws objected on the ground that the white men wore hard shoes and might tread upon their toes. Nevertheless, the Treaty of Hopewell provided that the United States would protect the Chickasaws, who would in turn recognize that the United States was the true protector of the Chickasaw Indians from thence onward.

On October 24, 1801, a treaty was made at Chickasaw Bluffs that resulted in the creation of the historic Natchez Trace that was to go from Nashville, Tennessee, to Natchez, Mississippi. This treaty gave the President of the United States permission to survey and construct a wagon road through Chickasaw land between the Mero District settlements in Tennessee and those of Natchez in Mississippi Territory. Later in the year, a similar treaty was signed with the Choctaws and the United States government allowing the use of their land for the southern part of the Trace. This road was to be a highway for both white Americans and the Indians.

When President Jefferson took office, the government advocated a policy of trade between the Indians and the white settlers who were gradually moving into Indian country. Chickasaws were encouraged to adopt civilized ways. To encourage these actions among the Indians, to represent the government, and to promote friendly relations with the Indians, the federal government employed Indian agents and stationed them at key points.

At the agency stations, traders set up shop and began to receive Indian produce, such as honey, beeswax, nuts, bear oil, and skins. In exchange, the Indians got cheap dry goods, tools, firearms, and ammunition. The Indians were encouraged to buy freely even on the credit. Two purposes were served. First, the Indians acquired those implements -- axes, plows, and other farming aids -- which would be needed in the settled life that the government was promoting. Second, every credit meant increasing debt for the Chickasaws. Soon, they had to give up more of their land to settle their accounts. This was to release large tracts of land for white settlers coming into the area. Alas, the Indians were too gullible and were ineffective traders with the whites. President Jefferson realized this too late, and a policy of gradual Indian extinction had been put into force.

Indian indebtedness and pressure on the federal government to supply more land for white settlers resulted in the Treaty of 1805. A vast territory, stretching from the mouth of the Ohio River along its left bank to the dividing ridge between the Ohio and Cumberland Rivers, and running hundreds of miles eastward, was ceded to the federal government. The consideration was $20,000 paid to the Chickasaws and the payment of their debts due to the merchants and traders. Some financial incentives were also given to chiefs.

The Treaty of 1816 was signed under similar conditions at the Chickasaw Council House near the present city of Pontotoc. Under it, the Chickasaws gave up a strip of land in west Alabama and northeast Mississippi from the Tennessee River south to the Choctaw boundary line. Andrew Jackson, Jesse Franklin, and David Meriwether represented the United States. King Chinnubby, Chief Tishomingo, George Colbert, and Levi Colbert (Chief Itawamba) represented the Chickasaws.

When Mississippi officially became a state on December 10, 1817, the Chickasaws owned much of north Mississippi. This was to change in forthcoming years. By the Treaty of 1818, the Chickasaws ceded to the American government all of their lands lying in Tennessee and Kentucky west of the Tennessee River. This area like much of the present Belmont area had been used previously as Chickasaw hunting grounds. This treaty, the so-called Jackson Purchase, validated the Rice Grant of about 5,000 acres of land and enabled the title holders of the grant - Andrew Jackson, John Overton, and Marcus Winchester - to become owners of Memphis, formerly Chickasaw Bluffs, when the treaty was officially ratified in the United States Senate in 1819.

When Andrew Jackson became president in 1829, the Indian removal became a national issue; and the Chickasaws, long-time friends of the white people, began to foresee their impending doom. President Jackson met with the Chickasaws on August 19,1830, at Franklin, Tennessee. After three days of social formalities, Secretary of War, John Eaton, and General John Coffee warned the Indians on behalf of President Jackson that they would be forced to move west or else abandon tribal laws and customs. The Indians would have to submit to the laws of the State, and white men would occupy most of their lands. After about a month of negotiations, a treaty was signed with the condition that a home be provided for the Chickasaws in the West. Since the Chickasaws later balked at having to occupy land with the more populous Choctaws, the Franklin Treaty became void; and Indian removal was delayed.

Meanwhile, a number of white settlers filtered into Chickasaw country, which included the area in which we now live. The Chickasaws after much deliberation agreed to give up their homelands in northeast Mississippi with the Treaty of Pontotoc Creek that was held between John Coffee, representing the government, and the Chickasaw Nation in council at the Council House on Pontotoc Creek on October 20, 1832. The solemn treaty signing that marked the transfer of the Chickasaw land into the hands of the government for our forefathers is described as follows: lshtehotopah, the last King of the Chickasaws, first walked up with a sad face and with a trembling hand made his mark. Noble Tishomingo, the War Chief whose judgment the King highly respected and followed, advanced next with "solemn mien" and signed. Slowly, one by one, the other chiefs, including the renowned Colberts, signed the treaty. Levi Colbert was seriously disturbed about the treaty; but after angrily rejecting a hinted bribe from John Coffee, he hesitantly signed the treaty.

Under the Treaty of Pontotoc Creek, the lands of the Chickasaw Nation, over six million acres, were to be sold. The proceeds, less expenses of sale and expenses of the Indian Removal, were to go to the Chickasaws. It was provided that the Indians were not to be disturbed in their homes while the government was locating a new home for them in the West. This was not strictly enforced because a new influx of white settlers moved into our area not long after the treaty was signed.

Before the treaty was ratified, Levi Colbert (Chief Itawamba) and some other Chickasaw leaders were still seriously upset about certain facets of the treaty. A meeting was held at the home of Levi Colbert at Buzzard Roost on the Natchez Trace in the edge of Alabama. From this meeting, a delegation went on to Washington to try to get the terms of the treaty amended and to express their discontent at the means through which the treaty was executed. Their efforts and petition in Washington to have the treaty amended were denied. However, the Treaty of Washington in 1834 reassured the Chickasaws that they would be protected from hostile Indians in their moving West and that their people would be protected in the sale of their lands. In the meantime, Levi Colbert became sick and died at the home of his son-in-law, Kilpatrick Carter, at Buzzard Roost.

The Chickasaws eventually located land in Indian Territory. By the Treaty of Doaksville, near Fort Towson in present day Oklahoma, on January 17, 1837, the Chickasaws agreed to pay $530,000 to the Choctaws for a large track of land in the western portion of the Choctaw land.

Then, the sad day of Indian exodus came. King Ishtehotopah and Chief Tishomingo were in the westward procession of Chickasaws that went through Arkansas to their new home in present Oklahoma. Tragically, the venerable Chief Tishomingo died on the trip, possibly near Fort Coffee.

The proud, unconquerable Chickasaws abandoned their warriorlike ways and signed treaties which sold their birthright for very little and finally put them on the road to exile. The startling decline of the Chickasaws, completed in less than 50 years, can be accounted for in part concerning the weakness of the older generation. Instead of transmitting age-old tribal values, they abandoned them for half-understood European virtues and vices – with emphasis on the latter. This broke the chain of generations of Chickasaw pride and set in motion a rapid decay which made these proud and unconquered people of old into a declining, exploited race.

When the Chickasaws moved to the West, they left behind a proud heritage of land ownership involving the land upon which we now live in Tishomingo County. They left contributions in some of their principles and customs. With their decline, they left a solemn lesson which we of this complex modern time would do well to learn well. When the Chickasaws left, our white forefathers steadily continued to come into this country from Alabama, Tennessee, North Carolina, Virginia, South Carolina, and Georgia. Preserving part of the Chickasaw heritage, the early pioneer leaders named the county in which present-day Belmont is located after the last great warrior chief and "prime minister" of the Chickasaws - Tishomingo.

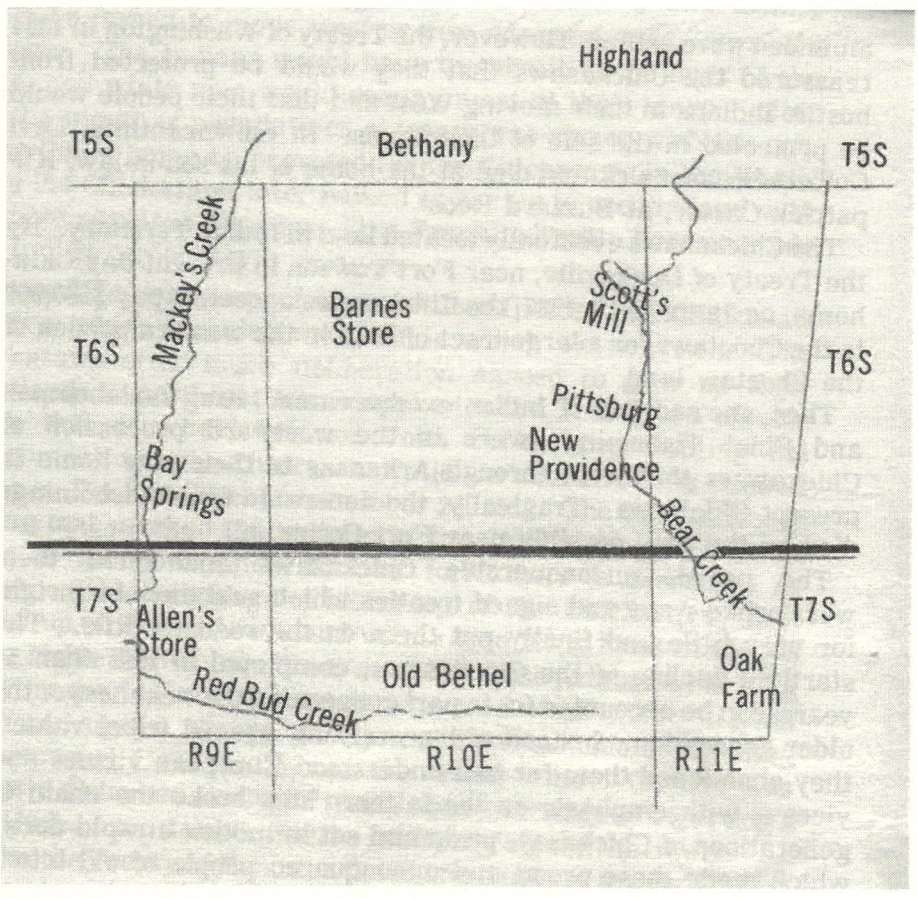

Some early settlements of what was to become the present south Tishomingo County.

CHAPTER 3

EARLY SETTLERS AND SETTLEMENTS

Although the Treaty of Pontotoc provided that the Chickasaws were not to be disturbed while the government was finding them a new home in the West, several impatient white settlers came into this area. They selected homesites and built log cabins in the wild expanse of the ancestral Chickasaw hunting grounds. Then, they began clearing land for farming. These sturdy pioneers, true to their ancestral faith, did not neglect religious services. School and church were often held in the same log building. Some church services were often held in homes until a church building could be erected.

Before Tishomingo County was officially formed, some pioneer homes were existent in this area. When the federal land office was opened at Pontotoc, Mississippi, white settlers hastened to purchase title to the acreage which they occupied. Then, on February 9, 1836, more than a year before Chickasaw removal to the West began, the Mississippi legislature divided the Chickasaw Cession into ten counties. These were Tippah, Marshall, De Soto, Tunica, Panola, Lafayette, Chickasaw, Pontotoc, Itawamba, and Tishomingo. An act organizing these ten counties was passed on February 14, 1836.

In this county formation, the Township seven lands of the present day Tishomingo County Fifth District were in Itawamba County. This included what is now south Belmont, Golden, New Bethel, Old Bethel, Moore's Mill, and Fanchertown. This land was to stay in Itawamba County until Reconstruction county revisions in the early 1870's.

Tishomingo County, including much of the land upon which present Belmont is built, was the largest county in the state. It had 923,040 acres. Due to its size, it was often called "the Free State of Tishomingo" and included much of the present counties of Tishomingo, Prentiss and Alcorn.

A board of police was soon elected, consisting of a member from each of the five districts. With duties comparable to our present supervisors, the board of police proceeded to carry out the business of the budding county with the assistance of a sheriff, coroner, treasurer, tax collector and assessor, ranger, and surveyor. Circuit and probate courts along with their respective clerks protected the rights of the people. On the district level, justices of the peace settled minor property disputes, wrote deeds, and maintained law and order with the help of the constables.

Armistead Barton donated sixty acres of land to the newly formed Tishomingo County. Lots for a settlement were sold. The county seat, Jacinto, was situated on this property. The name of Cincinnati was originally selected, but many citizens took exception because they felt their city would become a metropolis rivaling the Cincinnati in Ohio in size and trade. Thus, the settlers named their city, Jacinto, in honor of the Battle of San Jacinto, where Texan independence was won. Caleb Lindsey was given the contract to build a log courthouse at a cost of $199.00 with the expressed consideration that there would be no extras. Later, around 1854, the first brick building in Old Tishomingo County replaced this log courthouse. J. J. Blythe was awarded the final contract of $6,798 to build this brick building, the Jacinto Courthouse. It still stands today, thanks to the preservation and restoration efforts of several people. Dr. Joe K. Stephens, a Belmont native who now lives in West Point, saved the courthouse from being destroyed in 1964. He paid $2,000 for the old courthouse and then donated it to the Jacinto Foundation, Inc., a non-profit organization. Among the many others who worked to preserve the Jacinto Courthouse were Mrs. Fayette Williams, O. T. Holder, and Frank Simmons.

Subsistence farming characterized the early days of Tishomingo County. On this developing frontier, nearly everything was grown at home -- cotton, corn, wheat, sorghum, tobacco, and an abundance of vegetables. Horses, cattle, sheep, hogs, mules, geese, and chickens were commonly raised. The settlers tanned animal hides from which they made most of the shoes they wore. The spinning wheel and the homemade loom saw use in the homes in helping the women make clothing for the early settlers.

Both settlers and land speculators were involved in the earliest land entries in 1836 in the present Belmont-Fifth District area. Among these were the following: W. H. Files, Henry Cook, Isaac H. Bell, Micajah Lindsey, John Joel, William Suggs, Jesse Hallmark, William Carroll Lindsey, John Reager, Hugh Rogers, Jesse W. Garth, J. Kemp, T. M. Reynolds, Phillip O'Riley, and O-nah-ho-chubby. Early in 1837, Ephraim H. Wygle, Silas C. Byram, and Benjamin Condry entered area land. Benjamin Condry on March 6, 1837, entered the SE¼ of section 35, Township

6 south, Range 10 East upon which downtown Belmont is now located. O-nah-ho-chubby, a Chickasaw Indian, entered the entire section 13, Township 7 South, Range 10 East on February 6, 1836. This is the land that includes the Charles Bostick farm, Waldrep property, and Burgess Cemetery extending eastward.

With a growing population and with a deserved feeling of accomplishment, our early settlers saw in the Christmas of 1836 a great occasion for rejoicing. They had in the Chickasaw wilderness erected their log houses, established homes, and attained a degree of security with a recognized government to protect, not deprive, their rights.

The southeastern part of Old Tishomingo County, basically the fourth district then, was to later furnish the foundation for the emergence of a place called Belmont along with the northern part of old Itawamba County.

One early settler of this area was Alfred Smith, who died in 1847 and is buried in the old McRae Cemetery on the present Ross Sparks farm. Alfred Smith reportedly lived around there when he died and is reported to have been a close relative of Amanda McRae, wife of John McRae who later lived on this place near Rock Creek.

Two of the very first white settlers around here were Micajah C. Lindsey (1775-1845) and his wife, Elizabeth McClurkin Lindsey. They lived, reportedly, in the vicinity of the present Lindsey Cemetery among the hunting Chickasaws before the Indian Removal. After the land office opened at Pontotoc, Micajah Lindsey entered in excess of 3,000 acres of land in a matter of a few years. In March, 1840, he sold seven various quarter sections of land to William Carroll Lindsey, his son, for $2,500. Micajah Lindsey died in 1845 and was probably the first person to be buried in the present Lindsey Cemetery between Belmont and Dennis.

In addition to being a loyal member at New Providence Primitive Baptist Church, William Carroll Lindsey was a respected, dependable public servant who held several positions of leadership. He is reported to have lived on the place overlooking Bear Creek where the Oco Horn home now is. His land transactions were strategic in helping open up this area for development. In addition, W. C. Lindsey in 1853 established a ferry across Big Bear Creek on the then new road from Frankfort, Alabama, to Carrollville, Mississippi. The ferry was to be named the Pittsburg Ferry. For ferriage, a man and horse were to be charged ten cents. A wagon or oxen and driver were to be charged twenty-five cents.

Daughters of Micajah and Elizabeth Lindsey were Jane (Mrs. Matthew Davis), Mary (Mrs. David Franklin), and Elizabeth (Mrs. John Joel). James Lindsey, Holland Lindsey, and Bazzle L. Lindsey were also sons of Micajah Lindsey and his wife.

Bazzle L. Lindsey (1805-1892) reportedly lived on the present Jerome Mitchell place. On the roadside of this place is the grave of Mary Lindsey (1848-1853), the daughter of Bazzle L. and Elisabeth Lindsey. B. L. Lindsey was a church clerk, a justice of the peace, and a prominent land owner. His sons included T. B. (Tom) Lindsey, M. C. (Clabe) Lindsey, M. W. (Mike) Lindsey, and Carroll Lindsey. The first three raised families and grew with the rest of our area. Most assuredly, the integral contributions of the Lindseys to this area from pioneer times to the present have been very valuable.

One of the very earliest settlements was Pittsburg. In June, 1837, the county board of police ordered that a precinct for receiving votes be held at Pittsburg. Ephraim Reid, John Joel, and Micajah Lindsey were appointed inspectors. They were authorized to hold all elections at that place for a two year term. In 1839, Silas Byram was judge, and Bazzle L. Lindsey was a clerk at a Pittsburg election. The Pittsburg election holders in 1841 were John White, Isaac Toland, and John P. Smith.

In the Pittsburg settlement was New Providence Primitive Baptist Church, which was about two miles north of present Belmont. On May 19, 1838, William Carroll Lindsey deeded two acres for the purpose of locating a church house for New Providence and for school site purposes for citizens of the surrounding vicinity with spring privileges to them. In 1839, Silas Byram was a deacon of New Providence. Thomas Thorn and B. L. Lindsey were church clerks in 1839. In January, 1841, William Carroll Lindsey was church clerk and served ably until his death in 1867.

Some general prices of trade in 1837-1838 in the Pittsburg settlement were as follows: beef (front cuts), 4 cents per pound; beef (hind cuts), 5 cents per pound; flour, 8 cents per pound; molasses, one dollar per gallon; pork, 10 cents per pound; and salt, about 7 cents per pound. A cow and calf sold for sixteen dollars. Travelers were charged 37 1/2 cents per meal. Horse care and feeding were about 75 cents per day, while boarding and meals for the traveler -- reduced price -- were one dollar per day.

Another early pioneer of the area was Silas C. Byram (1791-1882). He; his wife, Martha Blythe Byram; and their family had moved before 1838 from near Allsboro, Alabama, into the Pittsburg settlement. The Silas Byram children included John, Alden, William, Alfred, Martha, Erasmus, and Cavalier. A double wedding involving this family took place on July 19, 1838. Martha Byram married G. W. Hallmark. Alden Byram married Kiziah Hallmark. Kiziah Hallmark and G. W. Hallmark were children of Jesse Hallmark and Mary Hallmark, early settlers whose descendants were to later become contributing leaders in a place called Belmont. The Hallmarks may have settled on the Bear Creek flats northeast of present Belmont in the general vicinity of the Byram (Rob Epps) Ford. Jesse Hallmark entered in excess of 1,200 acres of land in and around present Belmont. In later years he is said to have lived in the vicinity of the present Hopkins property south of Belmont.

Other early landowners who owned the land upon which a place called Belmont was to later form included the following: Benjamin Condry, Isaac Maulden, Hiram Maulden, William M. Campbell, Benjamin Hopkins, Micajah Lindsey, Bluford Reynolds, William Carroll Lindsey, Willie D. Melton, Ransom Hill, Jephtha Robins, John B. Fry, Jesse Evans, James Anderson, Jo Hunt, David McClung, J.M. Hodge, D. G. Greenwood, William Martin, J. W. Clement, and C. Reynolds. Benjamin Condry of De Soto County in about 1840 sold the SE¼ of section 35, Township 6 South, Range 10 East in which the downtown business center of Belmont is now located to Hiram Maulden for $250.

Benjamin Hopkins (1812-1862) would surely have to be a significant early settler. His family moved from Kentucky down through Tennessee into south Tishomingo County. A daughter, Lucinda A. (Bam), was reportedly born here in 1845. Ben Hopkins owned several hundred acres of land in and around present Belmont. His children in later decades were to own much land in and around Belmont, and their families were to be a part of the emergence of Belmont. The children of Ben Hopkins were John I. C. Hopkins, W. A. Hopkins, B. F. (Frank) Hopkins, L. A. (Bam) Vinson, Mary Jane Gilbert, H. B. Hopkins, Larkin C. Hopkins, Margaret M. Mitchell, J. A. Hopkins, and R.S. Hopkins.

In September, 1850, Benjamin Hopkins bought from Hiram

Maulden for $500 the south half of section 35, Township 6 South, Range 10 East. A few weeks later, Ben Hopkins bought the NE¼ of section 35, Township 6 South, Range 10 East from William Carroll Lindsey for $300. Evidently, Ben Hopkins knew the value back in the 1850's of the land upon which Belmont was to be located over a half century later. In 1856, he continued to buy land upon which Belmont corporate limits were to be later. He purchased from John Bradford Fry for $80 the SE 1/4 of section 34, township 6 South, Range 10 East. In 1859, Ben Hopkins bought for $150 from Fry the West ½ of the NE¼ of section 34, containing buildings, spring, and spring lot.

   William M. Campbell bought the East ½ of the NE¼ of section 34, Township 6 South, Range 10 East from John B. Fry for $150 in 1859. In 1849, "Uncle Billy," as he was affectionately called by friends and kin, had bought for $100 the NW¼ of section 35, Township 6 South, Range 10 East from Ransom Hill. This land was to furnish the future site of not only the old Gum Springs school in Belmont, but also the site for the present Belmont Blue Springs City Park.

   William M. Campbell (1820-1903), a true Scotchman at heart and in principle, had moved into the area with his wife, Rachel Angeline, around 1840. Their daughter, Mary, who married Frank Hopkins in later life, was reportedly born in late 1840 in Mississippi. Additionally, Rachel Angeline Campbell was a daughter of Solomon Shook. Her brother, William Wiley (Bill) Shook, was the father of a later prominent Belmont builder, C. C. Shook.

   Back in 1853 when the Pittsburg Ferry was established on Bear Creek, W. M. Campbell was overseer of the Frankfort-Carrollville Road in the Pittsburg area. Uncle Billy Campbell kept abreast of change, yet he staunchly upheld a firm set of principles. Like many of his descendants, he made the day much brighter for those around him.

   The Shooks were pioneer families that were to have a profound influence on the area, and, in fact, the actual being of a place called Belmont. Two brothers, Solomon Shook and Noah Shook, moved from Alabama with their families in the 1840's. Solomon Shook in November, 1845, lived in Franklin County, Alabama. Then, he bought land from David McClung on the Bear Creek flats in the vicinity of the present Bill Ezzell place. His son, William Wiley Shook, is reported to have lived at the old house site across the road from the present Claude Carr home. Some Shook families lived in the Rock Creek-McRae settlement. Mike Shook lived in later years at the edge of "the Shook fields" northerly across Rock Creek from the present Ross Sparks home. On Rock Creek, Mike Shook operated a water mill.

David Phillips settled in the 1840's west of present Dennis. John A. Russell (1772-1846) is buried in the Pittsburg Cemetery. The twin sons of William and Mary Clingan that died in early 1846 are also buried at Pittsburg Cemetery. Robert Moore (1803-1870), Callaway A. Moore (1826-1910), and Stephen R. Moore were early settlers in the greater Bay Springs area.

North of Bay Springs was the home of John William Stephens. In early 1839, John William Stephens left Maynard's Cove in Jackson County, Alabama, with his wife and their nine children. They headed westward in an oxen-drawn wagon to the Free State of Tishomingo. John William Stephens and William Stephens, who had arrived in 1836, were land buyers on the same day of adjoining plots of land approximately two miles north of Bay Springs. Northerly from the Stephens families, W. A. H. Shackelford settled in about 1842. Northwesterly from Bay Springs near the Natchez Trace was Cape Horn. A stagecoach route reportedly went through here. John R. Martin lived in the vicinity of Cape Horn and also served several terms as justice of the peace.

Another group of early settlers centered around the Bethany Presbyterian Church near the present home of Fourth District supervisor, M. R. Whitehead. Prominent among these settlers were the Padens. About 1833, Robert W. Paden, Dan Paden, Alexander Paden, David Paden, and their families moved from their home near Greenville, South Carolina. Some lived for a while in Tennessee. In time, they settled and bought several tracts of land in the vicinity of Bethany in south Tishomingo County.

One of the first things they did was to cut and hew logs to build a church house. This rustic log structure, used as both a church and school, was about 20 by 30 feet and stood about 40 yards south of the present building. Both the floor and the seats were made of old-time puncheons (split logs with their faces smoothed). The building had one door and two windows that closed with wooden shutters. The pulpit was built on the old Scottish model -- a semi-circle front with the puncheon floor elevated several feet and mounted by a flight of steps. Candles were used for lighting, and there was no heat. Winter services were provided with a fire built outdoors.

The Bethany Presbyterian Church reportedly held its first service in December, 1840. Rev. James B. Stafford was the organizing minister. The charter members included Elizabeth Paden, Daniel A. Paden, Catherine Paden, Margaret Paden, Isabelle Wylie, and Hugh P. Paden. Robert W. Paden and Alexander Savage were ruling elders. Many of these early settlers and their family members rest today in the Bethany cemetery.

In 1845, Cornelius Carmack, an Indian fighter with Andrew Jackson and a former member of the Alabama legislature, moved from Alabama to the Bethany settlement. In 1846 when the state legislature inaugurated the public school program, Cornelius Carmack was appointed to the Tishomingo County school commission. This man was an able public servant and a brilliant orator. While presiding over a convention in Jackson, Cornelius Carmack died suddenly on December 19, 1851.

Meanwhile, E.W. Carmack, a son of Cornelius Carmack, had established Euclid Academy at Bethany. This progressive school met at first in the Bethany church building and could accommodate up to fifty people. In January, 1851, the trustees of Euclid Academy named E. W. Carmack to teach. He had the previous year taught at Spring Creek Academy about three miles west of Good Springs. Euclid Academy boasted of good water, good health, and good morals. Students boarded with Cornelius Carmack, whose home was about 300 yards from the school, and with other neighboring residents. Board was thirty dollars for a five month session.

Professor Carmack agreed to teach orthography, reading, writing, arithmetic, and vocal music for $6.25. Students instructed in English grammar and geography were to pay eight dollars. Natural sciences, higher math, philosophy, rhetoric, logic, and ancient languages cost a little more. Euclid Academy intended to give moral restraint and have less temptations to vice than at other schools. A debating society was to be formed, while the well-qualified E. W. Carmack was to introduce declamation and compositions into the school program.

In August, 1853, H. P. Paden deeded to E. W. Carmack that portion of the NE¼ of section 34, Township 5 South, Range 10 East which lay west of the Jacinto-Russellville Road, including fifteen acres upon which Euclid Academy was standing. In another Bethany development in September, 1853, James F. McDougal and Mary McDougal deeded seven acres in the NW¼ of section 34, Township 5 South, Range 10 East to Alexander Paden and David Paden, deacons of Bethany Presbyterian Church.

Shortly after the untimely death of Cornelius Carmack, Professor E. W. Carmack moved Euclid Academy to Jacinto. Later, he entered politics and became an outstanding public servant noted for his integrity and brilliant ability. Everything considered, E. W. Carmack was one of the most outstanding citizens in the history of Tishomingo County. The fact that his career began around Bethany is a source of pride for the people of south Tishomingo County. Additionally, the descendants of the old Bethany settlers were later to have important roles in the development of places like Burnt Mills, Barnes Store, Hillside, Highland, Paden, Tishomingo, Dennis, and a place called Belmont.

In the Township seven lands of our area which were in Itawamba County until the early 1870's, one of the early settlers before 1840 was Rev. Thomas Pharr, a well-educated Presbyterian minister from South Carolina. His son, John Christian Pharr, became a Methodist minister. In 1844, John Christian Pharr married Elizabeth Womack, whose family were also early settlers around present Old Bethel. The early Old Bethel settler, Nathan Womack (1795-1854), had married his first cousin, Louvicia Womack, several years before moving to Mississippi. Their son, Andrew J. Womack, was one of the earliest to be buried in the cemetery of Old Bethel in April, 1849. The Womack family of Old Bethel was destined to make a very memorable sacrifice years later in Civil War times.

Another respected Old Bethel settler was Alexander Houston Montgomery (1807-1872). The contributions of him; his son, George Houston Montgomery (1844-1896); and their families were most valuable not only to the development of Old Bethel but also to the later development of a place called Belmont. For example, Booker Montgomery, a son of G. H. Montgomery, was to live later in Belmont and become a contributing Belmont merchant for several years.

A few of the other families that settled in this area included the following: Wigginton, Ivy, Shook, Reeves, Allen, Cole, Pate, Bailey, Vinson, Burgess, Stewart, Hammett, Abel, Clement, Samples, Calvert, Bates, Cobb, Bennett, Jackson, Weems, Whitehead, Seviles, and Lynn. Back of the present Phillip Reeves home and easterly from present Old Bethel is a very old cemetery in the woods. Sarah Hammett relates that her great grandfather Weems is buried here. A Pharr lady who married a Bailey is reported to be buried in this old cemetery. In fact, there is some conjecture that an early church may have been located at this place. Furthermore, in the neighborhood vicinity of the old Alton Hammett and Columbus Hammett homeplaces was a Baptist Church located in the SE¼ of section 8, Township 7 South, Range 10 East. This Baptist church was located on six acres that William Abel deeded in or before 1857.

In July, 1850, John Stewart and his wife, Mary, in consideration of love and good will they bore to Cumberland Presbyterian Church gave a plot of ground containing five acres and sixty poles in the northwest corner of the NE¼ of section 16, Township 7 South, Range 10 East to A.H. Montgomery, James B. Bailey, and Andrew Maulden, trustees of the Cumberland Presbyterian Church. This land, somewhat northwest of a present church on Red Bud Road, Chapel Hill Church of God of Prophecy, was to be used in 1850 for the construction of a house of worship for the Cumberland Presbyterian Church. More specifically, this old Presbyterian church property was located in the hills northerly from the present Dallas Wigginton home. In later years, a school and possibly another church may have been located in this vicinity.

The Old Bethel Methodists built a church in the late 1840's. On February 9, 1849, Joseph Abel and his wife, Mary Abel, deeded to Nathan Womack, Alfred Stephens, Joseph Abel, James Haney, and William Farley, trustees of the Methodist Episcopal Church South at Old Bethel a piece of land for a church house site, containing and laid out for one acre and 77 poles. Church men cut trees, hewed and rolled logs, put up the walls, and completed work on the one-room, log church with no windows. Church women furnished dinner on the ground in this manifestation of love and Christian devotion.

Further down Red Bud Creek from Old Bethel, another settlement existed. In the general vicinity of present Moore's Mill, Edmond Gannaway was postmaster of Cotton Ridge in early 1843. The Cotton Ridge post office was discontinued in September, 1855. In time the name of Cotton Ridge faded away. Meanwhile, the identity of Allen's Mill, later Allen's Store, was emerging.

Joseph Allen (1799-1860); his wife, Sarah; and their family had moved from near Woodruff, South Carolina, about 1842-1844 to settle near Red Bud Creek in the present Moore's Mill community. From the outset the contributions of Joseph Allen and his family were noteworthy. The family contributions were destined to continue to present Belmont. Joseph Allen operated a grist mill and gin on Red Bud Creek and served also as justice of the peace in 1847 and 1848 in Itawamba County. A store was established near the water mill, and the settlement became Allen's Mill. Later, it was known as Allen's Store and kept this name into the 1880's.

The children of Joseph and Sarah Allen married into several of the pioneer families of the area. One daughter, Keturah, married W. P. Womack. Another daughter, Isabella, married John A. Beachum. His father, John Beachum (1789-1845), was a prominent early settler who lived near and is buried in the Mitchell (Beachum) Cemetery. Kiever Allen married Barcia, the daughter of one of the local settlers, John Hood. Three other Joseph Allen children -- Wister, Cordelia, and Charnel Hightower -- married into the family of the respected old settler, John Strother Gaines, who lived at present Pleasant Valley in Prentiss County. C. W. (Wister) Allen and his uncle, Holland Allen, became Primitive Baptist ministers. C. H. Allen and his brother, L. B. (Benona) Allen, attended Louisville Medical College and were qualified to practice medicine. Dr. L.B. Allen went to Hill County, Texas, and practiced there. Although qualified to be a doctor, Charnel Hightower Allen chose to operate the mill and store. In time, he improved and added to the mill to better serve the people of the community around Allen's Store (Allen's Mill). The proximity to Bay Springs and Old Bethel created many friendship bonds for the early settlers of Allen's Mill. In fact, several of the settlers of Allen's Mill and Bay Springs worshipped at the old Mackey's Creek Primitive Baptist Church north of Bay Springs.

Obviously, many other settlers made valuable contributions to our overall area. From the virgin forests, they and the settlers mentioned built homes, constructed churches, and cleared farming land. No doubt, many of these pioneers helped lay a foundation upon which "life, liberty, and the pursuit of happiness" could be pursued. As more people moved into the area, settlements became more evident. Despite the importance of all settlements to the growth pattern and eventual emergence of a place called Belmont, the dominant settlement of this period was to be Bay Springs.

CHAPTER 4

HEYDAYS OF BAY SPRINGS

Visitors to Bay Springs can readily understand why the early settlers took a liking to this scenic area with its development potential. Dr. William Clifford Morse, State Geologist in 1935, described Bay Springs on Mackey's Creek in the following way: "Perhaps no small area in the state is so picturesquely beautiful as this Bay Springs region." The Highland Church sandstone outcrops form cliffs and gorges through which Mackey's Creek meanders. The most famous cliff is Lover's Leap, which is steeped in Chickasaw legend. According to this legend, a Chickasaw brave and his beautiful sweetheart met here. The brave, in time, went off to battle. The Chickasaw maiden continued to go to the large rock ledge alone. She dreamed of the day when her lover would return and linger with her on the ledge while the waters of Mackey's Creek babbled sweet songs below. When the warriors eventually returned, she anxiously looked for her beloved; but to her sorrow, he had been killed in battle. Heartbroken, the Chickasaw maiden went to the ledge (Lover's Leap) and plunged to her death according to the legend.

The white settlers viewed Bay Springs with more optimism. In September, 1836, W. H. Files entered the SW¼ of section 26, Township 6 South, Range 9 East. This is the Bay Springs quarter section-- the 160 acres upon which many of the buildings were to be located. Mackey's Creek flowed through this quarter section and provided an abundance of water power potential. Ephraim H. Wygle entered the quarter section south of present Bay Springs in January, 1837. He may have established a water mill on this property.

About 1838, George Gresham and his family moved from the present Mars Hill area near Florence, Alabama, and settled on Mackey's Creek near where the present Highway 4 crosses the creek at Bay Springs. Some think that George Gresham lived on the road just north of Gin Branch. He quickly saw that the high sandstone cliffs made this spot an ideal location for a dam to furnish water power. At first, George Gresham probably operated a watermill on Gin Branch which drains into Mackey's Creek. Being well-respected, he was appointed in 1840 to be overseer of the road from Gresham's Mill to the county line.

George Gresham entered about 640 acres of land in the Bay Springs area. Since he had a rather domestic nature, George Gresham turned over the development mostly to his son, James Files Gresham. James Files Gresham (1820-1891), one of the most successful promoters of his time, went to work. In 1839, he bought from his kinsman, W. H. Files of Itawamba County, the Bay Springs quarter section for $800. In fact, Gresham bought several hundred acres around Mackey's Creek. Long would Tishomingo County, and especially Bay Springs citizens, remember James Files Gresham and the results of his shrewd business acumen.

In the early 1840's, James Files Gresham and George Gresham erected a sawmill and grist mill on Mackey's Creek. This was to help not only the Greshams but also the area settlers. Since this mill was the only one in that part of the county equipped for the manufacture of flour, the pioneers brought their wheat for quite a distance to have it made into flour. The Gresham water-powered sawmill supplied the neighborhood with lumber for the construction of new frame houses and barns. Greshams also sawed a large portion of the lumber used in the later construction of the factory and other buildings.

A village, Gresham's Mills, sprang up. A blacksmith shop, a cotton gin, and a general store were built. The settlers were adjusting to their new homes; and progress was starting to show, especially at Gresham's Mills.

About four miles southwest of Gresham's Mills was the home of Robert Lowry on the present Rob McKinney place. Here were bay trees and clear springs in profusion. Lowry operated a store in which the first post office in that vicinity was established in 1844. The post office was called Bay Springs, and Robert Lowry served as postmaster. When he moved to Carrollville in 1845, the post office was moved to Gresham's Mills without a change of name. The budding trade center on Mackey's Creek was thereafter called Bay Springs. James F. Gresham then became the postmaster of Bay Springs. (Incidentally, the son of the elder Robert Lowry, also Robert Lowry, was to later become governor of Mississippi after Reconstruction.)

On August 16, 1845, several interested in the Predestinarian Baptist faith met at the George Gresham home at Bay Springs and formed the Mackey's Creek Church. Ministers who met with the interested people were Sanders Mills, Charles Riddle, James Lindsey, and Gainer Jeffreys. Founding members were Moses

Holland Allen, William H. Riddle, Joseph Allen, Sarah Allen, George Lee, Andrew McCreary, Frances McCreary, John Allen, and Rachel White. Two deaths shortly thereafter necessitated a burial site and resulted in the selection of a church site. Keziah Lacy Gresham, wife of James Files Gresham, died September 17, 1845, a few weeks after her baby son, W. G. C. (Billie), was born. Lucy McDougal Moore, wife of Stephen R. Moore, died October 19, 1845. Both were buried on a plot of land north of Bay Springs. Land transactions for the burial ground site where they were buried and for a church site were finalized in September, 1846. Then, John R. Martin and Elizabeth Martin donated three acres and sold six more acres for six dollars to the church trustees-- Joseph Allen, John Allen, and William H. Riddle. John Allen was the first church clerk. J.M. Riddle and W. C. Lacy were to follow him as church clerks. This early church of the greater Bay Springs area was located adjacent to what is now known as Old Mackey's Creek Church Cemetery.

In the meantime, the issue of spirituous liquors surfaced at Bay Springs. No license was required to sell wine and hard liquor in quantities of one or more gallons. Stores and saloons retailing liquor by the drink or bottle were charged fifty dollars per year. The average wholesale price on whiskey was between 15 and 20 cents per gallon, making it comparatively cheap in relation to other articles of commerce.

The Tishomingo County board of police in the winter of 1847-1848 granted James F. Gresham authority to retail spirituous liquors at his store at Bay Springs. A retail liquor license was issued to William Thompson of Bay Springs in1850, and another license was issued there in1851. Then, Rev. E. C. Gillenwaters, a Cumberland Presbyterian minister, came into the area, preached with much religious fervor, and succeeded in rallying the people in favor of his prohibitionist views. In fact, the zeal with which Rev. Gillenwaters waged war on the liquor traffic led to the closing of the saloon at Bay Springs in 1852.

By this time, the shrewd James F. Gresham had turned his interest to county politics, having been elected to the board of police. Then, he entered into a most daring endeavor. In April, 1850, James F. Gresham and John Briggs, a prominent Eastport merchant, entered into a copartnership, Briggs and Gresham, for the purpose of carrying on a cotton manufacturing business, cotton ginning, and lumber sawing. At Bay Springs, Briggs was to furnish machinery for 300-500 spindles and furnish the means to put it in operation at the cotton mill called Bay Springs Union Factory. Gresham for his part of the capital was to furnish about 680 acres of land and tenements, comprising Gresham's Mills and valued at about $3,000. James Files Gresham was to be chief active manager of the concern and was to receive $250 for the first year. Gresham was to agree not to gamble, bet or be a noisy politician. Instead, he was to pursue an honorable calling with a view to profit and a "general benefit to our fellow men."

Concerning working conditions at Bay Springs Union Factory good order and uniformity were to be strictly observed with moral and proper treatment to the factory hands. The working hours were to be twelve hours.

Shortly, John Robinson bought an interest in the concern. In April, 1851, Briggs, Gresham, and Company made articles of agreement for the Bay Springs Union Factory. The interest of John Briggs consisted of money and machinery he actually expended on the factory and mills up to the time of commencing operations. The interest of James F. Gresham was $3000 for land, mills, and buildings; $2,000 for the building of the factory; and other sums he might spend later by mutual agreement. John Robinson secured a one-sixth part of the Gresham interest and a one-sixth part of the Briggs interest.

Furthermore, John Robinson was to receive three hundred dollars annually for his services in superintending the factory in every department, keeping the company books, and "devoting the whole of his time in promoting the interest of the said factory exclusively." James F. Gresham was to continue to receive his salary for services rendered. The operations of the Bay Springs Union Factory were to commence on the first day of July, 1851.

On February 28, 1852, the state legislature approved an act to incorporate the Bay Springs Union Factory Company for "the purpose of erecting, furnishing, and carrying on at Bay Springs…the manufacture of cotton and woolen yarns and fabrics; and also, for the making of all machinery necessary for manufacturing purposes, and for the erection, furnishing, and carrying on of saw or grist mills ... "The capital stock of the company was to be fifty thousand dollars to be divided into shares of one hundred dollars each. The act further stipulated that no person was to lawfully retail vinous or spirituous liquors within one mile of the Bay Springs Union Factory.

In April, 1852, James Files Gresham and his wife, Savilla Tipton Gresham, made the deed to John Briggs, James F. Gresham, and John Robinson, trading under the name of Briggs, Gresham, and Company, in consideration of $3,000 for about 680 acres of land and improvements. In the fall, Ephraim H. Wygle and his wife sold to Briggs, Gresham, and Company the quarter section down Mackey's Creek for $900. Improvements had been made on this land, and a water mill may have been on this property. Things were definitely looking up around Bay Springs, especially to Briggs, Gresham, and Company.

The Bay Springs Union Factory was built reportedly in an east-west direction on the east side of Mackey's Creek south of the old bridge. To provide this suitable location for the new structure, the original sawmill and grist mill had to be torn down. A dam about eleven feet high with a breast wheel twelve feet in diameter was built across Mackey's Creek to furnish power for the factory. The factory, more than one story tall, manufactured cotton yarns, commencing with 360 spindles, increasing to about 744, and possibly reaching 1,000 spindles years later. These cotton yarns, familiarly called "factory thread," were used in the old hand looms of the country to make cloth. Ropes were made here later.

After incorporation, the factory added a set of wool cards and set up a sawmill. To further use the abundant water power, Briggs, Gresham, and Company built a short distance downstream from the factory a grist mill with two sets of stones and a cotton gin. Furthermore, a blacksmith shop, general store, and post office continued to function in this thriving village.

In the Bay Springs post office on the east side of the creek, mail was obviously picking up. Isaac W. Wright was postmaster in 1851. Henry Collier followed him in 1852. Isaac W. Wright again became Bay Springs Postmaster in 1856.

In 1853, the Bay Springs Masons obtained a charter. Charter members of the Bay Springs F. & A. M. Lodge No. 167 included the following: Lewis R. Pate, Worshipful Master; John R. Martin, Senior Warden; Hugh Moore, Junior Warden; A. W. Hardy; W. H. H. Tyson; James F. Gresham; C. G. Pardue; and George Tankersley. The original lodge meeting place was on the east side of Mackey's Creek in the second story of either a store or a cotton
warehouse of the cotton mill.

Around 1853, George Gresham died and was buried in the Old Mackey's Creek Cemetery north of his home at Bay Springs.

About 1855, John Briggs died. The Briggs heirs in March, 1856, sold their interest at public auction in the Bay Springs Union Factory to James F. Gresham for $4,500, giving him control of the enterprise. The successes that the cotton mill and related enterprises achieved are definitely tied to his business ability and untiring efforts.

Bay Springs and the surrounding neighborhoods continued to grow. Southwesterly from Bay Springs lived James Henderson Caveness, E.W. Caveness, and their families. The Tiptons were also early Bay Springs settlers. Easterly, J. H. Jordan operated a gin and grist mill at his home on Jordan Creek on the present old McRae place south of Jourdan Hill. This quarter section that Lewis Jackson Deaton entered in 1838 attracted several land buyers. Both Kenneth McRae, a large landholder, and J. Carroll Terry, a prominent Eastport-Iuka land speculator and merchant, owned this property.

Northeast of present Jourdan Hill, a new post office was established in August, 1854. This was Barnes Store, northwest of present Dennis in the vicinity of the Harlon Brazil place. Samuel Barnes, owner of the rural store, was appointed the first postmaster. He also served as a justice of the peace in 1856-1859. In July, 1860, Samuel A. Barnes secured a license to peddle goods in his wagon. Assuredly, his store and the post office there furnished a new supply of goods and a means of communication for the people from Bay Springs through the present Belmont area to the Alabama line. Then too, Samuel A. Barnes may be credited with having run the first "peddling truck" in our area in his wagon.

The Aberdeen to Eastport stagecoach route came through the Bay Springs-Barnes Store-Highland route northward. About 1855, a four-horse coach traveled this same route three times a week. Voting precincts in the Tishomingo County Fourth District in 1857 were Cape Horn and Barnes Store. The next year the Scott's Mill voting precinct was established in the Bear Creek vicinity. Many settlers living on what was to become Belmont would have voted at Scott's Mill in all probability. In 1859 the Cape Horn precinct northwest of Bay Springs was renamed Cape Fair.

In the late 1850's, the state legislature passed an act requiring the board of police in each county to organize their counties into patrol districts and appoint captains. Serving this area as captains were J. George Kelly, George Tankersley, J. T. Wright, and

A. J. B. Wright. Since these patrols were actually slave patrols, these captains had very little to do in view of the relatively sparse slave population of the area.

Efforts were also made to improve basic education. Teachers were first required to secure certificates before being employed to teach in the public schools of Tishomingo County in 1858. To get one of these certificates, a teacher had to pass an examination in "the rudiments of an English education" before a committee of three competent persons whom the school commissioners appointed. Joab Hale and John McRae were teachers in the rural area that was someday to have a place called Belmont. Joab Hale had students from the following families: Vinson, Hopkins, Hampton, Campbell, McClung, Moore, and Shook. Among the students of John McRae were two brothers, John Shook and Columbus Shook. C. C. (Columbus) Shook must have learned well from John McRae because he was later to have a key role in the emergence of Belmont.

In 1859, E. W. Carmack deeded a parcel of land to New Providence Primitive Baptist Church on the Eastport and Aberdeen Public Road for church purposes and for a school in the neighborhood if desired. The log church-school at New Providence had split log benches. This early school was the embryonic beginning of an educational movement that was to grow into our present school at Belmont.

The county board of school commissioners at the July, 1860, meeting at Jacinto appointed trustees of common schools in their respective townships. These trustees were given the task of choosing teachers, based on qualifications, for their respective townships. They were also responsible to superintend the schools in their respective townships and make the necessary rules and regulations. At this time C. C. Malone was the fourth district school commissioner. Appointed as trustees of common schools in our area for Township 6, Range 9 were John R. Martin, Isaac Wright, J. F. Gresham, W. H. Woodruff, and Stephen R. Moore. From Township 6, Range 10 were Samuel A. Barnes, Robert Bullen, P. Smith, William McClung, and B. F. Hopkins. Trustees from Township 6, Range 11 were W. C. Lindsey, W. A. Russell, W. Embrey, J. Toland, and H. J. White.

Meanwhile, another group of Masons had formed a lodge, probably in the vicinity of Banner in Itawamba County. This lodge was in later decades through some moving about to settle and become the present Belmont Masonic lodge. On January 18, 1859, Pleasant Hill F. & A.M. Lodge No. 237 was chartered with the following charter members: S. L. Houston, Worshipful Master; Joshua Stevens, Senior Warden; Martin Bailey, Junior Warden; O. W. Stewart; James W. McCulloch; David McClung; J. D. Reagor; and William Benson.

A new post office operated about 1858 in the present Fanchertown community. The post office was Oak Farm, and Hardin Patterson was the postmaster. This post office was to continue through the Civil War until it was discontinued for a while in 1867.

Back at Bay Springs, new developments were occurring. Dr. Charles Ryan, having graduated from the Memphis Medical College, located around Bay Springs. Dr. N. B. Warren practiced in the area also. Dr. Ryan, in time, moved a few miles west of Bay Springs around the present Friendship Church in the East Prentiss community which in the latter years of the life of Dr. Ryan was to be known as Elma.

In 1860, war talk was everywhere. Tishomingo County actively began war preparations. The county assessor was ordered to determine the number of persons in the county subject to military duty. The first work of the board of police at their December meeting was to order a special election for the secession convention to meet in Jackson on January 7, 1861. Although many hoped there would be no war, the events of the next few weeks would make it inevitable.

James Files Gresham pondered his future at Bay Springs and began making preparations if the seemingly inevitable war should come. For sure, the Gresham families had witnessed a heyday of development and prosperity in their Bay Springs business involvements. In 1861, the Bay Springs area; the sparsely populated, rural area that was later to become Belmont; Tishomingo County; and the entire South were soon to face a struggle that was to change their way of life -- the Civil War.

Courtesy Margaret G. Rogers

James Files (Uncle Jimmy) Gresham, one-time owner of the Bay Springs Union Factory in its heyday at Bay Springs. He was one of the shrewdest promoters our area has ever had.

CHAPTER 5

CIVIL WAR AND ITS AFTERMATH

The inevitable Civil War was to have a deep-cutting, devastating impact on both the way of life and the economy of this area. In 1860, Tishomingo County was, reportedly, one of the wealthiest in the South. The population had increased to 24,149. The number of free white eligible voters between 21 and 50 years of age was 3,260. Assessed valuation of land was $3,750,000. The valuation of personal property, exclusive of slaves, was $1,577,000. The valuation of the 4,673 slaves under 60 and over 16 years of age was $4,673,000. Their total owners in the county were 686 citizens.

Some typical prices of trade in 1860 were as follows: butter, 25 cents per pound; live beef cattle, 8 cents per pound; coffee, 13-20 cents per pound; corn, 50 cents per bushel; chickens, about 20 cents each; cotton, 9-13 cents per pound; eggs, 12½ cents per dozen; flour, $4.50 per barrel; live hogs, 8 cents per pound; molasses, 45 cents per gallon; lard in barrels, 11 cents per pound; sugar, 8-9 cents per pound; and tobacco, 40 cents per pound. This was to change because the gathering clouds of Civil War were about to bring their terrible storm.

Representing Tishomingo County at the state convention on January 7, 1861, were delegates favoring secession from the United States provided all Southern states withdrew from the Union together. They were opposed to taking any action in Mississippi until the other Southern states made their positions clear. Therefore, these delegates with mixed feelings voted against secession. However, the Tishomingo County delegates with even more mixed feelings later signed the Articles of Secession on January 9 after the majority had voted for secession.

On February 8, 1861, the Provisional Government of the Confederate States of America was organized at Montgomery, Alabama. The next day, Jefferson Davis of Mississippi was elected the President of the Confederacy; he was inaugurated on February 18. On March 29, Mississippi joined the Confederate States of America.

Though against impulsive secession, Tishomingo County responded to the call for volunteers with admirable loyalty to the Southern cause. More than 2,000 men answered the request. Some of the first Confederates were sent to Virginia and Tennessee to help the Confederate cause. A later group of volunteers, organized in 1862, soon saw action in the Corinth and Shiloh campaigns.

The colorful, respected Arthur E. Reynolds, over 300 pounds of statesman from Jacinto, visited the Confederate capital at Richmond, Virginia, and secured permission from President Jefferson Davis to organize a regiment of infantry. Arthur Reynolds was unanimously elected its colonel in September. Colonel Reynolds with the assistance of F. M. Boone, who became the lieutenant colonel of the regiment, proceeded to effectively organize the gallant Twenty-sixth Mississippi Infantry. This regiment had ten companies and was to be involved in many strategic battles of the Civil War.

At Bay Springs, a chapter of history was ending. James Files Gresham was considering selling his factory. He organized a company of soldiers and became captain of this group called the Cape Horn Grays. This company was mustered into the Confederate States army at Iuka on August 16, 1861, and was to become Company H, 26th Mississippi Regiment. Before long, Captain James F. Gresham became the regimental quartermaster. W. A. H. Shackelford took his place as captain of Company H. Likeable R. J. (Will) Moore was to become company captain in later years of the war.

Company H of the 26th Mississippi Infantry probably had more members from this area than any other company. The captain of Company K was Ben J. Kizer of the present Pleasant Valley community in Prentiss County. He and Captain R. J. (Will) Moore married sisters, the daughters of John Strother Gaines. Members of this family were to help later in the early growth of a place called Belmont. Several area men served in Company K, Company G, 32nd Mississippi, several Mississippi and Alabama cavalry units, and other various Confederate groups.

When Colonel Arthur Reynolds rallied the 26th Mississippi Infantry to meet at Iuka in August, 1861, the volunteers were eager to fight although they were rather poorly armed. Many of the soldiers had cap-and-ball rifles, flintlock muskets, and Hall rifles. Others had only squirrel shotguns and rifles.

Before long, war news gave way temporarily at Bay Springs to news that James Files Gresham had sold the Bay Springs mills. On November 7, 1861, he sold for $14,000 to J.C. Terry and W. J. Hart, well-known Eastport-Iuka businessmen, the Bay Springs property embracing the cotton factory, cotton gin, grist mill, sawmill, and other improvements. Aware of the financial success at Bay Springs, Terry and Hart held high hopes when they bought the Bay Springs enterprise. The Bay Springs heyday under the

Greshams was history. A new day had dawned there, but it was to be darkened with the clouds of the expanding Civil War.

While Company H was camped at Iuka awaiting battle action, another land transaction of note occurred in the Pittsburg settlement. William Carroll Lindsey and his wife, Martha Bullen Lindsey, on November 30, 1861, sold to J. W. Toland the SE¼ of section 22, Township 6 South, Range 10 East, except one acre. This acre on the east boundary line was accepted for a graveyard including some graves that were already there. These graves, for sure, included those of the early pioneer, Micajah Lindsey, and his wife, Elizabeth. In addition to revealing the respect of a son for his parents, this transaction also marked the recognition of the present Lindsey Cemetery on the west side of Highway 25 between Belmont and Dennis. Men who fought for the Confederacy who were later to be buried here included M. C. (Clabe) Lindsey, T. B. (Tom) Lindsey, and A. J. Wood.

The 26th Mississippi encountered full-scale action at Fort Donelson in Tennessee. G. N. G. Gresham, a son of James F. Gresham and the third lieutenant of Company H, had died at Russellville, Kentucky. At Fort Donelson with the Rebel yells resounding, the regiment fought bravely; but the overwhelming Union forces prevailed. Reportedly killed in the battle from Company H were G. B. Epps, Frank Ferguson, and S. R. Maulden. Henry Shook and G. W. Clingan, Sr. were wounded. After the Confederate surrender at Fort Donelson on February 16, 1862, the 26th Mississippi was sent to northern prisons. Commissioned officers were sent to Camp Chase and Johnson's Island, Ohio; other officers and privates were sent to Camp Morton in Indiana. They were exchanged later in the fall of the year. With very little delay, the regiment reassembled at Jackson, Mississippi, and was sent to Holly Springs. General Lloyd Tilghman praised the good judgment and their impetuous gallantry at the ensuing Battle of Coffeeville. The 26th Mississippi was to fight later with honor in the Vicksburg campaign.

Back in Tishomingo County, the board of police had set up a military relief fund to help families in need while their men were off to war. A county militia was formed; and in May, 1862, W. C. Lindsey and W. A. Tankersley were appointed from the southeastern part of the county to enroll and report the names of militia subject to military duty under the Confederate law known as "the conscript act." The citizens at home were also faced with the problem of staying out of the way of Union troops in the county.

During the Civil War, Dr. Charles Ryan had an extensive practice. The doctor was exempt from military service on account of his crippled arm that was paralyzed when he was about eight. Dr. Ryan and Dr. N. B. Warren were two of the very few doctors left in the area, and they frequently had to ride 30 miles to see a patient. To more fully appreciate their efforts, one has only to think about the physically fatiguing practice of medicine combined with the mentally troubling threat of harassment from Union raiders and Tories.

The Battle of Shiloh was fought in April, 1862. About this time, both Union and Confederate soldiers were traveling through this area along with raiding bands of southern Unionists who were often called Tories.

In early August, 1862, as part of a reconnaissance prior to the Iuka encounter, a detachment of Union soldiers turned from scouting the Memphis and Charleston Railroad to raid Bay Springs and the surrounding area. The commanding officer reported to his superior that he had inflicted damage on the factory at Bay Springs to such an extent that repair could not be made without assistance from New England. He could well have exaggerated to his superior this boastful claim. In fact, mysterious indeed is the reason why the Yankees did not put the torch to the entire Bay Springs installation. Many local stories related that, possibly after a repair period, the factory functioned on through the latter part of the war without repairs from New England. My great grandmother, Sallie Harris McCreary (1852- 1953), recalled that as a young girl of about twelve she swept the factory. Her older sister and several other women, reportedly, worked at the factory in the latter part of the war.

Before and after the Battle of Iuka on September 19, 1862, the Fulton and Iuka Road was used very much. Hugh Rogers, an early settler of the present Moore's Mill area, lived on the present Allen farm. Yankee raiders troubled him and his family so much that they had to hide and even bury most items of value and utilization to keep the marauders from stealing them. Other roads of the area were having a steady flow of Tory ransackers and Union soldiers.

On September 12, Confederate general Henry Little camped his troops at Bay Springs. He talked of a weak bridge, rain, and bad roads. On September 13, after repairing the bridge, this force marched on to Iuka, where General Little was killed in the battle. In the Battle of Iuka, the Confederates under the command of General Sterling Price once again fought bravely with success before retreating ahead of large Union reinforcements.

After the Battle of Iuka, the larger part of the Price army retreated by way of Bay Springs to Baldwyn. During this movement, a heavy ammunition wagon, pulled by six mules, had an accident crossing the weak bridge over Mackey's Creek at Bay Springs. A rear wheel of the wagon ran too close to the edge of the bridge flooring and broke through. The wagon fell into the stream below and pulled the team of mules down upon it. After somewhat hasty adjustments, the Confederates moved on.

In this area, however, the economy did not move on. It was at a near standstill. The home folks had many trials and tribulations in finding food and in carrying on their everyday living while many of the men were gone. Serious corn and salt shortages bothered the people. When salt was available, it sold for 25 cents per pound. To further complicate life on the local front in the Civil War at this time, the problem of raiding Union soldiers and especially Tory ransackers got no better. One lady with shotgun in hand confronted the raiders and kept them from taking the only cow she had for milk and butter for her children.

Over at Bethany Presbyterian Church, Porter Paden sought a safe place to hide his meat from the raiders. He pried up the floor of the church pulpit and hid his meat underneath the pulpit. The Union raiders camped later at the church. They used the church and walked ever so near many times to the cleverly hidden meat. After the Yankees moved on, Porter Paden again pried up the pulpit floor, found his meat intact, and went home with it. He graciously thanked God for the house of worship that had also served in this trying time as a house of security against thieves.

Young W. T. Clark reportedly kept and fed the family horses in a secluded place on a swampy, wooded knoll between his home and Bear Creek to prevent the raiders from taking them. Hallie Yarber recalled that her grandfather, John Norman, was killed in the Civil War. Her grandmother, Phebe Norman, lived in the present Ridge-Fanchertown community. Union ransackers took corn, wool blankets, and coverlets. Another day, Mrs. Norman was at the home of a relative on a hog-killing day. The raiders reappeared. Leaving only one old mule, they took cattle, horses, chickens, saddles, bridles, and even the hog meat. Tory and Union raiders are said to have done much overall damage to the property of Hardin Patterson and Mr. Leslie.

A few miles down Mackey's Creek from Allen's Store, the Yankees burned the mills of Isom J. Warren, a Confederate cavalry captain, about February 14, 1863. Near Bay Springs, the Union troops took the old settler, Stephen R. Moore, father of Captain R. J. (Will) Moore, from his home. They sent him to prison at Alton, Illinois. He died there in 1863, four months after his imprisonment.

A very uneasy condition really existed when Union sympathizers (Tories) continued to band together and further threaten the subsistence living of the home folks. The Tories hanged Jack Collier, a Confederate soldier. They stole so many horses in the area that women and children faced a very difficult matter in making crops and providing food for themselves. Some Tory raids were nothing more than pure menace disguised as Union support. In this area as elsewhere, many families became very bitter due to the mixed feelings they harbored regarding local Confederate support versus Union support. In a sense, Civil War life on the home front around here centered around worry for loved ones fighting the war, thoughts of food and meager living, bitter thoughts about the Union sympathizers, and nagging fear of Union or Tory raids.

On the real war front, the 26th Mississippi was involved in the Mississippi River campaign and other action relating to Vicksburg. David Barron was said to have been killed at the Battle of Baker's Creek (Champion's Hill) in May, 1863. Other embattled Confederates were to see action at Jackson, Meridian, and Demopolis, Alabama, before reporting to Virginia in the spring of 1864.

The 26th Mississippi was also at the Battle of the Wilderness in Virginia in May, 1864. Here, T. J. Allen, James Voyles, and other brave sons of our homeland gave up their lives carrying out their patriotic duty for a cause in which they believed. Lieutenant Colonel F. M. Boone, who ably led the regiment, was shot in the forehead and died instantly. After his burial and after the Battle of the Wilderness was over, a search party was unable to find his grave since the crude marker had been destroyed. Although F. M. Boone was from north Tishomingo County, he was highly respected among the Confederates from the present Belmont area. In fact, he was held with such esteem that years later the Confederate veterans of the Belmont area named their camp in his honor-   F. M. Boone Camp No.1694.

At the Battle of Weldon Railroad in August, Joab Hale was killed; and G. T. Millican reportedly lost a leg. David Matthews and Joab Hale were named to the Regiment Roll of Honor for their valiant efforts. William Alexander Stephens of Company K, 26th Mississippi was one of two men to make the Regimental Roll of Honor for gallantry in the Battle of Bethesda Church.

In the summer of 1864, the bloody, prolonged Petersburg battle and siege near Richmond, Virginia, involved the stout-hearted efforts of Company H, showing a strength of about 125 men. Here, they and their fellow Confederates of the 26th Mississippi and other units fought overwhelming forces with diminishing means for months. Captain R. J. (Will) Moore was injured, captured, and sent to Johnson's Island prison. Lieutenants George L. Womack and Samuel A. Barnes were killed at Petersburg. The siege of Petersburg prolonged through the winter. The pendulum of momentum had swung toward the Union forces, despite Confederate heroics on many fronts.

Several present Belmontians have mentioned that they had the following kindred to fight for the Confederates in addition to those in Company H: Captain Alexander Fancher, B. F. (Frank) Hopkins, Andy McCreary, Julius Taylor Clark, Sam Vaughn, Joe Stockton, James Sparks, Dave Ardis, M. C. Lindsey, T. B. Lindsey, O. L. Phillips, James H. Cobb, J. T. Montgomery, Dave Allen, Michael Shook, A. J. Wood, G. H. Montgomery, Holland Pharr, L. J. Cain, Alford W. Byram, William A. Sartain, T. J. Selby, and J. T. Butler. Obviously, hundreds of other area men fought in the Civil War with equal honor and bravery.

Maudie Stacy Osbirn relates that both of her grandfathers, T. F. Stacy and J. C. (Jack) Credille, fought in the Civll War. J. C. Credille was reportedly imprisoned and offered a release if he would go West to fight the Indians. Fortunately, the war ended before he had to make a decision; and J.C. Credille was released to come home. Our present area includes many descendants of J. C. Credille.

Levi Epps, grandfather of W. Elbridge Epps, was a Confederate scout in this area and was killed in action. He is buried in a small cemetery in the Ridge-Banner vicinity. Another Confederate who helped protect the home folks was Dr. Middleton M. (Mid) Davis 1833-1919). Once, when approaching his home near present

Dennis, Dr. Davis saw his little girl, Becky, running after the geese. Actually, the little girl was running to tell him that Union soldiers were down the road. To avoid confrontation with the raiding soldiers, he stayed all night in a nearby pine thicket. In a land transaction that was to have much importance to the later early emergence of Belmont, Dr. Middleton M. (Mid) Davis in December, 1864, paid $2,000 to John Winegar for the SE¾ of section 10, Township 6 South, Range 10 East northerly from present Dennis on the Phillips place.

The Womack family of the Old Bethel community sent five sons to fight for the Confederacy in the Civil War. All of them lost their lives except William P. (Bill) Womack. He was wounded and lost a foot in the battle at Kennesaw Mountain in Georgia. James H. Cobb, who married Martha Womack, also died in the Civil War. Martha Cobb later married Jim Tom Montgomery, and they were residents of Belmont in its early years. Later her daughter, Mary Lou (Mollie) Cobb, was to marry an early Belmont builder, W. T. Clark.

W.R. Akers relates that his grandfather, Jackson M. Akers, and Columbus Akers, a brother of Jackson, served with Company E, 42nd Mississippi in the Civil War. In a March, 1863, letter from Virginia, Jackson Akers wrote that the camp soldiers got a half pound of meat and about a pint of flour per day with sufficient salt and sometimes a little rice. The water was good, and the soldiers got it from wells dug about three feet under the ground surface. Corn was two dollars per bushel, and bacon was 65 cents per pound. The soldiers in his company were punctually paid eleven dollars per month every two months.

The Confederate government furnished the soldiers with shoes, socks, and clothing. Preaching was held two to three times a month. Each 25 men reportedly entitled a company to one furlough; and since Company E lacked a few in having 50 men, they only got one furlough. The overall situation was to worsen very much as the battles raged and as Southern supplies lessened. Jackson M. Akers was wounded in the arm at Gettysburg, was imprisoned and paroled, and finished the war with the army of Robert E. Lee. The principled Jackson Akers in a very exemplary manner lived to be 97 years old.

In January, 1865, Captain W. A. H. Shackelford of Company H, 26th Mississippi Regiment wrote that all was quiet along the lines at Petersburg and Richmond. In a rather melancholy mood of grim realism, Captain Shackelford wrote to his friend, William Harmon Riddle, that the weather in Virginia was beautiful then. The pretty weather led him to ponder why men could not be about their domestic pursuits at home, such as mending up their old fences, clearing off their farms, and making their farms ready for seed planting. Alas, this was not the case. Instead, the men were huddled in squads over little smoky campfires, thinly clad, and poorly provided with "the staff of life." He felt the soldiers were worrying seriously about the plight of their loved ones back home and spending their lives in much displeasure, both physical and mental. In grim realism, he wrote, "Sometimes, when I survey it in all its features, it seems to verge close upon one complicated mark of nonsense. But I could not be right and everybody else wrong so I must agree with the majority." Agree he did because Captain Shackelford remained a true Confederate and a community leader after the war.

Despite the spirited battling of the Confederates with many losses, Petersburg fell; and the end of the Civil War was in sight. After this ferocious fighting, very few of the gallant 26th Mississippi were able to follow Lee to Appomattox, where the Civil War ended on April 9, 1865.

Among those in Company H, 26th Mississippi who died in the Civil War and were not mentioned previously were K. T. Allen; Guthrie Allen; Mart Choate; G. W. Clingan, Jr., who was killed at Perryville; John Dailey; A. J. Embrey; Sgt. A. F. Farmer; Tom Purdy; Pete Smith; Jake Toland; and W. J. Bellamy, who died on the way home after the surrender. Some of the area men who survived the war included James F. Gresham, quartermaster; R. J. "Will" Moore, captain; W. A. H. Shackelford, captain; J. H. Russell, lieutenant; J. W. McDougal, sergeant; W. P. Pardue; D. C. Apperson, drummer; J. H. Allen; Cavalier Byram; J. M. Byram; W.W. Barron; Andy Cunningham; Riley Cunningham; J. W. Duncan; James Ferguson; James Gable, fifer; E. A. Howell; Abe Howell; Charlie C. Harris; William Harris; Jake Hill; John Hill; David Hunt; J.M. Jourdan; W. A. Jourdan; D. N. Matthews; William Millican; Fayette Moody; Jeff Moody; William Rushing; Elliot Riddle; George Russell; James M. Russell; C. C. Shook; S. T. Shook; Henry Shook; Erwin Searcy; T. F. Stacy; J. W. Stacy; Albert Taylor; Mitch Taylor; Wesley Taylor; J. H. Tipton; James Williams; W. M. Williams; Thad Woodruff; Fred Woodruff; J.M. Wilson; and J. K. Wright.

The end of the Civil War when General Lee surrendered to General Grant at Appomattox Court House in Virginia was received with mixed feelings. Mrs. Ruth McCreary Mayo recalls that her grandfather, Andy McCreary, was one of the Confederates who were captured while trying to help Jefferson Davis escape. True to his cause to the last, Uncle Andy expressed his feeling in no uncertain terms to the Union captors. Still, in a short while, Andy McCreary was one of the thousands of Confederates who were released to go home to "pick up the pieces."

Many returning "sons of the Confederacy" found their livestock gone, their homes in disrepair, their farms grown up in weeds, their families in need of more food, many parents dead from the strain of the war, bitterness over Tory marauding, and their previous way of life gone forever.

The Tishomingo County government began to function more actively with the war ended and the soldiers back at home. Men from our area served ably in government. James F. Gresham was sheriff and tax collector; while E. W. Carmack, formerly from Bethany, was probate clerk. George Tankersley, John Byram, D. G. Pardue, and W. A. Paden were justices of the peace who functioned from this vicinity. Joseph Hunt and William Storment served on the board of police. A. J. Wood and Samuel Pounds were area constables.

At the close of the war, prices on some products were the following: clear side bacon, 20 cents per pound; shoulder, 15 cents per pound; ham, 25 cents per pound; butter, 25 cents per pound; coffee, 33 cents per pound; corn, 75 cents per bushel; eggs, 20 cents per dozen; corn meal, one dollar per bushel; flour $8-16 per barrel; lard, 25 cents per pound; molasses, $1.25 per gallon; tobacco, $2.50 per pound; and coal oil, one dollar per gallon. Some of the price increases were due to Civil War inflation.

In January, 1866, J. C. Terry of Memphis sold his one-half interest in the Bay Springs enterprises to his partner, William J. Hart, for $5,000. In December, Hart sold a two-thirds interest in the Bay Springs business to Alexander R. Wiggs of Tishomingo County and Moses J. Wicks of Memphis for $6,666.66 and two-thirds cents. The next year John Robinson of New Orleans gave a quit claim deed to Wicks, Wiggs, and Hart concerning his previous interest in the Bay Springs cotton factory, land, sawmills, grist mill, out buildings, and other improvements. The Bay Springs factory was on its way back up after the Civil War setbacks.

Additionally, Elizabeth Wright was in charge of the Bay Springs post office on the eastside of Mackey's Creek in 1867.

Mackey's Creek Primitive Baptist Church along with other area churches had essentially suspended most church activities during the Civil War. James. M. Riddle, the church clerk at Mackey's Creek before war broke out, died in the war. In September, 1865, members of Mackey's Creek Church agreed to build a meeting house on the same ground where the old house stood. Possibly, raiders destroyed the old church. In time, the area churches were resounding with old-time hymnal music and sermons.

In 1866, area justices of the peace included John McRae, Joseph Hunt, J. N. Wilson, and W. A. Paden. John Byram and W. P. Pardue were two of the district constables. In November, 1866, David McClung sold to Sarah Ann Clark (Mrs. James M. Clark) 160 acres of land involving much of present north Belmont in consideration of 1,200 pounds of good seed cotton delivered at the Hardin Patterson gin the following November. Three sons of Sarah Ann Clark - John Henry Clark, W. T. Clark, and G. A. "Dick" Clark - were in later decades to be noted Belmont builders. Another land transaction in February, 1867, involved the SW¼ of section 36, Township 6 South, Range 10 East. M. D. L. Adams bought it for 3,000 pounds of lint cotton. This quarter section sold for $300 in 1876 to a Confederate veteran named C. C. (Lum) Shook.

In the Allen's Store community, which is presently called Moore's Mill, a post office existed in September, 1867, about 60 yards on the north side of Red Bud Creek. It was on the Iuka to Ryan's Well route over which John M. Thompson carried the mail once each week. John M. Redden was the Allen's Store postmaster and continued on into 1872.

With the death of the former postmaster, Samuel A. Barnes, in the Civil War, the Barnes Store post office had a new postmaster, Ransom Davis, in 1867. The influence of Ransom Davis (1800-1877); his son, Dr. Mid Davis; and their families was to be very influential and memorable in many ways.

For the years 1867-1868, Joseph Hunt, John McRae, W. A. Paden, and W. P. Pardue were justices of the peace. John Byram was re-elected constable. John McRae (1818-1905) was on the new county board of police that took office the first of May, 1869. In about a year the Free State of Tishomingo ended its illustrious existence. In these Reconstruction times, an act of the Mississippi legislature, approved on April 15, 1870, provided for the division of Old Tishomingo County into Tishomingo County, Prentiss County, and Alcorn County. At 1870, Reconstruction problems seriously posed many hardships on the people. Many developments, both good and bad, lay ahead in the troubled 1870's in the Fifth District of the new Tishomingo County where a place called Belmont was to be located later.

CHAPTER 6

THE TROUBLED 1870'S

After much political maneuvering at state and national levels, Mississippi had been readmitted into the Union in 1870. Public unrest, however, continued until the Reconstruction government ended around 1876. The Freedman's Bureau, passed in 1865 theoretically to look after the interests of recently freed slaves, continued to function until about 1872. All too often, the officers of the Bureau turned out to be adventurers who cared more for political and financial gain than for the welfare of the blacks. In a sense the Freedman's Bureau did not function on a powerful scale. The destitution and the predominantly white population probably caused the bureaucratic zealots to bypass Tishomingo County in favor of counties with large black populations. In 1870 the population analysis of Tishomingo County revealed 7,350 people-- 6,609 whites and 741 blacks. The number of eligible white voters was 690 compared to 94 black voters with 273 people disqualified.

Prior to 1870 the functions of Loyal Leagues in Tishomingo County to help the blacks harassed and irritated many whites. Then too, a few gangs of ruthless desperadoes roamed the county, terrorizing and raiding homesteads and farms. To counteract these threats to their homes and way of life, the Ku Klux Klan was formed in Tishomingo County in the spring of 1867. It had about 1,500 members. Some sincere efforts of the Klan kept life and property from being at the mercy of the outlaws and profiteers of Reconstruction times. Many Klan actions went beyond the "realms of right." On the other side of the ledger the actions of the desperadoes, carpetbaggers, and scalawags also made life miserable for many persons wanting only "life, liberty, and the pursuit of happiness."

The Constitution of 1869 went into effect in 1870. It brought several changes to the county governments, including Tishomingo. A board of supervisors, consisting of a member from each of the five districts, replaced the board of police. Our area was in the Fifth District in the new Tishomingo County. The chancery court replaced the abolished office of probate judge; the chancery clerk replaced the probate clerk.

John McRae was the first supervisor of the Fifth District in the newly formed Tishomingo County. Other Fifth District supervisors in the trying 1870-1880 period were William Hartsell and Hardin Patterson. The justices of the peace for the Fifth District in this time included John Wilson, Joseph Hunt, W. W. Gilbert, Alexander Fancher, Enoch Jordan, F. Bennett, P. G. Pardue, and T. B. Lindsey. G. W. Vaughn, Jr. was named constable of the Fifth District but declined to qualify. Willis Davis was appointed constable in 1871. Other constables in this decade were J. C. Moody, J. I. Hopkins, John A. Byram, George Regan, and A.G. Clark.

Provisions for a public school system came from the Constitution of 1869. The establishment of the public school system in the state is one of the truly good things that came from the Reconstruction government. Nevertheless, this system ignored local needs and imposed one system on the entire state. Like many Reconstruction enactments, this extravagant system was to be unusually burdensome on poor counties like Tishomingo. A lack of money connected with the burden of the dual school system aroused resentment against the proposed policy of putting a schoolhouse on "every high hill and under every green tree." Overlooked was the ability or willingness of the people to pay for the schools. This policy can take much blame for lots of the backwardness toward education prior to 1900.

For a while, schools were either scarce or badly conducted. Some referred to these crude one-teacher, log schools as "roasting ear schools" because they lasted little longer than "roasting ears" were in season. The schools were not the only segment of society to suffer. Provisions of basic living were scarce and too high. Society was not good, and hard times characterized the early 1870's.

Then too, a mistake had occurred in the Revised Code of 1871 in defining the boundary line between Tishomingo and Itawamba counties. A portion of the territory of Tishomingo County was included in Itawamba County. This involved land was in part of Township seven generally from the Allen's Store area on the west to Oak Farm and the Alabama line on the east. Present day Moore's Mill, Old Bethel, New Bethel, Fanchertown, Golden, and south Belmont are located on this land that was included in Itawamba County.

Map of southern Tishomingo County, including land added from Itawamba County. The Tishomingo County land south of the Township 7 line was originally in Itawamba County until Reconstruction county revisions. An error in the Revised Code of 1871 had this land again in Itawamba County.

On March 5, 1872, the Mississippi legislature corrected this county line mistake. The boundary line between Tishomingo County and Itawamba County was to be as follows: a line commencing at the southwest corner of section 14, Township 7 South, Range 9 East and running east on the section lines to the state line of Alabama. The territory lying north of this line in Township seven officially became part of the Fifth District of Tishomingo County. In 1872, the Fifth District settlements included Bay Springs, Barnes Store, Pittsburg, Providence, McRae-Moore settlement, Oak Farm, Old Bethel, and Allen's Store.

Down in north Itawamba County, Dr. Thomas E. Copeland and his wife, Alice Copeland, became parents of twin sons-Orlando and Alcanda--on March 12, 1870. Alice Copeland called Alcanda "Little Bit" because he was the smaller of the two. Other family members misunderstood Mrs. Copeland at times and called Alcanda "Little Dit." When the twins were about three, they had scarlet fever; and Orlando died. Alcanda "Dit" Copeland grew up to become a doctor as did his brothers, Jim and Oscar. Their impact on north Itawamba County, the Red Bay area, and our Belmont area was to be very noteworthy in the decades ahead.

East of Bear Creek in the present Valley community, a new Baptist church was formed. Old Union Church was organized July 11, 1874, at Barber's Chapel. Elder W. F. White and Rev. J. S. Stockton, presbytery, called for letters to come forward and the following responded: W. F. White and Mary White, J.E. Spencer, Sarah Weatherford, Jane Russell, W.J. Clingan, Sarah Elizabeth Clingan, S. J. Clingan, G. W. Weatherford and S. N. Weatherford, S. B. Monroe and Wincy Monroe, Nancy Cranford and S. J. Cranford and Margaret Hopkins. W. H. Harris, J.M. Harris, and C. P. Harris were received by experience and baptism. W. F. White was selected as pastor, and J. S. Stockton was moderator. J. C. George was the church clerk protem. W. M. Clingan deeded about three acres to the Union Missionary Baptist Church and gave free access to a certain spring of water situated approximately 200 yards to the southwest of the church.

Several interesting developments occurred in the area post offices. Frank E. Gipson was postmaster at Allen's Store in 1872. Later in the year, C. H. (Hightower) Allen (1845-1884) became postmaster of Allen's Store and served very capably until his death in January, 1884. At his death, the post office was closed; and mail went to Bay Springs.

In late1873 or early 1874, the Barnes Store post office name was changed to Hillside. Ransom Davis continued as postmaster until his death in 1877. His daughter, Catherine R. Davis, then became Hillside postmaster. In 1879 John C. Harris was Hillside postmaster.

The Oak Farm post office, located where present Fanchertown is, was in 1873 on the Iuka to Pikeville, Alabama, Road. H. S. Brooks picked up the mail once a week, and J. F. Patterson was the Oak Farm postmaster. About 1877, the Pleasant Ridge post office began at Nabers Store near the present Ridge Road, and Oak Farm faded away. W. N. Nabers was the Pleasant Ridge postmaster; and the mail route from Hillside to Shottsville, Alabama, went through there once a week.

Courtesy Gertrude Ozbirn

Dr. M. M. (Mid) Davis, the first Belmont postmaster in 1873.

In 1873, the birth of Belmont, Mississippi, in the Fifth District of Tishomingo County occurred. Ironically, Belmont did not begin at Belmont! It was at Davis Store on the present Phillips place northerly from present Dennis. Dr. Middleton M. (Mid) Davis was the first Belmont postmaster in November 17, 1873, at his store located in the SE¼ of section 10, Township 6 South, Range 10 East. It was on the Iuka to Pikeville mail route on which H. S. Brooks carried the mail one time per week. The Highland post office was about five miles north. Oak Farm post office was nine miles in a southern direction; and Barnes Store was three miles in a western direction. The Belmont post office was on the west side about 100 yards from the surveyed railroad route and was to serve a population of approximately 200. Evidently, something went awry on the railroad survey because the reported site of the first Belmont post office is today on the east side of the railroad. At Davis Store and Belmont post office, Dr. M. M. Davis also had an early type horse-powered gin which his daughters often operated.

Many people of the area around Belmont post office southward to the county line saw the necessity of education and about 1872- 1874 set out to have a free school. The one-teacher log school was about two miles north of present Belmont where the old New

Providence Primitive Baptist Church once stood. Actually, school could have been held in the old church building which stood where the present Verna Wood Crow house is located on the west side of Highway 25.

About 1875, steps were taken to move the school within the corporate limits of Belmont in or near the present Belmont Blue Springs City Park. The one-teacher school was called "Gum Springs school," taking its local name from a spring just down the hill behind the school where most school children got water. Some students also got water from Blue Springs southwesterly from the school. Many local citizens "pitched in," hewed logs, and built the 18 by 24 feet school house. It had a stick-and-dirt chimney and other usual rough fixtures of the time. The school patrons also split logs to make luncheon benches for the students.

In August, 1875, William M. (Uncle Billy) Campbell deeded the property for the school, for all orthodox churches, and for the Grangers one day in each month or more if necessary. Churches and Grange were to have free access to the springs not to conflict with the days of each other. He further stipulated that the Mormons could preach in his blacksmith shop.

In 1876, the same year Reconstruction ended, L. R. Davis, a son of Dr. Mid Davis, was the teacher at Gum Springs in the opening session. He taught the children how to spell in the old blue-back speller and how to do sums by Rule of Three. He was back the next school year; and W. T. Clark, who had returned from the West, succeeded him.

In 1876, W. T. Clark (1848-1923) became Belmont postmaster at his home in present Belmont on Old Highway 25 where the Grover Pounders home is now located. In 1877, M. J. Hopkins and John I. Hopkins were Belmont postmasters. Some think the post office may have been at the John I. C. Hopkins Store that was south of present Belmont and east across Highway 25 from the Carl Sartain home. In 1879, John Henry Clark (1850-1924) became the Belmont postmaster where W. T. Clark, his brother, previously had it.

In the late 1870's, cotton brought about 11 cents per pound. Cross ties were about 35 cents, and lumber sold for $7-11 per thousand. Still, despite the hard times of Reconstruction, the Bay Springs factory and other enterprises were beginning to return a good profit. Ownership changed hands several times in the 1870's. For example, Alexander R. Wiggs and William J. Hart sold their interests to their associate, Moses J. Wicks, in July, 1870. Others who owned interests at various intervals in the decade were Sarah Wicks, W. J. McGavock, Sam Tate, Jr., Lizzie C. Tate, and John M. Nelson, Sr. John M. Nelson (1813-1882) seemed to have been in charge of company operations and had full ownership in the Bay Springs factory and enterprises about 1877.

    E. H. Reno was Bay Springs postmaster in 1871 and was bookkeeper for John M. Nelson and Company in the first part of the 1870's. Thomas H. Ladd became postmaster in 1876, while Robert C. McMechan followed him in 1877. McMechan signed a store receipt for John M. Nelson and Company, lending some credence to the fact that the post office may have been located in the factory commissary, or store. In 1879, the store operated as Nelson and McMechan, and John M. Nelson, Jr. worked there.

    Meanwhile, the Bay Springs Masons purchased for $600 in about 1874 a half acre from John M. Nelson and Company upon which was built a two-story hall. This structure still stands today in weather-worn disrepair. It is on the west side of Mackey's Creek a little south of where the store stood. Ransom Davis, the county surveyor, surveyed the lot for the lodge building. The Masons used the stairway and upper story for lodge purposes, while the bottom floor was used for church services for all denominations. Hardin Patterson, a Methodist minister, and an evangelist named Bass are reported to have preached here many times. In the twentieth century, the Church of Christ was to meet here.

    Life at Bay Springs and, in fact, the entire area in 1875 was characterized with bad times, financial embarrassment, and destitute conditions. The hard times of Reconstruction led many people to go West, especially to Texas. Still, the benevolent Masons gave the Friendship Grange No. 305 the privilege of holding monthly meetings in the lodge free of charge for the rest of the year. As Reconstruction ended, things began to improve little. As 1880 rolled around, some felt that the Bay Springs mills under John M. Nelson, Sr. could become one of the largest enterprises in the state and in the South. There was even talk of building a railroad through Bay Springs.

    The budding settlement to the east which some called Belmont was beginning to develop some leaders. However, the true identity around which sound development comes was not there because the post office was being moved rather frequently. In July, 1880, the Belmont post office was again moved. This time, it was located at Clark's Gin in the NW¼ of section 10, Township 7 south, Range 10 East near the North Fork of Red Bud Creek in the vicinity of the present Goodwin place. Thus, in 1880, Belmont had emerged as a name; but it had not settled down to its eventual identity location.

Courtesy Joe K. Stephens

The Bay Springs Masonic Lodge.

CHAPTER 7

THE EMERGENCE OF BELMONT

The emergence of Belmont gained much momentum between 1880 and 1900. Belmont gained a locational post office base around which to identify and grow. In 1880 many changes were taking place in the Fifth District of Tishomingo County. People were learning to adjust to their way of life. Interest increased in schools and churches. More country stores were showing up in the area. More people were going to Iuka, Booneville, and other trade centers to transact business. The population was on an upswing. In 1880, the population of Tishomingo County was 8,774 with 1,359 residing in the Fifth District where a place called Belmont was to emerge. Ten years later, 9,302 people lived in Tishomingo County with 1,587 in the Fifth District.

Only 13.3 per cent of the land in Tishomingo County in 1880 was tilled. The predominant crop with 15,965 acres in cultivation was corn. Cotton occupied only about one-fifth of the cultivated acreage as 7,555 acres were planted. Oats were grown on 3,237 acres, and wheat was grown on 702 acres. Still, the people looked through hope and tradition to cotton as the "money crop." To sell their cotton, most of our area farmers went to Iuka around 1880. With money earned from the cotton crop our farmers brought back mercantile items that were to gradually upgrade the local way of life. Nevertheless, this change was to be very slow until the coming of the railroad through the Belmont area in the twentieth century.

Actually, farm transportation was very slow. The people were equally slow in adjusting to new farming ideas. Around 1890, the first shipment of commercial fertilizer came to the Iuka market. It was purely bone meal and was reportedly shipped in 200 pound sacks. The obviously foul smell, the origin of the bone meal, and fear that the fertilizer might be poisonous or cause disease led many to hesitate about using it until the early 1900's. In the years around the turn of the century, there was much talk about the new stock laws. Previously, cattle, hogs, and sheep were allowed to roam free range. Rail fences were built around fields. With the new stock laws, things changed. Stock was fenced in, and fields began to be left open. Sheep raising declined. Farm feelings were very mixed regarding the stock laws, but the benefit eventually prevailed.

Farm situations worsened in 1892 when crops failed. Land sold cheap. Many of our people went West again, especially to Texas. The statement, probably exaggerated, is made that Hill County, Texas, had more Tishomingo County citizens than Tishomingo County had. In November, 1892, in Iuka the following prices of trade prevailed: cotton, 7 ½ cents per pound; corn, 40 cents per bushel; meal, 50 cents per bushel; butter, 12 ½ cents per pound; eggs, 12 ½ cents per dozen; chickens, 10-15 cents each; calico, 5 cents per yard; cloth checks, 4½ cents per yard; and gingham, 8 and one-third cents per yard.

Despite the agricultural and living hardships, the Fifth District trade centers were to witness much change in the years before 1900. Many of the people and later their descendants were to help bring out the emergence and growth of Belmont.

Serving the growing Fifth District as supervisors from 1880 to 1900 were Enoch Jordan, T. B. Lindsey and W. T. Clark. Some of the justices of the peace were T. B. Lindsey, W. A. Paden, J. Epps, John Henry Clark, J. D. Mann, J. T. Vaughn, W. A. Martin, Lemuel Trollinger, C. C. Shook, W. H. Lindsey, W. B. McCollum, and J. T. Flurry. Some of the constables were J. C. Hallmark, J. F.Vinson, J. W. Hale, W. M. Davis, J.C. Tittle, and O. L. Phillips. In 1880, the population around Allen's Store on Red Bud Creek was listed as 22. With the death of the Allen's Store postmaster, Charnel Hightower Allen, in 1884, the post office closed. His son, L. P. Allen (1881-1969), was destined in future years to do very much to help Belmont and the area grow. In fact, L. P. Allen was to be one of the most outstanding builders to ever live on our "beautiful mountain" at Belmont. At the Red Bud settlement, Steve Moore took over the operation of the water mill. Thus, this settlement on Red Bud Creek, formerly Allen's Store, came to be known as Moore's Mill and is still Moore's Mill today.

A new post office, Emma, was opened in the Moore's Mill community in 1894, and Willy Robert (Will) Moore was the postmaster. His wife, Emily A. Moore, became the Emma postmaster in 1898. An event that caused much conversation the previous year was the issuance of a patent to Francis M. Bennett. Francis Bennett, who assigned ½ interest to Emily Caveness, got patent No. 582,153 on May 4, 1897, on a combination ballot box and register. This ballot box-register would provide an automatic registering mechanism in connection with a ballot box so every ballot would be properly registered and an accurate count insured.

The population at Bay Springs in 1880 was listed at 65. Here, these formative times saw one sad change for the worse. Many continued to have high hopes for Bay Springs, but fate finally caught up with the Bay Springs factory in the 1880's. In 1881, John M. Nelson served as Bay Springs postmaster. He was reportedly making a real nice profit from his factory and mill enterprises. He had a beautiful two-story house that was located where the Jack Searcy family lived decades later in a neat white house south of Gin Branch at Bay Springs. Nelson owned a gin, a sawmill, a grist mill, a flour mill, a well-stocked store, and the cotton factory with a wool-carding machine and many spindles for making yarn and thread. Although no cloth was manufactured, John M. Nelson, Sr. was planning to put in looms. Before he could carry out his plans, John M. Nelson died on April 1, 1882.

This changed the ultimate course of Bay Springs. John M. Nelson, Jr. did not possess the drive and business sense of the elder Nelson. In fact, much of the actual management of the enterprise is said to have fallen to the hands of Mrs. Marion E. Nelson, the widow of the elder Nelson, and to an in-law. Some conjecture that Jessie E. Paden, a daughter of John M. Nelson, Sr., and her husband, Ramsey Paden, may have been involved in the operation. For sure, Marion E. Nelson became the Bay Springs postmaster. She served until the post office was discontinued and mail went to Tynes on July 28, 1885. In the meantime, the factory which is said to have once employed 50-100 people began to decline. It is said that the actions of John M. Nelson, Jr. displeased many. Employee relations with the new management became worse. Local people had been bringing cotton to the factory and putting it in stalls for several years. About 1885-1886, a fire of suspected incendiary origin destroyed the factory. H. R. Davis recalls that his father, G. W. Davis, lost two bales of cotton that were at the factory when it burned. Others also lost stored cotton in the fire. The Nelson loss was much greater. W. W. Shook recalled before his death that, as a boy with his father, Mike Shook, at their home on Rock Creek, they saw the entire night sky in the Bay Springs direction glow red from the raging, destructive fire. Shortly, the Nelson family moved away from Bay Springs. The dam was in time removed from the creek. The death of John M. Nelson, Sr. had also sounded the death knell to the Bay Springs factory and other enterprises. The plentiful water power remained. The picturesque beauty remained. The Masons still met at the lodge. Church was still held downstairs from the Masonic lodge. Confederate reunions were held at Bay Springs. People came there for family outings. A road from Booneville and points west came through Bay Springs and meandered to the emerging settlement around Belmont. Nevertheless, Bay Springs suffered because it had no entrepreneur like James Files Gresham or John M. Nelson, Sr.

Ironically, some of the best interest in Bay Springs at this time came from the first mayor of Tupelo, Harvey Medford. In 1887, Mayor Medford proposed that the state penitentiary be moved out of Jackson to Bay Springs. He suggested that convicts be put to work there quarrying building stone. Medford also issued one of the earlier calls for the state to have good roads, suggesting that the roads be improved with local "misdemeanor convict" labor. Mayor Medford stated that at Bay Springs in Tishomingo County piles on piles of building stone were available. This huge mass of rock would be near inexhaustible. Convict labor would be able to peck, saw, and blast rocks to furnish the building stone. Moreover, impenetrable and fireproof prison walls could be made from rocks right on the spot.

Courtesy Mittie H. Searcy

Scene at a Confederate Veterans Reunion at Bay Springs.

Courtesy Margaret G. Rogers

Remains of the factory and dam on Mackey's Creek at Bay Springs in the late 1800's.

In his statement in 1887, Medford further praised Bay Springs: "There is no better water power anywhere. Good timber is in great abundance. Close by are beds of the finest clays... With that water power the cotton factory and mills could be established and do a good business. From Baldwyn to Bay Springs is about twenty-four miles. There is a railroad charter to Marietta about half way. The famous Purple Shell Springs are here. Let this charter be extended to Bay Springs (Acts 1884, page 883). Let the state build this road with convict labor and with what other help can be had from outside."

While the plea of Harvey Medford was not accepted in other parts of the state, he had certainly made an interesting proposal for thought. Even today, some very valuable efforts for the Tennessee-Tombigbee Waterway project, which includes a dam and lock at Bay Springs, have come from many segments of the Tupelo leadership.

West of Bay Springs in the present East Prentiss community, the Elma post office was existent in 1881 with Captain R. J. (Will) Moore as postmaster. B. F. Wright was a later postmaster of Elma and was to be a valuable builder in early Belmont. Near Elma at present day Friendship Church, Dr. Charles Ryan continued his medical practice. At his home on his farm, Dr. Ryan operated a store where he sold both general merchandise and medicine.

Hillside post office, northeast of Bay Springs, had Catherine Davis back as postmaster in 1886. Hillside had a big spring. It was or had been a stagecoach inn for the convenience of passengers on the stagecoach route that went through Hillside in the last half of the nineteenth century. Dave Ardis was reportedly a stagecoach driver on this line. Mrs. C. H. Hester, a granddaughter of Dave Ardis, and her husband recalled going to Hillside post office in the vicinity of the old Fulton-Iuka Road. In 1892, James T. Butler was Hillside postmaster; and James D. Ardis succeeded him in 1893. W. R. Akers, a former rural mail carrier from the Dennis post office, saw some of the old hewed logs which were taken from the old inn-post office after it closed. Otis Pardue used some of the logs in building his house many, many years ago. Ruth Brazil recalled finding the name board "Hillside Post Office" on the Brazil property several years ago. In 1898, Robert W. Fowler was the new Hillside postmaster, and the office was at a new site on the present Deck Byram place.

Southeast of Bay Springs near Rock Creek was Tynes post office in the office of its postmaster, Dr. Henry Tynes. The Davis brothers contracted to pick up the mail at Tynes two times weekly. Dr. Tynes had sons who were also to become doctors. One son, Carl Tynes, was later a dentist in Belmont. Dr. Henry Tynes practiced when quinine and calomel were prominent medicines. He reportedly was unusually good in breaking up colds and pneumonia.

On July 18th, 1887, the Tishomingo County courthouse at Iuka burned. The board of supervisors, including Fifth District supervisor, T. B. Lindsey, voted at their August, 1887, meeting that the storehouse on the public square in Iuka that Dr. N. B. Warren owned was to be rented for eight dollars per month. E. S. Candler, Sr., agent for Dr. Warren, was present and agreed to the rent. This storehouse was designated as the Tishomingo County courthouse until further order of the board. In time, a new courthouse was constructed.

In the late 1880's the way of life in the Belmont area centered around farming (including much sharecropping), livery stable work, storekeeping, timber-related work, and the operation of water mills. John McRae had a two-story water mill on Rock Creek on the present Ross Sparks place. A. J. Trollinger, a son-in-law of John McRae, was to own and operate this mill later. This mill building contained a sawmill, gin, flour mill and grist mill. The gin head and the bolting shaft were upstairs. The sawmill was downstairs. Down Rock Creek from this mill was the Callaway Moore mill, which functioned several years around the turn of the century.

    Callaway Moore is reported to have donated the land on which the first Cotton Springs school, a one-teacher log structure, was located north up the road from the Tynes place. George Vaughn and Curg Oaks were two of the first teachers. Additionally, the Bay Springs voting place in 1895 was deemed inconvenient. It was moved to the Cotton Springs schoolhouse on the Eastport and Fulton Road, retaining the Bay Springs name. Bay Springs and Providence were to remain the Fifth District voting precincts in the late 1880's.

    Easterly from Cotton Springs a few miles on Perry Branch behind the present Hubert Ruple house was a water mill. On the west side of Perry Branch in the SW¼ of section 21, Township 6 South, Range 10 East was the first Mineral Springs School. On March 31, 1891, L. B. Looney deeded two acres to G. M. Perry, W. H. Lindsey, and E. L. McCulloch, the Mineral Springs trustees, to be used for a public free school. All orthodox denominations were permitted to preach there when the services would not conflict with school.

    The Mineral Springs School had a nearby freestone spring; and the mineral spring was easterly across Perry Branch, reportedly on the present Young farm. W.W. (Billy) Shook taught here. K. F. McRae, a son of John McRae, went to Mineral Springs as a student and later taught at Mineral Springs. Dr. K. F. McRae was destined to be one of "the founding fathers" of the village of Belmont. Later, the Mineral Springs School moved to two other locations.

    About 1881, Dr. M. M. (Mid) Davis sold the quarter section on which his old store and the first Belmont post office had been located to his son-in-law, O. L. Phillips. Dr. Davis owned land around present Dennis before purchasing forty acres in 1892 from F. L. Harris in the Belmont settlement around where the

Elizabeth Williams home presently is. Here, Dr. Davis had probably the first store on the present corporate limits of Belmont.

O. L. Phillips was a constable in the late 1800's and an election commissioner early in the 1900's. Also interested in education, he donated a little over an acre in 1889 to John Holt, E. C. Cornelius, and H. S. Deaton, trustees of Foster School, in consideration of a public school house being built upon the land. In 1891, O. L. Phillips donated 1¼ acres around where the present Ray Denson home is to W. H. Gurley, J.M. Harrison, and R. L. Anglin, the Foster School trustees at that time. Some of the teachers at Foster School included Curg Oaks, Frank Gardner, Grady Oaks, Mrs. Frank Gardner, and Charlie Flurry.

West of present Dennis on Highway 4 near the present L. G. Phillips home, Zeke Harrison home, and old Gilley place, N. S. (Pole) Davis and L. R. (Babe) Davis had stores. They were sons of Dr. M. M. (Mid) Davis. L. R. Davis was in the lumber business, and the settlement around 1890 was called Davis Mills. L. R. Davis, an early educator, was trained to be a doctor and practiced medicine for a while. Later, he decided to establish a post office in the Davis Mills settlement. For some reason, possibly because of a similar name elsewhere, the proposed Davis Mills name did not meet government approval. L. R. Davis was a dedicated member of New Providence Primitive Baptist Church, and the pastor at New Providence was at that time the respected Dennis W. Crane. According to J. T. Lindsey, L. R. Davis decided to name the post office for his pastor; and the name of Dennis was born.

On May 15, 1893, L. R. Davis (1855-1942) became the first postmaster of the newly formed Dennis post office. The names of Dennis and L. R. Davis were destined to be closely associated until his death in 1942.

Late in the 1800's, John Henry Shook and Jack Moody had been converted to Christianity in Texas and joined the Christian Church (Church of Christ). John Henry Shook, a son of Mike Shook, returned to our area and began to preach. Later, Jack Moody joined him in this work. About 1889, T. B. (Tom) Lindsey (1843-1915) provided land south of Dennis upon which a church building was constructed. The question arose about a name for the church. Since many had helped to put up the building and since all were sincerely seeking heaven, the name of Liberty Christian Church was selected to indicate that all could have liberty in Christ, (Decades later, the church was renamed

Liberty Church of Christ to distinguish it from the groups that used instruments of music in church services.)

At this time, a man's word was as good as his signature, and T. B. Lindsey certainly lived up to this in his dealings. On October 31, 1895, T. B. Lindsey donated to C. M. Burleson, John H. Shook, and J. C. Johnson, trustees of Liberty Christian Church in a deed about ½ acre of land for their church purposes. Singing schools and an early school are also reported to have been held at Liberty. In December, 1895, R. D. Flurry donated ¼ acre of land to the trustees of the Christian Church at Liberty. (This land was to be taken up later for railroad purposes when the railroad came through.)

Courtesy Ethel Campbell Hurd

Singing School at Liberty in the 1890's. Identified on the front row are the following: 2nd, Cora D. Byram Campbell; 3rd, Lillie Cleo Davis Flurry; 4th, Ella Sartain Hamilton; and 7th, Ada Phillips. On the second row are, 1st, Dema Cornelius Phillips; 5th, A.G. W. Byram; 7th, John Henry Shook; 8th, Bent Hamilton; 9th, William Martin (Uncle Billy) Campbell; and 10th, Dave Phillips. Identified on the back row are, 5th, Luvenia Carr; 6th, Goodlow Hughes; and 11th, S. S. (Tinker) Byram.

T. B. (Tom) Lindsey was a very respected public figure. He had served as justice of the peace, district supervisor, and county school board member. Tom Lindsey operated a general store between present Dennis and Belmont west across Highway 25 from Joel Cemetery in the vicinity of the present Massey Groover home.

About 1895, a young man who traveled through this area buying cattle and sheep made his headquarters with T.B. Lindsey. Mr. Lindsey assured the young man that he always had a standing invitation to visit or board in his home. Along about this time, the young man was reportedly refused credit at Iuka to buy a stove for about four dollars and a half. With rededication to purpose, he worked even harder after talking the matter over with friends like Tom Lindsey. Then, he moved to Iuka in about 1897 to enter business. This young man became a very successful business man and prominent Tishomingo County leader, J. C. Jourdan. J. C. Jourdan never forgot the friendship and counsel of T. B. Lindsey and always held him in highest esteem. T. B. Lindsey continued his own leadership and public service, later moving to and becoming a builder in a place called Belmont.

In another church development, the benevolent T. B. Lindsey donated an acre of land in 1899 to J. T. Sartain, J. F. Byram, and N. H. Frederick, trustees of Mt. Pisgah Methodist Protestant Church for church purposes on the west side of the Iuka and Pikeville Road. The Mt. Pisgah Methodist Protestant Church, probably called locally Red Hill Church, was on the southern side of Joel Cemetery about where the railroad was to be later. John Byram was a preacher there as were two other preachers named Conwill and Duckworth. The nearby Joel Cemetery, where many of the "founding fathers" of the area are buried, was named for a Mr. Joel who was reportedly the first person to be buried there. Near the southern part of Joel Cemetery, J. T. Sartain had a general store about the turn of the century. His father, W. A. Sartain, earlier operated this Store.

M. W. (Mike) Lindsey lived south of Joel Cemetery across the present Old Highway 25 from the Sidney Pruitt home. In December, 1888, he agreed to give land to the Sardis School patrons for a school house site. Then, in March, 1889, he gave ¼ acre of land to the Sardis School trustees, T. B. Lindsey, D. W. Crane, and E. L. McCulloch, for a building site for the Sardis School. The Sardis School, a log structure, was located behind the present Jack McKinney home in the Pittsburg community.

In his later years, the likeable old settler, William M. (Uncle Billy) Campbell, lived in the Pittsburg community. On his 75th birthday, he barbecued a beef or a hog for the festive occasion. With spirit to let, Billy Campbell arose from eating his birthday dinner and boasted, "I will do anything the rest of you can do and lots of things you cannot do." On the last day of the nineteenth century his family was involved in another happy occasion. A grandson, Lawrence L. Campbell, and Cora D. Byram were married December 31, 1899.

The Sardis School gave way in time to the Pittsburg School. In August, 1899, W. A. Sartain deeded a plot of land to C. M. Anglin, W. D. Campbell, and J. H. Shook, trustees of Pittsburg Public Free School for public free school purposes. It was further stipulated that all public gatherings could meet in the school house. Orthodox preachers could preach there, provided they did not conflict with the school. However, no denominations were to hold an organized church in the Pittsburg school house. This school was located between the present Jack McKinney home and the Kenneth Embrey home on the westerly side of the road near a spring. Many later Belmontians went to school here, and Pittsburg eventually merged into the school at Belmont in the late 1920's.

On the present Oco Horn place is the Pittsburg Cemetery on Campbell Branch. The cemetery has burials tracing back to at least 1846. In March, 1894, in a noble act, J. P. Hester and his wife conveyed approximately 2 acres of land for the exclusive use for a public cemetery to R. L. Anglin, L.A. Deaton, and J. F. Byram, trustees of the Pittsburg Cemetery.

On the Harrison (Mauldin) Branch on or near the present A. B. Campbell farm northwest from Dennis Bear Creek Bridge, the Mauldins early had an overshot water mill. Deatons and Harrisons later operated the mill. A store and boarding house were also there. Cotton was ginned at a reported rate of about two or three bales per day. Cotton was carried in baskets to a screw press that baled it. Then too, Mr. Mauldin reportedly made shoes from leather and wooden pegs.

The road from the old "Cowhide" Williams place going easterly went under the flume (water trough) of the mill and continued to the Flat Rock on Bear Creek. A ford was here, and the road continued on through the present Valley community into Alabama. A fish trap was near the Flat Rock, and another fish trap was later on Bear Creek at about the present Cain place.

In the time around the turn of the century several fords were on Bear Creek. Among the fords were the Pittsburg (Lindsey) Ford on the present Rob Parrish place, the Byram (Rob Epps) Ford, the Bill Wood (Hale) Ford, the J. I. Epps Ford about where the Golden Bear Creek Bridge now is, the Stanphill Ford, the Gee Ford, and the Patterson Ford. Many travelers crossed these fords, and a few had the misfortune to have drowned horses or mules. Many early baptisms were held in these fords and nearby stream waters. The Patterson Ford is said to have had a hand ferry operated with a steel cable. J. I. (Jim) Epps lived near the ford on his place and had a store and gin on the west side of the creek. His home was where Mrs. Ozema Epps Hale now lives. J. I. Epps had a skiff on Bear Creek with which he and his family carried travelers from one side of the creek to the other.

In 1892, a new post office, intended at first to be called Whitfield, was begun at the home of John D. Mann. The post office, located where the present new Steve Cain home is, was named Mann; and John D. Mann was the first postmaster. An early school was once in the vicinity of the Mann home. Additionally in 1891, W. A. Mann deeded one acre to W. E. Mann and the other trustees of Prospect School for school purposes. This school was located east across the present Bob Timbs Road from the present new Bill Acklin home near the Prospect (Mann) Cemetery near Fowler Branch. Prospect Church was later in this vicinity. In fact, a settlement existed around the turn of the century around Brumley Branch and the road that went eastward to the present old Charlie Timbs house.

Here, Whitfield E. Mann (1838-1920) lived. He and his son, Emmett, are reported to have had a grist mill and cotton gin on or near Brumley Branch. Another son, J. R. (Rufus) Mann lived nearby and was a strong advocate of the Farmers Union. In his home he operated a farm co-operative store. Later, Rufus Mann became a state representative from our county. John D. Mann, Henry Mann, Charlie Mann, and Amon Mann were also sons of Whitfield Mann. Amon Mann lived in Golden and operated a sawmill about where the present H. W. Vaughn home is. Amon Mann also operated the hotel in Golden at one time. Charlie Wofford, who later owned much of the land of the Prospect area, had a thriving sorghum mill in Golden where the Mann sawmill was.

In 1893 in the old Oak Farm settlement (present Fanchertown), a new post office was established. The names of Luck, Hill, and

Flat were considered. In the final decision, the post office became Golden; and H. B. "Bud" Fancher was the first postmaster of Golden. The post office was about three miles off the main route from Hillside to Rara Avis over which mail was carried twice a week. Elijah Mayhall was postmaster of the Pleasant Ridge post office which previously handled mail transactions from what was to become Golden. The Golden post office was later moved to the store of Dr. V. S. (Vince) Stanphill about where the Bobby Woods home now is. Dr. Stanphill also became the Golden postmaster in 1898.

In the early Golden (present Fanchertown) community, the Patterson Chapel Methodist Church was organized in about 1884. It was named in honor of Rev. Hardin Patterson, a respected minister and early area builder. He reportedly delivered the first sermon at the church and was very helpful in the locating and starting of the church. The first membership of the church was composed mostly of members from Mt. Zion Methodists Church, which had been located over in the edge of Alabama and was destroyed in a ravaging storm. Early families of Patterson Chapel were Fancher, Nabers, Mink, Pate, Patterson, Messer, Bostick, and Epps. An early school, Patterson Chapel Public Free School, functioned in this community. W. F. Bostick donated the land for the school in 1899 to the school trustees, H. B. Fancher, W. B. Dickinson, and J. F. Messer.

Around 1890, another school existed near Golden. W. T. Martin deeded to Dr. V. S. Stanphill, C. L. Pate, and A. W. Patterson, trustees of Martin Free Public School a plot of ground on the north side of the old Eastport and Pikeville Road upon which a log schoolhouse was located. From these and other Belmont area developments, the fact is evident that the people were placing increasing importance in more churches and schools as growth became more widespread and the population increased.

A church and school also became available for the black residents of the area. In 1897, W. J. Hale deeded a little over an acre of land near the present Red Bud Road for public school purposes to George Spears, Willis Thomas, and Enoch Haley, trustees of Macedonia Public Free School. About 1899, W. J. Hale deeded one acre for church purposes to Enoch Haley, Jerry Leslie, and James Warren, trustees of Macedonia Missionary Baptist Church. Tom Ramsey and Garland Davis were reportedly two of the early preachers at Macedonia Baptist Church.

Later, in the 1930's, Benny Warren gave property near his house for the location of the Macedonia School there.

Down Red Bud Creek, a new frame structure replaced the old log church at Old Bethel Methodist Church in about 1893. A young man whose descendants were to be very valuable to his community and the Belmont area as well worked on the church on his twentieth birthday. This person was the likeable James G. "Uncle Jimmy" Montgomery. Marion Waddle, Sr. reportedly was construction foreman on the church work. Among the others who helped were Holland Pharr, John Ivy, Booker Montgomery, Jim Pharr, Henry Whitehead, Bill Campbell, and Bill Pharr.

An early school also existed in the community and was reportedly in the hills north of the present Dallas Wigginton home. This school was called either Bethel or New Bethel. It was later moved across the North Fork of Red Bud Creek to the Henley site near the present Horace Stepp home. Some of the teachers here included Jim Mitchell, Martha Clark, C. B. Wright, Lee Hicks, Chester Hallmark, Bertie Hallmark, Arthur Jackson, and possibly Jesse Jackson.

The Coke post office was in operation at different sites down Red Bud Creek. M. C. Conwill was the first Coke postmaster in 1895. James N. T. (Turner) Pharr was the second Coke postmaster in 1896. The Waddles operated a water mill on Red Bud near here. A. F. Cole may have operated this mill earlier; it was located southerly from the present Beatrice Joslin home. Further up Red Bud Creek, the friendly, respected J. H. (Holland) Pharr had a water mill and store. It is said that Bill Pharr operated this mill several years earlier before he moved to Prentiss County.

The New Bethel Baptist Church started at its present site about 1898. On November 25, 1898, Mahala A. Whitehead and Joseph Whitehead donated a square acre of land to M. D. Cranford, P. E. Hammett, and John McRae, trustees of the Bethel Baptist Church for a church site. Around the turn of the century, their son, Sion Whitehead, had a store near the church in the vicinity of the present New Bethel parsonage or the nearby road. Around the turn of the century, W. H. Holcomb lived in the New Bethel community. Today, an overwhelming majority of this thriving community are descendants of W. H. Holcomb or are married to his descendants.

In the late 1800's, several general stores began to appear in the vicinity of Belmont. The store of John I. C. Hopkins south of Belmont on the present Carl Sartain land did a good business for the times. In 1886, the Merora post office was in the Hopkins store; and John I. C. Hopkins was the first Merora postmaster. For about one month in 1888 Merora handled the Belmont mail. John Campbell was named Merora postmaster in 1893. Later in the year the post office was discontinued, and mail went to Belmont.

From 1880 to 1900, the young Belmont settlement continued to gain attention. In the decades to come, the growth and movements into Belmont were to increase the population markedly and make Belmont emerge from its embryonic stage. The population at 1880 of Belmont was listed in one source as about 20. This could be misleading because the Belmont post office was then at Clark's Gin near the present Goodwin place on Red Bud Creek, not in the budding Belmont settlement that was to develop.

In 1886, W. T. Clark moved the Belmont post office three miles northeast back to his old home where the Grover Pounders family now lives in Belmont. Here, the Belmont post office was on the Rara Avis to Hillside route upon which L. N. Sweat carried mail twice weekly. The Belmont post office at the Clark home was to serve about 250 people. This log house had part of the porch boxed in for a post office. A hole, or slot, was made, through which patrons could drop letters or cards. For sure, post office practice was not too time-consuming or complex in those days.

In early January, 1888, Belmont mail temporarily went to Merora; but the Belmont post office was functioning again on January 31, 1888, with W. T. Clark continuing as postmaster. Across the road from his home, W. T. Clark had a horse-powered cotton gin in a two-story building. Cotton was stored upstairs. A screw press baled the cotton. He later had a threshing machine for wheat. Around the turn of the century, W. T. Clark had a store in present north Belmont across Highway 25 from Billy P. Sartain Grocery in the vicinity of the Reno Crossing on the railroad. In addition, W. T. Clark served very capably on the county board of supervisors from the Fifth District for sixteen years from 1888-1904. Combined with his later contributions to the village and town of Belmont, the big-hearted, civic-minded W. T. Clark would have to be a builder in the truest sense of the word.

His brother, John Henry Clark, was another builder of early Belmont. He was a highly respected surveyor and justice of the peace. His son, J. U. (Julius) Clark, was to serve several terms as justice of the peace about a half century later. In 1892, John Henry Clark became the Belmont postmaster and served until shortly before 1896 when he became county surveyor. Mary L. D. (Mollie) Clark, the wife of W. T. Clark, became the Belmont postmaster in late 1895 and continued until 1903.

North up the road from Clarks, a progressive family had moved in November, 1892. The George S. Jackson family in a wagon pulled with a yoke of oxen moved from Pogo, Alabama. Jesse and Belle, two of the older children, rode on horseback. Luther, only two years old, sat in the lap of his mother, Amanda Millican Jackson, in the wagon. George Jackson drove the wagon through the murky, leaf-filled water of Bear Creek at the Byram Ford, which was to be called later the Rob Epps Ford.

The Jacksons settled on the present Old Highway 25 east across the road from the present Jim Sartain home. In fact, George Jackson operated a store a little southeast of the present Jim Sartain home. Some of the Jackson neighbors were the Jenkins Byram family, the G. A. "Dick" Clark family, the Jesse Cummings Hallmark family, the Frank Looney family, and the Ed Gilbert family. North of them up the road, Frank Looney also had a store near the present Leon Northington home. Carters later operated a store here and served the surrounding area with a peddling truck.

Several years earlier, the Valley Methodist Church, a log building, was organized on the flatwoods just off the present Bear Creek Road on the south side about ¼ mile southwesterly from the home of Mrs. Ben Patterson. It is said that the Valley Methodist Church may have started as far back as 1849; some feel that the Valley Methodist Church on the flatwoods was organized about 1881. Although the official starting date of the Valley Methodist Church is not conclusively known, we do know that a woods fire destroyed its log church house on the flatwoods easterly from Belmont. In November, 1892, G. A. "Dick" Clark and his wife, Julia Ann Clark, deeded about 1¼ acres of land to J. T. Montgomery, R. F. Flurry, and E. L. McCulloch, trustees of the Methodist Episcopal Church South at New Valley Grove Church. On this property the Methodists built a frame structure of oak boards near the present home of Mrs. Dalton Wood on Old Highway 25 north in the forks of the road. A grove of large shade trees was in the church yard.

One of the early Methodist pastors was Rev. Thomas E. Yancy, who boarded with the Jacksons and even helped them pick cotton. Another early Methodist pastor was Will Wood. In 1888, W. T. Clark and Mollie Clark had deeded to George S. Jackson, W. H

Gurley, and J. M. Gurley, trustees of the New Valley Methodist Church, some property about where the Robert Williams family now lives for a residence for the pastors of the New Valley Methodist Church. Rev. T. J. Hopper was reportedly the first to live in this Methodist parsonage.

South from New Valley about where John E. Eaton now lives at the old Luther Taylor place, Sarah (Sallie) Hopkins, wife of the early pioneer, Ben Hopkins, lived in a log house. Nearby, her son, Frank Hopkins, and his family lived in another log house. Mrs. Myrtle Clark Shook recalls that Frank Hopkins pulled teeth at times for people in need. Neighbors called his wife "Mary Frank" to identify her from her neighbor, Mrs. C. C. "Lum" Shook, whom they called "Mary Lum."

In 1892, Mrs. Sarah Hopkins succumbed to cancer. In 1893, the Ben Hopkins estate sold through court the SE¼ of section 35, Township 6 South, Range 10 East upon which present downtown Belmont is located to W. T. Shook and R. L. Shook for $441.00. W. T. Shook later sold his interest to R. L. Shook. In 1900, R. L. Shook sold 95 acres on the south side of the quarter section to his father, C. "Lum" Shook. The twentieth century influence of the Shooks on this land was to be a driving influence in the Belmont development, as the influence of the Ben Hopkins family had been in the pioneer development. In fact, the Vinsons, the Cranfords, the Gilberts, and other members of the Hopkins family were to continue to contribute to the emergence of Belmont.

Meanwhile, the school at Gum Springs continued as a one teacher set-up in the original log structure. Among the teachers of this period starting around 1880 were, reportedly, W. M. Hundley, Charles Hughes, Joe Kay, J. T. Vaughn, P.A. Gates, R. M. Perry, and W. T. Shook. W. T. Shook was the teacher at the log school during the 1894-1895 term. This log schoolhouse faced east and was located north of the present main entrance to the Belmont Blue Springs City Park. The stick-and-dirt chimney was on the north side of the building. There were only two windows, and there were no steps as the schoolhouse was built on or near the ground. The roof was of boards. Inside the building were about five or six benches. The benches were simply split logs rasped smooth and then fitted with wooden peg legs. The teacher had a homemade desk at the front, and a blackboard was on the wall. The students, about twenty-five of them, wrote on slates with special pencils. Blue-backed spellers and mental arithmetic books were prominent in this early learning atmosphere.

In the fall of 1895, a new Belmont school building, which many called "the Ebenezer school" due to its location near the Ebenezer Baptist Church, faced east and west. A few more years found the rather small frame structure not large enough to accommodate the growing educational needs.

In November, 1899, Governor A. J. McLaurin signed the charter of incorporation of the Belmont High School. Charter members included R. L. Shook, W. T. Clark, W. L. Cranford, J. C. (Cummings) Hallmark, C. C. Shook, John C. Hallmark, G. A. Clark, J. M. Wood, and C. S. (Carter) Shook. The incorporation of school patrons had the power to purchase and own real estate necessary to carry out its objectives, not to exceed $10,000. The general objectives of the corporation were "the education and improvement of the youths." The directors were to fix the capital stock, which was to be divided into shares of ten dollars each. Interesting is the fact that several "founding fathers" of the Belmont area chose to establish a high school and build another school building for improved, expanded education opportunities as the nineteenth century came to a close.

From the first Ebenezer school building a short distance, the area citizens constructed a much larger building which together with the older one, would accommodate approximately 200 students. These structures were about where the present K. H. "Bud" Pardue home and Jim Wall home are located. The new school building faced north and south. With the expanded school facilities and the expansion of the school to a two-teacher school, the willingness of the Belmont people to support better education became even more evident. This willingness to support better education has characterized Belmont down through the years and forms an integral part of the proud heritage of a place called Belmont.

R. L. Shook and his wife, Ann Lindsey Shook, were principal and assistant when the two-teacher expansion was underway. Walter Elledge, according to Luther Jackson, was one of the first principals at the two-teacher school. The curriculum, ungraded, consisted of spelling, writing, reading, arithmetic, and geography. Teacher salaries ranged from $20-$35 per month. Near the turn of the century, or shortly thereafter, the courses of study were expanded to include the approximate range of the present elementary school with perhaps a few subjects on the high school level. The school year is said to have been about four months. It lengthened in time. In addition, girls and boys played separately at early Ebenezer school in Belmont. Dinner was brought in lard buckets usually. It is said that students were assigned certain trees or other places where they were to eat their lunch.

Between the two Ebenezer school buildings a platform was erected for the presentation of plays. Minstrels were popular, especially with the boys. Once, a concert and magic show were held on the school platform. A homemade coffin was on the platform, and Anthony Yarber volunteered for the magic trick. He was placed inside, and the coffin was sawed in half to the awe and serious concern of many onlookers. Actually, Anthony had gone out a hole in the platform before the sawing began. To the amazement, and relief, of many, Anthony soon appeared in the crowd. Then, the gathering continued to enjoy the magic show.

Games at school included tag, "gulley bug", town ball, "Ring around the Roses," "Fox and Geese," and "Red Rover." Often, the chase and tag games wandered too far from school for the students to get back before the bell rang for "books." A dose of "hickory tea" usually awaited; or if the students were lucky, only a "stern tongue-lashing" resulted. After all discipline was then stern -- expected and meant to be respected! Most of the time, a second whipping awaited the child at home if he or she, got one at school.

The last day of school was enjoyable to the early students in many ways. They lined in a circle, always trying to stand near the one each "claimed." The students marched to music after which the teacher gave each student a piece of candy. Compared to our advanced society and event-filled schools, these early school days might seem rather simple or uneventful. To the students at the turn of the century, their school days were a time of development, learning, and happiness in a rather stern, austere world.

Just north of Ebenezer school on the present Wilbur Tesseneer place was Ebenezer Baptist Church. It is said that Ebenezer Baptist Church may have started as far back as 1872, but the official starting date is not conclusively known at the present. J. S. (Joe) Stockton was reportedly an early preacher at Ebenezer Baptist Church. W. W. Gilbert preached some at Ebenezer and also at other churches in the area all the way to present Fairview. Gilbert; his wife, Mary Jane Hopkins Gilbert; and their family lived northeasterly from the present Dillard Credille home near Ben Martin Branch. His son, W. E. (Ed) Gilbert, was a deacon in the Ebenezer Baptist Church. Exemplifying the energy and dedication of an early preacher, W. W. Gilbert would plow until noon on Saturday, saddle his horse, ride to the Fairview area, preach that evening, preach Sunday, and return home on Monday. In addition, W. W. Gilbert, like many of his fellow ministers, learned the Bible by the light of a pine knot fire.

At 1899, his health was failing because he was unable to deliver the sermon at an association meeting. At this association meeting some of the churches and their representatives were the following: Ebenezer - W. E. Gilbert, J. F. Looney, and W. T. Shook; Union -- W. T. McClung, E. L. Cain, and W. A. Leatherwood; Bethel -- J. S. Whitehead, C. H. Cranford, and T. J. Johnson; Prospect -- J. C. Long, J. R. Mann, and F. M. McDonald; and Red Bud--R. L. Williams, R. J. Hammett, and F. M. Bennett. A. F. Cole, whose daughter, Paratine, later married Hatley M. Shook, was minister at Salem, Evergreen, and Bethel. In 1899, W. R. Whitehead was the Bethel church clerk, and the church had about 50 members. Red Bud had 32 members, and R. J. Hammett was the Red Bud church clerk. J. S. Stockton was the pastor at both Ebenezer and Prospect. J. D. Mann was the Prospect church clerk, and Prospect had about 25 members. J. R. Cranford was the clerk of Ebenezer Baptist Church, which had 55 members. J. M. Harrison was the Union pastor, and W. A. Leatherwood was Union church clerk. Union had 60 members.

Church services were held at Ebenezer on Sunday afternoon many times. As in many early churches, men sat on one side; and women sat together on the other side. Pallet space was provided for young children. Older children sat attentively with their parents. For a long time, there were no song books or Sunday School literature. Hymns were sung from memory until song books became available. Several members had Bibles. The preacher read verses, and the members repeated them. In time, the minister preached a rousing, well-received sermon. No doubt, the deep-rooted belief in God and the Bible in many of our area people enabled our section of the country to be a part of the Bible Belt. This and the wholesome sight of people going in family groups to and from the church of their choice at the turn of the century constitute an integral part of the proud Belmont heritage.

As Belmont faced the dawning of the twentieth century, things were beginning to take shape. A solid foundation was being established in homes, churches, and schools. The inevitable growth of a place called Belmont seemed promising as 1900 rolled around. The emergence of Belmont was, for all practical purposes, a reality.

CHAPTER 8

DAWNING OF THE TWENTIETH CENTURY

The dawning of 1900 found Belmont a growing community. A settlement was also situated around the present Dennis as was a settlement eastward from present Golden. The population in Tishomingo County was 10,124, compared to 9,302 in 1890. The population in 1900 in the Fifth District was 1,969, compared to 1,587 in 1890.

For sure, the area was basically rural. The people were mainly Scotch-Irish. They were self-sufficient, proud, and slow to accept change they did not understand. Many families still used the spinning wheels, wash troughs, cedar buckets, and quilts handed down from their ancestors. With no modern conveniences, most of our forefathers around 1900 raised their food, quilted their bedding, and often spun the cloth for their simple clothing. Some fairly modern conveniences for the times were brought from places like Iuka and Booneville, and the rural stores stocked some conveniences. By and large, simple, subsistence living prevailed.

The home and the church were the centers of all social life, but the school was beginning to have some impact on the rural society around Belmont. House-raisings, quiltings, singings, and bold holiday serenadings were among the popular activities. The principal music expressions were the singing of hymns, ballad singing, and fiddling. Visitors to the M. L. (Fayette) Harris home were often privileged to hear Mrs. M. L. Harris play the concertina. Organ music was also enjoyed in many area homes. Many of the locally sung, or played, ballads were of an entirely local origin, being vigorous and earthy. Many had a broad sense of humor, and many were "outlaw songs" brought over from the Freedom Hills east of Bear Creek. Many times, neighbors or area groups gathered at "singings." Moreover, it was not uncommon to hear ballads being sung, whistled, or hummed from farmers plowing the fields, women washing the family clothes in an outdoor wash pot, or a carefree youth walking or playing along a country road.

Many of the houses were still made of logs (later of clapboards) with a wide-swept hall, called a "dog-trot," running through the center. The cook room (kitchen) was in the rear. "Dog-trot" houses are part of the heritage of our area and constitute a contribution to American architectural types. The simple log cabin was an indivisible unit. As children were born and the need to expand the house arose, another log room had to be built. That the hillbilly should lay his two log cabins parallel and roof the open space between the two to make a hallway ("dog-trot") was natural. The cooling effect of the hallway was noted as a decided benefit. The threat, or fear, of fire dictated that the cook room be separated. This and the desire to have a fire in the living room showed that time and saved steps for the wife did not dominate the thoughts of the early settlers. In time, this changed because cook rooms were annexed to the back of the houses.

To sheathe the logs with clapboards was the first sign of societal progress that thawed the frontier. When the "dog-trot" was walled in and a porch was added, progress was well under way. As the population began to forge ahead, many two-room houses were expanded to four-room or five-room frame structures with a porch across the front and sometimes the rear. A chimney was on each end of the house, and the enclosed "dog-trot" often became a center hall or room. Complementing these rustic houses were beds of flowers like verbena, old maids (zinnias), phlox, and four o'clocks. In addition, some yards had natural grasses; while others were scraped "pen neat" clean to the bare earth. Picket fences or similar enclosures were around some of the yards of the houses in the Belmont area.

Courtesy Jerome Mitchell

The M. M Davis home in what was to become Belmont

Singing schools furnished outlets of expression for several people. "The Sacred Harp," a song book of several hundred pages presenting songs with the ancient "form notes," was often used. Those attending singing school, often held in churches, learned the "fa, sol, la" songs brought down from Elizabethan England. These songs were written in four parts on separate staffs with each part carrying to a degree a melodic pattern of its own. The singing master taught the singing participants to "pitch," to know tone lengths, and to know tone shapes. Then too, the singing master taught songs adapted to various occasions as "Ye Who Are Weary," "Glory For Me!," "Just Beyond the River," "Heaven's My Home," and "Come Ye Faithful".

At the turn of the century and for several decades thereafter, Old Harp singings furnished much entertainment, relaxation, and tension outlet. From Old Harp song books, the participants sang. After the tune had been pitched, the gathering sang unaccompanied. Singings of this nature would usually last until mid-afternoon and include dinner on the ground.

At New Providence Primitive Baptist Church, the annual foot washing services on the third Sunday in May drew large gatherings and continued into the twentieth century after the coming of the railroad. Following the foot washing ceremonies, a sermon and communion were held. In addition, dinner on the ground usually was noteworthy at these memorable gatherings. Later, even larger crowds attended the New Providence services on the third Sunday in May, including many who came on the "Doodlebug."

Assuredly, one of the proud contributions of our forefathers around Belmont was the respect for Sunday. Mule-drawn wagons, horse-drawn wagons, and oxen-drawn wagons carrying families to church on Sunday were surely heartening sights. To exemplify this in our area, the road to Patterson Chapel from the east was crowded with people in wagons or on foot going to church at Patterson Chapel Methodist Church on Sunday. For Sunday dinner in our area, the woman of the house would "kill a chicken" and "put the big pot in the little pot." The bountiful meal might consist of baked or fried ham, fried chicken, chicken and dumplings, peas, green beans, corn, mashed potatoes, biscuits, cornbread, coconut cake, chocolate pie, egg custard, banana cake, or banana pudding. This was topped off with sweet milk cooled in the spring or iced tea.

After the delicious, very filling meal, the family gathering might after a short rest play a game of town ball down in a level part of the pasture. More than likely, the gathering of up to a dozen, or even more at times, would sit on the front porch to rest, to rock, or to gab about "goings-on." Gatherings of this nature strengthened the value of the home as an institution and showed that the parents still valued togetherness with their children.

In essence, the people of the Belmont area around 1900 and for decades to come reflected their raising. Until the progress brought with the railroad and the new ways brought back from soldiers going to the wars, our forefathers preferred the independence and isolation of hilly retreats to the ways of a world that might jeopardize their "life, liberty, and pursuit of happiness." Scattered on basically small farms with the trading centers hardly more than the country stores, the people retained with remarkable purity their traditions. Having little financial means with which to supply leisure needs, the residents of our section supplied some of their inner artistic expression in such useful handcrafts as woodwork for the men and quiltmaking for the women.

Each person proved his worth and usually thought as the land "thought." The faith of our area fathers around 1900 was essentially in God and the hopes for the next crop which might enable them to continue their quest for "a satisfied mind." With pride beaming, they were born with an inherent regard for the Constitution. However, their own interpretation was preferred to that of others. Deep within most lay an interest in politics. Like many of us today, they vehemently criticized politics and politicians. Yet, they would hitch up the team of mules to the wagon and drive for miles in order to hear and applaud the thunderous, hand-waving outcries of a candidate who they knew deep down they were going to vote against. Still in all, they were not hypocrites because they would stand up for principle and conviction when the situation necessitated firm decisions. The candidate speakings furnished a social function for the early citizens. The resultant hard feelings and occasional fights at times at the speakings created an unneeded source of problems.

The greatest worry about earthly things still proved to be the weather. People treasured the calendars and almanacs which storekeepers gave them. True to their heritage, many people relied on folk traditions regarding plantings. Hog jowl and black eyed peas were eaten on New Year's Day to bring prosperity. Many believed the first twelve days of January represented the weather to be expected in the respective twelve months of the year.

Moonlight during Christmas meant light crops, while darkness at this time meant heavy crops. If the wind was from the south on March 22, the year would be dry; and the farmer could look to plowing hot, dusty fields with the slim hope of rain. Some felt that each day with thunder in February would have a corresponding day of frost in April. If the sun set behind a bank of clouds on Sunday, the people expected rain before Wednesday. If it set behind a bank of clouds on Wednesday, rain might be expected before Sunday. A red sunset, like a rainbow in the morning, brought wind rather than rain; while a rainbow in the afternoon streaked sunset brought fair and dry weather respectively. Winter was supposedly over if the ground hog did not see his shadow on Ground Hog Day, or when the fig trees began to leaf.

Obviously, many early citizens of the area relied on the birthday almanac they got at the country store. They looked for the January thaw to plant cabbage plants, greens, and onion sets. On St. Valentine's Day, many planted Irish potatoes, provided the moon was right. To them, leafy vegetables did better when planted in the light of the moon, while root vegetables did better when planted in the dark phase of the moon. Good Friday was a holy day and would bring them good fortune in planting beans and other early vegetables, provided they were planted before the night set in. When the whippoorwills started to "holler," farmers knew that they could start getting ready to plant cotton. While the belief in folk traditions and "the signs of the moon approach" to planting are discounted in many present circles, they did furnish basis around which people believed until more scientific approaches came to light.

From 1900 into 1904, our area suffered a very serious epidemic of "slow fever" (typhoid). Many people died. Mrs. Maudie Osbirn relates that her father, Billy Stacy, and three of his brothers died from typhoid. Her mother and sister also had it, but they recovered.

George Jackson and W. O. Stockton had the fever, but they recovered. Mrs. J. C. (Elizabeth) Hallmark lay with "slow fever" 64 days before recovering. Margaret Stacy, who later married Andrew Credille, lay for 84 days, reportedly, with the dreaded typhoid before recovery. In 1904, Ed Gilbert died from typhoid. The typhoid epidemic killed several other area people. Some felt that typhoid was rougher on men than on women. Those stricken with "slow fever" were allowed to eat very, very little. For our age of immunization, the terrible effects of typhoid are hard to comprehend. For those who remember the epidemic around 1900, it was an agonizing period of very trying times.

After the turn of the century, several new postmasters assumed their duties. At Emma, Irene Caveness became postmaster in 1900. John T. Caveness was Emma postmaster in 1901, and the post office was in his house in the present Moore's Mill community. Late in1902, the Tynes post office was moved to Emma to be effective January 15, 1903. Later, in December, 1905, the Emma post office closed; and mail went to New Site. In the Moore's Mill community in November, 1902, Belle D. Ferguson donated an acre of land for school purposes to W. C. Moore, E. A. Cole, and Will Ferguson, trustees of the Red Bud School. This school was located southeast of the Pete Allen Hill (John Brown Hill) on present Moore's Mill Road.

Over in the Valley-Prospect area easterly from Belmont, W. L. Brakefield was the Mann postmaster in 1901. Later in the year, Mary E. Loveless became Mann postmaster at a site about 2½ miles southeast of the previous location. Marion E. Mann was the postmaster in 1902 at a site near the Whitfield Mann place. Then too, J. R. (Rufus) Mann and his wife in 1902 deeded the acre of land on which the Prospect Baptist Church prospered near the Baldwyn and Pleasant Site Road to the Prospect church trustees --J.C. (John) Long, M. E. Mann, and W.R. Dodd.

In August, 1902, C. C. (Lum) Shook and his wife, Mary E. Shook, deeded one acre of land on the east side of the Fulton and Iuka Road to O. L. Phillips and T. J. Selby, deacons of Ebenezer Church for church purposes and to C. L. Pate, Worshipful Master; J. C. (John) Long, Senior Warden; and G. W. Sims, Junior Warden of Pleasant Hill F. & A. M. Lodge No. 237 for Masonic purposes. This Masonic lodge had moved from the old Pleasant Hill to Pleasant Ridge back around 1880. In 1902, the Pleasant Hill Lodge moved to Belmont in the upper room of a frame two-story building in the vicinity of the present First Baptist Church parsonage on Main Street. Charlie Flurry was reported to be the first man to become a Mason at this new site.

In July, 1902, the county board of supervisors voted to move the

Providence voting precinct about one mile south on the Fulton-Iuka Road to New Valley Methodist Church. The precinct was still to be called Providence.

In the early 1900's a church house was located in the vicinity near the present Luther Sparks home and was reported to have been called Jackson Free Will Baptist Church, or locally Jackson Meeting House. The Ezekiel Jackson family is reported to have headed the building of the frame church and were regular members there. Tommy Jackson, a son of Ezekiel Jackson, was a preacher at this church.

Not too many years after the turn of the century, a modern convenience came to Belmont. George Jackson built a telephone line into the Belmont area from Iuka for a telephone company. The exchange was first at Iuka. George Jackson had the first telephone in the Belmont area. Since he bought cotton, the telephone early proved worth its nominal expense and then some. George Jackson once made $100 on a cotton deal when an Iuka cotton buyer called him about selling some cotton before the price changed. The phones of this time were the old-fashioned box wall phones with cranks and protruding mouthpieces. Others in the Belmont area with early telephones were T. B. Lindsey, C. C. Shook, R. L. Shook, and G. A. Clark. When the line was run to the New Bethel-Moore's Mill area, Columbus Hammett reportedly had the first phone.

Most assuredly, the coming of the telephone had an impact on this rural area. Some of our citizens were going to Iuka to trade although an overnight journey was necessitated from the wagon, horseback, or buggy transportation. This, combined with the coming of the telephone, brought outside ideas and values into the Belmont area. Still, neither of these was to have the powerful impact that the coming of the railroad was to bring. The coming of the railroad "made" Belmont! Belmont and its neighboring towns of Golden and Dennis became functioning realities after the railroad was completed.

Courtesy Gertrude Ozbirn

Patterson Chapel School group in 1901-1902. Carroll Gilbert was the teacher.

Courtesy Ora Johnson and Bonnie Johnson

New Bethel School group in the early 1900's. Arthur Jackson was the teacher

CHAPTER 9

THE COMING OF THE RAILROAD

In October, 1903, the honorable old Belmont settler, William M. Campbell, died and was buried in the Joel Cemetery. He had been somewhat of a mystic in his later years. Billy Campbell prophesied that, although he might never live to see it, people would fly in the air like birds and that people would soon move down the roads in objects without any oxen or horses pulling them. He also said that people would someday be talking through the air with no connections of wires. One day, Billy Campbell told Carter Shook if he would come to his grave after his death at a certain time he would talk to Carter. In his first three predictions the self-educated, old pioneer was accurate. In getting a response from the promised grave talk, we will never know because Carter Shook assured him that he would not be finding out. Whether or not Billy Campbell ventured into predicting the specific future of our area, we do not know for sure. We do know that with the coming of the railroad Belmont entered into a new era of growth and progress. The railroad "made" Belmont!

The coming of the railroad was to have a long-lasting effect on Belmont. The Illinois Central Railroad Company decided to run its track and train service through Corinth, through our Belmont area, and on to Haleyville, Alabama. The railroad from Corinth to Haleyville was referred to as the Mississippi and Alabama Railroad Company, but the Illinois Central Railroad Company was actually in possession of and operated it. Survey work began about 1903-1904. Right-of-way property was purchased in 1906. Many changes were destined to occur in the Belmont area until the railroad was completed in the fall of 1907.

Over large areas of this country, huge virgin pines grew thickly. Large oaks, poplars, chestnuts, hickories, and other hardwood trees were found on many hillsides and in stream bottom lands. Sawmills appeared more and more. Many logs were rafted down Mackey's Creek into the Tombigbee River to the larger mills at Amory and Aberdeen. The logs were rolled into the creek, bound together with spike and chain in batches, and rafted down the stream. If the creek was at certain levels, difficulty was often encountered at Bay Springs where remnants of the old dam caused log jams to form. Jumping safely ashore and breaking up the jams to get the logs on their way again posed nagging problems for loggers. They also involved a serious amount of danger for the loggers. Nevertheless, the coming of the railroad was to eliminate the need for this type of transportation.

North of Bay Springs on Mackey's Creek, the Harris Crossing bridge was built. Turner Harris recalled helping build the first road and first bridge at the Harris Crossing. Northeast from this bridge was Lancaster (pronounced "Lankster" by many) Cemetery. Lancasters lived near here and were probably the first to be buried in the cemetery. Trollingers also lived near here around Billy Goat Hill and were buried later in the cemetery.

Mrs. Lancaster was a "baby-catcher" or "night-rider" (midwife). She rode a horse to the homes of those wanting her help. Sarah Byram was another midwife. In fact, other area people delivered babies in addition to Dr. Thomas Mayhall; Dr. Willie Mayhall; Dr. Bill Hodges; Dr. V. S. Stanphill; Dr. Levi Epps; Dr. Henry Tynes; Dr. K. F. McRae; Dr. R. L. Montgomery; and Dr. A. E. Bostick. Dr. A. E. Bostick received the Stork Doctor of the Year Award for delivering the most babies in the state one year. In furtherance, John D. Mann delivered babies in the Valley community when the service was needed. Ruby Byram states that he delivered her mother, Laura Bridges (Mrs. W. H. Clingan in married life), into the world. Myrtie Lindsey, a daughter of John D. Mann, served her community around Dennis well in helping when many babies were born.

John D. Mann of Valley functioned in many areas of community service, having previously been a teacher, a postmaster, and a justice of the peace for several terms. He was later to serve as Fifth District supervisor for three different terms, and his first supervisor term was 1908-1912. In 1904, J. N. Patterson was Fifth District supervisor. W.W. "Billy" Shook was county treasurer, and John Henry Clark was county surveyor. J.C. Miller and C. C. Shook were the Fifth District justices of the peace for the 1904-1908 term, and J. A. Clingan was constable. Previously serving our area as justices of the peace for the 1900-1904 term were C. C. Shook and L. F. (Lee) Sartain. G. A. Clark was on the county school board about this time. In the 1908-1912 term, J. C. Miller and A.G. W. (Green) Byram were Fifth District justices of the peace; and Carter S. Shook was constable.

Several developments were occurring in the area post offices. Amelia Fowler was Hillside postmaster in 1902. Then, Cora L. Harris became Hillside postmaster in late 1903. She operated the

Hillside post office in a little room on the porch of the Harris home where her brother, George Harris, later lived. The historic old Hillside post office ceased to exist in 1905. Mail went to Hunt, where William Henry Hunt was postmaster. Hunt post office closed in 1906, and the mail reportedly went to Burnt Mills (near present Paden). A relocation of some routes may have occurred also.

Shortly after the turn of the century, the Mineral Springs School had moved to a new site southwest from the original site. In October, 1904, E.G. Fuller and his wife deeded an acre of land to W. L. Pate, W. P. Dickinson, and A. C. McRae, trustees of the Mineral Springs School for a school site. They reserved all rail timber on the land. Later, the Mineral Springs school site was again changed to the present homesite of Durell Johnson. In August, 1917, Ambrose Vinson and his wife conveyed an acre of land here to W. Hester, E. G. Fuller, and Ambrose Vinson, trustees of Mineral Springs School for a school site.

On October 11, 1907, W.W. (Billy) Shook and Martha I. (Belle) Shook donated two acres of land on which Joel Cemetery was located to W. A. Sartain, J.P. Hester, and G. M. Perry, trustees of the Joel (Jowell) Cemetery. Many area citizens were buried and were to continue to be buried at Joel, including Michael Shook (1834-1904), the father of W. W. "Billy" Shook.

Down on Red Bud Creek, the friendly, big-hearted J. H. (Holland) Pharr (1845-1924) became the Coke postmaster in 1905. Holland Pharr, in addition to operating a water mill, also had a store, probably the post office site, about where the present Whitehead house is. In 1906, the Coke post office closed; and mail went to Dennis. Further down Red Bud Creek, where Turner Pharr earlier had the Coke post office, the Jim Allen family was to operate a store.

The Golden mail went to Dennis on December 14, 1904, to be effective January 14, 1905. Eastward across Bear Creek at Prospect, James R. Mann became the Mann postmaster in 1905. The Mann post office closed in 1906 with the mail going to Mingo.

Over in the present Valley community, C. M. Armstrong in October, 1904, deeded a parcel of land for school purposes to E. L. Cain, W. M. Toland, and Charlie Armstrong, trustees of Union School. Union School may have merged into Valley School because in August, 1905, H. S. Deaton, G. H. Bridges, and Mrs. J. A. Bridges donated about an acre of property to the trustees of Valley School.

At Patterson Chapel Methodist Church, the old building about 1904 was deemed inadequate for the growing membership. During the pastorate of Rev. T. B. Young, J. R. "Bob" Cranford with help from several church members constructed a new frame building. In November, 1905, W. F. Bostick and M. A. Bostick deeded an acre of land to J. P. Stanphill, N. B. Mink, and W. F. Bostick, trustees of the Methodist Episcopal Church South at Patterson Chapel for the site on which the church house was built.

Back at Belmont, Amanda Millican Jackson, wife of George Jackson, became the Belmont postmaster about 1903 and operated the post office in the Jackson home north of New Valley Methodist Church. Belmont mail went to Dennis effective December 31, 1904. Charlie Flurry delivered the mail on Route 1, Dennis, at this time through our area.

Courtesy Edna Flurry

Friendly Charlie Flurry, rural mail carrier for many years, delivering the mail on Route 1, Dennis. For a few years before the coming of the railroad, Belmont had no post office; and Charlie Flurry delivered our mail on Route 1, Dennis.

Learning at the Belmont school at the Ebenezer site was progressing under educational leaders like N. L. Phillips, Charlie Flynt, T. A. Clark, Jeff Busby, J.P. Matthews, and Willie Elledge.

N. L. Phillips, who later became county superintendent and sheriff, was said to be "nice, but he meant what he said." Charlie Flynt taught with Miss Mae Adams at Belmont. Later, they were married. T. A. Clark was a Belmont native whose father, G. A. "Dick" Clark, was a prominent early Belmont builder. The students respected T. A. Clark, who later became a prominent lawyer who practiced in both Belmont and Iuka. Professor J.P. Matthews reportedly came from Iuka about 1906 and organized the first graded school. He boarded with the George Jackson family. Professor Matthews liked horticulture and enjoyed teasing the Jackson children about being able to grow "white blackberries and white tomatoes," Professor Charles Lynch, who is said to have taught at Belmont, had the motto: "Make the big ones do, and the little ones will follow." Willie I. Elledge, a kind Baptist minister, according to a former student, was "a real good man who had the deepest respect of nearly everyone." These early principals and their assistant teachers sowed and cultivated the seeds of education upon which Belmont was to develop into the twentieth century.

Courtesy Myrtle C. Shook

Stapps Writing School at "Ebenezer school" in Belmont shortly after the turn of the century.

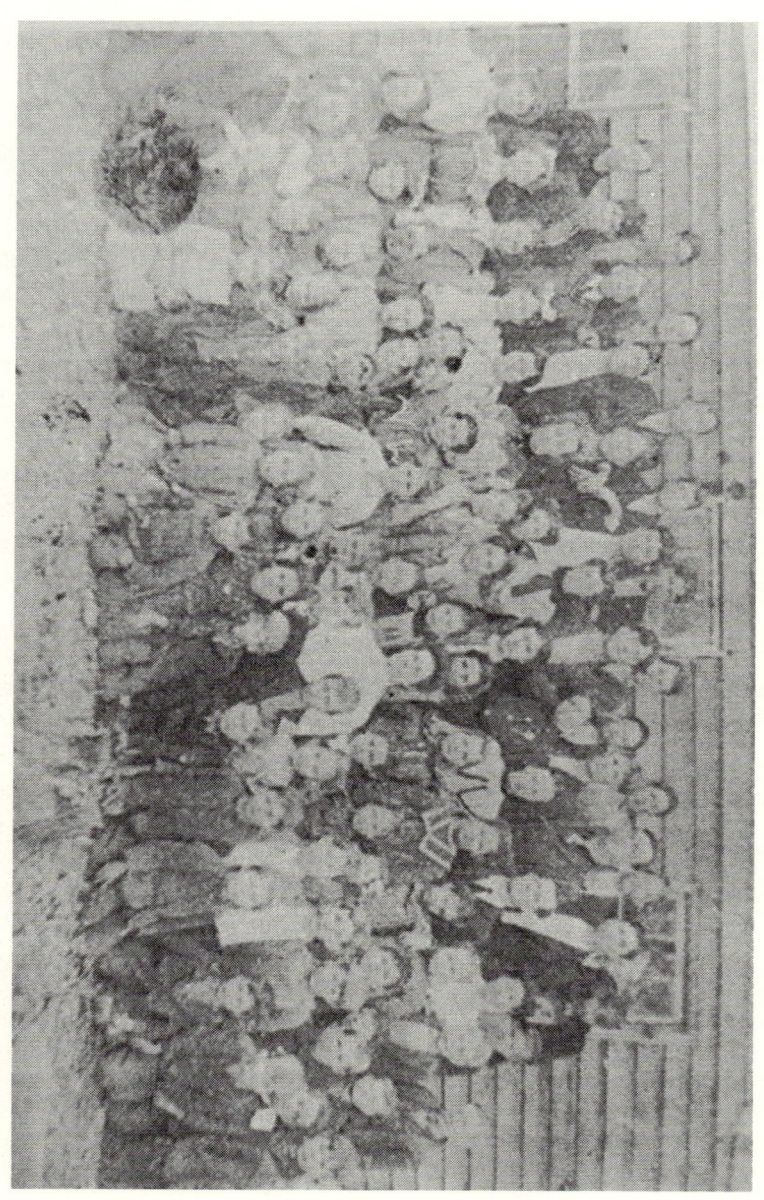

Courtesy of Bertie H. Taylor

Students and teachers at Belmont Public Free School ("Ebenezer School") about 1907. Willie I. Elledge was principal, and Mrs. Ann Shook taught primary subjects.

Willie I. Elledge was minister of the Ebenezer Baptist Church from 1904 to at least 1907. His salary in 1905 was $57, the highest in the Tombigbee Baptist Association at that time. Ebenezer had a membership of 84. Squire C. C. "Lum" Shook was the church clerk. At the Tombigbee Baptist Association held at New Home Church at Clay in Itawamba County on October 14-17, 1905, the following Belmont area churches were represented: Red Bud --M. B. Waddle; Ebenezer -- G. W. Yarber, C. C. Shook, O. L. Phillips, and J. S. Stockton; Bethel - W. H. Holcomb and J. S. Henley; Union-- W. M. Toland, E. L. Cain, and R. T. Mauldin; and Prospect--M. E. Mann. J. S. Stockton was the pastor at Salem in Itawamba County with 93 members and at Highland with 49 members. J. M. Harrison was the pastor at Union with 57 members; L. A. Cain was Union church clerk. W. H. Hamilton was pastor at Red Bud with 28 members and at Bethel with 57 members. G. W. Holcomb was the Bethel church clerk, and M. L. Parker was the Red Bud church clerk. A. A. Gray was pastor at Prospect, and C. M. Long was church clerk there. Prospect had 60 members.

On the south side of Belmont, Dr. Mid Davis, the first Belmont postmaster who had formerly practiced medicine in the Dennis area, operated a store near the present Elizabeth Williams home. His store was a white frame building and had a stock of general merchandise brought in from Iuka. This store, operating before the coming of the railroad, was outside the picket fence around the nearby Davis home. Dr. Mid Davis practiced medicine very little when he moved to Belmont. South of Dr. Davis, about where the Hugh Nichols home now is, was the home of Major Davis, a son of Dr. M. M. Davis. A few years later, Major Davis and his family along with the Dr. Mid Davis family moved to Golden. Major became a depot agent there after the railroad came through.

In the late 1800's, F. L. Harris operated a gin back of the present James Stephens home which he sold shortly after the turn of the century to J. N. (John) Patterson. J. N. Patterson was the Fifth District supervisor for the 1904-1908 term. According to Hallie Yarber, his daughter, J. N. Patterson built the Belmont Bear Creek Bridge in his term in office. It was built about 1907 on the W. C. (Bill) Wood place. Vincennes Bridge Company had the contract, and J. G. "Bud" Harris furnished lumber for the bridge. Being a supervisor in the period of the coming of the railroad was evidently no easy task; but J. N. Patterson, true to his ability, did a highly commendable job in this formative time.

Courtesy Gertrude Ozbirn

The M. M. Davis and Son Store, the first store in what was to become Belmont. Dr. Mid Davis stands in front of the store steps with his wife, Mary Jane Davis.

Courtesy Evie H. Cleveland

The M. L. Harris home in Belmont. Mrs. Parthenia Harris and her daughter, Evie, stand in front of the house.

The M. L. (Fayette) Harris family lived at this time about where the present home of Mrs. C. M. (Oniece) Harris is. Parthenia, the wife of M. L. Harris, was a daughter of Dr. M. M. Davis. Fayette Harris, a son of pioneers Basil and Polly Ann Harris, followed the dental profession into the 1920's after having taught several years before the coming of the railroad. He attended Nashville Dental College and was one of the first dentists in this area. He was a traveling dentist and drove a wagon that carried his dental equipment from community to community. From house to house he went, mending and pulling teeth. M. L. Harris had a foot-powered drill with which he cleaned and prepared teeth for filling. With gold foil, he hammered in gold dabbed on the gums. Quite a contrast exists between the near painless techniques and modern dental advances of our present dentist, Dr. Billy V. Stephens, and those early dental practices of M. L. (Fayette) Harris.

About the time of the coming of the railroad, Dr. Snow and Dr. Bennett practiced under M. L. Harris. Later, Dr. W. Cleveland, who graduated from dental school in 1919, practiced with M. L. Harris between terms of school.

M. L. (Fayette) Harris was also a farmer. In later years, he had several hundred hogs roaming the Bear Creek bottom lands, fattening on acorns, beech mast, and other wild foods. M. L. Harris had a most unique ability in animal husbandry: he was the best person in the country in being able to tole hogs, some semi-wild, from one place to the other. He would drop corn or feed along the way the hogs were supposed to go. The hogs usually followed along, eating the corn and being moved from one place to the other. Several early settlers could tole hogs. M. L. Harris was one of the very few who could reportedly tole a hog across a foot bridge.

Most assuredly, the family of Dr. M. M. (Mid) Davis was to have a big impact on this area. His son-in-law, M. L. Harris, was a dentist and prominent land owner. His son, Major, was to be a depot agent. A daughter, Lucy, married O. L. Phillips, a respected law enforcement officer and merchant around Dennis. Other daughters of Dr. Davis were Becky Mitchell, Nancy Davis, Mary Davis, Martha Jane Ozbirn, Vinnia Davis, and Roxie Long. Two sons, L. R. Davis and N. S. "Pole" Davis, were very prominent merchants in the Dennis area. A son-in-law of L. R. Davis, Charlie Flurry, was a respected rural mail carrier for years and years. Belle, the wife of L. R. Davis, was a daughter of John Byram. Her sister, Sarah, was the wife of Dr. V. S. Stanphill, who practiced medicine in, and had one of the first stores in, the present Golden area. Dr. Stanphill first had his store about where the Bobby Dean Woods family now lives, but it was later moved to Golden proper near the railroad.

About where the Harold Davis family now lives near Golden was Martin School. A log school was there first, but a frame building replaced it years later. Church was held there for a time. At school, a rowdy situation existed for a while. Outsiders and overaged students caused sincere educators to leave after one term. Then, Lee Hicks and Thomas Oscar Lindsey were hired. Both were single at the time. They rode their horses up from Belmont to Martin School. Thomas Oscar Lindsey gave a little talk to the students: "We have come here to teach and have school... Lee and I will be here when it is all over." A "bulldog fight" soon happened among some students. As in previous times outsiders took up the fight. Still, T. O. Lindsey and Lee Hicks stood their ground and would not let the "rowdies" run over them. School prevailed! The trustees came in a few days and upheld the teachers. School went on at Martin School better than ever before. With the coming of the railroad, a new two-story building was constructed where Golden Manufacturing Company now operates in Golden.

On the present Claude McAnally farm north of the old Vaudrie Davis place, W. T. Shook, a son of Squire C. C. Shook, had a general store. Near here lived Andrew White, the father-in-law of W. T. and a respected, prosperous farmer. W. T. Shook also owned a dry good and general merchandise store in Belmont with his brother, Hatley Shook, that was to be one of the first stores in the Village of Belmont. Later, W. T. Shook was a prominent merchant and community leader in Golden. For sure, the valuable contributions of W. T. Shook as an educator and a community leader in both Belmont and Golden helped our area to prosper.

In the meantime, south of the present Belmont school down Griffin Street near Ben Martin Branch lived some of the first black people in the area: G. M. (Mart) Luster (1856-1914) and his wife, Adline Luster. Their children were Dolphus, Jonah, Walker, Viola, Arvilla, Alrada, Len, and Isom. Near where the Web Thomas family now lives on Red Bud Road was a black woman called "Aunt Barb" who told fortunes with coffee "grounds." Ann Beachum also told fortunes at her home. If in their fortune telling they had foretold about the changes to be with the coming of the railroad, few people would have believed them. Yet, changes were definitely forthcoming.

Right-of-way work for the railroad through our area followed the surveying and right-of-way purchases in 1906. The right-of-way clearance destroyed a chestnut grove west of the George Jackson home. Squire C. C. "Lum" Shook had to move his home westward off the right-of-way when the railroad came through. It seems that different contractors bid off so many miles of construction. Barber had a camp near New Providence. The Belmont segment was reportedly under the direction of Palmer. The Palmer railroad construction camp was northeasterly from the water well in the present Shady Cove area and was mostly on the west side of the railroad.

Will Clark, a son of W. T. Clark, recalls being a water boy for one of the grading gangs. When the Belmont trestle was built, it consisted, at first, of green timber. This temporary trestle was later replaced with a better one. With the mules of his father, Will Clark hauled lumber for the section houses in Belmont on Front Street where Blue Bell now is. The depot was built about this same time.

In the building of the railroad, many deep cuts had to be made. Several mules were hitched to massive plows or slipscrapes in the earth-moving process. Many black workers cut the right-of-way and worked on the grade in places. The drivers of the teams of mules could hit any mule with the crack of their whips without much effort. Since this work was done before bulldozers, the work was most interesting, even amazing, to the local people. The rowdy atmospheres around the camps left much to be desired. Still, the people of the area watched and wondered as the rails were put in place.

There was much concern, conjecture, and even consternation about where the villages or towns would be located on the railroad. One idea was that the new settlement would be located cross from the present Liberty Church of Christ workshop building to the east. Another idea would have placed the town in present north Belmont across present Highway 25 and the railroad from Billy P. Sartain Grocery northward. Another plan, supposedly following talks among area leaders, would have put the new town between present Belmont and Golden near the John T. Griffin home and southeast from there. By this plan, L. R. Davis and N. S. Davis would consider moving their stores from the present area around Dennis to here as might Dr. Stanphill and W. T. Shook from the present Golden area along with the stores existing in the Belmont area. This plan was not put into action.

In 1906, Joseph Lennon and W. E. Small had taken land options from area residents regarding land for a possible townsite and depot site. Among those who gave options were C. C. Shook, M. L. Harris, Dr. M. M. Davis, J. N. Patterson, and R. L. Shook. Eventually, the Village of Belmont would locate at its present site; while Dennis and Golden would locate at their present sites.

It is said that a Belmont Townsite Company was formed around 1906-1907 and consisted of C. C. Shook, Joseph Lennon, R. L. Shook, Jordan M. Boone, W. E. Small, and possibly a few others. They got townsite property from C. C. Shook and R. L. Shook. This company ceased to exist after a while; and the property stayed in the hands of its original owners, C. C. Shook and R. L. Shook.

Courtesy Evie Cleveland

F. L. (Finess) Harris and his wife, Anna Harris. Finess Harris, a son of Basil Harris, sold the property upon which Dr. Mid Davis had the first store in what was to be Belmont. He sold the gin to J. N. Patterson which was located behind the present James Stephens home. With the coming of the railroad, Finess Harris had a sawmill east of the railroad which processed the logs cut off the Noel Survey where downtown Belmont was to locate.

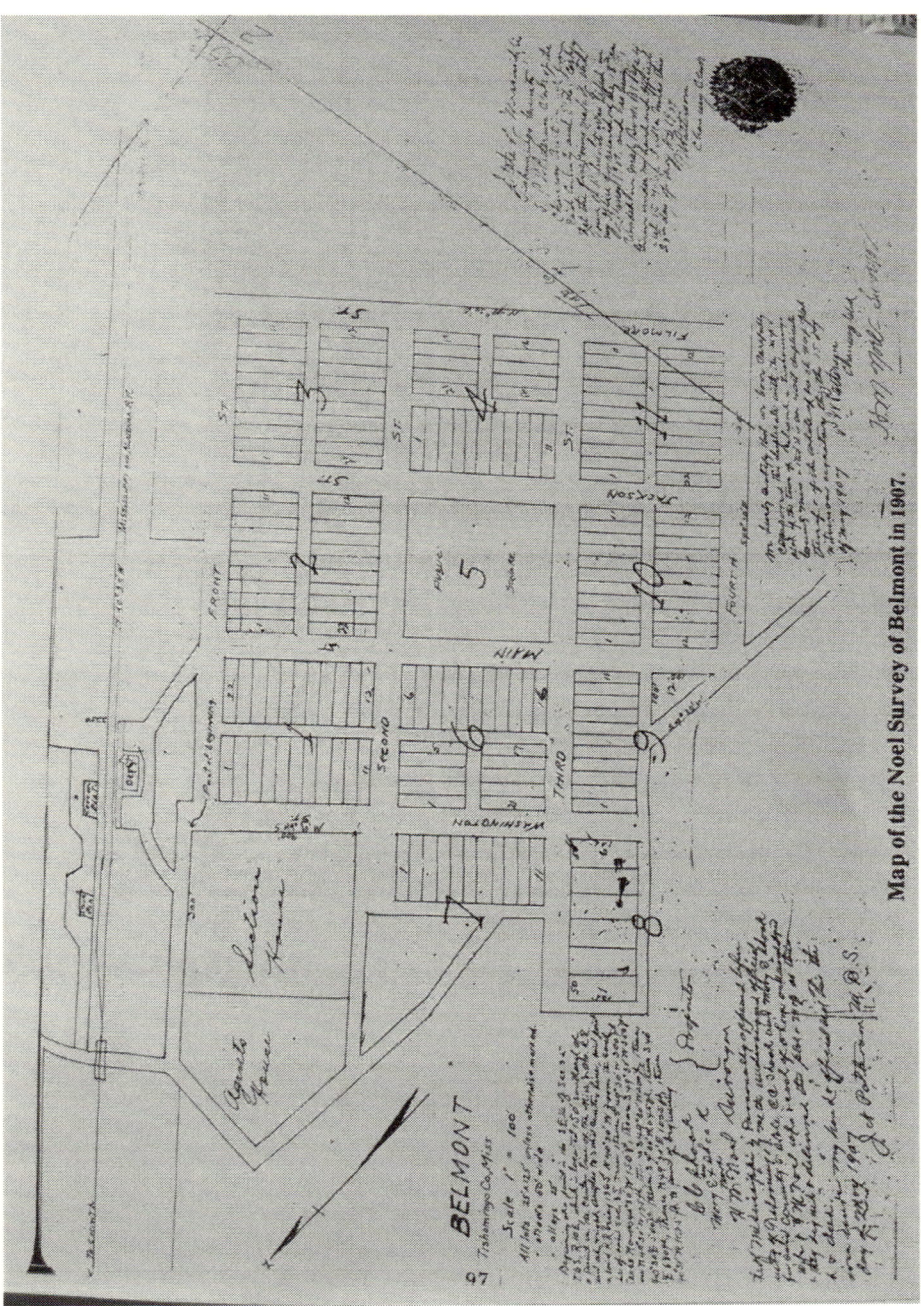

Map of the Noel Survey of Belmont in 1907.

Belmont was laid off in blocks for a village. H. M. Noel, a short young civil engineer for the railroad from a northern state, did the Belmont survey, relying many times upon the assistance and counsel of John Henry Clark. This survey, the Noel Survey, encompassed the present downtown area of Belmont and involved the scrub woods pasture of C. C. Shook. On May 15, 1907, C. C. Shook and Mary E. Shook signed and delivered the platted map of the Noel Survey. On May 31, 1907, R. L. Shook, Mary A. Shook, C. C. Shook, and Mary E. Shook signed and delivered an addition plat and map for Belmont adjacent to the Noel Survey. John Henry Clark had surveyed this property May 23, 1907. Work was begun removing the timber off the pasture of Squire Shook. O. M. Cain recalls hearing his father, Marshall Cain, tell about hauling logs off the present Belmont court square to the F. L. Harris sawmill eastward across the railroad. Others were reportedly involved in the log hauling. Soon, C. C. "Lum" Shook would offer lots for sale in downtown Belmont, especially on Main Street. Soon, more and more people would come to the settlement the "beautiful mountain." Soon, Belmont would be born officially.

Dennis and Golden were also laid off in blocks. Original Golden was supposed to have been named Wamsley or Wambi. Then, shortly after the railroad came through, a daughter was born to Mr. and Mrs. Jim Wiggins. Jim Wiggins, a brick mason lived across the road from Dr. A. E. Bostick. Dr. Bostick, who lived where the Tom Hellums family now lives in Golden delivered the baby girl, Golden Patrie Wiggins, on January 18, 1908. Through the encouragement of Dr. Bostick, Golden came to be named for Golden Patrie Wiggins. No doubt, the Golden name from the earlier area post office was also a contributing factor.

In June, 1907, several Golden area residents had formed the Golden Townsite Company. Dr. V. S. Stanphill was the trustee of the company. The stockholders included Dr. V. S. Stanphill, Dr. A. E. Bostick, N. B. Mink, J.P. Stanphill, J. I. C. Hopkins, M. J. Hale, D. D. Paden, W. H. Patterson, J. I. Epps, J. M. Nix, Lille Hale, Dr. Loammi Harris, S. T. White, J. R. Davis, A. J. Long, J. A. Byram, T. A. Stanphill, B. F. Patterson, J.B. Hopkins, W. A. Mann, W. E. Mann, and T. Hall. Shortly, D. J. Hale and his wife N. A. Hale, sold land along with Dr. V. S. Stanphill to the Golden Townsite Company. John Henry Clark surveyed the plat for the Town of Golden on this land. On June 25, this plat and map was recorded in the chancery clerk office.

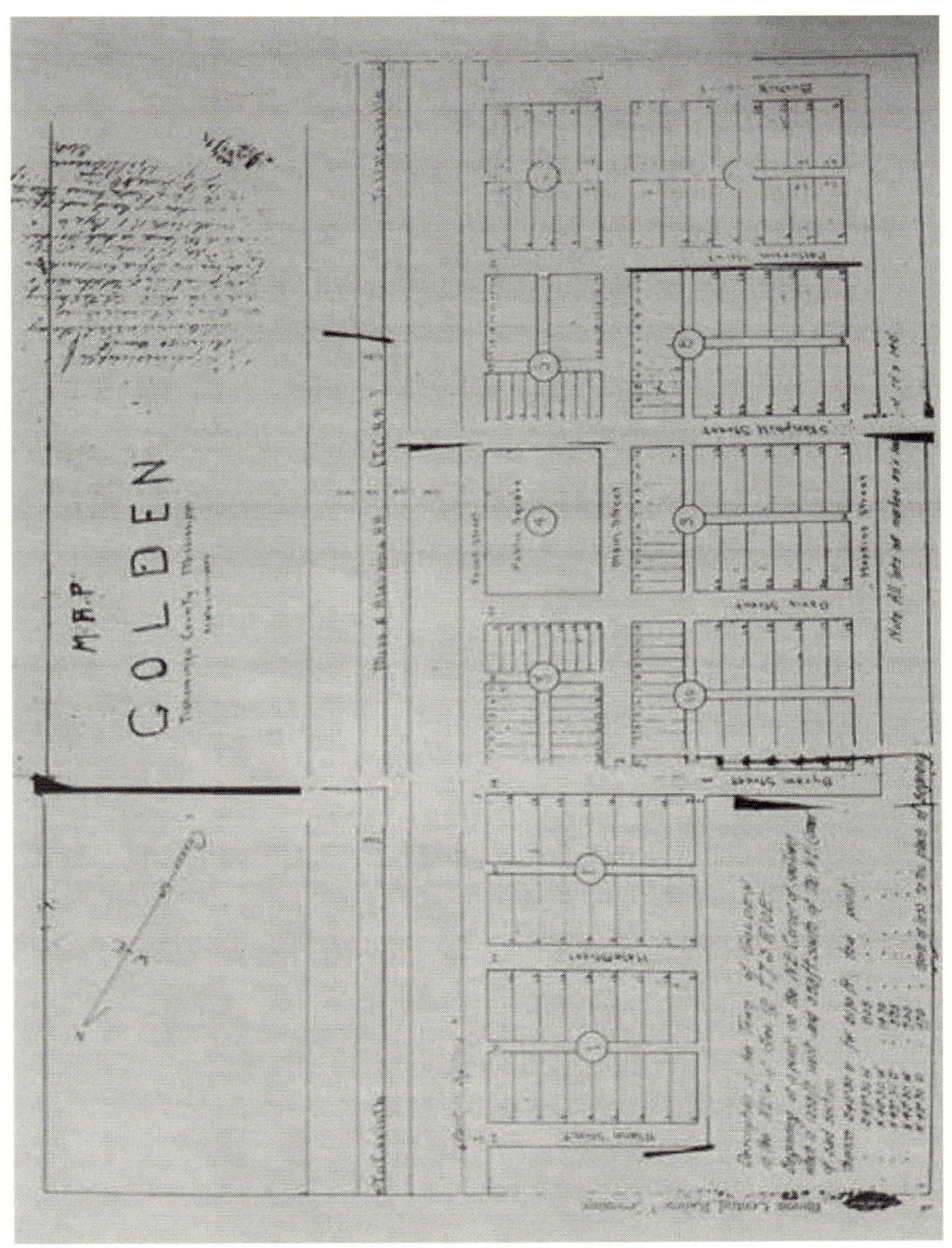

Map of Golden in 1907.

L. R. Davis had previously named Dennis in honor of the New Providence pastor. Being the postmaster and a highly success businessman as well, L. R. Davis could be called "Mr. Dennis" without fear of overstating the point. He was to be a dominating force at Dennis until his death in 1942. In November, 1907, L. R. Davis, Belle Davis, Charles Flurry, and Lillie Cleo Flurry recorded the plat and map of the town of Dennis which John Henry Clark had surveyed and laid out. In late 1907, L. R. Davis moved the Dennis post office about a quarter of a mile northeast of the old site and about ten rods west of the railroad on the new townsite. John T. Blanchard, a prominent Primitive Baptist preacher and public servant, became the Dennis postmaster in January 1908.

In December, 1907, Samuel Porter (Sam) Beaty became the first Belmont postmaster in the new Belmont located in the Noel Survey. Dr. Loammi Harris became the Golden postmaster in early 1908.

Courtesy Lalla Allen

The store of L. R. Davis in Dennis in 1904.

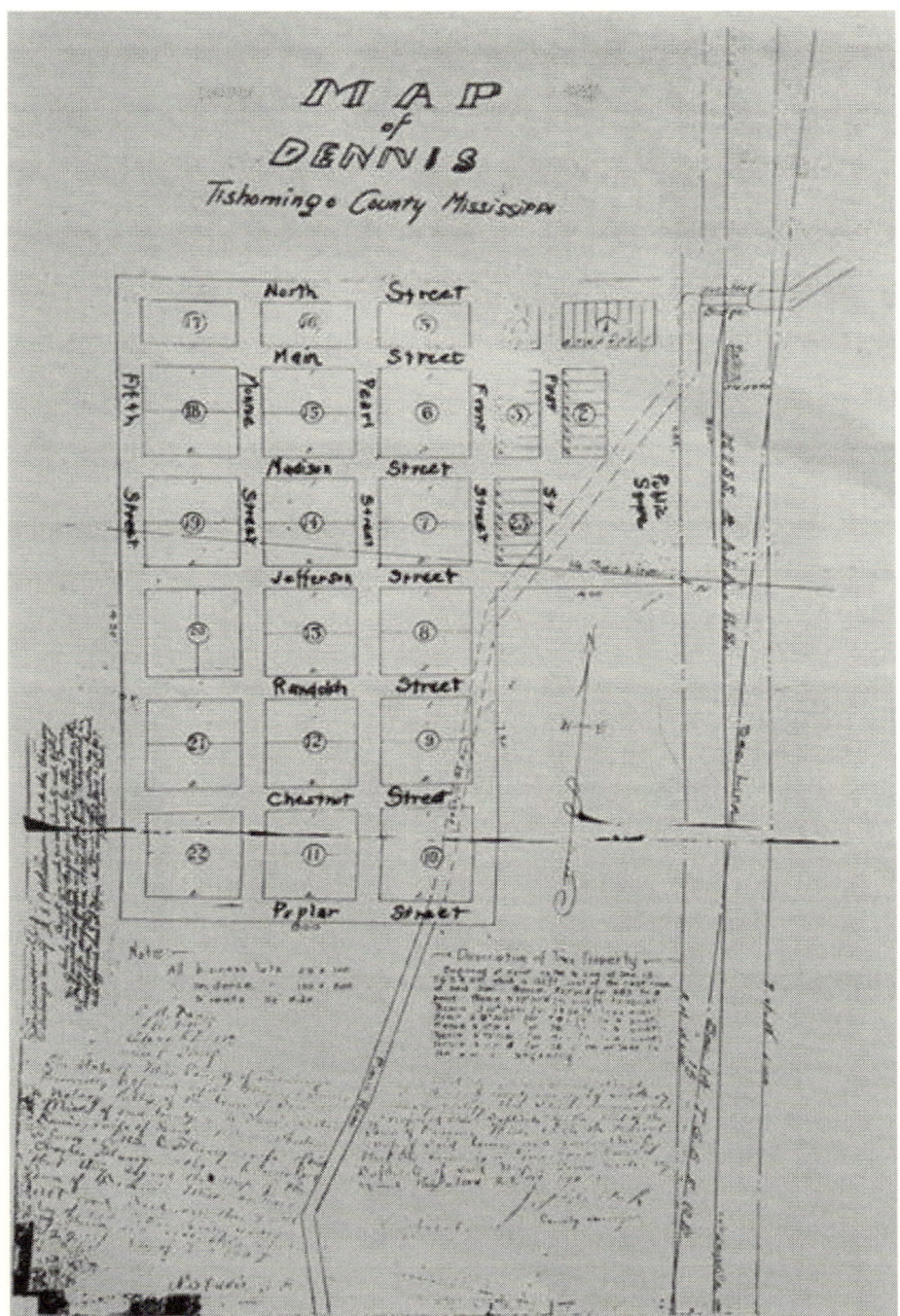

Map of Dennis 1907.

Courtesy Mr. and Mrs. J. T. Lindsey

The early Dennis depot.

In 1907, the boll weevil invaded Mississippi. At the time this caused little concern for the Belmont area people, who were more interested in the progress of the railroad. In the fall of 1907, the first train passed through Belmont. A Mr. Johnson was reportedly the first depot agent. Short, mixed trains were on the line first. The memorable "Doodlebug," beloved in the hearts and minds of many, arose from these early trains. Other faster trains operated later on the Illinois Central Railroad through here, like the Seminole and City of Miami; but the little "Doodlebug" train is the one our area people recall with fondest memories. The "Doodlebug" consisted of three or four as follows: an engine, a mail or baggage car, and one or two passenger cars. It usually ran around 9:00 A. M. going north; and many people went to Dennis, Neil, Tishomingo, and Corinth for pleasure and business. About 3:30 in the afternoon the "Doode" came through Belmont going south to Golden, Red Bay, Vina, Hackleburg, and Haleyville. The "Doode" furnished a means of travel, while it stopping in Belmont furnished a gathering place and simple social atmosphere at the depot. Down through the years, many were to gather at the depot to watch people get off the "Doode," called "short train," and the Seminole, called "the fast mail." The coming of the railroad was surely going to have a solid influence on the Belmont area in terms of travel, commerce, and the learning of new social ideas.

Courtesty O. L. Strickland and Cecil Sumners

The memorable "Doodlebug."

Courtesy De Etta Wigginton

The Belmont depot.

Meanwhile, an organized village was starting to form on the converted pasture of Squire C. C. "Lum" Shook. People had to dodge stumps on Main Street for a while, but they were to continue to come to town to trade in the new stores that had opened. W. T. Shook and R. L. Shook were among the first to buy business lots on the Belmont townsite property. The W. T. Shook store – W. T. Shook General Merchandise – was located about where Rhodes Barber Shop and Tesseneer Station are presently located. The R. S. Shook store – Shook and Lindsey – was situated where Yarber Rexall Drugs now is. Moreover, W. T. Shook General Merchandise was the first store building erected in downtown Belmont in July, 1907. The store of R. L. Shook was built in September, 1907.

Courtesy Forest Wright

Construction on the W. T. (Willie) Ferguson house in Belmont about 1909. Willie Ferguson is the second from the right; and his stepson, Ernest Keith, is on the right. On the left is L.P. Allen; while Rollie Anderson is third from the left. Bob Ferguson, son of Willie Ferguson, sits calmly on the lower level. Moving from Ozark in Itawamba County, W. T. (Willie) Ferguson had a general store – one of the early Belmont stores – where the present Belmont Hotel is located. He also operated a gin in the vicinity of the present Belmont post office and Western Auto store. His cousins, Dick Ferguson and Frank Ferguson, were also early lumber men in Belmont. Reportedly around 1910, Willie Ferguson sold his house, one of the best in Belmont, to Dr. Lee Montgomery.

Courtesy of Bertie H. Taylor

Downtown Belmont about 1910. L. P. Allen is visible in front of his store, the second on the left. The fourth store, left to right, W. T. Shook General Merchandise, was reportedly the first store in downtown Belmont, in the Noel Survey.

It is said that the first residences built on the Belmont townsite were those of Dr. R. L. (Lee) Montgomery about where Forest Wright now lives and Dr. K. F. McRae where the present Deaton Funeral Home is. Ironically, the home of Dr. McRae was built about where the gate to the old Lum Shook wooded pasture once was. Others who early purchased lots in the Belmont townsite area included B. F. Wright, L. P. Allen, Dr. L. S. Greene, Iuka Hardware Company, J. M. Pharr, J. T. Montgomery, W. T. Clark and James A. Clark (W. T. Clark and Son), G. A. Clark, Annie O. Gilbert, T. A. Gilley, J. N. Patterson, W. W. Shook, and A. G. W. (Green) Byram. Several others followed shortly thereafter. Most assuredly, the railroad made Belmont! It furnished the catalyst which enabled a wooded pasture to be transformed with human effort and co-operation into an enthusiastic village of people interested in making their world a better place. The coming of the railroad started a new era in a place called Belmont. At the helm of this new era was the long-time justice of the peace and respected community leader, Squire C. C. "Lum" Shook.

Courtesy Mr. and Mrs. Irby Shook

Squire C. C. "Lum" Shook, first mayor of Belmont. Downtown Belmont emerged on the wooded pasture land of this likeable early Belmont builder.

CHAPTER 10

THE SQUIRE SHOOK ERA

The coming of the railroad had excited people. They were enjoying the trips on the "Doodlebug" and the Sunday afternoon gatherings at the depot to see who was getting off and getting on the "Doode." The trains were helping commerce. A new era had dawned. The central person of this era was in all probability Squire C. C. "Lum" Shook.

C. C. "Lum" Shook was born January 21, 1846. From Alabama his father and mother, William Wiley Shook and Mahala Shook, moved their family to the present Belmont area in the 1840's. His grandfather, Solomon Shook, is said to have owned at one time some of the real estate where Birmingham, Alabama, is today. Solomon Shook wrought in steel and owned a plant there before moving into this area. C. C. Shook fought in the Civil War in Company H of the 26th Mississippi Infantry. In the years after the Civil War, Lum Shook was very active in the Confederate Veterans gatherings at Bay Springs and Belmont. In fact, he was camp commander of the F. M. Boone Camp No. 1694 of the Confederate Veterans in our area. Lum Shook was a longtime justice of the peace in the Fifth District. From this office, he probably earned the title "Squire." In law enforcement he was said to be fair, yet firm. C. C. Shook was very active in the Ebenezer Baptist Church, serving as church clerk, helping in church activities, and rarely missing a church service. In addition, he was instrumental in helping various aspects of progress to our area. Squire C. C. Shook was a builder in the truest sense. His influence and the influence of his family were to be very strategic to the progress of Belmont.

C. C. "Lum" Shook married Mary Anglin. To this union were born nine children. Two children died in infancy. Sons of C. C. and Mary Shook were W. T. (Tommy) Shook, R. L. (Lee) Shook, H. M. (Hatley) Shook, and M. A. (Arthur) Shook. Their daughters were Mrs. Aderine (Flora Belle) Bostick, Mrs. W. O. (Lottie) Stockton, and Mrs. Charles H. (Laura) Yarber. The valuable contributions of these people and their children form an important part of the Belmont heritage.

When the railroad came through, Lum Shook had to move his house off the railroad right-of-way. This house, probably the oldest in Belmont, stands today on the property of Mr. and Mrs. J. P. Fulton, Jr. Ruth Stockton Fulton is a granddaughter of C. C. Shook, and the old Shook house is southeast of her home on the north side of Yarber Street (formerly County Line Road) in Belmont. Lum Shook operated a sorghum mill on the east side of the railroad but later moved it to where the Deaton Funeral Home now is. From there the Shook sorghum mill was moved back of the present home of Jewell Shook, another granddaughter of C. C. Shook. The Lum Shooks moved to a house that stood where the present Kenneth Mayhall home is.

Squire Shook was, according to those who knew him, "somebody you could count on . . . a good booster. . . He was strict and fair. If you got in trouble, you got fined. He rarely missed a church service and loved to jest and be around young people." Once Evie Harris (later Mrs. Webster Cleveland) carried him some squirrels which her father had killed that day. Mr. Lum was seated on his porch, swatting autumn flies. He remarked to Evie and laughed, "I do believe these flies sharpened their bills down at Doss Pate's blacksmith shop." Essentially, the Squire Shook Era marked the foundational beginning of the Village of Belmont and the Town of Belmont. Fortunate indeed was Belmont to have a man with the likeable personality, leadership drive, and solid principles of C. C. Shook at the helm.

In late 1907 or early January, 1908, several citizens of Belmont signed a petition seeking incorporation and mailed it to Governor Edmond F. Noel. January 22, 1908, is a famous day in the history of Belmont. A proclamation of Governor Noel on January 22, 1908, granted a charter of incorporation to the Village of Belmont. Secretary of State, James W. Powers, later certified this charter on February 7, 1908. The number of inhabitants at incorporation was 110. Two-thirds signed the petition seeking incorporation. The first municipal officers of the Village of Belmont were as follows: Mayor – C. C. Shook; Marshal – J. H. (John Henry) Clark; Treasurer – J. A. Clark; and Aldermen – S. P. (Sam) Beaty, Dr. R. L. (Lee) Montgomery, and Dr. K. F. McRae.

At first, Belmont, Golden, and Dennis were villages. This reason was explained in the Mississippi Code of 1906, Chapter 99. Municipal corporations were divided into three classes: cities, towns, and villages. Those municipal corporations with 2,000 or more inhabitants were cities. Those having less than 2,000 and not less than 300 inhabitants were towns. Those corporations having less than 300 and not less than 100 inhabitants were villages. A municipal corporation could not be created with a population less than 100 inhabitants. Thus, with 110 inhabitants in 1908, Belmont was at first the Village of Belmont.

On September 4, 1908, the Village of Dennis was officially incorporated with 130 residents. William H. Lindsey was the first mayor of Dennis. The Dennis marshal was John C. Cornelius, and Ransom Young was the treasurer. The first aldermen of Dennis were J. A. Byram, L. F. Sartain, and R. F. Flurry.

On February 8, 1908, the Village of Golden was incorporated with 124 residents. James T. Vaughn was the first mayor of Golden. R. A. Miller was marshal, and W. H. Patterson was treasurer. Dr. Loammi Harris, M. J. Hale, and N. B. (Bascom) Mink were the first Golden aldermen.

About 1908 in Golden, Rev. Dave Bass held a tent meeting; and the Golden Methodist Church was organized shortly thereafter. Services were held in the Golden School building until about 1915. Some of the early families who were members of the church were reportedly the following: Bostick, Epps, Mink, Patterson, Wiggins, and Creel.

Courtesy Mr. and Mrs. Irby Shook

Wright and Winsett store in early Golden. Evidently, E. E. Wiginton also operated a store here at one time.

Courtesy Flossie Hollingsworth

View north up the railroad from Golden, showing the home of M. M. Davis and Major Davis on the left.

Courtesy Flossie Hollingsworth

Charlie Wofford sorghum mill in Golden.

At the February 2, 1908, Belmont meeting held at the office of Dr. McRae, W. T. Clark swore in Mayor C. C. Shook. On February 3, W. W. (Billy) Shook was unanimously elected village clerk. R. L. Shook was elected street commissioner, and J. H. Clark was named tax collector. With no village meeting hall, the March meeting was held at Shook and Lindsey Store that R. L. Shook and his father-in-law, T. B. Lindsey, owned. The following ordinances were passed. All offenses against the criminal laws of the State of Mississippi occurring in the Belmont limits not amounting to a felony were unlawful in the said village and were in violation of village ordinances to be punished as provided by state laws. In addition, each male resident between 18 and 55 was subject to street duty and to perform annually 6 days labor of 10 hours each on the streets, alleys, and avenues of Belmont. In lieu of failure to fulfill street duty, the man was to pay three dollars to the street commissioner to be turned into the village treasury.

At a June meeting of village officers at the office of Dr. Lee Montgomery, the Separate School District formed within the Village of Belmont annexed some patrons of the Belmont Free School outside the corporate limits into the Belmont Separate School District. Among the patrons outside the corporate limits of Belmont signing the petition to be annexed to the Belmont Separate School District were George S. Jackson, B. L. (Fayette) Hicks, John C. Hallmark, J. S. (Joe) Stockton, W. L. Cranford, Jesse Cummings Hallmark, W. C. (Bill) Wood, S. J. (Sid) Wood, C. S. (Carter) Shook, J. Yarber, T. M. Stanphill, Annie O. Gilbert, and W. T. Stacy. A board of trustees was named as follows: R. L. Shook, three year term; S. J. Wood and T. A. (Tom) Gilley, two year terms; and W. T. Clark and W. L. Cranford, one year terms. The board of aldermen approved at the August meeting the issuing of $3,000 in bonds for the purpose of raising money for the erection and equipment of a public school building in Belmont. R. L. Shook and C. C. Shook later gave the property for the new school site. This school, which many locally called in later decades "the Clement school," was located on the property the J. E. Clement later owned where the James Timbes family now owns and lives. The school building was a two-story frame building with an auditorium upstairs and classrooms downstairs. C. W. Davis was reportedly the first principal here, and D. R. Shelton followed him.

Courtesy Grady White

The new school building of Belmont Separate School about 1909. Principal C. W. Davis and Ben Brumley stand at the doorway.

Courtesy Rae Yarber

Belmont school group about 1909 or 1910. Principal C. W. Davis is on the middle right. Fourth from the right on the back row is Clay Wright, and third from the right on the back row is Arthur Shook. Later, these two were to be the first to graduate from Belmont in about 1911 or 1912 under Principal D. R. Shelton.

The first tax levy for Belmont was made at the September meeting. The levy for the year beginning October 1, 1908, and ending September 30, 1909, was three mills for the Belmont Separate School District and one mill for general taxes. In November, W. T. Clark was unanimously elected tax collector for the 1908-1909 year. In another appointment, A. G. W. (Green) Byram was named trustee on the school board to fill out the unexpired term of T. A. Gilley, who moved from the school district. At the December meeting, J. H. Clark, street commissioner, reported $111 street tax collected during the year 1908, showing that 37 men preferred paying the annual three dollar street tax to working on the streets.

On Tuesday, December 8, 1908, the first municipal election was held in Belmont at W. T. Shook's Store. Hatley M. Shook, W. T. Clark, and T. B. Lindsey held the election. The next day, the village officials met at Belmont Hardware and Furniture Company to canvass the election returns and declare that for 1909 and 1910 the following officers were elected, all with 11 votes each: Mayor – C. C. Shook; Treasurer – J. A. Clark; Marshal – G. C. Martin; Village Clerk – W. W. Shook; and Aldermen – Dr. K. F. McRae and T. B. Lindsey. At a special election on January 20, 1909, Village clerk, W. W. Shook, was elected alderman also.

A calaboose (jail) was constructed on the court square. Squire C. C. Shook had donated the land for the court square. He was also to donate land for the Baptist Church, the Church of Christ, the Methodist Church, the school, and the park where the bandstand was to be built around 1909.

Belmont Church of Christ started in a frame building constructed in 1909 on the land that Mayor Shook donated. This building was located where the present downtown Church of Christ building is. Among the charter members were Mr. and Mrs. A. J. Trollinger, Mrs. R. L. Shook, T. B. Lindsey, Mr. and Mrs. W. W. Shook, and Mr. and Mrs. Dick Ferguson. Early elders of the church were T. B. Lindsey, R. L. Shook, and W. W. Shook. Early deacons of the church were A. J. Trollinger, M. L. Shook, and J. H. Lambert. At first the church had only a part-time minister, R. L. (Lee) Shook. John Henry Shook and Frank Baker are reported to have preached here also. Of further interest is the fact that T. B. (Tom) Lindsey, who was very instrumental in helping start the Liberty Church of Christ, served a similar role in helping start the Belmont Church of Christ. Two of his daughters,

Mrs. R. L. (Ann) Shook and Mrs. W. W. (Belle) Shook, were charter members of the church.

Another daughter of T. B. Lindsey, Elizabeth, was the wife of A. G. W. Byram. They were active in the Baptist Church. In addition, in about 1909, A. G. W. Byram had the first hotel in Belmont. It was a two-story, frame building located on the present Wright property between the present hotel and Blue Bell on Front Street. In 1910, A. G. W. Byram sold the hotel to Charles Googe.

In May, 1910, C. C. Shook donated the church property south of the present Belmont Library to J. T. Montgomery, J. C. Jackson, and J. N. Patterson, trustees of the Belmont Methodist Episcopal Church South of Belmont. The Methodist Church building was completed about 1911.

In March, 1909, Mayor Lum Shook had appointed a school building committee consisting of Chairman R. L. Shook, W. L. Cranford, S. P. Beaty, J. N. Patterson, and J. C. Jackson. They reported shortly to village officers who accepted the lowest responsible bid of J. W. Shook for $740 for completed work (labor) on the two-story school building. An estimation of material was $1,600. The building committee was authorized to buy dressed lumber and other materials responsibly. Consequently, construction of the new school building was under way in the summer of 1909.

In 1909, Fannie I. (Belle) Jackson (later Mrs. B. N. Patterson) became the Belmont postmaster. Then, in 1911, Sam Beaty again assumed the job as postmaster. T. C. Stanphill succeeded him as postmaster in the fall of 1913.

Around 1909-1910, the first Model T Ford cars came to Belmont. Dr. K. F. McRae probably had the first car – a chain-operated vehicle that was rarely seen. M. L. (Fayette) Harris had a T model that operated off four dry-cell batteries. M. L. (Mark) Shook also had one of the first T models in Belmont and operated a taxi service. G. W. "Bill" Martin, my father, hauled freight from the depot. He recalls hauling the first gasoline brought into Belmont to Allen-Wright Hardware, purchasers of the six drums of gasoline. Behind Allen-Wright was probably the first garage in Belmont. Ed Pate and Troy Pate are reported to have operated this garage. Moreover, Allen-Wright Hardware Company, Shook and Lindsey, and Tishomingo Banking Company – all on Main Street – are reported to be the first brick store buildings in Belmont in about 1912.

The Belmont mayor and each alderman were allowed six dollars per year for services in 1909. The village clerk was allowed six dollars additionally. The marshal was allowed $1.25 per day for each day engaged in actual work on the street and a 2 percent commission on all street tax collected in 1909. J. A. Clark, village treasurer, was allowed one percent on all money that he received in 1909 except money for the school building. Actually, the village officials were more concerned with helping bring growth than in their salary. Showing a concern for cleanliness and peaceful surroundings, village officers passed some ordinances. It was unlawful for anyone to leave any horse or mule hitched to any vehicle of any description on any of the principal streets of Belmont without its being securely hitched in the usual way. In addition, all persons living in the corporate limits of Belmont were required to clean up the premises over which they had control. All closets (toilets) and out houses were to be kept in sanitary condition with the use of some good disinfectant. Furthermore, all rubbish whatsoever description was to be kept off the principal streets in use and off all alleys and vacant lots adjacent to business houses. In September, another ordinance was passed making it unlawful for any person to play any ball game or throw or knock any ball on any of the principal streets of Belmont.

Courtesy Mr. and Mrs. John Trollinger
Belmont Drug Company, reportedly the first drug store in Belmont. Owner, W. W. (Billy Walker) Williams, is at the left.

Any violator was subject to a fine not exceeding $10 and an imprisonment not exceeding 10 days in the village calaboose.

The 1909 tax levy for Belmont totaled five mills, consisting of three mills for the Separate School District, 1 ½ mills for Separate School District Interest, and ½ mill for Belmont Corporation. In October, W. T. Clark and W. L. Cranford were re-elected trustees at school for a term of three years beginning August, 1909. In December, 1909, W. W. (Billy Walker) Williams was appointed tax collector for the year 1909-1910.

Courtesy Jewell Shook

A gathering of downtown Belmontians around 1909. Pictured on the back row, left to right, are John Seago, Sam Beaty, Jim Shook, (Unidentified), George Jackson, C. C. Shook, Lee Shook, and Jim Clark. Left to right on the front row are Lee Hicks, Hatley Shook, Billy Walker Williams, Dick Clark, Billy Shook, Green Byram, Benton Green, and Tom Lindsey. The young lad in front is Herbert Shook, who was to be later one of the most outstanding Belmont educators, serving very capably as superintendent from 1931-1940.

Late in 1909, a new Masonic lodge name was born in Belmont. Pleasant Hill F. & A. M. Lodge No. 237, which was formed back in 1859 in Itawamba County, became the Belmont F. & A. M. Lodge No. 237. The lodge met upstairs in the building about where the First Baptist parsonage now is before moving downtown. In 1919, the Masonic lodge was situated downtown above the office of Dr. D. D. Johnson and the T. C. Stanphill Store.

In the meantime, T. A. Clark in June, 1908, stood the bar exam of Chancery Court in Tishomingo County. T. A. Clark obtained a license to practice law. About 1910, the Mississippi legislature created the office of county attorney. Governor Edmond F. Noel appointed T. A. Clark to the post in Tishomingo County. Tom Clark did his first law practice in Belmont. He later went to Iuka and entered into a law partnership with W. T. Bennett. His father, G. A. Clark, bought the hardware from Iuka Hardware Company in October, 1908, and renamed it Belmont Hardware and Furniture Company. He incorporated the hardware, owning controlling stock. W. W. Shook and G. J. Tankersley were the other stockholders. In late 1910, G. A. Clark sold the hardware to B. L. (Fayette) Hicks.

In the early days of Belmont, B. F. (Ben) Wright moved his family to Belmont from the Elma community (present East Prentiss community). There, he had a store and gin. He and his wife, Martha Ann Wright, had operated the post office at Elma. B. F. Wright was a solid, very successful business man and was able to "sum up a person" with remarkable accuracy. His impact on Belmont was to be very outstanding. Shortly, L. P. Allen of Moore's Mill heritage who had been working at Barnett Supply Company in Booneville moved with his wife, Annie, a daughter of B. F. Wright, to Belmont. Mrs. T. A. (Carrie) Gilley, also a B. F. Wright daughter, lived in Belmont. Another daughter of B. F. Wright, Anna, was married to Dr. L. S. Greene; but she died in 1912. Three sons of B. F. Wright – B. E. (Ellis) Wright, E. Clay Wright and Toy Wright – made valuable Belmont contributions. Toy was a gifted athlete and baseball pitcher at the University of Mississippi. Ellis Wright and Clay Wright were to be outstanding civic leaders in Belmont. In fact, Clay Wright and Arthur Shook, the youngest son of C. C. Shook, were the only members of the first graduating class about 1911 under Professor D. R. Shelton.

L. P. Allen began business in Belmont about January 1, 1910, in a building about where the O. E. Sparks Grocery was located in later years. About this time, J. N. Patterson operated a gin and grist mill across the road from the present Lessie Reed home and behind the present James Stephens home. On the property where the old Clement planer buildings presently are, George Isbell had a brick-making business. A deep hole was there, and many youth around 1910 went swimming there. Quite a contrast exists between the old Isbell swimming hole, one of the first used in Belmont, and the beautiful Belmont Blue Springs City Park swimming pool of today. We have progressed!

The population was also progressing. In 1910 the population in Tishomingo County was 13, 067, and the population in the Fifth District was 2, 982. The census report showed Golden with a population of 209 and Dennis with a population of 147. Belmont had a census population of 367, compared to 110 when the village was incorporated in 1908.

At Moore's Mill, the water mill continued to grind corn and make meal under the efforts of Steve Moore. In June, 1910, Edwin W. Caveness and Stephen Moore, Sr. deeded a parcel of land north of the mill on the west side of the Fulton and Iuka Road to the trustees of Red Bud School for a school site. This frame school served the Moore's Mill area until a few decades later when it merged with South Tishomingo School.

When Belmont was just getting started, C. A. (Dolphus) Millican had moved to Belmont and entered the lumber and sawmilling business. His home was about where the present Lester George home is. His mill was located behind the present home of Dr. Billy V. Stephens. Later, William Millican, the father of Dolphus Millican and a brother of Mrs. Amanda Jackson, moved to Belmont from the Blythe's Chapel community in Prentiss County. The Belmont home of this Civil War soldier and his family was a two-story building located where the present N. C. Deaton home is. William Millican, who had a hearing problem, was nevertheless, a gifted blacksmith. True to his ability, William Millican at one time repaired the boiler at the family sawmill, saving them a costly bill. In addition to the sawmill, the Millicans had a flour mill and a grist mill near the William Millican home.

John Hellums was another timber man who early came to Belmont. His son-in-law, Bob Crouch, moved to Belmont from Marietta and lived near Mr. Hellums where the present L. S. Short home is located near the old Belmont park. R. C. (Bob) Crouch became a contributing merchant with his jolly manner that was to brighten the day for many in Belmont. Indeed, Belmont was fortunate when people like the Millicans, John Hellums, and Bob Crouch moved here. Ironic is the fact that many Prentiss Countians would continue to move to Belmont and come through historic Bay Springs where a previous growth area had once prospered.

Courtesy Ethel C. Hurd

Condederate Veterans Reunion at Bay Springs from 1910. Identified are the following: front row, 1. Tom Lindsey, 3. Cavalier Byram, 4. Andrew J. White, 5. Charlie C. Harris, 6. W. Thankersley, 7. Frank Hopkins, and 17. C. C. Shook, commander of F. M Boone Camp No. 1694; back row, 1. Rev. Joe S. Stockton and 12. Clabe Lindsey.

About the summer of 1910, the annual Confederate Soldiers Reunion was held once again at Bay Springs. The reunions were to be held annually for years to come. Confederate gatherings were also held at the Belmont park. To play at gatherings like this and to enjoy music expression, the Belmont Concert Band was organized about this time. C. A. (Dolphus) Millian played a major role in the organizing of the band, and Fred Martin was the band director. Among the band members were C. A. Millican, A. G. W. Byram, Charles H. Yarber, Anthony Yarber, R. C. (Bob) Crouch, Arthur Jackson, Claude Shook, Herbert Shook, Olen

Yarber, M. L. (Mark) Shook, John L. Hallmark, Otis Byram, Claude Yarber, Kirk Crabb, Carroll Yarber, Dr. Carl Tynes, Audie Fugitt, and possibly a few others. Many late afternoons, the hills of Belmont was truly alive with the sound of music, sour notes and all, as the members of the Belmont Concert Band practiced individually on their instruments.

Courtesy John L. Hallmark

Belmont Concert Band in session in front of the old telephone exchange about where C and P Auto Supply is presently located. Band members (L-R) are as follows: A. G. W. Byram; Anthony Yarber; Charles H. Yarber; R. C. "Bob" Crouch; Arthur Jackson; Herbert L. Shook; C. A. "Dolphus" Millican; Claude Shook; (Unidentified); Olen Yarber; Mark Shook; Otis Byram; John Lumpkin Hallmark; and Fred Martin, band director.

Herbert Shook recalled playing the cornet which his father, W. W. Shook, had bought for him from a mail order house for $8.98. To play for the Confederate Soldiers Reunion and to experience the adventurous, rousing spirit of the reunion carried a youngster like Herbert L. Shook to the very zenith of happiness and delightful excitement. After all, the annual reunion of Confederate veterans of the area at Bay Springs was an unforgettable experience to young and old alike. The event reportedly took place on the last Thursday and Friday in August. People came from miles around on horseback or in their wagons and buggies pulled by horses, mules, and oxen for the two-day festivities. Many came to spend the night. Some slept in the lodge. Some slept on the ground. Some did not sleep at all.

The second day featured the real highlights. Noted fiddlers and banjo pickers came from all over the area. The air at scenic Bay Springs was filled with the strains of "Cotton-eyed Joe," "Billy in the Low Ground," "Sally Goodin," "Eighth of January," "Chicken in the Straw," and other popular renditions of ballads of the day. In this festive atmosphere, the staunch, proud Confederate veterans organized and paraded in rank with appropriate music, furnished at first from the brass band around New Site but around 1910 from the Belmont Concert Band. Spines tingled with goose pimples when the band poured forth its rousing rendition of "Dixie." Then, the aging Confederates responded with their famous, blood-curdling Rebel Yells.

Following the marching of the Confederate veterans came political speeches galore. About 1910 at the Confederate Reunion at Bay Springs, the colorful Theodore G. Bilbo, James K. Vardaman, and Governor E. F. Noel all unleashed their oratorical thunder. Often, speakers praised the Confederate efforts to keep their way of life and vehemently blasted the hardships of Reconstruction. It is said that Dr. Carroll Kendrick, a prominent legislator from Alcorn County who also represented our area, defiantly proclaimed that he was a member of the Ku Klux Klan and mighty proud to admit it.

Dinner on the ground was enjoyed thoroughly. Lemonade stands, often 30 to 40 strong, were always in evidence. The vendors had rectangular enclosures of pine boards or heavy cardboard in the more strategic locations around the lodge to better sell their products. M. L. Shook of Belmont was one of these vendors. From all over the area around the Bay Springs lodge came the cries, "Ice cold lemonade, made in the shade, stirred with a silver spade!" The price was the best feature – two large glasses for a nickel! Many are the forefathers of our area who on a hot, dusty day in August at Bay Springs quenched their thirst with a glass of lemonade served with tin dippers from wash tubs of lemonade with large chunks of ice floating in them. Greater bargains prevailed in the late afternoon when the reunion was breaking up – four glasses for a nickel.

Still, beverages less expensive were easily available. Near the bridge on the east side of Mackey's Creek was a copperas spring. Up the creek in a deep shade was "the drip spring," where water almost ice cold dripped steadily from the overhanging bluff. On the west side of the creek in a deep ravine through which Gin Branch flowed was a strong, bubbling spring.

Usually, there was an unneeded overabundance of another beverage that did not come from the springs or the lemonade stands. Some drank too much of it, and free-for-all fights erupted. Law enforcement was needed and was present. The negative results of the drinking and fights were overshadowed with the positive enjoyment of the Confederate Veterans Reunions. After all, the Confederate Reunions at Bay Springs were not only reunions for the aging Confederate soldiers but also massive social gatherings for thousands of acquaintances and friends which time and space separated.

Courtesy Tom Thrasher

Early Belmont scene at the junction of Main Street and Front Street near the depot.

Courtesy Bob Yarber

View of early Belmont from the depot westward up Main Street. The Hicks building is on the left.

   Back in Belmont, J. T. Sartain was elected marshal and street commissioner; and T. A. Clark was elected a school trustee to fill out terms. Additionally, G. W. Davis of Bay Springs was on the county school board at this time. In March the corporation limits of Belmont were enlarged with the addition of a plot of land on the south side of the village. In May, 1910, R. L. Shook, who had taken a current census of Belmont, reported a population of 405. In June, T. A. Gilley became a street commissioner. The tax levy for 1910 in Belmont, passed in October, totaled six mills, consisting of three mills for Separate School District and three mills for Interest on School Bonds.

   An ordinance was passed in October prohibiting anyone from exploding fireworks or shooting fireworks or firearms of any description on the Main Street or within 400 feet of Main Street in any direction. School matters continued to be prominent as Preston Yarber, M. J. Mayhall, and T. L. Upton were granted permission to be added to the Belmont Separate School District. The personable, respected W. W. Williams was re-elected tax collector for another year. Then, at the November 8, 1910, meeting, the village fathers took another step forward. They approved the construction of a village courthouse and voting place not to exceed $200. Aldermen Dr. K. F. McRae and T. B. Lindsey were appointed a committee in charge of plans and specifications.

Courtesy Ruth S. Fulton

Main Street in downtown Belmont facing the east. On the left is the telephone exchange building. On the right is the W. T. Clark and Son Store. The well on the court square is partially visible at the right of the buggy.

On November 25, 1910, an important part of Belmont history took place. Governor E. F. Noel issued a proclamation raising the Village of Belmont to the Town of Belmont. At the December 6, 1910, Belmont meeting, clerk W. W. Shook was authorized to copy the proclamation raising the Village of Belmont to the Town of Belmont. The town was entitled to five aldermen instead of three as a village. The Town of Belmont ordered that five aldermen be elected in the election on the second Tuesday in December, 1910, and thereafter at regular elections. The Town of Belmont was now official! The town officers elected for two year terms beginning in January, 1911, were these: Mayor – C. C. Shook; Marshal – H. D. Pate; Treasurer – J. A. Clark; and Aldermen – Dr. K. F. McRae, G. A. "Dick" Clark, T. B. Lindsey, Dr. R. L. Montgomery, and W. W. Shook.

In the summer of 1911 the two-story, frame courthouse

was completed. In August, W. W. Williams and W. O. Stockton were elected school trustees for two year terms, and C.S. (Carter) Shook was elected for a three year term.

About this time, much of the financial transaction was done with the Tishomingo Banking Company. James H. Faircloth was head of the bank, and W. W. Shook operated the branch of this bank at Belmont. It is said to have opened in Belmont around December, 1908. In the latter part of 1911, the Tishomingo Banking Company failed and closed its doors, due reportedly to the failure of the parent bank. Many area people who were beginning to get ahead were shocked and very disturbed at losing their money. One Belmont family is said to have lost over $3,000. A local merchant reportedly lost part of the money he recently borrowed to go into business. Luther Jackson recalls planning to get married only to lose better than $250 in the bank failure. Still, he went ahead under some temporary hardships and was married in January, 1912, to Ollie Kizer, a sister of Mrs. W. W. Williams and a daughter of the noted Civil War captain, Ben Kizer, who had lived before his death in 1908 in the Pleasant Valley community in Prentiss County. The financial setbacks from the bank failure of 1911 hurt many people, causing hardships, distrust, and some ill feelings. Yet, the Belmont people forged ahead in spite of financial problems and mixed feelings among the people.

At a special town meeting in December, the town board granted the Cumberland Telephone and Telegraph Company permission to erect, maintain, and operate a telephone exchange in the Town of Belmont. George Jackson was in charge of the exchange maintenance and operation in general. Benton Greene and his wife operated the first telephone exchange in Belmont, reportedly. In April, 1912, a franchise was granted to the Stantonville Telephone Company.

A new county administration began in 1912 with personable Lee F. Sartain, a staunch Democrat, as Fifth District supervisor. He had previously served as justice of the peace for the 1900-1904 term, and his descendants were to make many valuable contributions to our area down through the years. J. A. Clingan was constable, and he had served a previous term around the turn of the century. H. L. Pate and T. H. Dean served ably as Fifth District justices of the peace. N. L. Phillips, a Dennis native, began his first of two terms as county superintendent in 1912.

In July, 1912, county superintendent, N. L. Phillips, and the county school board – J. F. Oaks, G. W. Bishop, W. H. Lindsey of the Fifth District, W. T. Storment, and E. F. Parnell – decided to move Foster School to Dennis to become Dennis School. School trustees of the newly created Dennis School were Ransom Young, J. P. Lindsey, and G. P. Deaton. The first teachers were B. A. Brumley, principal, and Ruth Kirk.

The Dennis Methodist Church was located east of the railroad on property that Willis M. Davis and Harriet Davis deeded in 1910 to the church trustees, W. H. Gurley, Sr., Ransom Young, and R. F. Flurry. In further Dennis developments, John A. Bruton became postmaster in 1910. Thomas Oscar Lindsey became Dennis postmaster late in 1914.

A few miles northwesterly up the railroad from Dennis was the lumber town of Neil. The Pines post office was established at Neil. James E. Haynes was Pines postmaster in June, 1909; and John W. Haynes, Jr. became the postmaster later in the year. James G. Flurry was Pines postmaster in 1910, and Thomas E. Bottoms followed him in late 1911. The Pines post office was discontinued in July, 1916; and mail went to Dennis.

In March, 1912, new territory was added to the corporation of Belmont on the north side from a petition of A. G. W. Byram, Joe Yarber, John C. Hallmark, B. L. (Fayette) Hicks, and R. E. Wamsley, who had bought the George Jackson place. (Some of this property was eliminated from the corporation later in July.) Another plot of land was added to Belmont in April. An ordinance was passed allowing the street commissioner permission to take up all stock found running at large in the corporate limits. He was to receive 25 cents each per head taken up. Still, the town decided to have a watering trough made near the public well on the court square. Henry Googe, who had a livery stable about where Effie's Café is today, reportedly made the watering trough. In other town matters, W. O. (Oscar) Stockton was appointed town marshal in July. In August, Preston Yarber was elected a school trustee for a three year term.

In November, 1912, Woodrow Wilson was elected President of the United States. He along with all the world was to be faced with a terrible world war. A few years later, this was to have a marked influence on the future and lives of Belmontians, especially our young men.

The respected Squire C. C. "Lum" Shook was beginning to show signs of slowing down. He had sold several plots of his property in Belmont and decided not to run for mayor again. On the first

Tuesday in December, 1912, the municipal election was held. Election holders were J. N. Patterson, Charles H. Yarber, J. T. (Tom) Sartain, and John C. Hallmark, bailiff. Election commissioners at this time were J. T. Sartain, R. L. Shook, and C. H. Yarber. Town officers elected for the years 1913 and 1914 were the following: Mayor – G. A. Clark; Marshal – W. O. Stockton; Treasurer – J. A. Clark; and Aldermen – T. B. Lindsey, J. N. Patterson, L. P. Allen, W. W. Shook, and Dr. K. F. McRae.

Thus, the Squire Shook Era came to an end. It had witnessed the beginning of the Village of Belmont and the Town of Belmont. It had withstood a financial depression in 1911. It had witnessed the emergence of people working together for the good of the Town of Belmont and the surrounding area under the capable leadership of men like Squire Shook. On March 11, 1913, C. C. Shook fell dead on the porch at his home. He was buried with a Masonic funeral in the Joel Cemetery.

His fellow Masons of Belmont F. & A. M. Lodge No. 237 appointed A. G. W. Byram, L. P. Allen, and S. P. Beaty as a committee to adopt a resolution as an expression of feeling and sympathy to the family of the beloved C. C. "Lum" Shook. Their tribute to Christopher Columbus Shook included the following well-deserved praise: "C. C. Shook was honored, revered, and loved. For so many years he displayed characteristics and true principles of citizen, brother, friend, and neighbor. He was patriotic, serving his country to the best of his ability in peace and war. As a citizen he was always conservative and ever endeavoring to array himself on the side of right in all questions – moral, political, civic, and economic. As a neighbor, C. C. Shook was unexcelled – genial, sociable, and lovable. As a Christian, he was faithful and true to his church, cheerfully rendering every service required of him and leaving a record of which his family, friends, and "fraters" may be and are justly proud. Although his body sleeps in the silent chambers of the grave, he has gone to receive his just reward and dwell forever in realms of light and life eternal. Let us imitate him in virtuous and amiable conduct in unfeigned piety to God that we may welcome the grim tyrant, Death."

"C.C. Shook was one of the senior citizens of Belmont, being preceded to the grave by most of the older settlers who with him cleared the virgin forests of this area and, out of the same, made beautiful farms. His frail form trembling under the infirmities of age and ill health had long been a familiar figure, yet his smiling countenance and kindly greeting were pleasing to all – old and young. He ever had a kind word and a warm grasp of the hand for all who knew him. Squire Shook, or Esquire Shook, as he was commonly known, will be missed more than anyone of the town. His home was the scene of generous hospitality. In all the affairs of the town, he was a moving and active participant, having served as mayor of the town from incorporation until shortly before his death."

For sure and certain, Squire C. C. "Lum" Shook was a builder in the truest sense of the word. Fortunate indeed was Belmont to have had an outstanding leader of the ability and principles of C. C. Shook in its beginning, formative years. The Squire Shook Era was a very integral part of the proud Belmont heritage.

Courtesy Paul Allen

Several early Belmontians gathered in front of Allen-Wright Hardware and Furniture Company. The Shook and Lindsey Store is on the left.

CHAPTER 11

GROWING UP DESPITE WAR WITH THE HUNS

The death of the respected founding father, C. C. "Lum" Shook, on March 11, 1913, ended a most important era in Belmont. Ironically, a natural occurrence two days later was to speed up change faster than was anticipated in the area. A devastating cyclone tore up Tishomingo and destroyed much of Marietta, leaving a wide path of destruction. At Tishomingo, Dr. Dayton Waldrep and R. C. Edmondson were reportedly killed when the Nash Store blew down on them. Jeff Smith was in the store and was hurt. Many houses and the Tishomingo School were severely damaged. Annie Wren, a teacher, had a broken arm and damage to her head while getting students located when the storm hit. Marietta was nearly demolished as the tornado came through. Before the storm, I. C. (Clint) Files operated a hotel above the historic mineral springs at Marietta and had a store in the hotel. The devastating tornado of 1913 destroyed the hotel.

At Belmont the storm was evident in boiling black clouds and wind. Some damage occurred; but compared to the damage at Tishomingo and Marietta, Belmont was very fortunate. The sky was dark as night. School at Belmont was dismissed. S. L. "Bud" Sumners, who had moved to Belmont a few weeks earlier, was caught in the storm while going to town. He got on the back porch of the B. F. Wright home just as the well box and a shed blew down. Later, the unnerved people learned that the storm had nearly blown away Tishomingo and Marietta. People from Belmont, Dennis, Golden, Red Bay, Iuka, Booneville, Burnsville, Corinth, Kossuth, and many other places went to Tishomingo and Marietta to offer their assistance. They worked in a most admirable way to restore Tishomingo and Marietta to functioning towns.

Huge virgin pines and other trees were blown down in countless numbers. Sawmilling was picking up in our area before the tornado of 1913. With all the huge trees on the ground from the storm and with an urgent need for lumber to rebuild at Tishomingo, Marietta, and other places in this general area, the lumber business accelerated from necessity much faster than previously figured.

In Belmont, the likeable G. A. "Dick" Clark was proving a

worthy successor to his friend, C. C. Shook, as mayor. With the help of his son, attorney T. A. Clark, and the aldermen, Mayor Dick Clark got several ordinances restated and brought up to current legal specifications. New election commissioners were Bony Patterson, R. L. Shook, and J. T. Sartain. W. W. Shook was reappointed town clerk. The streets of Belmont were being improved and graveled. Belmont was not just growing. It was "growing up." A nice little town serving the needs of the people in a troubled time had sprung up, and new stores were appearing right along. In July, 1913, the granting of a franchise to Union Telephone Company went into force.

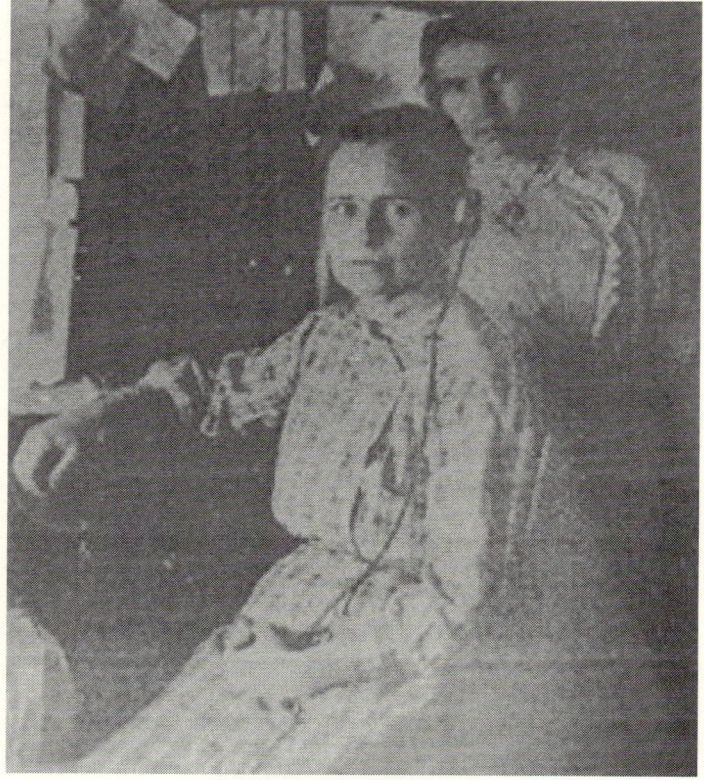

Courtesy Eula F. Long

Mrs. Lucy Fugitt at the switchboard of the Union Telephone Company in Belmont. Savilla Wood is behind Mrs. Fugitt.

The Union Telephone Company, a partnership of Dr. Oscar Copeland and William Boydson, operated in the old exchange building. Mrs. Lucy Fugitt ran the telephone exchange with the help of her daughters, Eula and Gladys, from 1913 to mid-1915. The exchange building had living quarters in the back of the first floor and also upstairs. The telephone exchange was in the front of the first floor. On the left side was the business area for discussing problems and paying bills. On the right side was the switchboard. There were no telephone books. On each side of the exchange board were papers with phone number. The board had 80-100 little drops and 50 or more plugs. The telephones in the home were hand crank wall types. When someone rang, the drops would fall. The exchange operator would plug up and answer the ring. Then, the operator rang the number of the party being called and connected another plug to the number being called. A combination of long rings and-or short rings determined the identification number of the person being called, especially on party lines. Among the communities that the Union Telephone Company served were Belmont, Dennis, Golden, Moore's Mill, Old Bethel, New Bethel, Red Bay, Valley, and Pogo. The Valley community had approximately nineteen phones on one party line. Party line phone owners were responsible for line upkeep. The company would send repairmen to keep up private lines. Telephone bills were collected once a month. There were some long distance calls. Lee Shook and Tom Sartain, local cotton buyers, spent 25 cents a call to get the current cotton market. The telephone exchange closed about 10:00 – 11:00 o'clock at night except for emergencies. For sure, the early telephones in Belmont furnished a means of communication for the people of our area and for area people carrying on trade and commerce.

    One of the first brick buildings in Belmont, Allen-Wright Hardware and Furniture Company, housed a thriving business. B. F. Wright and his son-in-law, L. P. Allen, started the business. B. E. (Ellis) Wright joined the firm, reportedly, after completing a course of study at a college in New York. Around 1913, E. Clay Wright is said to have become a member of the firm. He had recently graduated from Birmingham School of Pharmacy with honors and a pharmacy license. Allen-Wright had the Ford dealership and sold many early T Models in the Belmont vicinity. They also had the International truck dealership.

    Miss Mary Whitehead ran a millinery store that was located in the new bank building next door east of Allen-Wright. Hatley M. Shook had a nice two-story brick building and dry good store about where Tesseneer Texaco is. After the death of C. C. Shook, his son-in-law, Charles H. Yarber, operated the sorghum mill behind the H. M. Shook home. Later, he moved to the location of the present Sartain Texaco north of the present Belmont Cleaners and operated a grist mill, feed store, and grocery store before going into the dry goods business. East of the present Belmont Fabric Shop where a parking lot now is, B. L. (Fayette) Hicks operated a grocery and feed store in a nice brick building near the depot. Several other stores were in Belmont at this time, giving proof to the statement that Belmont was not only growing but also growing up.

Through the guiding force of Dr. Oscar Copeland, The Bank of Belmont was incorporated in 1913. Incorporators were Dr. Oscar Copeland, L. P. Allen, and George S. Jackson. Dr. L. S. Greene is reported to have been the cashier of The Bank of Belmont which reportedly existed about three years.

Courtesy Byrd G. Moore

Dr. L. S. Greene, cashier of The Bank of Belmont around 1913.

In the summer of 1913, Dr. K. F. McRae moved to Corinth. Dr. Homer H. Goyer came to Belmont to practice a few years until Dr. McRae returned about 1915. In the winter of 1912-13, Dr. Alcanda (Dit) Copeland had moved to Belmont with his wife, Mittie, and their four children, Winona, Morton, Fae, and Walter Kelley. In Fulton, Dr. Copeland had practiced with a cousin of his wife, Dr. John Senter, who was also an uncle of our present Dr. Jack Senter. Dr. Dit Copeland purchased some medical supplies and the two-story home of Dr. R. L. Montgomery, where Earl Campbell presently lives. Dr. Copeland opened his office on the south side of east Main Street in Belmont, and Dr. Lee Montgomery moved away. Dr. Copeland mixed his own medication in the back of his office.

In 1914, Dr. Alcanda (Dit) Copeland bought an open Ford roadster which he used during the summer months to call on his patients. During the winter months, he rode horseback, taking along his saddlebags loaded with medication to make house calls over the area. Many times the only pay the early doctors received for their services was some food from the farms. Dr. Dit Copeland especially liked watermelons and cantaloupes. The people remembered him and his fellow doctors in the harvest with farm produce, some money when available, and a sincere appreciation of the valuable deeds of the doctor.

In 1913, George S. Jackson replaced Dr. McRae on the board of aldermen after Dr. McRae moved. H. M. (Hatley) Shook and J. H. (Jim) Lambert were elected trustees at school for two year terms. In October, W. L. Cranford was elected a school trustee for a term of three years. In the fall of 1913, I. C. (Clint) Files and his family moved from Marietta to Belmont. They bought from W. G. Green the two-story wood hotel building that faced the railroad and was behind the present hotel. C. A. (Dolphus) Millican; his wife, Dora; and Clyda Cooper had operated the hotel previously. Clint Files was a salesman for a meat packing company in the Midwest and won several bonuses for being a top salesman. In addition, Belmont now had a newspaper, **The Belmont Herald,** with R. L. Page, Jr. as editor. Mr. Page was given free use of the upper story of Town Hall for one year from December, 1913, provided he used it for printing a newspaper.

Earlier, Dr. Levi Epps had a small medical office at his home just west of Lindsey Cemetery. He gave up his practice about this time and moved to Belmont in a house that stood near the present Brooks Griffin home. In June, 1914, Dr. Dit Copeland was elected local health officer for the Town of Belmont for the rest of 1914, serving without receiving any pay. The 1914 graduating class of the University of Tennessee Medical School, which had taken in the old Memphis Hospital School, included three men who were to be prominent physicians and civic leaders in our area: Dr. Claude Cromeans, Dr. D. D. Johnson, and Dr. Z. L. Weatherford. Most assuredly, the overall contributions of our area doctors down through the years into the present in professional administering to the sick, in words of encouragement, in understanding, and in community service form a vital artery to the very heartbeat and existence of our "beautiful mountain" and the surrounding vicinity.

The Town of Belmont under the leadership of Mayor G. A. "Dick" Clark continued to make improvements. The park that C. C. Shook donated previously was enlarged with the purchase of two more lots from H. M. Shook. Bridges were constructed around town across ditches and washes. C. L. (Lee) Hicks, B. F. Wright, D. R. Shelton, and Charles H. Yarber signed a petition on March 7, 1914, asking the town to lay out a street 20 feet wide beginning at the street going north and south at the residence of Mollie Tynes, running between her and Professor Shelton and further between B. F. Wright and Charles Yarber to C. L. Hicks. This street petition was granted. A. G. W. (Green) Byram was elected on the school board for a three year term. Wister Elledge operated the Belmont depot in a very efficient manner. In fact, down through the years, Belmont depot agents were to contribute well to Belmont and "brighten" the Belmont scene daily.

The growth in Belmont was obvious. Yet, the outbreak of World War I in Europe in 1914 troubled people. President Wilson encouraged America to remain neutral. Despite a general sympathy for the Allied Powers and a strong propaganda campaign against Germany, the United States remained out of the war until 1917.

Domestic progress dominated the area scene. In November, 1913, B. N. Roberts and his wife sold two lots and also one acre south of Bostick Street in Golden to D. N. Grissom, W. F. Bostick, G. A. Clark, and J. H. Pharr, trustees of the Methodist Episcopal Church South of the Belmont Circuit for the site of a parsonage for preachers of the Belmont Circuit of the Methodist Episcopal Church South. In November, 1914, Dr. A. E. Bostick and his wife, Mary Bostick, conveyed five lots in Golden to N. B. Mink, W. H.

Patterson, and Dr. A. E. Bostick, trustees of the Golden Methodist Episcopal Church South. Upon this property the Golden Methodist Church was soon built during the pastorate of Rev. W. W. Hartsfield. Dr. Loammi Harris gave the bell for the church.

In the Old Bethel community, the Pharr School property was deeded in October, 1914. John Ivy, Sim Ivy, and Arnelia Ivy donated to J. H. Pharr, D. W. Clement, and James Allen, trustees of the Pharr School one-half acre of land known as the Protestant Methodist Church property. The members of the church were reserved the right to hold meetings in the school house, but not to conflict with the public school. In another area school development, F. R. Webber and Mrs. M. E. Coffin deeded to the trustees of Cotton Springs School in March, 1915, 1.7 acres of land for school purposes. The provision was made that the Missionary Baptist Church reserved the right to hold their services in the school house, but not to conflict with the school.

In January, 1915, a new town administration had taken office in Belmont. Charles Googe was the new mayor. The new board of aldermen were J. N. Patterson, George S. Jackson, C. A. (Dolphus) Millican, L. P. Allen, and B. E. (Ellis) Wright. Ellis Wright was named the town clerk. J. A. (Jim) Clark was still town treasurer, and S. L. "Bud" Sumners was marshal and tax collector. The election commissioners were R. L. Shook, J. T. (Tom) Sartain, and Bony Patterson. R. A. Nelson was elected to fill a vacancy on the school board that the moving of A. G. W. Byram created. In April, W. W. (Billy Walker) Williams was elected a school trustee to serve a three year term.

Mayor Googe appointed George S. Jackson, J. N. Patterson, and L. P. Allen to a committee to go with marshal S. L. Sumners to purchase an acre of land for a dumping ground for the town. On February 2, 1915, S. L. Sumners was allowed $30.90 for 1 ½ acres, more or less, for a dumping ground just off the present Moore's Mill Road when the deed was executed. The garbage problem was an indicator that the community was using more items of trade and using more canned goods. An ordinance to combat the growing garbage problem was passed. It specified that all rubbish should be kept off the principal streets, all alleys, and vacant lots adjacent to business houses in town. Owners of business houses and adjacent lots were required to dump rubbish into sanitary garbage cans and empty the garbage outside the corporation limits twice a week or as often as the marshal deemed necessary.

In May, 1915, Mayor Charles Googe resigned to move to another city. In his short tenure in office, Mayor Charles Googe displayed capable leadership like his predecessors. His moving away was an obvious loss for Belmont. The respected T. W. (Tom) Hunicutt, who lived where the Walton Montgomery family now lives, was elected mayor in a special election on June 10. Once again, Belmont had survived a setback. Once again, the mayoral leadership was available in a reliable man like Tom Hunnicutt; and Belmont continued to grow.

The T models were becoming more common in town, and many were carelessly driving them. In August an ordinance was passed that regulated the running of automobiles within the corporation limits at a speed greater than 15 miles per hour. It was unlawful to run around any street corner or over any street crossing at a greater speed than 10 miles per hour without first blowing the horn or sounding the alarm. Also unlawful was the driving of an auto in town between the hours of sunset and sunrise without lights on front and rear. Another ordinance made a violation of jumping on or off any auto while it was in motion in Belmont. In addition, the town officers passed an ordinance in September that authorized the marshal to take up all stock running at large within the corporation limits of Belmont with state stock laws applying. This measure was taken because stock running at large was destroying the crops, hedges, and truck patches.

T. L. Selby had a general merchandise store across Main Street from Allen-Wright. Crouch and Hellums had a drug store in a building east of the present old theater building. The jolly Bob Crouch made daily life in downtown Belmont much brighter with his witty, friendly ways and his jokes. In another town development, at the request of J. N. Patterson, Anthony Yarber, and Bony Patterson, a street was opened at the southeast corner of the public square that ran across the lands of M. A. Shook, M. M. Davis, Jr., M. L. Harris, Anthony Yarber, and Bony Patterson through the J. N. Patterson land to the Pikeville Road. The street would also extend from the southeast of the public square southeast to the County Line Road and also intersect the road through M. L. Harris by Anthony Yarber and Bony Patterson going south to the Pikeville Road. With the construction of new streets, the town board stressed the need to collect street tax or get lieu work from those not paying the tax.

In 1916, James R. (Rufus) Mann was a state representative. Lee F. Sartain began his second term as Fifth District supervisor.

Carter S. Shook was constable. T. J. (Tom) Moore and Charlie H. Cranford served as justices of the peace. Worthy of mention is the fact that justices of the peace in addition to administering justice performed many marriage ceremonies and prepared deeds. Supervisors also "wrote up" deeds and performed several marriages. From before the turn of the century until post-Depression years, many of our citizens were married in either supervisor or justice of the peace ceremonies. Mayors at times used their ex-officio power to perform such marriages. Still, many people like the majority in the present time chose to have a minister perform their marriages.

In 1916, the first walking cultivator for one row was introduced into Tishomingo County. The first boll weevil was spotted in the county this year. Also, in 1916 a compulsory stock dipping law was passed to combat ticks. One dipping vat was below the depot in Belmont. Another was on the Allen place near Rock Creek, and other dipping vats were located throughout the area.

Courtesy Elvie H. Cleveland

Third Street view of Main Street in downtown Belmont about 1916

In February, 1916, R. L. (Lee) Shook, W. T. (Tommy) Shook, and M. A. (Arthur) Shook petitioned for and were granted a street 35 feet wide at the east end of Jackson Street running east across Front Street across the M. A. Shook strip 100 feet wide. The street then continued across the Illinois Central Railroad across the R. L. Shook and W. T. Shook land, intersecting the Belmont and Pleasant Site Road at the corporation line. In April, John Henry Shook was appointed an election commissioner. T. A. (Tom) Clark was elected a school trustee for three years. T. H. Dean was elected a school trustee for two years, and C. S. Shook was elected for a one year term. In May the board ordered the marshal to tear down a dangerous, unsanitary livery stable at the expense of the owner, showing the concern of our officials for sanitation. In October, 1916, C. A. Millican resigned as alderman to take another office; and W. O. Stockton was elected to fill out the term.

Property of J. L. Yarber and Ira O. Harris was added to the Belmont Separate School District in November, 1916. Also this month, a petition for a street from C. B. (Ben) Wright, John Henry Clark, Julius U. Clark, and M. L. Shook was granted approval for a 16 feet wide street – Shook Street – in the vicinity of their property.

Subscriptions to the **Belmont Herald**, a weekly newspaper, were one dollar per year in 1916. R. L. Page, Jr. was the editor, and R. L. Page Music Company was the publisher. R. L. Page was a sincere, yet witty, newspaper man. He wrote of Belmont, "We love this town too well to sit down and wear holes in her sidewalks."

About this time, the town merchants had a trade day. Sam Goodwin received the premium chair on trade day from Allen-Wright. T. J. Brown received the silver set prize at Belmont Drug Company from owner, W. W. Williams. Miss Willie Mae Nelson received the set of vases given as a premium to the most popular young lady on trade day. The friendly, good sport, R. L. Page, Jr., got the pipe as a premium for the ugliest man in town on trade day. He said that, had the judges of the contest included "varmints," the pipe would have gone like "Ward's Ducks." Editor Page concluded, "We thank you, gentlemen."

R. L. Page, Jr. enjoyed gospel singings like many others and attended them throughout the area. Gospel singing became very popular. In fact, the Tri-County Singing Convention under the leadership of men like Carter Shook was one of the best in northeast Mississippi or northwest Alabama. Later, the Tishomingo

County Singing Convention functioned well. Fall singing conventions were held in Belmont for many years with men like N. C. Deaton furnishing very capable leadership. Large crowds attended these singing conventions into the 1950's. People enjoyed many happy hours of fellowship in addition to the gospel singing of the conventions.

Around 1916, prices were rather interesting for the sake of comparison to prices of today. Cotton was 17-18 cents per pound. Young fryer chickens were 14 cents per pound, and hens were 11 cents per pound. Eggs were 20 cents per dozen, while butter was 15 cents per pound. Stock peas were one dollar per bushel.

In January, 1917, a new town administration took office to give their efforts to the "growing up" process under way in Belmont. They were to be faced with a forthcoming American involvement in World War I. The new mayor was the personable S. L. "Bud" Sumners. J. A. Clark continued as town treasurer. B. R. Anderson was marshal and tax collector. The board of aldermen was composed of W. O. Stockton, T. W. Hunnicutt, B. E. (Ellis) Wright, J. N. Patterson, and George S. Jackson. Ellis Wright continued as town clerk. The election commissioners were John Henry Shook, Bony Patterson, and G. A. Clark. C. B. (Ben) Wright was retained as legal counsel for $175 per year. R. L. Page was elected a trustee at school for a three year term.

The war clouds were heavy now. On April 2, 1917, President Woodrow Wilson addressed Congress, asking them to declare war on the German Empire. He stressed serious concern that German submarine warfare was warfare against mankind. The American involvement would be directly against the "military masters" of Germany in "a war to end all wars." On April 6, 1917, the United States Congress declared war on the German Empire. Our soldiers went to war to fight for the better life, the principles of what was good, and our French and British allies. They wanted to destroy evil in the form of the barbarous German "Huns," who had killed defenseless Belgian women and children. In a short matter of time, wartime machinery dictated that several of the promising young men of our area leave our area in its "growing up" period and go off to fight the Huns in the "war to end all wars."

The reality of the war became more evident when Roscoe Turner of Corinth landed an airplane in the Hatley Shook pasture east of the depot. This was the first plane most Belmontians had ever seen, and many called it an airship. It is reported that people got up at 4:00 A. M. and started gathering in the Shook pasture to await their first look at the airship. Some thought it looked like a huge orange crate. To people today, it would have been relatively small; but to the people of that time the plane seemed massive.

Along about this time, Professor E. (Ed) Strickland had come with his family to Belmont to head the school. He was previously at Kossuth in Alcorn County. His father, Benjamin P. Strickland, had moved into Old Tishomingo County way back in 1848 from Georgia and had served in the Confederate army in the 32nd Mississippi Infantry in General M. P. Lowrey's Brigade. Ed Strickland was prominently known in Alcorn County and came to Belmont highly recommended as one of the ablest teachers in the state. He also contributed to the wartime effort in Belmont and was one of the Minute Men of Tishomingo County. Professor Strickland was modest, conservative, and well-balanced. His love for education and young people was complemented with his love for God, farming, and good livestock. Fortunate indeed was Belmont to have an outstanding educator like Professor E. Strickland at the head of the school to insure that the young people of our area would have a solid educational foundation upon which to grow.

In July, 1917, an Old Harp Singing was held at the Methodist Church in Belmont. Beginning July 9, an Inter-County Normal for teachers was held for six weeks at Corinth. On August 10, 1917, the Annual Confederate Veterans Reunion of the F. M. Boone Camp No. 1694 was held at Belmont. Speaking in the morning at the park dwelled on the War of 1865 and on the war that confronted the people in 1917. Old Confederate soldiers, instead of marching, were carried in autos in an auto parade. The Belmont Concert Band led the parade.

In the fall of 1917, J. M. Woodruff, a successful business man from Burnsville, moved to Belmont to be superintendent of one of the planing mills of his company located in Belmont. J. M. Woodruff was one of the Minute Men of Tishomingo County and served on several war committees, never receiving a penny for his services. He was also a commissioner of the Burnsville Good Roads District. On September 12, 1917, the Belmont aldermen passed an ordinance co-operating with the commission of the Belmont Road District in the construction of good roads under Chapter 176, Acts of the Legislature, 1914. This covered the construction of a main highway through Belmont described as follows: On 2nd Street, said highway after leaving said street would follow the Iuka and Fulton Public Road through Belmont in the way of helping to grade said street. A public meeting was held to better inform the people of this important development.

Shortly, our young men went off to war. On September 20, 1917, the first 37 drafted from this county area went to Camp Pike. The second 86 left in October. At home, the local people were also making sacrifices. Conserving food for the war effort, they gave up meat, wheat, and sweets on certain days. To support the war effort financially, the government sold Liberty Bonds and War Saving Stamps. In Tishomingo County, the First Liberty Loan quota of $19,000 was oversubscribed $28,950. The Second Liberty Loan was also oversubscribed, while the Third Liberty Loan went over the top with 269 percent of her quota. People sacrificed at home and abroad to bring victory with an enduring peace.

In November, 1917, Anthony Yarber was elected a school trustee to fill the unexpired term of T. A. Clark, who moved to Iuka. G. C. (Chester) Hallmark, a former teacher at several schools of the area, was elected a school trustee to serve until April, 1920. About this time, W. T. Gober moved his family from Leedy to the old B. L. Hicks house off present Old Highway 25 northerly from the Patrick house. They lived here about a year before moving to the two-story Copeland house where Earl Campbell now lives. W. T. (Bill) Gober was to become one of the most prominent, respected merchants of Belmont.

In the summer of 1918, the Marion Grissom family moved back to Belmont to the exchange building. Lucy Grissom and her daughters once again operated the telephone exchange located in the vicinity of the present C and P Auto Supply building. About this time a terrible flu epidemic hit. The flu hit the construction workers at Wilson Dam at Muscle Shoals and also the army camps. Thousands died. Rows of seriously sick soldiers were said to have been in the army camps. Quarantine is said to have been effected at times. A woman from this area visited her son in the camp at Arkansas and got to see him before the quarantine was effected. Her son later died. In Belmont the doctors instructed the telephone operators to take the names of those needing treatment the most. This agonizing flu often started with nosebleeding. In many cases, pneumonia often followed.

Dr. Dit Copeland is said to have told several to cut a piece of fat meat in a round shape and stuff it up each nostril to stop the nosebleeding until he got there. During this flu epidemic, Dr. Copeland could not ride his horse over the frozen roads of winter at times. He reportedly put nails in his boot soles and walked to the homes of those suffering from the influenza or other sicknesses. Meanwhile, Dr. Copeland contracted the influenza and was very ill for several weeks. According to his daughter, Fae, his family thought the high fever may have affected his heart and may have led to his death in 1921 at the age of 51. In time, the flu epidemic broke, but not before an agonizing experience of hardship and sorrow for many of our people.

In 1918, the Belmont board of aldermen had passed an ordinance prohibiting the running or operating of any stationary gasoline, kerosene, or steam engine within 90 feet of Main Street. In May, 1918, T. H. Dean and R. A. Nelson were re-elected school trustees for three year terms. At this meeting, the aldermen also passed a very stiff ordinance to suppress and prohibit the running of billiard tables and pool rooms in the Town of Belmont. They specified a misdemeanor against the town for any person, or persons, corporation, or partnership, to run or cause to be run in the said town billiard tables, pool rooms, bowling alleys, itinerant sellers of medicine, corn doctors, fortune tellers, gift enterprisers, feather renovators, peddlers, flying jennies, pistol or shooting galleries, ten pin alleys without regard to number of pins used, and skating rinks. The fine was not less than $25 or more than $100 for each offense. The operator was to have his business closed; and his property in the house, tent, or place where operating was to be forfeited to said town, sold, and placed in the school fund of the Town of Belmont. In July, 1918, Mayor Sumners appointed a committee to locate a graveyard (cemetery) site that consisted of Chairman G. A. "Dick" Clark, George S. Jackson, J. N. Patterson, and C. A. Millican.

Despite the terrible war in Europe, Belmont had grown up lots and had adjusted financially to the growth. World War I came to an end when the armistice was signed on November 11, 1918. Despite the efforts and hopes of President Wilson, the war was not to be "a war to end all wars." Peace did bring the boys back home and joyful happiness prevailed. In Belmont, bells were ringing, and horns were blowing all over town. Dynamite was exploded. People were cheering, crying, and rejoicing. A truck with side frames, loaded with about 50 people from Belmont, rode to Red

Bay. Much yelling and cheering was heard. A merchant rolled out a barrel of apples and gave apples to all. People between Belmont and Red Bay met them to receive the good news that the war was over. Surely, the news of the end of World War I was a time of rejoicing.

In the December 19, 1918, **Belmont Herald,** the ad of J. C. Jourdan Drug Co. of Iuka had a most appropriate expression, "The clouds of gloom are lifted. There has not come to this generation a more perfectly Merry Christmas than this." The family of M. Arthur Shook, a young man full of vim and go, received word from him in France that he was safe and sound and would greet all real soon. Tom Skinner, who sailed for France in the army two days before armistice was signed, had returned home to his family. Edgar Epps was home from the army and enjoying the fireside of his parents, Dr. and Mrs. Levi Epps. As at other places, there was much happiness in the Belmont area as the boys came home from the war.

At this time, the **Belmont Herald** had a "humor column" in which Editor Page delighted in poking fun at local merchants. Interesting is a look at 1918 humor compared to present humor. The "humor column" revealed that hickory switches seemed to be showing up more at the school building. W. W. Williams, the drugstore keeper, had been keeping strict order recently and had barred all "unreasonable" tables around the stove since the stove pipe was not safe. Anthony Yarber had sold his Ford car and was trying to get lightning rods for his sidewalks to keep the rain from getting them wet. R. C. Crouch thought that looking into a well was a sight cheaper than having a personal picture made – not to mention the overall economizing factor. L. P. Allen said that opportunity might knock at a person's door now and then; but more often, it will be some neighbor wanting to borrow a pinch of salt or get a good meal. Politics was ebbing again in Belmont. Charles Yarber "stole three planks" out of the Pomp Franks platform and was elected alderman. James A. (Jim) Clark of W. T. Clark and Son was astonished reportedly to have gotten the following note from a citizen of this area: "Send me a sack of flour, five pounds of coffee, and one pound of tea. My wife gave birth to a fine boy last night, also 5 pounds of corn starch, a screwdriver, and a rat trap. It weighed 10 pounds and a few potatoes and the neighbors say it looks like its pa and a piece of meat. The people of Belmont at the end of World War I could still laugh together. They were also working together and overcoming the recently agonizing situations. Moreover, they could plan together and fraternize.

The Belmont W. O. W. Camp No. 518 met on Saturday before the third Sunday in December, 1918, to elect officers for the new year as follows: C. A. Millican, Consul Commander; G. C. Hallmark, Adv. Lieutenant; R. L. Page, Jr., Banker; M. M. Shook, Clerk; James A. Clark, Assistant Clerk; W. A. Shook, Escort; T. L. Selby, Watchman; T. O. Shook, Sentry; T. W. Hunnicutt, Manager; T. H. Dean, Manager; E. Strickland, Manager; Dr. D. D. Johnson, Camp Physician; and Dr. K. F. McRae, Camp Physician. Then, on December 12, 1918, several Belmont business men met to organize a Business Men's Club. G. B. Smith was temporary chairman. Officers elected were J. M. Woodruff, President; C. B. Wright, Vice-president; and W. W. Shook, Secretary-Treasurer. The board of directors was composed of L. P. Allen, M. P. Haynes, R. L. Shook, J. C. Seago, and B. L. (Fayette) Hicks. The constitution and bylaws committee members were B. E. (Ellis) Wright, G. B. Smith, and R. L Page, Jr. The public improvements committee was composed of C. A. Millican, B. E. (Ellis) Wright, and Dr. D. D. Johnson. Membership dues were only one dollar per year.

Belmont had grown up very much in the matter of a few years. It had witnessed the damaging effects of the tornado of 1913; and its people had big-heartedly helped the people of Tishomingo and Marietta, where the storm hit the hardest in our general area. The Belmont people withstood the sorrow of World War I and overcame the serious flu epidemic. In spite of all this, Belmont had matured under the leadership of some very dedicated builders. Certainly, Belmont had grown up despite the terrible war with the Huns.

CHAPTER 12

PEACETIME ADJUSTMENTS

With World War I having ended, Belmont had gone through both a trying time and a time of growth. The returning soldiers brought back new hopes and ideas. Radios and motion pictures began to appear. Change was in the air as our area started to make peacetime adjustments. The lumber business really boomed. Sawmills were located all over the area. Steam sawmills became more common. People were anxious to move ahead while carrying on their quest for "life, liberty, and the pursuit of happiness." Old ways of life were slowly giving way to a new way of life centered around the timber boom and automation. About this time, the Trollinger water mill on Rock Creek was torn down principally through a lack of demand. The Callaway Moore mill was no longer existent.

On February 26, 1919, the Bank of Belmont was chartered and operated in a brick building adjacent to and east of Allen-Wright Hardware and Furniture Company. The original stockholders included A. M. Grimsley from Fayette, Alabama; R. L. Page, Jr.; J. M. Woodruff; J. C. Seago; M. P. Haynes; B. L. Hicks; W. T. Gober; Dr. D. D. Johnson; W. W. Williams; S. S. Strickland; D. W. Clement; C. A. Millican; B. E. Wright; L. P. Allen; E. Strickland; Dr. A. E. Bostick; J. E. Clement; B. F. Wright; W. O. Stockton; J. N. Patterson; A. R. Hall; H. M. Shook; and I. J. Wright.

C. A. Millican operated a hardware with his brother-in-law, T. W. Hunnicutt, in a building where Claude's Dollar Store now is. In the fall of 1918, C. A. Millican and his wife, Dora, took in a school teacher boarder, Mrs. W. R. (Edna) McCormack. Edna McCormack was active in music in addition to being a gifted, respected teacher. She was in the R. L. Page Quartet along with the Millicans, Mr. Page, and others later. Furthermore, Amy Deaton, Verona Deaton, and Verda Mae Deaton formed a singing trio in this period. W. R. McCormack, the husband of Edna McCormack, returned from the war in France to Belmont in the fall of 1919. At first, W. R. (Rady) McCormack helped R. L. Page, Jr. with the **Belmont Herald** and kept books for Mr. Page.

R. L. Page owned property north and east of the Millican store. On the property east of Millican, R. L. Page had a building in which R. T. Sparks reportedly had a grocery in the front. The Page printing office was once in the back of this building. Earlier, the Page printing office was said to have been in the vicinity of the present Denson Radio and TV store. In addition to the **Belmont Herald,** the likeable R. L. Page, Jr. also printed song books. Two of the books that he printed in Belmont were "Songs of Amazing Grace" and "Shining Gems for Jesus." For sure, R. L. Page, Jr. helped Belmont in many ways, including printing the paper and encouraging the W. R. McCormacks to locate in Belmont.

C. A. Millican and C. L. (Lee) Hicks operated the first motion picture in Belmont in a frame building near the Millican store building. Rady McCormack operated the projector for this theater that faded away in a few years.

About 1920, J. A. (Jim) Clark, C. A. Millican, and W. R. McCormack formed a lumber business that was located in the Millican buildings. The company was named Jacaw Lumber Company, using both initials of J. A. Clark, both initials of C. A. Millican, and the first initial of W. R. McCormack. Lee Hicks may have been in the business at one time. W. R. McCormack was the Jacaw bookkeeper. Jim Clark and Dolphus Millican bought lumber for the company, and it was sold to out-of-state firms mostly. Later, Lumpkin Hallmark, a son-in-law of C. A. Millican, had a store in this building at the corner of Main and 3rd Street. R. S. (Bob) Mayhall became a partner in this grocery business and later bought the business. L. L. Davis had a grocery store and sold school books in the store adjacent to the Mayhall building. Later, Grady Oaks reportedly had the first Gulf distributorship in the vicinity of the back of the Mayhall building.

In 1919, Dr. Webster Cleveland, who had worked between terms with M. L. Harris in Belmont, graduated from dental school. He started his dental practice upstairs in the S. L. Sumners building. His dental office was in later times in the Selby building and beside the office of Dr. D. D. Johnson. Even later, Dr. Cleveland was to have his dental office where the south part of the Belmont Steak House now is.

A new town administration had taken office in 1919. S. L. "Bud" Sumners continued as mayor of Belmont. The board of aldermen included J. N. Patterson, Charles H. Yarber, B. E. (Ellis) Wright,

W. O. Stockton, and T. W. Hunnicutt. Ellis Wright continued as town clerk, and J. A. Clark remained town treasurer. B. R. Anderson was marshal, street commissioner, and tax collector. C. B. (Ben) Wright was retained as town legal counsel. Dr. K. F. McRae was elected a school trustee to fill out an unexpired vacancy. Anthony Yarber and Chester Hallmark were elected trustees to serve three year terms.

On July 5, 1919, the business firm, Stanphill and Johnson (T. C. Stanphill and Dr. D. D. Johnson), deeded the second story of their building to C. S. Shook, Worshipful Master; C. B. Wright, Senior Warden; and T. C. Stanphill, Junior Warden, for and on behalf of the Belmont Masonic Lodge No. 237. The Masons were to complete the bricking improvements of their part of the building and keep the second story in good repair. At last, this lodge had officially found a long-standing home that the present Masons still occupy today.

Additionally, Belmont Woodmen of the World Camp No. 518 with headquarters upstairs in the adjacent building in conjunction with M. L. Shook, owner of the first story of the adjacent building, agreed to tear down the old frame building in 1919 and erect a new brick building on that lot. The Woodmen had moved to the upstairs of the frame building when it was constructed around 1908.

Improvements were made on ditches, culverts, and bridges in town. In another development, the Belmont Telephone Company, a partnership, was assigned a 25 year franchise on October 8, 1919. In December, 1919, Copeland Telephone Company was granted a franchise to operate and maintain a telephone system in Belmont. This was located where the present new library is on Third Street. In November, 1919, Anthony Yarber was granted the privilege to blueprint his plot of land in south Belmont and record it in the chancery clerk office.

In the fall election of 1919, Professor E. Strickland was elected state senator for the 1920-24 term. W. R. McCormack was named principal to fill out the 1919-1920 term. Reportedly about December 12, 1919, the Belmont educational system suffered another big loss: the school building burned. Ironically, Mrs. Belle Strickland, wife of Ed Strickland, and her son, J. B., had an unusual experience in getting J. B. to go to school. From the Strickland home west of Belmont on Moore's Mill Road, J. B. set out to school when deep down he did not want to go. Getting to the Daniel Threadgill home, he turned back and told his mother he did not feel good. She knew better and sent J. B. off to school again. He got a little further up the road this time before turning around and going back home. This time Mrs. Strickland "laid down the law" and told J. B. that she would whip him if he came back again. This time he met one of the sons of T. J. Brown who told him there was no need to walk to school because the school house had burned. Faced with a real dilemma, J. B. very hesitantly returned home. His mother asked what was wrong this time. Fearing a whipping, he tearfully uttered, "The school house burned." Mrs. Strickland soon found out officially that the school house had burned. J. B. escaped a whipping and got out of his dilemma. The Town of Belmont and the Belmont Separate School District had a tougher dilemma. A few years and much unrest over bond issues were to pass before a new school building could be constructed. Children in this time went to school in local churches, the town courthouse, and the old Ebenezer school building. Peacetime adjustments in Belmont involved many adjustments in education after the school burned at what was to be later the J. E. Clement property.

At the February, 1920, town meeting a petition of January 20, 1920, for an election on the issuance of bonds for construction of a school building was approved. A special election was called for February 21, 1920. In addition, R. L. Shook was elected a school trustee for a three year term.

At the March 2nd meeting, petitions were approved granting new streets in Belmont. One street, sixteen feed wide, began on 2nd Street where the road ran just north of the B. F. Wright property and residence. It followed this road 240 feet in a westwardly direction to the B. R. Anderson land. This is the present Wright Street between the Sexton family and the Etha Mann family. Another street extended Washington Street across the land of J. C. Seago. It began at the west end of Washington Street, being 50 feet wide, and ran in a westwardly direction, intersecting the Belmont and Bay Springs Road at the J. C. Hallmark place.

To further improve the streets of Belmont, the town board passed an ordinance co-operating with the commission of the Belmont Road District . . . concerning construction of a main highway leading into Belmont from the west. This highway, beginning at the corporation line on the Belmont and Bay Springs Public Road, was to run east with the road and intersect Washington Street at the J. C. Hallmark place. Then, it would continue east on this street, intersecting 2nd Street or 3rd Street, going south on 3rd Street to Main Street. The road continued east on Main Street to 2nd Street or to the alley just west of the Christian Church and south on the said alley to Main Street, continuing east on Main Street to 2nd Street or all. Most assuredly, a better system of roads through Belmont was in store.

In April, L. H. Deaton became an election commissioner to fill out the term. In May, J. C. Seago was told that the Seago Annex was received to west Belmont. Still, the school bond issue was not resolved. A $35,000 bond issue followed a proposed $40,000 bond issue. In June, an ordinance issuing school bonds for $35,000 was passed; and the bonds were offered for public sale. Readvertisements of school bonds in August, September, and October failed to find buyers. Consequently, the fate of the school was somewhat clouded.

The town did get an option and purchased a little over six acres of land from Mary Almedia Cranford in October. The 1920 tax levy for Belmont increased from 11 mills in 1919 to 15 ½ mills, consisting of School, 6 mills; General Corporation, 2 ½ mills; and Bond Interest, 7 mills. J. H. Lambert was elected a school trustee to fill the unexpired term of Chester Hallmark, who moved out of the school district. At a special meeting in November, 1920, the aldermen agreed to buy some property for the Belmont Separate School District. They voted to purchase 3 ½ acres from Jesse C. Hallmark for $600. Then too, they voted to buy from John C. Hallmark a strip of land from the north side, provided it could be bought for $50. On December 27, 1920, J. E. Clement bought the old school site consisting of six lots in Block 14. Although the bond issue situation was not resolved at the end of 1920, the town and school officials had taken steps to get property upon which to locate the proposed school.

In Dennis developments, James M. Burleson was the postmaster in late 1920. Charles Flurry, a long-time rural mail carrier, accepted the postmaster job at Dennis in March, 1925, and served until 1928. Mrs. Esta Kate Flurry Campbell then became the postmaster of Dennis, serving kindly and efficiently until her retirement on August 31, 1965.

Over at Golden, James W. Harris was postmaster in November, 1920. John E. Collum was acting postmaster in 1921, and James W. Harris succeeded him later in the year. In late 1920, the Golden Saw Mill Company commenced an operation that was to have a major impact on the area for over a decade. W. H. Patterson and P. T. Hargett sold land upon which this far-reaching sawmilling operation centered. Among those involved in the Golden Saw Mill leadership were R. L. Curtis, Hubert Young, W. D. Henry, Mr. Ayres, H. F. Quinn, and the Louis Werner Saw Mill Company of St. Louis, Missouri. In the early 1920's, sawmilling continued to be a major force in the area economy; and the Golden Saw Mill became the major force in area sawmilling.

In the fall of 1920, women had the right to vote for the first time in the presidential election as a result of the adoption of the 19th Amendment granting women the right to vote on August 28, 1920. The women of our area were rather slow to vote at first, thinking this to be the job of the men. The 1920 census report showed 15,091 people in Tishomingo County. The Fifth District had 3,590, including 459 in Belmont, 217 in Dennis, and 194 in Golden.

In 1920, most people in the absence of electricity got their light from coal oil lamps, candles, and fireplace light. L. P. Allen and W. L. Cranford had power plants that generated their own electricity for their houses. L. P. Allen had a hydraulic ram in the B. F. Wright pasture at Blue Springs in the present Belmont Blue Springs City Park. Allens had a water supply tank at their house and a pump house near Blue Springs. In fact, remnants of the pump house are evident in the new park. In earlier years, the Church of Christ had baptisms near Blue Springs. This is evidenced in the fact that Elder R. L. (Lee) Shook baptized E. Clay Wright here in February, 1916. It is said that there were lights at Blue Springs, enabling the Church of Christ to have baptisms at nights.

To treat the sick, Belmont was fortunate to have at about 1920 very capable doctors like Dr. D. D. Johnson, Dr. Dit Copeland, and Dr. K. F. McRae. Dr. A. E. Bostick continued his successful medical practice in our area, centered around Golden. In 1920, Dr. Claude Cromeans moved his practice from Cliff, his boyhood home at present Ryan's Well in Itawamba County, to Dennis. He was to practice five years in Dennis before moving to Belmont. Like most area doctors, Dr. Cromeans made his rounds in a Model T if the roads permitted. He had a pair of horses for buggy or horseback travel on roads impassable for auto traffic. Dr. Cromeans was to deliver in excess of 4,000 babies in the years to come in homes in our area. The first fee he charged for delivering babies was five dollars plus lodging for a night. The fee remained in effect for about 10-11 years after he started practicing medicine. In addition to his ability to treat and medically help the sick, Dr. Claude Cromeans always seemed to have a laugh or joke for nearly every occasion. He recalled spending the night at the home of a man whose wife was expecting. Upon going to the table the next morning and finding the entire meal consisted of lard gravy and biscuits, Dr. Cromeans joked the man, "I expected a better breakfast since you have had nine months to get ready for my visit."

My father, G. W. "Bill" Martin, drove for Dr. D. D. Johnson about three years on his medical rounds in the area. Roads permitting, they traveled in a Model T. On bad roads in the winter, they rode in a two-horse buggy. Two bricks were warmed and wrapped upon which to set the feet to keep warm. The bricks were rewarmed at each stop. Cough syrup and quinine capsules were commonly used. Dr. D. D. Johnson, in addition to being a very capable doctor, always seemed to have a friendly smile and a kind word of encouragement. For sure, the Belmont area has been blessed down through the years with the presence of a dedicated, most capable group of physicians who have treated our sicknesses and helped ease our pain and agony in a most outstanding manner.

Nationwide, problems arose from the peacetime adjustments. A slackening of government price guarantees combined with less demand for agricultural products resulted in a serious situation. Many farmers failed to sell their crops before a serious price drop and suffered financial disaster. Prices rose on manufactured products until consumers could not afford to buy. A "buyers strike" in 1920 caused a big drop in business. By 1921, a depression was affecting many people. Around Belmont, timber men suffered serious losses. Times were rather troubled financially, and the concern over the local school bond issue reflected the depression times. The depression was short-lived, and America entered into a period of new heights of prosperity based on an economic policy of whatever business wanted to do was bound to be good for the country.

Meantime, 1921 was to be a very eventful year in Belmont progress despite the depressed national economy. A new town administration was in office. The personable M. Arthur Shook, a young man of "vim and go," was the new mayor. The board of aldermen consisted of C. L. (Lee) Hicks, J. L. (Lumpkin)

Hallmark, T. W. Hunnicutt, J. M. Woodruff, and B. E. (Ellis) Wright. Ellis Wright continued to serve very capably as town clerk. B. R. Anderson continued as marshal and tax collector. For the first time since the formation of Belmont as a village, there was a new treasurer. The reliable J. A. (Jim) Clark gave up the job after serving since 1908. His handling of the town funds in the formative years in a very efficient manner was a big help to the ultimate growth of Belmont. The respected W. W. (Billy) Shook became the new town treasurer. C. B. (Ben) Wright was retained as legal counsel for the town.

In February, 1921, Dr. Copeland sold to V. L. Matthews and H. L. Matthews his entire telephone plant known as the Union, or Copeland, Telephone Company at Belmont. This telephone exchange was located where the Belmont Library now is. In the transaction were the exchange property, one switchboard, all office fixtures, about 100 Kellogg telephones, telephone poles, and other related items of value. Some of the later telephone exchange managers included, reportedly, J. S. Whitehead, Sixty Yarber and Rae Yarber, Avie Shewbart, Virgil A. Shewbart and Ila Shewbart, and W. A. "Blackie" Livingston and Verda Mae Livingston.

In the March 21, 1921, meeting of the town board, action was taken on the school bond issue problem. The $35,000 bonds ordinance was repealed, and an ordinance issuing $28,000 in school bonds was passed. In April, M. P. Haynes and S. S. Strickland were named school trustees. Later, a new ordinance was passed, issuing bonds of the Belmont Separate School District for $25,000 to build and equip a school house. A petition was filed against issuing the bonds, so the town officials ordered a special election for August 5, 1921, to determine the matter about the school bond issue.

In the meantime, Belmont had concluded the cemetery purchase project. The property of J. N. Patterson, then a pasture of pine and sassafras interminglings, was under serious consideration. Some confusion about purified water problems caused this site not to become the cemetery. Today, this area is the beautiful Shady Cove area in southeast Belmont. In 1921, there were those who opposed locating a cemetery in Belmont at all because of doubts about water purity. The town officials felt differently and on July 5, 1921, they voted to buy a certain tract of land of about 13 acres from Dr. W. Cleveland, the Belmont dentist.

Mayor Arthur Shook appointed a committee of J. L. Hallmark, J. M. Woodruff, and C. L. Hicks to negotiate the land deal. Dr. Cleveland had bought this plot from Marion and Lucy Grissom, who lived nearby and had reportedly planted part of this property in corn and peas. The remainder was in woods and pasture. Jesse Cummings Hallmark was seriously ill with cancer, so cemetery plans were rushed along with this in mind. If the town had not bought the cemetery land, the Hallmark family had decided as an alternate idea to bury Mr. Hallmark on his property about where the school football field is now. Jesse Cummings Hallmark died on July 10, 1921, and was the first person buried in the new Belmont Cemetery. The green corn stalks had to be removed in the hot summer weather for the burial of J. C. Hallmark. Jess Cummings Hallmark was one of the founding fathers of the Belmont area, serving as a rural merchant north of town in the late 1800's and as a merchant in Belmont in the early 1900's. His children and their families have made countless valuable contributions to the Belmont area down through the years. The burial of Cummings Hallmark marked the beginning of the Belmont Cemetery that was to grow from a corn field to the neat, restful cemetery that we have today. On July 11, 1921, the town board had also finalized the cemetery land transaction when they approved the payment of $1,000 for the property.

Courtesy Evie H. Cleavland

First Baptist Church baptism scene at Yarber Pond about 1921. Pastor A. M. Nix is seen on the front right.

In August, the school bond matter was resolved. In the special election on August 5, a total of 107 votes were cast with 84 votes for the issuance of the bonds and 23 votes against issuance of the bonds. The town board promptly effected an ordinance providing for the issuance and sale of $25,000 bonds of the Belmont Separate School District for the purpose of building and equipping a school building. Later in the fall, the town board voted to negotiate to try to purchase the J. C. Hallmark property for $1,500 and the J. W. Crane property for the school property. Tom Hunnicutt, Lee Hicks, and Lumpkin Hallmark comprised the committee to negotiate the school property proposals. The students continued to go to school in churches, the courthouse, and the old Ebenezer building. Still, a new school building was forthcoming in the next year.

On September 6, W. T. "Bill" Gober was elected an alderman to replace J. M. Woodruff, who resigned to move back to the northern part of the county. Renovation of the public square was undertaken. Mayor Arthur Shook had the calaboose painted. Just eastward from the courthouse, the calaboose was a rather simple building around ten feet by twelve feet or slightly larger. There was one door and a step-up entrance in the frame structure with no windows where law violators were put. While the calaboose was being painted to improve its looks, a critic griped that Mayor Shook was going to bankrupt the town in spite of everything. This failed to bother the friendly, big-hearted Arthur Shook; and he resolutely went on with his efforts to make Belmont a better place.

On November 24, 1921, the cornerstone was reportedly laid; and a well-attended ceremony was held for the new Belmont school. Mrs. Mary Almedia Cranford, a daughter of Mrs. L. A. "Bam" Vinson and a granddaughter of the early pioneer, Benjamin Hopkins, furnished a gold piece to go with the Bible, a copy of the **Belmont Herald**, and other items that were placed in the cornerstone area at the ceremony. In addition to furnishing the gold piece for the ceremony and some of the land near her home where the new school was to be built, Mary Almedia Cranford also sold a lot of the land upon which west Belmont was to develop. Additionally, the Cranford log home, one of the first in Belmont, was located just east of the present south entrance to Belmont Schools. At the east entrance to present Belmont Schools, about where the Safety Bug Park now is, was the home of the Jesse Cummings Hallmark family. Like their early pioneer ancestors, Benjamin Hopkins and Jesse Hallmark, the Cranford family and the

Hallmark family contributed to the Belmont heritage and advancement when they made land available for the badly needed Belmont school facility.

Courtesy Theda Rocco

Belmont School building construction about 1922.

Assuredly, the cornerstone ceremony for the new Belmont school marked the beginning of brighter days and educational advances there. In January, 1922, Tom Credille dug the well for the school. Dr. K. F. McRae and W. L. Cranford were elected school trustees in May for three year terms. Property of Henry E. Mayhall and J. L. Yarber was added to the Belmont Separate School District. In the summer of 1922, the new brick school building at the present site was complete. There were approximately 13 classrooms and an auditorium. The first superintendent at the new Belmont school for the 1922-23 term was J. D. Langston. The first faculty was reportedly composed of Edith McRae, Mrs. J. C. (Louise) Patterson, Mrs. B. L. (Lera) Johnson, Mrs. Bill (Dezzie) Davis, and Mrs. A. G. W. (Elizabeth) Byram in addition to Superintendent Langston. Twelve units of standard high school work were offered. This was increased the following year, 1923-24, to 16 when the first class graduated. Member of this class were Evelyn Gilley, Nell Rose Pilley, and Ellis Deaton.

C. W. Baley, a circuit-riding Methodist minister, came to Belmont to serve in the fall of 1922. C. W. Baley, Jr., his son, recalls the rainy day in the fall of 1922 that astride the big horse of his father he rode from Guntown over muddy, sandy roads through Bay Springs into Belmont from the west and stopped at Mayhall's Store. With help, the Baleys found the new Methodist parsonage, which Luther A. Jackson had recently constructed for the Methodists.

The new brick school building with plenty of windows in large rooms impressed the students. There was no gymnasium; the teams played on outside dirt courts. C. W. Baley, Jr., who had played some football at Macon before moving to Guntown and Belmont, was amazed when he found that few of the high school boys knew the difference between a touchdown and a kickoff. Some questioned allowing six points instead of two for a touchdown. They could not see why the football had to be punted instead of the player running with it. The well-elevated west end of the auditorium furnished a basement room where the boys dressed for athletic events. There were no basketball uniforms. The boys usually played in overalls and bought their own tennis shoes. Several used lightweight Boy Scout shoes. The girls basketball team used one of the classrooms to change into blouses and dark "bloomers." At this time, the girls fared well in their games, while the boys found the competition tougher. The tough, rangy Patterson Chapel boys team was especially good.

The Belmont school building was quite a center for community events and activities – singings, civic speakings, box suppers, cake walks, townspeople plays, senior plays, and other school plays. The auditorium was usually full and on some occasions overflowing.

In the fall of 1922 the Seago Annex was added to the Town of Belmont. J. C. Seago was employed to oversee the graveling of the remainder of Washington Street. Careless driving was becoming a nagging problem. The town passed an ordinance regulating traffic on the streets of Belmont. All animal-drawn or motor-propelled vehicles were to obey "Keep to the Right" signs in town. They were not to be on or across walkways or intersections. All motor-driven vehicles were to be parked with the rear of the car standing against the curb. All motor vehicles were to be equipped with mufflers, and none would be permitted to run without mufflers. Furthermore, no "cut-outs" would be permitted to be used.

Peacetime adjustments after World War I were to advance the way of life around Belmont. In a progressive manner like the administrations of his father, C. C. Shook, Mayor Arthur Shook in his administration had brought many valuable, long-lasting changes to Belmont. A new school and an expanding educational system spoke well for the future of Belmont. People were getting around and looking to more prosperity and pleasure. New heights of prosperity and progress lay ahead.

Courtesy Jewell Shook

The Hatley M. Shook building, home of Shook Brothers Supply Company, that burned in downtown Belmont in the mid-1920's

Courtesy Claire D. Griffin

Belmont school group in 1925. Members of the faculty on the back row are the following: left to right Mrs. A. G. W. Byram, Mrs. C. W. Baley, Elizabeth Hagins, Dixie Dexter, Beulah Stockton, Edith Herring, Superintendent L. D. McCoy, E. G. Senter, and Charlie Gilbert.

CHAPTER 13

NEW HEIGHTS OF PROSPERITY

In the 1920's, people strove to reach new heights of prosperity. The timber business recovered to a large extent after the short depression of the early 1920's. Agriculture was relatively good with fairly stable prices and yields. An increase in farm mechanization was noticeable. Commercial fertilizer was being used more with the introduction of ammonium nitrate.

Battery-operated radios appeared in several homes. The Crosley of Tulon Bostick and the Atwater Kent of A.B. Campbell were two of the first radios in Belmont. Tulon Bostick with the audio "bug" in his ear related from hearing his radio the results, round by round, of a heavyweight boxing match to several nearby persons. Many went to local motion picture shows at the Millican theater and also later at the Tulon Bostick theater in the back of his drug store about where Steve's Surplus Sales is presently located in Belmont. Others including many of the ministers shunned the picture shows and had doubt concerning their moral value. It was a carefree, prosperous time in which people sought "the higher pursuit" of life, liberty, and happiness.

Arthur Shook, the Haynes boys, and several other local men had always loved baseball. They organized an independent team and played their home games east of the depot on the flats. They played "far and wide" and faced many opponents in very aggressive action. They are said to have played Sheffield, Tishomingo, Corinth, Haleyville, Cherokee, Savannah, Tupelo, and others. Some of the players were Arthur Shook, Bill Haynes, M. P. Haynes, Carl Files, Henry Yarber, Ernest Haynes, Henry Wood, and Tulon Bostick. Their game against Sheffield with a "Southern League-caliber" pitcher named Riddle was a tough one. Riddle had a wicked screwball and was "mowing" the Belmont batters down. Some Belmont players bragged too much on Riddle and irritated Arthur Shook, who was also pitching hitless balls for Belmont. He scolded them, "Why the heck don't you say something about old Shook, he hasn't given up a hit either!" Shortly, one of the best Belmont hitters, Bill Haynes, accepted the challenge. He told his teammates, "You pea pickers, watch your Uncle Damper show you how to hit." Bill

Haynes really walloped a Riddle screwball and sailed it over the center fielder. Another long-ball hitter, Carl Files, came up to bat saying, "If Uncle Damper can hit him, I can too." With his homemade bat, Carl Files lashed out an extra base hit into right field. Belmont went on to win the game that had some very aggressive base-running throughout. Later, some of these players joined a team at Baldwyn. On this team, Arthur Shook and Toy Wright from Belmont were two of the pitchers. Toy Wright, a gifted pitcher, had pitched for the University of Mississippi. M. Arthur Shook reportedly pitched in the Kitty League, possibly with Mayfield, Kentucky. He had a terrific fast ball, but he had problems controlling his sharp-breaking curve. Arthur Shook developed a sore arm that resulted in his giving up baseball and getting more involved in public service. Still, at this time, baseball was top sport around Belmont. Many good baseball players lived around Belmont, and baseball continued as an enjoyed pastime for many growing youth.

A new town administration began in 1923. Fifth District justice of the peace, G. C. (George) Martin, swore in the new mayor, A. G. W. (Green) Byram. The board of aldermen consisted of Charles H. Yarber, W. R. (Rady) McCormack, J. E. (Joe) Stephens, B. Ellis Wright, and C. L. (Lee) Hicks. W. R. McCormack became town clerk, and W. W. Shook was still town treasurer. W. A. (Austin) Shook became marshal and tax collector. He was to be allowed ½ the fines collected on corporation whiskey cases in 1923-24.

In early 1923, the Reuben Sparks store building burned on west Main Street. In April, L. P. Allen was elected to the school board. In June, the town bought a Ford tractor from Anthony Yarber. In July, M. Arthur Shook was appointed to the election commission. The town board voted in August to give $50 for the benefit of the County Fair to be held in Belmont in the fall of 1923.

Belmont had been without a newspaper for a while because the **Belmont Herald** had closed its operation. Then, in about March, 1923, **The Belmont Times**, a weekly newspaper, was established in Belmont. J. A. Vincent was reportedly the owner and editor later in the year. J. L. (Lumpkin) Hallmark became the owner with J. P. Johnson as editor in 1926. Johnson and Murray appeared as owners and publishers on May 27, 1927. Friday was the day of publication.

The 1923-24 school term found Professor L. D. McCoy as

superintendent at Belmont. In addition to being a good academic man, Professor McCoy had lots of common sense. Like his predecessor, the personable J. D. Langston, Superintendent McCoy enjoyed sports, coaching the boys basketball and football teams. In fact, L. D. McCoy was the first football coach of the first football team at Belmont in the fall of 1923. Professor McCoy ordered one football and about 14 football uniforms. By the time the equipment arrived, there had been at least one or more box suppers or related events to raise money for the football uniforms. A number of merchants donated generously to the cause. Even after the 1923 season, there were fund-raising drives and events to pay for uniforms – truly one tremendous manifestation of town loyalty and interest.

    The school provided football helmets, shoulder pads, jerseys, pants, and stockings. The players furnished their own shoes and kidney pads. Mayor A. G. W. Byram, who operated a shoe repair shop, made football shoes from either Boy Scout or lightweight plow shoes. Looking at a catalog picture of a football shoe, he did an excellent job of using varied widths of leather to build up cleats on the soles. The team had only one football the first year. By the end of the year, the shape of the football was somewhat changed. The players looked forward to a game because they got not only to test their skill but also to use a good football.

    The football and basketball games covered a large area in northeast Mississippi and northwest Alabama, probably against Tishomingo, Golden, Dennis, Booneville, Marietta, Cherokee, Sheffield, Hackleburg, Haleyville, and others depending upon the sport in season. An out-of-town football game, according to C. W. Baley, Jr., posed a transportation problem. Professor McCoy had a Chevrolet touring car, and Red Pharr had a Ford touring car that were nearly always used. Carey Stephens and Elledge Selby could get their family cars if needed. Marshal W. A. Shook would take some players to games not too far from Belmont. Something to see was three cars loaded with 14 players and football gear plus Coach McCoy and one or two drivers heading off to a football game with football equipment on the front fenders. Lots of unloading, pushing, and reloading could be expected both going and coming on the road to Booneville through Bay Springs. Some of the players avoided riding with Professor McCoy if possible because his auto had a power pulling problem, and they had to get out more and push.

Harold Shook was the captain of the first football team. The first football cheerleaders were Lera Shook and Ruth Gilley. The football team did not win any games in 1923. One of the first few games was against Tishomingo, which had Charlie Gilbert, Candler White, and other Belmont area boys playing on the team. Charlie Gilbert, a son of Annie O. Gilbert and Ed Gilbert, was an outstanding athlete in not only football but also track and basketball. It is said that he was very gifted in reacting instinctively with much natural ability. After graduating from Tishomingo, Charlie Gilbert came to Belmont as a football coach. He also worked with Professor McCoy in coaching basketball. Another stellar halfback for Tishomingo in 1923 was Candler White, who scored several touchdowns in the game at Belmont. Candler White returned to Belmont his senior year, 1924-25. This Belmont football team is said to have won about three games as the football program began to become established.

In October, 1923, the school had bought from Mary Almedia Cranford a little less than one acre of land for the school between the school property and the Belmont and Bay Springs Public Road. W. A. Clement served at this time as night watchman in Belmont. Teacher warrants were being discounted. This problem was to become even more acute in forthcoming years. In December, the town board passed an ordinance prohibiting persons from loitering or loafing in town after dark.

The town passed another ordinance authorizing the building of sidewalks. One sidewalk was to begin at Main Street and 2nd Street, running on the west side of 2nd Street across the front of the property of H. M. Shook, T. L. Selby, L. A. Jackson, J. R. Elledge, Belmont Public Park, B. L. Hicks, and W. W. Shook to the intersection of Cleveland Street. The sidewalk was to extend west on the south side of Cleveland Street across the property of W. W. Shook, Mrs. A. Copeland, J. E. Clement, Mrs. Martha Whitehead, T. W. Hunnicutt, Preston Yarber, John Hallmark, and the public school property to the school building. Another sidewalk in town was to begin at Main Street and 2nd Street and run south on the east side of 2nd Street across the property of Gober and Strickland, Threadgill and Ozbirn, Charles H. Yarber, and H. M. Shook to the bridge just south of the Patterson Mill and Gin. The sidewalk then crossed to the west side of 2nd Street continuing across the property of Anthony Yarber, W. A. Frost, L. L. Davis, Rollin Elledge, Dr. D. D. Johnson, and Bony Patterson to the intersection of the road which ran south to T. E. James. The gravel for the sidewalks was to be according to specifications, and the size of the coarsest gravel was not to exceed one inch in diameter. The gravel was to be laid 4 inches deep and 36 inches wide. Except on low grounds, excavations were to be made with the proper width and depth to hold gravel in place. Low places had to be filled or bridged, and culverts were recommended at proper places to permit drainage that might harm the walk. The failure of those affected to build a walk would reportedly result in the building of the walk by the town at the expense of the owner. Some feel that some of the sidewalks may not have been built in the end as the completion date of February 1, 1924, was reached. At any rate, Belmont was growing; and the completed sidewalks would help the safety of pedestrians.

Serving the 1920-24 term as Fifth District supervisor was John D. Mann. Ed Strickland served as state senator. J. O. Epps, a Golden native, became county superintendent of education at this time and was destined to serve a second term later as county superintendent in the early 1930's. Fifth District justices of the peace for the 1920-24 term were T. J. Moore and G. C. Martin. Constables were reported to be C. C. Hammett and W. R. Kennedy. Mayors of Golden in the early 1920's were Dr. A. E. Bostick, H. K. Holmes, and C. H. Cranford. At Dennis, Charlie Flurry was mayor in the period. W. P. Taylor was the Dennis marshal, and N. S. Davis was treasurer. Dennis aldermen at this time were J. T. Selby, L. F. Sartain, and C. L. Moore.

In 1924, Tom C. Pharr began his first of two successive terms as Fifth District supervisor. M. G. (Mack) Davis was Tishomingo County state representative for the 1924-28 term. S. L. Sumners also served two successive terms as Fifth District justice of the peace. W. M. Perry and W. H. Collier reportedly served as justices of the peace along with Mr. Sumners. W. W. Crabb served as constable and to serve again in this office in the 1950's.

About the fall of 1920, J. E. (Joe) Stephens had moved with his family from near Little Brown Creek in Prentiss County to Belmont. He first bought the J. W. Crane place, where the Grover Pounders family now lives on Old Highway 25. Like many of the Prentiss Countians who had earlier moved to Belmont, J. E. Stephens, a prominent lumber man, was to become a respected community leader and builder in Belmont. In addition to his lumber yard in Belmont, J. E. Stephens had a large lumber yard in Dennis. The L. R. Davis planer dressed lumber for him at Dennis. In a few years, J. E. Stephens bought a house from S. J. Graham, another area lumber man, and moved with his family to this nice house on Highway 25 south in Belmont. In time Joe Stephens had a lumber yard near his home.

In the early 1920's the lumber business was very important to the Belmont economy. Some of the lumber concerns included R. L. Shook Lumber Co., M. P. Haynes Lumber Company, McRae Lumber Company, and Clement-Woodruff Lumber Company. The planers were southeasterly down the railroad from the depot. My maternal grandfather, W. S. Etheridge, was in charge of the Haynes planer for a while before he moved. He had worked previously for Mr. Clement at Leedy (Berea) and for L. R. Davis at Dennis. In Belmont, J. E. Clement in time had the planer on the west side of the railroad where McRae Lumber Company was previously. His planer then became much larger. C. L. (Lee) Hicks was the bookkeeper, and J. E. Pilley was the planer foreman for the Clement operation. The capable ability of these men combined with the J. E. Clement leadership enabled the Clement planer to be a dominant force in the Belmont lumber business in the late 1920's before the approaching clouds of depression.

Over in the Valley community, sawmilling was also thriving. Marshall Cain and Raymond Hellums had a sawmill at Three Forks between Valley and Pogo, Alabama. John Gray was another Valley sawmiller. In fact, H. L. Deaton added an extra room to his house at Valley and operated a store to accommodate the sawmill families and neighbors. The Hicks-Mann Lumber Company of B. L. (Fayette) Hicks, A. V. Mann, and L. K. Cain reportedly prospered in the vicinity of Holly Branch. It is said that John William Mann was involved in the company at one time. Their office was in the Hicks Building in Belmont. B. L. Hicks was a well-known Belmont merchant. A. V. (Vivian) Mann was to serve two terms as supervisor in the 1940's. L. K. Cain was later to serve terms as justice of the peace and school board member. For the time being, they were involved in the prospering sawmilling and lumber business as Hicks-Mann Lumber Company.

Courtesy Paul Allen

Inside view at Allen-Wright Hardware and Furniture Company.

Courtesy N. C. Deaton

Singing School of the Hartford Musical Institute at Valley School in 1920's.

Belmont displayed its spirit around 1925 with a big Fourth of July celebration. The merchants and interested citizens really "put their shoulders to the wheel," making available several molasses barrels full of free lemonade. The festivities included square dancing, harp singing, exhibits, sack races, a greased pig contest, tug-of-war, a greased pole contest, foot races, and tables of food at the park. There were even weight-pulling contests for those who wished to show off the pulling strength of their oxen, mules, or horses. Downtown Belmont was alive with people. C. W. Baley, Jr., who worked for Thomas Drug Store, where Steve's Surplus Sales now is, recalls dipping 45 gallons of ice cream for customers that day. W. W. "Doc" Williams at his drug store southeast across the street from Thomas Drug Store also had a very busy day in selling ice cream. Obviously, the respect of Belmontians for their country and the love of fellowship with friends made the patriotic celebration a noticeable success. It was made all the more enjoyable with the ice cream at only a nickel a dip combined with the food and free ice-cold lemonade.

Traditionally, several men gravitated to the barber shops, the depot, or the post office on Sunday morning. John L. (Lumpkin) Hallmark, who served as Belmont postmaster from 1922-26, or his sister assistant, Bertie Hallmark, came down to put up the Sunday mail. Still, they rarely missed a church service in performing the mail service for the people. On Sunday afternoon, many men and women went to the depot to meet the "Doode." There was a lot of mutual friendliness and exchanging of ideas, not to mention the plain fun in the gatherings that met the "Doode." T. S. (Sank) Smith, the local depot agent, had a few years earlier replaced Wister Elledge as depot agent. Mr. Smith maintained the depot "spick and span" and always had a hot fire in cold weather in the stove in the depot waiting room. As a former Belmont resident said, "This and other acts of concern and helpfulness permeated the very being of Belmont people . . . So many did so many things unto so many others on so many occasions."

S. L. "Bud" Sumners and Luther "Peanut" Gamble operated cafes in Belmont about this time. The jolly M. L. (Mark) Shook later operated a café downtown. Some of the barbers included Hector Underwood, "Lef" Gober, Sixty Yarber, and A. B. Campbell. Allen-Wright had the only gasoline in Belmont for several years. Then, the Texaco distributorship came to Belmont under early Texaco distributors that included J. W. (Wells) Hallmark, J. C. Greene, H. M. Shook, and Walter Davis. Wells Hallmark for his distributorship headquarters built a nice brick building that included a service station. In fact, Peanut Gamble also had a café at one time at this site.

In the early 1920's, Cliff Eason was in charge of The Bank of Belmont. His sound banking principles were complemented with a refreshing sense of humor. A few years later, Ellis Wright and Clay Wright came into the bank to lend several decades of efficient banking service and community service to our area. Cliff Eason located in Tupelo and became a prominent banker and highly respected builder in that major growth area.

Seth Pounds was also a leader in the Bank of Belmont. At one time, he had the Ford dealership in Belmont. Later, Seth Pounds moved to Booneville and became not only a very prominent Prentiss County civic leader but also a guiding force in The Peoples Bank and Trust Company.

In 1924, a young Fifth District man, Omer J. Bullen of Fanchertown, became sheriff of Tishomingo County, succeeding another area native, N. L. Phillips. His ancestors, the Bullens and the Tatums, were early pioneers of the area. Omer J. Bullen later served another term as sheriff in addition to serving as chancery clerk. In the 1940's he became public service commissioner. Leaving the political arena, Omer J. Bullen became the guiding force of Sunshine Mills at Red Bay, Alabama. He was a devout church worker at Patterson Chapel Methodist Church and later at Golden Chapel United Methodist Church. Always ready to help in benevolent drives, church work, and efforts to improve our area, Omer J. Bullen has been a true area builder down through the years.

In April, 1924, M. P. Haynes and S. S. Strickland were re-elected school trustees for three year terms. J. D. Finch became superintendent of the Belmont school for the 1925-26 term. In November, 1925, another acre of school property was purchased from C. L. Hicks.

Back in May-June, 1924, the Belmont Hotel Company constructed the new brick hotel at its present site. The Belmont Hotel Company was a group of local business men who invested to make the new hotel available. The capital stock was fifteen thousand dollars, while the par value of a share of stock was fifty dollars. The company included L. P. Allen, W. T. Gober, S. S. Strickland,

A. Yarber, J. W. (Wells) Hallmark, J. E. Clement, M. P. Haynes, and Dr. D. D. Johnson. Nim Harris and his wife moved to Belmont to run the new hotel. On May 6, 1924, the Belmont Hotel Company was granted exemption from municipal taxation for a period of ten years. In time, several stockholders sold their stock. L. P. Allen became the president of the Belmont Hotel Company. In 1928, A. E. O'Brien bought the Belmont Hotel property; but Nim Harris continued to operate it.

At Belmont school, the first edition of the Belmont school paper, "The Student," came out in November, 1924. C. W. Baley, Jr. was editor of the "folksy" student paper with its sports, literary society news, jokes, poems, and other student-oriented news. It seems that Professor L. D. McCoy had instituted a "student idea" segment in morning chapel services devoted to suggestions, ideas, or peeves from the student body subject to further consideration from a faculty committee if necessary. The students overwhelmingly voted for the school paper, and the faculty committee approved. Professor McCoy named Miss Elizabeth Hagins, the stern, well-educated high school principal, to serve as counselor for the paper. So many – students, faculty, parents, patrons, and J. P. Johnson of **The Belmont Times** – worked so hard to make the school paper a most enjoyable success. In fact, this is one of countless examples in which "the Belmont spirit" has been manifested down through the years.

Courtesy Marcia Allen

The shoe shop of A. G. W. Byram in Belmont. Mr. Byram stands in the back.

In July, 1924, W. R. McCormack resigned as alderman and clerk; and T. C. (Tommy) Stanphill was named to fill out the unexpired term. Seth Pounds was appointed to fill a vacancy on the school board. In November, C. B. Wright, Olen Yarber, and T. A. Gilley were named election commissioners. On December 2, 1924, the town board voted to dispose of the treasurer's office in a legal way and to have the keeping of the funds advertised. Thus, Belmont had only two town treasurers from 1908 to December, 1924 – J. A. Clark and W. W. Shook. The Bank of Belmont on bid got the keeping of the town funds at one percent to be kept in separate accounts for the Town of Belmont.

In January, 1925, a new town administration took office. W. A. (Arthur) Jackson was the new mayor. Aldermen were C. L. Hicks, J. E. Stephens, G. M. (Murph) Moore, L. L. Davis, and B. Ellis Wright. G. M. Moore was named the town clerk, and W. A. Shook was marshal and tax collector. Dr. K. F. McRae was re-elected a school trustee. In April, a street was granted on the lands of B. L. Hicks, Mrs. Mary A. Sartain, J. T. Sartain, and J. U. Clark. The street went back into the Iuka-Fulton Road just east of the J. U. Clark house. In July, G. M. Moore resigned as alderman and clerk; C. B. (Ben) Wright replaced him.

Courtesy Cecil L. Sumners

Mrs. Luna C. Davis and several elementary school students at Belmont about 1925-1926.

The Ed Strickland family that had moved to Kossuth about 1922 moved back to Belmont to their home on Moore's Mill Road about 1926. E. Strickland had served as superintendent at Kossuth, had been ordained to preach at First Baptist Church of Kossuth, and is said to have become the first area missionary of Alcorn County. Back at Belmont, E. Strickland pastored several churches, farmed, and taught varied subjects as a classroom teacher. Professor Strickland raised some of the first lespedeza sericea in our area. He raised wheat, blueberries, apples, and a large amount of sweet potatoes which were kiln-dried in his potato house. The moving of the E. Strickland family back into our area was a definite asset to the educational, religious, and agricultural advancement in and around Belmont.

In July, 1926, Miss Bertie Hallmark succeeded her brother, John Lumpkin Hallmark, as Belmont postmaster. She served in a courteous, capable manner until 1932. Golden postmasters starting in late 1926 reportedly included Pearl Williams, Iva Hale, and Tom Hale. In about 1929, Miss Lela Epps began a long tenure as Golden postmaster, serving in a kind, efficient way until her retirement in March, 1962. Golden patrons also recall the assistance of her sister, Miss Cleo Epps, down through those years. For many years, A. P. Hale brought the mail from the depot to the Golden post office. At Belmont, Fred Woodruff brought the mail up the hill from the depot to the post office for several years.

Meantime, B. F. (Ben) Wright had died on July 25, 1926. His passing left a void in Belmont because he was not only a successful business man who contributed much to the early growth of Belmont but also a man who had a rare ability to analyze people and situations to reach objective conclusions. His wife, Martha Ann, lived until 1937 and was from all comments a kind and considerate person who epitomized motherhood in its truest sense. For certain, Belmont was blessed indeed when B. F. Wright decided to move here when the village was just getting started. The contributions of this builder and other builders in his family form a most valuable part of the Belmont heritage and progress.

About this time, Mississippi Lieutenant Governor, Dennis Murphree, and others led a movement designed to advertise Mississippi throughout the nation with the "Know Mississippi Better" Train. This train made goodwill trips at intervals in the summer. Beulah Stockton of Belmont was a member of the Teachers

College Band of Hattiesburg that went on the "Know Mississippi Better" Train in 1926.

In May, 1926, Seth Pounds and J. H. (Jim) Lambert were elected to three year school terms. In November, 1926, the Inland Utilities Company of W. H. Goodhue and Tulon Bostick was granted an electric franchise. Tulon Bostick was mainly in charge. Despite his electrical ability, Tulon Bostick was to encounter many headaches in trying to make electricity available because of natural problems. For example, the power lines often fell into the water or had fallen limbs on them. At times, the power flow was very weak. Betty Jo, the young daughter of Henry Yarber and Mae Bess Yarber, voiced the feelings of many Belmontians when the lights began to flicker, "Turn the lights on, Tulon." Eventually, the Mississippi Power Company was to furnish a stronger electrical source.

Also about this time, Olivia Wood recalled teaching under her sister-in-law, Arah W. Ivy, at Pharr School on Red Bud Creek across the road from the present Calvin Fuller home. At the present Fuller place, Sim Ivy then operated a store joined to his home. The old Holland Pharr water mill was nearby at Red Bud Creek. At the Pharr School the trustees at this time were reported to be C. L. Ivy, G. C. Montgomery, and Edgar Whitehead. Olivia Wood recalled teaching the next year at Mineral Springs on the hill northerly from Rock Creek about where Durell Johnson now lives. Trustees were reported to be Ed Ginn, Arthur Holcomb, and Ambrose Vinson. Arthur Holcomb was to serve later as both Fifth District constable and justice of the peace.

In January, 1927, a new town administration took office. L. P. Allen was the new mayor. Aldermen were J. E. Stephens, E. Clay Wright, J. W. Hallmark, Charles H. Yarber, and W. W. Shook. W. W. Shook became town clerk – a post he originally held at the beginning of the Village of Belmont in 1908. Election commissioners were named as follows: A. G. W. Byram, T. A. Gilley, and L. L. Davis. Henry E. Mayhall was elected a school trustee for four years, and T. W. Hunnicutt was elected a school trustee for five years. D. G. Threadgill was the new marshal and tax collector. In April, the town board resolved that it would match whatever amount the County Superintendent of Education put up for the improvements on the school building. In April, 1927, the board passed a resolution heartily approving the application of the Mississippi Power Company for a preliminary permit for construction of a power dam to be located below the mouth of Bear Creek. The board also agreed to take street lights from Inland Utilities Company. In June, W. T. Gober was elected an alderman to fill the unexpired term of J. W. Hallmark.

About 1927, or possibly a while earlier, the **Belmont Tri-County News** was established with Roy C. Colson as editor. He reportedly bought **The Belmont Times** from Mr. Johnson of Red Bay and consolidated the papers into the **Belmont Tri-County News**. The day of publication was Thursday. In April, 1931, Fred Goodwin bought the paper but sold it in a few weeks to A. H. Barham.

Courtesy E. R. Warren

The Golden Saw Mill.

Courtesy Mr. and Mrs. E. R. Warren

Golden Saw Mill employees around 1926. Front row, left to right: Ernie Davis, Henry Qualls, Frank Gardner, Claudius James, Arial (Bib) Thrasher, Rob James, Mr. Nobels, Ira (Hump) Spigner, E. R. Warren, Toy Thrasher, Will Akins, and Richard (Dick) Miller. Back row, left to right: Bob McCants, Kermit Hughes, Wayne Brown, Moman Black, Floyd (Dock) Thrasher, Bill Green, Shack Gatlin, George Turner, Audie Hale, Ed Jordan, Audie Davis, Bud Gatlin, Rob Hargett, Wallace Fish, Sid Warren, A. G. Hall, Vernon Williams, and Albert Miller.

The prospering Golden Saw Mill was located in Golden on what is now mainly the property of E. R. Warren. The office was located where the E. R. Warren house now stands. The commissary (store) was situated on the present highway in front of the Warren house. E. R. Warren recalls doing the work of a man at the Golden Saw Mill when he was fifteen years old. He learned to feed the flooring machine, earning $2.25 per day. Common laborers were paid about $2.00 per day. About 1926-1928, the Golden Saw Mill was at the height of production. It put out approximately 60,000 board feet per day. A whistle blew about five minutes before work was to begin. Five minutes later when the big work whistle blew, the log hit the saw. About 350 were working at the operation including the woods crews. Railroad spurs extended into the Freedom Hills and to the Salem area in Itawamba County to speed up the hauling of the huge virgin pine logs. For a few years, the mill had both a day crew and a night crew.

Work hands were hard to get, and company advertised for labor at $3.50 per day for a ten hour work day. At this time, Golden was thriving and enjoying new heights of prosperity.

Around 1928, the likeable Albert Taylor was mayor of Golden. In the late 1920's, S. L. (Bud) Sumners held justice of the peace court at Golden one Saturday per month. Uniquely for the times, Mrs. A. E. Bostick and a few other women served as jurors.

In January, 1928, Dr. K. F. McRae was re-elected a school trustee at Belmont. At a special town board meeting in February, a franchise was granted to Warrior Water Company to build and operate a water works plant in Belmont. In April, the Warrior Water Company accepted the terms of the town franchise.

On June 11, 1928, the town board received a petition asking for the dissolution of the Belmont Separate School District. Approval of the dissolution was granted. A consolidated school district under the continuing leadership of superintendent J. W. (Warren) Sumners, who became Belmont superintendent in 1927, was formed with the union of the Belmont territory and the Pittsburg School. In July, 1929, Mrs. M. A. Cranford sold about an acre of land for more school property to the following trustees of the Belmont Consolidated School: S. S. Strickland, S. L. Sumners, Seth Pounds, O. G. Campbell, and J. H. Lambert.

In September, 1928, the town approved a petition and granted a street 25 feet wide beginning at the street in front of B. R. Anderson. This street, present Ebenezer Street, ran south on the quarter section line to the street in front of the Bertie Hallmark place. In November, an ordinance was passed compelling every male resident of Belmont between 18 and 55 to perform annually 6 days of labor at 10 hours each day on the streets and alleys of Belmont. In lieu of work, the men were to pay five dollars per year. A street was granted in December north of the Belmont and Moore's Mill Pike between C. B. Gilley and M. P. Haynes further through the properties of G. M. Moore, Georgia Pate, Ira O. Harris, W. Arthur Jackson, and Spencer Strickland. This street is what we today know as Witt Road.

Down at Moore's Mill, one of the last area water mills in existence still ground corn into meal. Tom Hutcheson operated the mill. He opened the water gates, permitting water to rush through. . . Rushing water turned the old mill wheel and shaft, setting power into motion. From the grind rocks on the mill floor, a stream of pearly meal began to fall into the box placed below.

Some of those involved in the operation of the historic old mill before and after Mr. Hutcheson included Steve Moore, Jr., Ben Moore, Newt Johnson, W. T. Stacy, A. N. Milam, and Carl Turvaville.

Nevertheless, new heights of prosperity had come to the Belmont area. Communication was faster. Ford A models, Chevrolets, and Buicks were seen around Belmont. Telephone lines were expanded, and radio antennas rose above many homes. At historic Bay Springs, interest continued to wane. New heights of prosperity were realized as people found more inviting places to go and more varied things to catch their interest. Little did they know that in the not distant future this prosperous way of life would be taken from them in a severe way that few could imagine.

Courtesy THE DAILY CORINTHIAN

Main Street in downtown Belmont in 1929.

Courtesy Noel Caveness
South Tishomingo School group about 1929-1930. Principal Tom Duncan is at the left. Other teachers were Arah W. Ivy and Blanche Whitfield.

CHAPTER 14

DEPRESSION GLOOM

The prosperous Twenties changed to bleak despair with the Wall Street crash in 1929. The 1920's had harbored a breakdown in idealism – a letdown in moral standards, a decline in respect for the law, and a carefree, somewhat disillusioned pursuit of "the higher life." By late 1929, a prolonged slump in agriculture combined with an excessive wave of stock market speculation to help create the worst financial depression in the country since 1837. Many rich people were financially broken in a matter of weeks. Thousands lost their lifetime savings. Black Friday, October 24, 1929, marked the day that bedlam broke loose on Wall Street. Despite calming effects from bankers for a few days, the stock market crashed on October 29.

This was to change our rich, prosperous economy into one with unemployment, declining income, and slumps in production. A chain reaction was put into movement that resulted in closed factories and businesses, more bankrupt firms, and more people out of work. There were still things to buy but little or no money with which to buy. Sources of credit practically dried up, or either people feared to borrow. This financial panic – The Great Depression – was to shackle America and Americans into the 1930's. In Belmont, times were comparatively bleak; and people suffered severely from the need of basic necessities of life, not to mention some of the luxuries to which they had become accustomed. The Great Depression was, assuredly, a dark, dreary chapter in the history of Belmont.

These were times for leadership, and Belmont was fortunate to have leadership. Otherwise, the terrible effects of the depression would have been even worse. In January, 1929, a new town administration took office, unknowing that the Great Depression lay ahead with unforeseen, complex problems for Belmont progress. They, like the rest of the country, were to realize that the only thing "great" about the Great Depression was the magnitude of problems because times were to be very trying. Fifth District Justice of the Peace, S. L. Sumners, swore in the mayor of Belmont, L. P. Allen. Aldermen were W. T. "Bill" Gober, J. E. Stephens, Charles H. Yarber, E. Clay Wright, and W. W. Shook.

G. C. (George) Martin was marshal and tax collector. W. W. Shook served as town clerk.

Two of the prominent enterprises of Belmont at this time were associated with the name of Clement. The J. E. Clement Lumber Company was a manufacturing concern of no small proportions. J. E. Clement and his family also operated the Freedom Hill Stock and Poultry Farm. It is said to have had one of the largest flocks of chickens in northeast Mississippi. At this period, the prominence of the Clement operations constituted a matter of pride in Belmont. Instead of petty jealousies that often frequent small towns, the Belmont community in early 1929 was blessed with an exceptional spirit of "pull-together." As a consequence, Belmont was putting together improvements before the Depression that overshadowed those of many larger communities. Belmont was on the move before the Depression!

In March, 1929, George Moreland, a reporter for **The Commercial Appeal**, visited Belmont and was amazed at the enthusiasm and progressive spirit. Mr. Moreland was so infatuated with the hospitable little town of Belmont after his first thirty minutes that he "debated seriously about getting his other shirt and locating in Belmont." To him, Belmont folks believed in having people make speeches, and they really believed in feeding their guests. The people of Belmont, true to their heritage, did not know the meaning of "no," only "yes" when progress was at stake.

Several Nettleton citizens had moved to Belmont at this time. Capably operating the Belmont Hotel were Mr. and Mrs. Nim G. Harris, and they served meals every day of the week. Shearer Thomas ran one Belmont drug store. Another Nettleton person, the likeable Tom H. Young, operated The Dixie Store, one of the neatest, cleanest establishments in Belmont. The Dixie Store was a grocery and meat market. Rev. Charles Nelson, the Baptist preacher, formerly was also at Nettleton.

George Moreland in his Belmont visit in March, 1929, spoke to the Belmont Woman's Club at a banquet at the Belmont Hotel. Mrs. J. E. Pilley, a delightful, cultured lady, was president of the club that had seventeen members who were sincerely interested in the work of the club. They had lofty aspirations to build a better Belmont culturally and a more beautiful Belmont physically. Little did they know at this festive gathering that the forthcoming Depression would sidetrack their lofty goals that would have advanced life on "the beautiful mountain" so much.

The Mississippi Superintendent of Education, W. F. Bond, spoke at the Belmont school auditorium at this time; and G. W. Stricklin, County Superintendent, accompanied him. The highly respected Superintendent Bond spoke of the many "firsts" of Mississippi education in the nation. He presented ideas to show how he hoped to teach Mississippi how to continue to develop a public school system which was already the envy of parts of America. Belmont superintendent, J. W. Sumners, also made progressive remarks about Belmont education at this meeting. Nevertheless, the Depression was to darken this bright outlook for education.

In his Belmont visit in March, 1929, George Moreland was treated again at the Belmont hotel. Among the Belmontians in attendance were Mayor and Mrs. L. P. Allen, W. W. Shook, Editor and Mrs. R. C. Colson, Mr. and Mrs. Tom Young, and Rev. Charles Nelson. According to Mr. Moreland, the Harrises loaded the table down with so much good, delectable food that it positively groaned. He remarked that he ate so much chicken and dressing that folks would have thought him to be a Methodist minister if they had not known better. The jovial George Moreland jested Rev. Nelson, the Baptist pastor, stating that Baptist ministers, as well as Methodist ministers, loved chicken judging from the number of times the chicken and dressing was passed to him.

Concluding his short visit to Belmont, George Moreland doubted that he could ever find people who could possibly accord a reception of greater warmth than he received from the good people of the fine, little town of Belmont. In his article in the **Commercial Appeal** in Memphis, George Moreland praised Belmont and its hospitality while bringing out a part of the proud heritage of a place called Belmont. He remarked, "There is something about Belmont that creates pleasant memories and makes people want to come back to it."

Meanwhile, the progressive Mayor L. P. Allen and the town board proceeded with steps to continue Belmont progress. Several of the streets of Belmont were improved and paved. Much work was done at the cemetery. Mayor Allen appointed a committee to confer with Belmont business men concerning the hiring of a night watchman in town. In May, Vinson Smith requested and was granted permission to use the upper story of the courthouse with the understanding that he would render legal advice to the board, assist the tax collector at times, furnish his own fuel, and pay any electrical bill over $1.50 if he used electricity.

The town board approved curbing, guttering, and paving several streets at their May, 1929, meeting. Following a petition against some street improvements, the town finalized the improvements to most of the included streets. The paving project and street improvements resulted in property owners on the improved streets being assessed with tax for the paving project. In addition, G. G. Skinner was elected night police at $30 per month, beginning April 20, 1929.

In September, 1929, before the Wall Street crash, the Fifth District Special Consolidated School was formed from the merging of Belmont, Valley, and Cotton Springs. The board of trustees consisted of S. J. Davis, President; S. S. Strickland, Secretary; W. P. Taylor; W. V. Tiffin; and W. T. Stacy. J. W. (Warren) Sumners was the superintendent, and H. L. (Herbert) Shook was the principal. Roy Fleemon was coach. Among the teachers at Belmont at this time were Julia Gordon, Miss Billy Manley, Irene York, Mae Bess Yarber, E. Strickland, Frances Shook, Mrs. Blanchard Taylor, Eula Mae Caveness, Leighvelia Cook, Gertrude Woodley, Mrs. A. G. W. Byram, and Myrtle Mae Lane.

In July, 1929, C. L. Ivy and Ella Ivy deeded to B. D. Waddle, B. S. Pharr, and E. B. Henley, trustees of South Tishomingo Consolidated School five acres near the Baldwyn and Russellville Public Road (present Red Bud Road). The South Tishomingo Consolidated School was formed from Pharr School, New Bethel School and Red Bud (Caveness) School. Rebecca Ivy and Verna Wood were reported to have been the last teachers at Pharr School. The Pharr School trustees were Silas Wigginton, Edgar Whitehead, and B. S. (Smith) Pharr. Bill Mayhall reportedly taught the last school at New Bethel. Trustees there were Elbert Henley and Frank Pharr. The last teachers at the Caveness school were Principal Elmer Lacenberry and Burton Maxey. The trustees were A. R. Bennett, John Caveness, and George Ashley. After the Pharr School closed, the Tishomingo County Board of Supervisors reconveyed later, in November, 1936, the half acre of land to the stewards of the Bethany Protestant Church for the use and benefit of the church.

Christmas of 1929 in Belmont was marred not only from the effects of the depression but also from personal tragedy. The prominent, highly respected Belmont merchant, W. T. "Bill" Gober, his daughter, Era Mae; and Helen Whitehead, the daughter of Kelvy and Martha Whitehead, were killed in a train-auto accident at the Red Bay crossing on December 24, 1929. W. T. Gober was definitely a builder whose friendly personality and contributions to the growth of Belmont form an integral part of the Belmont heritage. The Gober-Strickland store is remembered well in the memories of the people of that time. The "Red Goose Shoes" sign on the brick wall of Gober-Strickland on Highway 25 was a well-remembered sign in Belmont even into later decades. Bill Gober had previously been a Ford dealer in Belmont. His fellow members on the town board passed a resolution. It stated that in the tragic death of W. T. Gober on December 24, 1929, the town and community had lost a beloved and useful citizen, while the Mayor and Board had lost one of their most useful members.

The 1930 census showed a population in Tishomingo County of 16,411 with a population in the Fifth District of 4,405. Belmont showed a population of 703. Golden had 569, and Dennis had 238. In the next decade this population was to decrease, principally through the harmful effects of the depression. A ravaging fire in Golden around 1930 also proved to be a deterrent to the growth there. The rampant blazes destroyed several store buildings on the west side of the court square in Golden.

Earlier in January, 1930, Belmont Special Street Improvement Bonds were sold locally at par. With recognition of the depression problems, the board notified the telephone company to take immediate steps to put telephone posts in safe condition. They resolved that the proper authorities of Mississippi Power Company investigate the meters in the Town of Belmont in lieu of complaints concerning meters. In March, R. S. (Bob) Mayhall was elected alderman to replace W. T. Gober. T. A. Clark of Iuka was employed as attorney for $100 per year retainer fee. In April, an ordinance was passed prohibiting the sale of goods, wares, and merchandise on the streets and sidewalks of Belmont or from trucks or other vehicles parked on the streets of Belmont, excepting those sales of home-grown products.

Ordinances were passed in June relating to traffic violations of failing to stop at signs downtown and of making turns in downtown streets. In June, Marshal G. C. Martin was employed to execute traffic laws at three dollars per day, running from sunup to sundown until the board changed its policy.

The 1930-31 budget for Belmont was about $5,259.95. The tax levy was 20 mills with 4 mills for General Corporation, 10 mills for Streets, 3 mills for Bond Sinking, and 3 mills for Bond Interest. In November, 1930, J. A. Clark and Preston Yarber were named new election commissioners.

The school board in January, 1930, consisted of J. E. Stephens, President; H. R. (Hubert) Davis, Secretary; G. F. (George) Harris; Henry E. Mayhall; and H. L. Deaton. In March, the school bought with the approval of the county superintendent, one acre of land from L. E. "Peanut" Gamble for $175 for additional playground at school. In July, playground equipment was ordered. Yet, school matters were getting serious by degrees because teachers had their checks discounted; and some refused to teach for the available salaries.

My father, Bill Martin, recalls working when the Depression hit for about $45 per month as a mechanic at the Haynes Chevrolet place where Pounders Department Store is presently located. With the Depression, there was little money. He worked on county school buses and traded work for groceries. Later, he worked at a service station from before daylight until after dark for seven dollars per week. Still, he was fortunate in some ways. Daddy worked for a good, honest man – C. W. Stephens – who often paid his workers ahead of time. Then too, many other jobs, when available, paid only fifty cents per day. Times were definitely very hard in the Depression.

Elbridge Epps recounts moving after the dry farm year of 1930 to farm for W. V. "Bud" Tiffin on Bear Creek in the Pittsburg community. Bud Tiffin told Elbridge Epps, "By gracious, Elzie, I don't want you just to farm; I want you and your family for neighbors." On the Tiffin farm, where Oco Horn owns today, W. Elbridge Epps farmed on the sharecropper system of ¼ cotton and one-third corn to the land owner. Bud Tiffin gave hay ground free. The crop on 30-35 acres cost Mr. Epps about $35. For personal usage, W. E. Epps and W. V. Tiffin raised tobacco, learning how to pull off "suckers" on the plants and pick worms off the plants. As sharecroppers, the Epps family worked hard to provide for their needs like many other families in our area. They sold chicken and eggs to the peddlers who drove their "rolling stores" to homes throughout the area. The Epps family bought flour and had money left. More especially, they dearly loved the landlord family, the W. V. "Bud" Tiffins. A close, lifelong friendship was nurtured and existed in this adverse time.

Rachel Epps Winchester told about growing up on a farm in the Depression. She mentioned about being the next to oldest of seven children. Her parents, like so many parents in the Depression, had to work and manage money very closely. They borrowed money to make a crop and were able to pay their debts in the fall. There was no electricity in their home, only lamplight and firelight. They carried clear, cold water from a good spring on the Tiffin farm where they lived. There were no innerspring mattresses; they slept on straw or "shuck" mattresses. Her mother, Annie Epps, kept a clean house and cooked good meals. She also managed to get a lot of clothes for her children through quilting for people.

The children worked in the fields as soon as they were old enough. The girls wore plow shoes for men, gloves, long-sleeved shirts, and bonnets to the field. They plowed with mules, hoed cotton, and thinned corn. These rather typical farm children cut off ditch banks, got in the winter wood, carried in wood for the cook stove, dug nut grass from the fields, hauled in hay, and helped clean out the barns. They picked enough cotton for other farmers to buy family molasses and to buy their own shoes. To get the big family order from Sears was always a highlight of the fall harvest.

When no flour was available for biscuits, the family ate cornbread for breakfast. They made ice cream each time the cotton was hoed over. Christmas was a happy time. Each child had his own spending money. Christmas presents included school pencils and paper. To school, lunch was carried many times in molasses or lard buckets. In addition, the children were healthy. Their mother made a salve to doctor colds and sore throats. She gave ginger tea and round of Raymond's pills in the spring of the year. (Other people gave their children sassafras tea and calomel in the spring.) Hard work and hard times were overshadowed with family love and togetherness. They loved their landlord, Bud Tiffin, and his family like kinsfolk. Despite the terrible effects of the Depression living, the Epps family, like so many, many families, proved the value of the home as a strong institution. Rachel Epps Winchester reflects in the following statement one of the good things to come out of the Depression times: "We are thankful for our parents and their teachings."

Another good source of pride in Belmont was the fact that when the banks were closing all around, The Bank of Belmont never closed its operation. The business of the bank was never suspended in the Depression. A tribute indeed is deserving to solid bank leaders like B. Ellis Wright, E. Clay Wright, and L. P. Allen, who worked with the support of our people to make The Bank of Belmont a functioning reality throughout the Depression and later decades. Citizens like Henry E. Mayhall and W. T. Gober also deserve credit in going about town encouraging people to keep their money in the bank in this troubled time.

In 1931, a new town administration took office. M.P. (Prim) Haynes was mayor. Aldermen were E. Clay Wright, B. N. Patterson, Charles H. Yarber, J. C. (Jess) Ward, and W. W. (Billy) Shook. Charlie S. Thorn was marshal and tax collector. W. W. Shook remained town clerk. The aldermen voted that all street lights were to be discontinued except three lights on Main Street with the understanding that objections at the next meeting would result in all street lights being discontinued. A committee was named to investigate light and power rates. Obviously, the town officials were girding for the effects of the Depression. There was reason for concern as corn dropped to 12 ½ cents per bushel. Cotton was to drop to three cents per pound or no price at all.

Night watchmen in 1931 were T. E. James, A. F. Ward, and T. C. Pharr. In December, Mississippi Power Company was authorized to disconnect park lights. The tax collector was to collect taxes in the upstairs of the courthouse, and V. B. Smith was asked to help him.

Courtesy Forest Wright

Belmont school group in the early 1930's Superintendent H. L. Shook is on the right on the back.

At the Fifth District Special Consolidated School, Herbert L. Shook was elected superintendent for the 1931-32 term. J. C. Ward became president of the board of trustees. Wiley Richardson was elected principal and coach. He was granted permission to buy football shoes from game receipts with the board responsible for the balance. Coach Richardson was authorized to put a concrete floor and a ceiling in the dressing room with the school board bearing the expense. In addition, Mildred McLane was elected music and expression teacher and granted permission to buy a piano. The piano was to be paid with public entertainment with the board responsible for the balance.

With time and little or no money, many people went to Haynes Lake west of Three Hollows off Moore's Mill Road for recreation and relaxation. M. P. Haynes built the lake of about ten acres several years earlier with mules and slip scrapes furnishing the force. In fact, Haynes Lake had opened in May, 1928, with a festive opening day consisting of free swimming, boxing, Charleston contests, trapshooting, and a big barbecue supper. Down through the years, many came to fish, swim, or just relax. At times, the crowds were rather large with many people from nearby Itawamba County. The dam to the lake broke decades later; but in the Depression, Haynes Lake off Moore's Mill Road was a source of some relaxation in a troubled time.

The Colored First Baptist Church of Belmont that was located on the present Trentham place on Moore's Mill Road had a finance drive and all-day singing with Tishomingo members on March 13, 1932. W. M. Keller gave the sermon, while topic discussion and singing were held in the afternoon. S. H. Hood was the Belmont pastor. John Ford was church superintendent, and Maggie Lou Hood was church secretary. A cemetery was started near this church. In later years a storm destroyed the church.

For the 1932-36 term, W. R. Creel of Golden was Tishomingo County state representative. J. D. Mann was Fifth District supervisor. Fifth District justices of the peace were J. T. Vaughn and W. A. "Tack" Smith. J. U. Clark was constable. About this time in Golden, H. F. Quinn was mayor. T. L. Hale was marshal, and W. T. Shook was clerk. Golden aldermen were W. F. Epps, G. C. Stephens, and J. A. Bostick. In a later term at Golden in this period, W. H. Collier was mayor. R. A. Miller was marshal. Toy Thrasher was clerk, and W. T. Shook was treasurer. Golden aldermen were W. H. Patterson, C. H. Cranford, and G. L. Bostick.

Back in 1932, the Belmont town board passed a motion to reduce the electrical energy rates of Mississippi Power Company, successor of Inland Utilities Company, by one-third to go in force from March 17, 1932. On April 15, 1932, the respected Belmont builder, W. W. Shook, tendered his resignation as alderman and town clerk. Another respected Belmontian, C. W. (Carroll) Yarber, replaced him as town clerk and alderman. Night watchmen at this time were Dave Haynes and his successor, Price Ward. The salary had dropped from $25 per month to $10 per month. The town reconsidered the matter that cut the light rates by one-third. They set a new schedule of compromise rates and decided upon the time that the new rates would become operative. In September, the mayor and board declared that the dance hall being operated in a building on the east side of town had become a nuisance and declared it closed.

In school matters, the board of trustees now consisted of J. C. Ward, Henry E. Mayhall, Hubert R. Davis, George F. Harris, and Levi M. Cummings. In July, there were problems arising from the decision to have divided school terms at Valley and Cotton Springs and a continuous term at Belmont. Several rural citizens were dissatisfied with the continuous term that conflicted with crop gathering, and they threatened to circulate a petition to remove the 10 mill school levy. The board responded and decided to open school on Monday, August 22, in a divided term. In August, the board voted to investigate the possibility of securing a gym. In September, the 1932-33 school salaries were set as follows per month: superintendent, $100; coach, $100; grammar school principal, $65; high school teachers, $60; and grammar school teachers, $40. Considering the discounts of warrants for salaries, teacher pay was to be even less.

In March, 1932, W. W. (Billy) Shook assumed the position of Belmont postmaster. Later, Mrs. Luna Cromeans Davis became Belmont postmaster in 1936. She served the Belmont postal patrons until she retired October 31, 1952.

At this time A. H. Barham was editor of **The Belmont Tri-County News**. With the capable assistance of his wife, Addie, A. H. Barham put out weekly a real good newspaper. Subscriptions were one dollar per year. The September 15, 1932, edition of the paper reflected some typical Belmont happenings.

The members of the Belmont Methodist Church had a pounding shower for their minister, Rev. W. J. Wood, and his wife. Evangelist L. E. Hall of Birmingham was to start a revival meeting on the next Monday evening at the Mayhall building which the Methodists were using as a place of worship until their church building was completed. The foundation of the Methodist church building had been laid, and the faithful workers were progressing. An all day Old Harp singing had been held the previous Sunday at Valley. Mrs. M. L. D. "Mollie" Clark wife of the early builder, W. T. Clark, died on September 10 at Pratt, Kansas. She was buried at Belmont Cemetery with L. P. Allen and Son, funeral home directors, in charge of arrangements. The Baptist W. M. U. gave a going-away shower at the T. H. Young home for Mrs. Charles Nelson, wife of the Baptist pastor who was moving with his family to Red Bay. Elder R. L. Shook was to deliver the Sunday sermon at the Church of Christ. Patterson Gin was running full-time with the cotton coming in rapidly. Middling fair cotton was 7 ½ cents per pound. Marshal Charlie S. Thorn warned that skating on the sidewalks and streets of Belmont was prohibited and should be stopped. Mrs. W. H. Hodgkinson, proprietor of the Belmont Hotel, wanted boarders. All conveniences of heat, running water, and lights were included for five dollars per week. Likeable John Dobbs, an active Baptist church worker and respected Belmont merchant, had an interesting ad in the paper. It stated, "Why fool with cheap, black flour when you can buy guaranteed flour at Dobbs Grocery Store, be satisfied, and have delicious biscuits at low cost?"

About 1933, the new frame Belmont Methodist Church was completed west from the court square on Third Street. A storm badly damaged the Golden Methodist Church. Services were again held in the Golden school building. During the pastorate of Rev. M. H. Twitchell, a new building was erected for the Golden Methodist Church.

Election commissioners at Belmont at this time were Dr. W. Cleveland, A. G. W. Byram, and James A. Clark. Bud Shelton and Dave Whitfield were the night police in the winter of 1932. Mayor M. P. Haynes and the aldermen proposed to give the Belmont residents some tax relief in these troubled times through lowering assessments and raising tax millage. Accordingly, the 1932 Belmont tax levy was 34 mills compared to 19 mills in 1931.

To face the financial problems of the Depression life in 1932,

Mississippi had a new governor – Martin S. "Mike" Conner. Governor Conner, inaugurated in 1932, instantly tried to combat the politics and problems of depression-ridden Mississippi, which was more than twelve million dollars in the red. He took a business approach to his unenviable task as governor and gained the passage of a sales tax to get the state needed money to salvage its credit. Governor Conner urged the people to depend on work and their own resourcefulness to combat the problems of the time. He also lessened the damaging effects of politics in state agencies and tried to improve the public image of Mississippi. Still, his business approach and sales tax enactment in 1932 aroused much bitterness and resentment among businessmen and financially burdened consumers. Eventually, the Conner administration proved its economic value because the state had a cash balance in the state treasury of about $3,243,661 when Governor Conner left office in 1936.

In March, 1933, Franklin D. Roosevelt became President of the United States. He instantly went to work with his New Deal to bring relief, recovery, and reform to the people and the country. Many programs were helpful; some may have had the wrong effects in long-term evaluation. In 1933, something had to get better. The people were suffering, and many were already financially ruined or unemployed. The New Deal and President Roosevelt brought new programs. The Agricultural Adjustment Act brought farm controls. Livestock was killed, and crops were destroyed or plowed up. Excessive production was discouraged to accomplish the farm controls that the government desired. In the Belmont area several of our young men joined the C. C. C. Later the W. P. A. was to have a boosting effect to Belmont improvement and furnish badly needed employment.

The Civilian Conservation Corps (C. C. C.) was essentially a relief agency under the direction of the War Department that furnished types of outdoor work to unemployed men between 17 and 28 years of age. These men set out trees, built reservoirs, made terraces, cut trails, and did related conservation work. Tulon Vaughn went to C. C. C. at Fort Benning, Georgia. Many later went to C. C. C. camp at Tishomingo State Park and built that very beautiful park and its rustic facilities. Joe Vaughn recalls leaving in July, 1935, to go to C. C. C. camp at Ecru, where he stayed about 45 months. Clyde "Peg" Yarber of Belmont also went to the C. C. C. camp at Ecru, which centered around soil conservation. The young men built terraces; set out pine trees, kudzu, and locust trees; sodded spillways; and made maps in addition to other related projects.

The C. C. C. men earned $30 per month plus lodging and meals. The men awoke to reveille followed with breakfast. They wore blue denim fatigues to work. Retreat ended the work day in the afternoon. The men wore khaki with black ties to retreat. Although the army controlled the C. C. C. camps, the overall C. C. C. program was one of the most pleasing to participants and one of the best of the New Deal.

In January, 1933, a new administration had taken office in Belmont. Fifth District Justice of the Peace, J. T. Vaughn, swore in the mayor, A. G. W. (Green) Byram. C. S. Thorn continued as marshal and tax collector. Aldermen were J. A. Mann, Dr. Claude Cromeans, C. W. (Carroll) Yarber, Dr. Webster Cleveland, and B. N. Patterson. Dr. W. Cleveland served as town clerk. The election commissioners were Carter S. Shook, Dr. K. F. McRae, and J. C. Ward. M. P. Shelton served as night watchman until July, when Luther A. Jackson was hired.

At the school in Belmont, Herbert L. Shook was still superintendent; and progress was being made despite the financially troubled times. The school board consisted of President J. C. Ward, Secretary H. R. Davis, H. E. Mayhall, L. K. Cain, and Levi M. Cummings. The board at first discussed the possibility of converting the school auditorium into a gymnasium. In May, 1933, the trustees met with Seth Pounds, supervisor J. D. Mann, Anthony Yarber, and R. L. Shook. They discussed the erection of a gym and the adoption of Smith-Hughes work. In view of the time element and another school's wanting the benefits, the school board voted that Smith-Hughes work be adopted. Since the school had secured 25,000 board feet of lumber from the H. M. Shook Athletic Park east of the depot and since supervisor J. D. Mann had promised labor in the construction from a government program, the school board approved a motion to borrow $1,000 at no more than 6 percent to be used in construction of a gym that would also house much needed classrooms to care for increasing high school attendance.

Shortly, J. F. Hubbard and Mr. Greene of the state department of vocational education met with the school board and superintendent to outline the organization of Smith-Hughes work at Belmont. The steps outlined included the following: arrangements for a teacher home, erection of a vocational building, equipping of the vocational building, and proper selection of teachers, preferably experienced teachers. In the summer of 1933, the school bought the J.T. Vaughn house and property joining the school property for $425 for a teacher home. Anthony Yarber was hired to construct the vocational building, which now serves as a band hall and Headstart classroom and which in 1933 was constructed on the west side of School Drive at the intersection of Washington Street. Suzie Parker of Booneville was elected the first vocational home economics teacher, and W. G. Jacks was elected the first vocational agriculture teacher at Belmont for the 1933-34 school year.

The East Prentiss School consolidated with the Fifth District Special Consolidated School District in the summer of 1933 and continued so until 1937. A. R. Sartain was elected high school principal at Belmont, and Willie B. Lindsey was named grammar school principal. Earl Ward became boys basketball coach. Football was dropped, mainly because of the paralyzing injury to Bill Phillips of Tishomingo in the Belmont-Tishomingo game in the fall of 1932. In July, 1933, a commercial department was organized for the high school at Belmont; and B. F. Brandon was hired as the first commercial teacher. The trustees authorized the construction of a basement room in the north end of the school building to house the commercial department.

The trustees in August explained regulations to the teachers. They promised to adjust teachers salaries according to training and experience when and if the state budget was large enough to justify. Salaries would be increased generally if the state budget were sufficient to do so and take care of the deficit at the same time. Realizing that salaries would suffer as a consequence of the $1,000 loan to erect a vocational building and as a consequence of additional expense of equipping, the board promised to retain for the next session all teachers whose work was satisfactory for the 1933-34 term. Suggestions from trustees to teachers stated that weekends were to be free with the hope that teachers would always watch their conduct. Teachers were to have no date or parties through the week and were to leave off social functions except during the weekends. If on special occasions teachers desired to have social engagements, they were to secure permission from the superintendent. For sure, the times were stern and trying to teachers.

In September, 1933, C. W. Yarber replaced Dr. W. Cleveland as town clerk. In a special alderman election on September 30, B. Ellis Wright was elected to succeed B. N. Patterson, who had recently died in a tragic accident. In October, the aldermen granted a 25 year franchise to Independent Utilities Corporation for natural and manufactured gas in Belmont.

On November 13, another motorist – the third one who had taken the plunge and escaped injury – drove off the "Charmed Life" bridge on the highway at Dennis, dropping about 21 feet to the Illinois Central Railroad track. The driver climbed unharmed out of the truck that was badly damaged. As 1933 came to a close, Mississippi Utilities Company had the telephone service in Belmont. Buck Moore had bought the Texaco Service Station from C. W. Stephens. Buck Moore was later to have the Chevrolet dealership in Belmont. The Depression was still troubling the populace very much; but progress, especially in school plant and school curriculum, had been made in the Belmont area.

At Golden, the depression was taking its toll very seriously. The Golden Saw Mill shut down in 1933 and completely closed in 1934 according to E. R. Warren, a long-time employee of the mill. Flashel Lumber Company moved part of the operation to Savannah, Tennessee. Part was moved to Spring City, Tennessee; and part went to Mobile. Without doubt, the closing of the Golden Saw Mill was another serious blow to the already serious area economy.

By early 1934, work on the brick veneer gymnasium at Belmont was under way with the help of C. W. A. assistance. In February, Hardie Moore, Lee Eaton, and Bud Brown were named to the local school advisory board at East Prentiss. The Allen Line School was in the Fifth District Special Consolidated School District in 1934. In June, Mrs. Sam Mayhall was hired as a full-time hall teacher. In years to come she was to be endeared to the hearts of many of her pupils of this area, in Itawamba County, and at Itawamba Junior College as a master math teacher.

Basketball players and sports fans at Belmont were pleased that the new gym was available for games in the 1934-35 term. This was a welcome change from the outdoor dirt court. The dirt court had been surrounded with a picket fence of wood boards that was several feet from the court. Lights were strung overhead. Oil barrels that burned coal furnished heat for the games in the night air of winter. Fans stood up – mostly around the heat barrels.

The players wore conventional basketball shorts and vests. With the smoke problem; the cold, wintry, night air; and the competition, players surely needed lots of dedication and stamina. The 1933-34 team that played on the outdoor dirt court under Coach Earl Ward in basketball included Raymond Yarber, Eber Mann, Frank Waddell, John Caveness, Jr., Hobson Tiffin, Hoyt Griffin, and Floyd Yarber. In another sports matter of pride, the 1934 Belmont high school baseball team under Coach Wiley Richardson was undefeated.

The 1934-35 Belmont basketball team under Coach Earl Ward got to play the first games in the new gym. This team included Frank Waddell, John Caveness, Jr., Clyde "Bill" Thornton, R. Q. "Crit" South, Floyd Yarber, Hoyt Griffin, Leon "Boots" Shook, and Millard Oaks. A summary of their games according to John Caveness, Jr., is as follows: Belmont 26 – Burnsville 5, Belmont 16 – Thrasher 12, Belmont 15 – Cherokee 7, Belmont 26 – Marietta 8, Fulton 20 – Belmont 12, Belmont 24 – Farmington 11, Belmont 16 – Fulton 10, Belmont 17 – Holcut 9, Belmont 19 – Tishomingo 18, Belmont 27 – Burnsville 17, Belmont 50 – Paden 10, Belmont 20 – Marietta 17, Tremont 13 – Belmont 12, Tishomingo 18 – Belmont 16, Tremont 24 – Belmont 12, Belmont 15 – Red Bay 7, Belmont 17 – Red Bay 11, Belmont 25 – Booneville 18, Vina 23 – Belmont 6, Belmont 14 – Vina 10, Belmont 30 – Tishomingo 25, Belmont 22 – Holcut 11, Belmont 26 – Baldwyn 12 (preliminary game at Baldwyn before Celtics game), Corinth 30 – Belmont 14 (preliminary game at Corinth before Celtics game), Thrasher 14 – Belmont 11, and Belmont 13 – Corinth 11. Belmont won the Smithville Tournament, defeating Smithville, 26-12; Tremont, 19-18; and Hatley, 18-16. In the elimination tournament at Baldwyn, Belmont defeated Baldwyn, 20-19; but Wheeler put them out, 30-12. Clyde "Bill" Thornton and John Caveness, Jr. made the All-Tournament team.

O. E. Sparks was to be not only a loyal Belmont sports supporter but also a prominent Belmont merchant down through the years. His grocery store was to be an integral part of the Belmont business community for decades. In about 1934, he opened the grocery store on Main Street in downtown Belmont north of the court square. When O. E. Sparks opened his grocery, a 24 pound sack of flour sold for seventy-five cents; and eight pounds of lard sold for sixty-five cents. Ten pounds of sugar sold for fifty cents, while 1 ½ pounds of coffee sold for twenty-five cents.

In June, 1934, C. E. (Claude) Yarber and Lee R. Harris were elected aldermen to replace Dr. W. Cleveland and C. W. Yarber. C. E. Yarber also became town clerk. C. W. (Carroll) Yarber moved from Belmont. This was a gain for his new employer but a definite loss for Belmont because Carroll Yarber is a true builder wherever he is. In July, 1934, S. L. "Bud" Sumners again became marshal and tax collector in Belmont. He filled the vacancy caused when marshal Charlie S. Thorn died. Luther A. Jackson continued as night watchman.

A new town administration was sworn into office in January, 1935. A. G. W. Byram was re-elected mayor. The board of aldermen consisted of Ellis Wright, J. A. Mann, G. W. (George) Barnes, C. E. Yarber, and Dr. Claude Cromeans. Dave Whitfield was marshal and tax collector. C. E. (Claude) Yarber continued as town clerk. The town attorney was C. B. Wright. Election commissioners were Charles H. Yarber, S. L. Sumners, and Carter S. Shook. The 1935 school board consisted of J. C. Ward, G. F. Harris, L.K. Cain, H. E. Mayhall, and Levi M. Cummings. Mr. Cummings resigned in the fall, and E. A. Byram replaced him. H. L. Shook continued as superintendent. Earl Ward was boys basketball coach, and Inez McRae was named girls basketball coach.

In February, 1935, the Fifth District supervisor and also president of the county board of supervisors, John D. Mann, died. His contributions to his beloved Valley area and to the Fifth District in general form a memorable part of the heritage of our area. B. D. Waddle was elected to fill out the supervisor term. B. D. (Boss) Waddle was re-elected supervisor to serve the 1936-1940 term.

In the mid-1930's, W. H. Collier was Golden mayor. R. A. Miller was marshal, and W.O. Shook was clerk. At this time the Golden aldermen were W. H. Patterson, S. B. Hargett, and Toy Thrasher. At Dennis, W. A. "Tack" Smith was mayor, and H. R. Clay was marshal. Dennis aldermen were M. J. Hale, R. E. Flurry, and A. L. Lindsey. J. U. (Julius) Clark was the Fifth District justice of the peace, and R. L. (Bob) Wood was the district constable.

In 1935, the Town of Belmont was to benefit from the New Deal Public Works Administration program and Works Progress Administration program. At a special meeting on June 10, 1935, the board voted to enter into contract with engineers, Totten and Loving, from Birmingham in the construction and installation of a water works system and a sanitary sewer system. In August, the board passed a resolution to execute an application to the U. S. of A. through the Federal Emergency Administration of Public Works on behalf of Belmont for a loan and grant to aid in financing the construction of water works, sewerage system, and a city hall. The board entered into contract with Thomas H. Johnston, Jr. of Corinth to draw plans, write specifications, and fill out all W. P. A. forms required on the city hall project. On August 28, the board passed a resolution adopting the application to the Federal Emergency Administration of Public Works for a loan and grant to construct a water works and sanitary system. At the next meeting, Mayor Byram was authorized to file an application with W. P. A. on behalf of the town for a paving extension project. Many jobs were to become available with the forthcoming projects, and Belmont was to progress accordingly.

In depression times, J. B. Strickland with help from "Hoss" Gahagan and Spencer Strickland built a dam and formed a lake where the present Deaton (Witt) Lake is and where Yarber Pond was previously located. Slip scrapes were used in building the dam. Its strength was lessened when Spencer went to work for T.V.A. and J. B. found work. One morning, a near water spout with several hours of hard rain broke the dam and washed up the Tom Gilley potato patch below.

At the end of 1935, many area people were still feeling the agonizing financial burden of the Depression. Times were plenty hard! The people persevered. The town had an election on January 31, 1936, to determine if the Town of Belmont was to construct, maintain, and operate a water works system in Belmont according to present plans and issue and sell not exceeding $24,000 in Waterworks Revenue Bonds to pay a portion of the cost thereof. The election results revealed that 149 voted with 148 voting for the bond issue and only one voting against. The board agreed to sell $20,000 in waterworks bonds to the United States of America and continued by way of loan and grant in financing the construction of a waterworks system. Then, the town officials fixed the waterworks rates to be charged for services with a minimum monthly bill of $1.75 for the first 3,000 gallons of water used and other rates thereafter. The board approved the issuance of the waterworks revenue bonds and made plans toward completing the waterworks system that was estimated to have a total cost of about $36,364. In March, J. A.

Mann resigned as alderman and became night watchman. Dr. W. Cleveland replaced him as alderman. In April, the town board took further steps to set rates for various kinds of work on the projects.

Courtesy Rae Yarber

The Belmont courthouse which was built in the Great Depression with a W. P. A. project.

The Belmont school board met on February 14, 1936, faced with the possible necessity of closing the schools because of a lack of funds. They discussed whether or not to go further into debt or whether to close school short of the normal eight months. Pending advice from state officials in Jackson and bothered seriously because of near impassable conditions on school bus routes, the board voted to postpone school one week. In March, the school board met with the faculty to discuss problems of bringing school to a close with the normal term and to discuss the use of the school share of the million dollar emergency appropriation. In a compromise measure which the faculty approved, teacher salaries were reduced 33 and one-third percent on time basis of last semester or last four months, equivalent to a donation of 1 and one-third months. If the emergency bill demanded and if the teachers must be paid all due them from the appropriation, the teachers would receive it. If not, any funds left from reduction pay would be applied to the deficit that existed. Bus drivers were reduced on a proportional basis to be arrived at definitely from the amount of the allotment from the emergency appropriation fund.

On April 5, 1936, a tornado at night devastated parts of Tupelo. The Belmont area had lots of rain and wind. The tornado went through the Ridge area into the Freedom Hills. Tin, clothing, quilts, paper, wood, and other objects of fragmentation from the Tupelo area were found around our area. For sure, the 1936 tornado unnerved many in our area justifiably. The tornado, like the troubled economic situation, did much damage in certain areas and was reason for worry in other areas.

Contracts were let on the waterworks system. Then too, the aldermen appointed the following to the Landscaping and Beautification of Court Square Committee: Mrs. T. S. Smith, Mrs. T. H. Young, Mrs. D. D. Johnson, Mrs. B. N. Patterson, Mrs. R. L. Shook, Mrs. Clay Wright, and Mrs. L. P. Allen. Mayor Byram and the board designated L. P. Allen as local representative on the site of Docket No. Miss. 1080-R in the projects of the Public Works Administration.

Meanwhile, the new school board consisted of President M. P. Haynes, Secretary G. F. Harris, B. Ellis Wright, H. Mann, and E. A. Byram. The school board recommended Belmont Drug Company as the agency for the purchase of textbooks. As if fiscal problems were not enough, a polio outbreak worried the Belmont area people in the summer of 1936. Dr. T. P. Haney requested churches, schools, singings, and shows closed by order of the State Department of Health on account of polio in July, 1936. School was delayed to begin about October 1.

Many W. P. A. workers in the Depression worked on drainage ditches, like the one through the park on Highway 25 and the ditch between the present Byram Ford place and Yarber Insurance Agency. At Gum Springs, the old gum at the spring was unearthed in the cleaning-up project. Cemeteries were cleaned, writing projects were carried on, and sewing projects were conducted. Additionally, other W. P. A. projects in public works improvements were conducted.

In 1937, a new town administration in Belmont started. L. P. Allen became mayor. The aldermen were C. E. Yarber, Dr. W. Cleveland, G. W. Barnes, S. S. Strickland, and Dr. Claude

Cromeans. A. D. (Dave) Whitfield continued to serve capably as marshal as did J. A. Mann as night watchman. C. B. Wright was named town attorney. The election commission consisted of Charles H. Yarber, Carter S. Shook, and S. L. Sumners. C. E. (Claude) Yarber served on as town clerk. The town board repealed the ordinance prohibiting pool rooms. They secured fire hose and related equipment. In May, 1937, the board passed a resolution approving completion of the town water project. J. C. Lentz was allowed $125 for town land acquired from him for the town well site. Floyd Shook was named waterworks operator, beginning September 8, 1937.

The Commercial Appeal in Memphis sponsored a Plant to Prosper contest for regional farmers about this time. In 1937, C. W. (Wilson) Armstrong from the Pittsburg community near Belmont was the winner. About 1939, W. A. Phillips of Dennis won the Plant to Prosper competition.

On September 7, 1937, the Belmont Church of Christ was extended the courtesy and privilege to use city hall for a place of worship during the construction of the new brick building which still stands at the west corner of Main Street and 3rd Street. Elders in this period were reportedly W. W. Shook, R. L. Shook, and Clay Wright. R. L. Shook was part-time minister at the Church of Christ at the time the brick church was built in 1937.

The Fifth District Special Consolidated School became smaller in 1937 when East Prentiss School withdrew from the system. Herbert L. Shook continued as superintendent as did grammar school principal, W. B. Lindsey. Beulah Stockton was named high school principal at Belmont in 1937.

Editor A. H. Barham in the December 9, 1937, **Belmont Tri-County News** wrote that the cold weather was making hogs very scarce and people sassy. W. A. "Blackie" Livingston was still local manager of the Belmont Telephone Company. Basketball was under way. In the opening games of the year, Belmont girls defeated Iuka, 20-6; and the Belmont boys defeated Iuka, 18-16. Then, they beat Burton. The girls won 29-14. The Belmont boys won 6-5 over Burton in one of the most defensively fought basketball games ever to be held in the Belmont gym.

By 1938, a lessening of the Depression was evident. The county power company was invited to install decorative Christmas streamer lights for Belmont for Christmas 1938. To many,

Christmas 1938 was a happy time as the effects of the Depression were beginning to wane. With the Depression ending, it would seem that things would now be all right. This was not to be the case. Despite improved economic matters, boiling war clouds in Europe in 1939 forewarned a terrible war that was once again to take many of our promising young men from their homes to fight in Europe and Asia for the cause of freedom and their country.

CHAPTER 15

BOILING WAR CLOUDS

As the Great Depression faded away, the economic outlook seemed brighter; and the hopes for pursuit of happiness seemed much better in 1939. Boiling war clouds suddenly darkened the situation. In August, 1939, the Germans under their Nazi dictator, Adolf Hitler, made a nonaggressive treaty with the U. S. S. R. In early September, the German Panzer divisions swept across and conquered Poland in blitzkrieg swiftness. On September 3, Great Britain and France declared war on Germany. World War II was under way. America was sympathetic to the Allied cause, agreeing to send arms to them. Yet, it was still to be a while before America got into the war.

Our local leadership and people were trying to recover from the effects of the Depression. The Golden officials around 1939 were the following: W. H. Collier, mayor; R. A. Miller, marshal; W. O. Shook, clerk; Irby Shook, alderman; Toy Thrasher, alderman; and P. A. Wigginton, alderman. At Dennis, E. W. Smith was mayor around 1939. H. R. Clay was marshal. Dennis aldermen were, reportedly, H. E. Lindsey, W. A. Smith, and R. E. Flurry.

Courtesy Fonza Smith

Dennis mayor, E. W. Smith, and Hardie Moore (left) in front of the Smith store in Dennis in the late 1930's.

Courtesy Fonza Smith
The "rolling store" of Hugh Nichols at Dennis.

Courtesy Fonza Smith

Casual scene of the
Dennis depot in the
In the late 1930's

Courtesy Fonza Smith

Kirk Crabb, Dennis
rural mail carrier.

Courtesy Fonza Smith

John Crabb, Dennis merchant, in front of his store south of Dennis post office.

Courtesy Fonza Smith

O. H. Byram, a long-time Dennis merchant

Courtesy Fonza Smith

Mrs. Kate Campbell, Dennis postmaster for many years.

Courtesy Fonza Smith

Thomas Oscar Lindsey, rural mail carrier at Dennis

In Belmont, a new town administration had taken office. L. P. Allen was re-elected mayor, and L. R. Harris swore him in. Aldermen were Dr. Claude Cromeans, Dr. Webster Cleveland, G. W. Barnes, S. S. Strickland, and C. E. Yarber. A. D. Whitfield served on as marshal and tax collector. The election commission was Charles H. Yarber, S. L. Sumners, and C. S. Shook. C. E. Yarber remained the town clerk.

About this time there was a garbage dumping place southerly back of the cemetery. Careless, unthoughtful dumping became a nuisance around the cemetery. In February, 1939, a town ordinance was passed making it unlawful to dump rubbish in the form of old sacks, cans, auto parts, refuse, or litter on Belmont Cemetery property. Later, the week of May 15, 1939, was declared Clean-Up Week in Belmont. In August, C. E. Yarber was elected tax assessor of the Town of Belmont and the school district.

The school board in 1939 was composed of President Ellis Wright, Secretary George Harris, H. R. Davis, C. W. (Carey) Stephens, and L. K. Cain. The passing grade at school was reduced from 75 to 70. In March, 1940, Dr. W. Cleveland replaced George Harris on the board; and C. W. Stephens became school board secretary. O. T. Eaton was named school superintendent for the 1940-1941 term, replacing the respected builder, Herbert L. Shook, who had served ably with integrity through the trying depression period beginning with the 1931-1932 term.

Superintendent O. T. Eaton served capably at Belmont for two terms from 1940-1942. During his tenure at Belmont, O. T. Eaton reorganized and improved the Belmont school lunchroom program to accommodate more students. He planned and held a night Red Cross Training program for young people and also adults. Certificates were given upon completion of the course. A bus driver training course was held each year between school sessions to improve busing safety of the children. Superintendent Eaton worked with coaches Howard Shook and Homer Snodgrass to improve sports and athletic activities.

T. A. Gilley was named to the Belmont election commission in January, 1940. S. L. Sumners was elected marshal to fill out the term with 88 of the 109 votes cast in a special election.

Across the ocean, France fell to the onslaught of the German armies in June, 1940. The Nazis and Hitler began to set their sights on conquering Britain. Americans began to realize if Britain fell America might have to fight the Axis powers without a single ally with much power. Our country began to mobilize for war.

American arms were rushed to our Allied friends, while our government refrained from sending our young men to foreign battlefields for the time being.

In September, 1940, the Belmont town board approved a petition that extended Main Street in length 690 feet from the northwest corner of Block 10 of the Noel Survey and broadened Main Street from 3rd Street to 4th Street with a five feet strip. Effective October 1, 1940, C. E. (Claude) Yarber resigned as town clerk for the remainder of the year. The 1940 Belmont tax levy was 15 mills with 6 mills for General Revenue purposes, 2 mills for General Improvement, 6 mills for Bond Sinking Fund and 1 mill for Bond Interest Fund.

When 1941 rolled around, another administration was under way at City Hall in Belmont. The respected L. P. Allen was again mayor. Aldermen were Dr. Claude Cromeans, Dr. W. Cleveland, G. W. Barnes, S. S. Strickland, and Lee R. Harris. Lee R. Harris served as town clerk. S. L. "Bud" Sumners was marshal and tax collector. Charles H. Yarber, T. A. Gilley, and Carter S. Shook were election commissioners.

In June, 1941, Belmont lost a "ray of sunshine" and true Belmont spirit when Annie O. Gilbert passed away. She was involved in her family, owned business and residential property in Belmont, and was always doing something good for others, rich or poor. "Ma Gilbert," as many called her, regularly visited friends, relatives, and the sick. Yet, despite losing her husband, W. E. (Ed) Gilbert, to typhoid in 1904, she reared children who made many contributions to Belmont in education, athletics, church work, and business. Annie O. Gilley Gilbert visited others often and had cheerful words of encouragement. As a mother, as a neighbor, and as a Belmontian, Annie O. Gilbert "brightened the day" in Belmont with her exemplary life.

The town officials made improvements on the court square, city park, and the cemetery. Dr. Cleveland and Lee R. Harris were named a committee to look after the cemetery, price the lots, and put the price on the cemetery map. Roy Allen was asked to help them. This committee was authorized to plot off part of the cemetery and designate it as Free Burying Place for those requiring it through necessity.

Mayor L. P. Allen and the aldermen adopted a resolution giving the State Highway Commission the right and privilege to construct or reconstruct that section of Mississippi Route No. 25 from a point designated as the beginning point of the project in the northern corporation limits known as Belmont-Dennis Road. Improved roads and highways would help our area. Our leaders were anxious to help bring about these improvements whenever possible.

In the late 1930's and early 1940's, M. Arthur Shook, a former Belmont builder with "vim and go" now lived in Corinth and served in the Mississippi Senate. At a night session, the highway bill was before the Senate. Highway 72 was about to be left out. Tempers were short. The senators were tired, and no one had been to supper. Arthur Shook rose and began to speak. One senator had ordered some soup and crackers brought to his desk. He proceeded to eat his crackers and soup. Another senator got up from his desk and moved over to talk to another colleague in rather loud tones. Senator Arthur Shook picked up a law book and hurled it through the air at the noisy senator, barely missing his head. Then he spoke in stern words, "Senators, this is Arthur Shook speaking! I have something to say! You take your seats and listen!" Facing the senator who was munching crackers, he spoke, "And you, senator, stop stuffing your mouth with crackers and listen for we are about to build a highway in north Mississippi. You will surely want to know where it is." M. Arthur Shook received a rousing round of applause that broke the tension of the session and gained approval of his proposal concerning Highway 72.

On another occasion, Senator M. A. Shook was awakened at his home about six in the morning. Some relatives of a man who was in the penitentiary for rape offered him a tidy sum of money if he would help get the man released from the penitentiary. Hearing why the man was in the penitentiary, Arthur Shook told the people in no uncertain terms where they could go. Obviously upset, he went back to the kitchen and told his wife, "Nina, hold the biscuits. I'm too mad to eat now!"

M. Arthur Shook is a classic example of Belmontians who went elsewhere and did well. Still, he always enjoyed his visits to Belmont with old friends and family. A place called Belmont meant so much to him as it has for countless others since its beginning.

In November, 1941, the Belmont Separate School District Bonds had been retired, and no assessment was made to this effect to the welcomed relief of the taxpayers. The 1941 Belmont tax levy was only 8 mills with 6 mills for General Revenue purposes and 2 mills for General Improvement. The vastly improved economic situation was intermingled with the continuing war clouds from abroad.

On Sunday, December 7, 1941, the Japanese bombed Pearl Harbor. Shortly, Congress declared war on Japan at the request of President Roosevelt. Consequently, Germany and Italy declared war on the United States. Congress without a dissenting vote accepted the grave challenge and declared war against these threats to world peace and freedom. Disproving some foreign feeling that the Americans would be soft and disunited, American servicemen fought courageously with honor to turn the tide in the war.

Back in Belmont, the 1942 school board consisted of Dr. W. Cleveland, C. W. Stephens, L. K. Cain, H. R. Davis, and J. M. (Mark) Wilson. A school grading system, provided it concurred with state laws, was established as follows: A – 92-100; B – 85-91; C – 75-84; D – 67-74; and F – below 67. J. O. Avery was named superintendent for the 1942-1943 term, replacing O. T. Eaton, who later served as Tishomingo County Superintendent of Education for two terms and made many valuable additions to the educational advancement of our area.

By now, the effects of the war were very evident in Belmont. Many young men had gone off to fight in the war. Mock air raid alerts, or "blackouts," were held locally; and all lights in town were to be turned off. People were encouraged to buy defense savings stamps and bonds. Victory gardens were planted. Several food types were rationed, and ration stamps were issued. In 1942, four "sweet days in May" were named to register for sugar. Gasoline was also rationed.

In April, 1942, State Superintendent of Education, J. S. Vandiver, gave the address at school graduation in Belmont. The April 4, 1942, Report of Condition of The Bank of Belmont showed $62,892.50 in loans and discounts, $345,357.59 in deposits, and $10,000.00 in common capital stock at par value. The bank continued to prosper under the capable foresight and leadership of

builders like Clay Wright, Ellis Wright, L. P. Allen, and S. S. Strickland.

The forest fire protection system in the area was extended with the construction of a fire tower north of Dennis, the Blue Hill fire tower in northeast Prentiss County, and the fire tower in the north end of Itawamba County. These with the towers at Woodall Mountain and Eastport definitely helped in better controlling the spread of fires.

Old harp singing was still enjoyed, especially in the Valley community. At Union Church, an old harp singing was held Sunday, April 19, 1942. Cemetery decoration at Union was the fourth Saturday in May. The graveyard cleaning and decoration at Prospect Cemetery was on Saturday before the third Sunday in May. The graveyard cleaning and decoration at the Byram Cemetery was on the second Saturday in May.

In March, 1943, E. A. Wigginton and his wife deeded about an acre of land on Red Bud Road to J. N. Pharr, S. A. Wigginton, and C. L. Fuller, trustees of the Church of God at Chapel Hill for general church purposes. A. J. Tomlinson was general overseer. Previously, S. A. Wigginton had reportedly donated this property for the church. A few decades earlier, the Chapel Hill Church was located southeasterly down a road across from the W. R. Shook home. Elmer Wigginton is reported to have been one of the early preachers here.

A new town administration commenced in Belmont in 1943. L. P. Allen continued as mayor for the fourth consecutive term and the sixth term in all as mayor. Aldermen were C. W. Stephens, G. W. Barnes, Lee R. Harris, Dr. C. Cromeans, and S. S. Strickland. Lee R. Harris was still town clerk. Election commissioners were Charles H. Yarber, T. A. Gilley, and V. T. Griffin. S. L. Sumners served as marshal and tax collector. In April, 1943, Lee R. Harris resigned as alderman and town clerk. C. B. (Ben) Wright was elected to replace him in both positions.

The school board was composed of Dr. W. Cleveland, C. W. Stephens, H. R. Davis, Mark Wilson, and R. K. Houston. In the spring of 1943, Belmont had the distinction of hosting the Mississippi boys state basketball tournament. Coach Bonner Arnold and the Belmont boys basketball team won the state championship in 1943, bringing this honor for the first time to Belmont. Members of this team were as follows: Henry Clark, forward; John "Bo" Prestage, Co-Captain, forward; Howard
"Ram" Cain, center; Kenneth Cain, Captain, guard; Brison Mann, guard; Jack Mann, center; Buster Davis, forward; Quinn Byram, forward; Lex Cain, guard; Guy Campbell, guard; and Ben Wright,

manager. John "Bo" Prestage and Kenneth Cain reportedly were named to the All-State team. The superintendent, J. O. Avery, was re-elected for the 1943-1944 term.

In October, 1943, the respected old area builder, W. T. Shook, deeded a church site on Washington Street in Belmont to H. L. Deaton, M. P. Pruitt, and A. S. Pounders, deacons of the New Baptist Church. Later, the church became the Ebenezer Missionary Baptist Church. Even later, this growing church became Calvary Baptist Church.

In April, 1944, the school board consisted of Rev. Clyde Sherrill, President; C. W. Stephens, Secretary; H. R. Davis; Mark Wilson; and T. C. "Billy" Boggs. They re-elected J. O. Avery to continue as superintendent for the 1944-1945 term.

War news was of serious concern. In the Pacific, war against the Japanese had resulted in fierce action in places like the following: Bataan, the Coral Sea, Midway, the Philippines, the Marianas, Guadalcanal, and New Guinea. On June 6, 1944, (D Day), the greatest amphibious force in history landed the Allies in Normandy on the coast of France. Resultantly, in time, the brutal Nazi war effort began to lose ground.

Back in Belmont, in August, 1944, the town officials passed a resolution providing for the imposition and collecting of privilege taxes upon certain privileges exercised in the corporate limits of Belmont. They repealed all resolutions and ordinances in conflict with the privilege tax resolution.

About this time, J. H. Tesseneer was mayor of Golden. J. E. Parker was marshal, and W. O. Shook was clerk. Golden aldermen were E. R. Warren, J. H. Saucier, and L. W. Thrasher. W. A. "Tack" Smith" was Dennis mayor. J. W. Tidwell was marshal. Dennis aldermen were H. E. Lindsey, R. E. Flurry, and D. H. Crabb. In time, Dennis disincorporated; and Golden gradually had corporate inactivity.

In 1945, a new administration and a new mayor occupied city hall in Belmont. Roy P. Allen, a son of L. P. Allen, was the new mayor; and the aldermen were as follows: Roy Davis, T. A. Gilley, A. B. Campbell, W. H. (Henry) Yarber, and S. S. Strickland. W. H. Yarber was named the town clerk. Election commissioners were Charles H. Yarber, V. T. Griffin, and D. D. Patterson. R. L. "Tobe" Yarber became operator of the Belmont Water System in March. On March 6, the town board authorized the issuance of waterworks bonds of the Town of Belmont in the aggregate of $18,000 for the purpose of refunding outstanding, unpaid 4 per cent waterworks revenue bonds of the town in the aggregate principal amount of $18,000.

In 1945, four great years of girls basketball play were climaxed when the Belmont girls won the Mississippi state championship. Over the four year stretch the team won 151 games, lost 9 games, and tied 2 games. Compiling a 40-1 record, they lost only to Derma in the North Mississippi semifinals. Bonner Arnold was the coach, and Rev. M. N. Hamill was his capable assistant. Eugene Sparks was the team manager. Members of this team were as follows: Captain Marie McAnally, who scored 919 points in the state championship year; Faye Cain; Stella Cain; Rosie Lee Yarbrough; Jeanette Clark, Sarah Harris; Lauree Hargett; Charlene Credille; Olivia Moody; and Margaret Cain. Marie McAnally and Rosie Lee Yarbrough made the All-State first team. In their championship state tournament, Belmont beat Bassfield, 35-31, and Macedonia, 24-23. In the championship game they are reported to have beaten State Line, 26-16.

On the afternoon of April 12, 1945, President Franklin D. Roosevelt died rather unexpectedly at Warm Springs, Georgia; millions all over the world paid their thoughtful respect. Overseas, the momentum of the war had evidently changed to the side of the Allies. The Allies captured Berlin, and Hitler reportedly committed suicide in late April, 1945. On May 7, 1945, German military leaders unconditionally surrendered.

In May, 1945, the Belmont Theatre under the ownership of J. E. Clement opened in Belmont. The first picture was reported to be "Passage to Marseilles." Other early movies at the Belmont Theatre were "This is the Army," "Northern Pursuit," "Destination Tokyo," "Shine on Harvest Moon," and "Uncertain Glory." Saturdays were busy movie days. There was a daytime show, usually a western "shoot-em-up." There was an early night show, followed by the Saturday night Owl Show. The Saturday night movies increased nighttime business activity and gatherings of people that were good for Belmont. The people were restless because of the war. Thus, "Saturday night in Belmont" was something to which many people looked forward.

Overseas, Iwo Jima and Okinawa, the last island outposts of Japan, fell to the heroic efforts of the Allied forces in very fierce fighting. On July 26, 1945, President Harry Truman urged Japan to surrender or risk destruction. The Japanese did not heed the warning and were to encounter the most terrible weapon the world then had ever seen. On August 6, 1945, an atomic bomb nearly wiped out the

Japanese city of Hiroshima, killing over 70,000 people. The Allies dropped a second bomb on the city of Nagasaki on August 9. V-J Day came on September 2, 1945, when the Japanese surrendered. At last, World War II had come to an end!

Verlia Dean Robbins of the Jourdan Hill Community wrote "Will We Remember Them?" about the terrible war. This very meaningful poem is as follows:

"When this awful war is over,
And the boys come marching home,
Will they all still be our heroes
As they were when they took Rome?

Will their hardships be forgotten,
Will no prayers for them be said?
Will we always hold in reverence
Memories of our hero dead?

Will we lend a hand to help them,
Even though they're maimed, or blind,
Giving courage and our sympathy,
Trying always to be kind?

Will we think of gallant heroes,
Buried 'neath some foreign sod?
Will we remember the invasion,
While our hearts say, 'I thank you, God.'

When the years have dimmed our sorrows,
Our loved ones passed away;
Will we remember why they left us,
Will we remember them to pray?"

The Belmont area and its people did welcome our soldiers home and rejoiced that the war was over. With the end of World War II, our area, like much of the world, had matured. Things would never be quite the same as previously. With the war over, the economy remained relatively good around here. Many now seemed restlessly to want change and expansion that would bring a supposed better way of life than they had. Many brought back new values and new ideas from other areas and from across the waters. Many thoughts were evident, but one predominated. Everyone was thankful that the war was over!

In September, 1945, the Town of Belmont sold the 1 ½ acre tract of land near Moore's Mill Road to Mr. and Mrs. Charles McAnally. The town board voted in October to accept the 1945 county assessment on all personal taxes.

At this time, the school board consisted of President L. E. (Ellis) Deaton, Secretary C. W. Stephens, T. C. Boggs, Kenneth E. Mayhall, and J. M. Wilson. They elected J. P. Fulton, Sr. as superintendent for the 1945-1946 school term.

When Thanksgiving 1945 came, our people had more reason than usual to count their blessings. The boiling war clouds were gone. At Christmas 1945, families continued to count their blessings as many of the servicemen were back home. World War II was over! An age of anxiety and expansion lay ahead.

CHAPTER 16

AN AGE OF ANXIETY AND EXPANSION

The end of World War II brought rejoicing to Belmont as it did to many other parts of the world. The servicemen continued to return to their families. An age of anxiety and expansion lay ahead.

Much interest centered around the prospects of industrialization. Many wondered if we could industrialize without disrupting the way of life, destroying old-time virtues, or destroying the beauty of the countryside. The prevailing view in favor of industrialization was that industrialization could adequately be accomplished with pride, objective leadership, and work.

In 1946, E. C. Davis was president of the Belmont Chamber of Commerce. At the February 25 meeting, the Chamber of Commerce elected Louie Slayton with 32 of 36 votes cast from four candidates as night watchman for the Town of Belmont. Town officials would employ him beginning March 1 with the chamber co-operating with salary supplementing. The Belmont Chamber of Commerce discussed the efforts required in obtaining one or more industrial plants for Belmont. The Action Kit of the B. A. W. I. was discussed at length. The members present decided to get a representative of the Mississippi A. & I. Board to come to Belmont to further discuss the industrial procedures.

W. E. Doty, who had served as depot agent at Belmont about three years, moved to Hackleburg, Alabama, to accept the agency there. W. E. Doty was kind, courteous, and very efficient. The moving of the Doty family was a loss for Belmont, but a definite gain for Hackleburg.

The ever friendly C. O. Mitchell, who began work at the Belmont depot around 1944, was now the Belmont depot agent. With his efficient depot service and warm humor, C. O. Mitchell made the day brighter for those around him. Personable Stanley Shackelford followed C. O. Mitchell as depot agent in the early 1960's and continued the long-standing Belmont depot agent tradition of efficient service combined with friendly disposition.

The home of Mr. And Mrs. C. E. Malone was filled to capacity on Sunday, February 24, 1946, in celebration of the homecoming of Sergeant Lumis Malone, who had been overseas for more than two years. In fact, there were several celebrations in one. The wedding anniversary of Mr. And Mrs. C. E. Malone was February 22, and the birthday of C. E. Malone was February 23. The birthday of the twins – Wayne and Winona – was February 26. Lumis was born in a leap year; and although he had no birthday in 1946, he, like all of his family, thoroughly enjoyed the happy homecoming and family gathering. Family gatherings of this nature were enjoyed throughout the area, honoring the returning servicemen and sharing the joys of family togetherness again.

In the Town of Belmont, repairs were made on Main Street; and needed gravel was put on other streets. In May, 1946, the Old Iuka and Fulton Road was declared closed or discontinued from Main Street on the south to 2nd Street on the north. In August, 1946, Belmont entered a program of industrial development. Mayor Roy Allen and the aldermen passed a resolution requesting the Mississippi A. & I. Board to issue a Certificate of Public Convenience and Necessity for the Industrial Development of Belmont. The application for the certificate was accompanied with facts showing natural resources that were readily and economically available, available labor supply, and the financial condition of the Town of Belmont.

In October, the board voted to double the county assessment tax roll on all real estate and personal taxes in Belmont. Some property on the west side of town of Mr. and Mrs. J. T. Ozbirn, Mr. and Mrs. Charles McAnally, and Mr. and Mrs. Carl Ozbirn was incorporated into the Town of Belmont.

In 1947, the Belmont basketball boys under coach and superintendent J. P. Fulton, Sr. won the Mississippi state championship, defeating Big Creek, 34-27. Team members were as follows: Bud Davis, Buster Davis, Herbert Hargett, Leland Clark, Coolidge Ivey, Billy Owens, Bryan Sparks, Bobby Lambert, and Charlie Gaines Patterson. Waldrep Beard was the team manager. Windle "Buster" Davis and Kindle "Bud" Davis were named to the All-State first team.

The new town administration consisted of Mayor N. C. (Noonan) Deaton and the following aldermen: T. A. Gilley, H. R. Davis, S. S. Strickland, O. G. Campbell, and W. H. Yarber. Henry Yarber continued to serve capably as town clerk. The board voted to execute a contract to clean and paint the exterior and interior of the elevated water tank. Town law enforcement officers at various intervals in this period were L. A. Slayton, Aubrey Patterson, and J. T. Ozbirn.

In the summer of 1947, Luther Kinard, county sanitation director, met with the town officials to discuss Belmont sanitation. The town agreed to spray each and every house with 5 percent DDT in addition to spraying breeding places of flies and mosquitoes inside the corporation lines.

In school matters, the Valley School building had burned on February 18, 1947. Valley students were extended the opportunity to come to school at Belmont. Members of the Belmont school board at this time were Ellis Deaton, Carey Stephens, Billy Boggs, Oscar Searcy, and Mark Wilson. Likeable J. P. Fulton, Sr. was re-elected superintendent for the 1947-1948 term.

The 1947-1948 Belmont girls basketball team under Coach Glenn B. Williams brought further athletic renown for themselves and for Belmont when they won the state basketball championship at Cleveland. They defeated the Cleveland girls of Coach Margaret Wade, 42-41, when Julia Clark hit a free throw in the waning seconds of play. Ironically, this was the last state championship Belmont has won to date although there have been several promising chances down through the years. Members of the 1948 girls team were Captain Jeanette Clark, Julia Clark, Bobbie Deaton, Maurine Pardue, Sylvia Hamilton, Vaudie Mae Cain, Bonifaye Deaton, Jean Flurry, Willard Faye Davis, and Lalla Garrett. Serving as team manager was Eugene Sparks. Chosen to the All-State team were Jeanette Clark, Julia Clark, and Maurine Pardue.

In 1948, Belmont had a new doctor. Dr. Webster Cleveland, Jr. came back home and practiced medicine for two years with Dr. D. D. Johnson. The young doctor then took a two year residency in surgery at Mercy Hospital in Vicksburg. Returning to Belmont, he practiced for two more years before entering the Air Force as a captain and Chief of Surgery at Shaw Air Force Base in South Carolina. Dr. Webster recalls an unusual experience in his practice in Belmont about 1949. In a twelve hour period, he delivered three babies in two states and three counties. More specifically, he delivered the three babies in Tishomingo County, Mississippi; Itawamba County, Mississippi; and Franklin County, Alabama.

S. L. (Sixty) Yarber of Belmont served as Fifth District supervisor for the 1948-1952 term. A game warden and Belmont business man, Sixty Yarber was bubbling with Belmont pride and worked with others to help bring more progress and industrialization to Belmont. Arah Wood Ivy was elected Tishomingo County circuit clerk for the 1948-1952 term. Julius Clark served as justice of the peace, and George Wooten was constable about this time. In 1952, Cecil L. Sumners began his first of two consecutive terms as county chancery clerk and was to serve later terms as state senator.

Belmont in 1948 took a giant step forward in industrialization. At the April, 1948, town meeting, the board agreed to buy 1.77 acres more or less from Hattie V. Smith (Mrs. T. S. Smith) for $7,000 for a factory site between Front Street and 2nd Street. This was to become later the site of the Blue Bell factory. Additionally, the town joined the Municipal Association of Mississippi. On July 6, 1948, the town board passed a motion to execute the deed for the factory property.

J. T. (Thomas) Ozbirn, who had served as district constable several years earlier, agreed to fill the unexpired term as town marshal. An ordinance was passed regulating the parking of vehicles on the streets of Belmont. No trucks were to be allowed to park on Main Street between Front Street and 2nd Street or on the north side between 2nd Street and 3rd Street except for loading or unloading not to exceed 30 minutes. An ordinance was passed in September setting rates on the water system. No water or fire protection service was to be furnished or rendered free of charge to anyone or to the Town of Belmont.

At school, any student not passing in four subjects was forbidden to practice for competitive games. The school board agreed to co-operate with the Veterans Farm Training Program. The school board now consisted of L. K. Cain, S. S. Strickland, Oscar Searcy, L. E. Deaton, and Mark Wilson.

A new town administration took office in 1949. N. C. Deaton was re-elected mayor of Belmont. The new board of aldermen consisted of S. S. Strickland, Hershel Harris, Hoyt Griffin, W. H. Yarber, and H. R. Davis. Henry Yarber served on in his friendly, capable way as town clerk. Election commissioners were T. H. Dean, V. T. Griffin, and S. L. Sumners. In 1949, the town purchased a fire truck, purchased fire equipment for the truck, and built a fire truck garage on the southeast side of the court square.

An obvious highlight of 1949 in Belmont was the fact that Blue Bell, Inc. opened its operation here. Murray C. Adams was the plant manager. The town officials, E. Clay Wright, Paul Allen, K. E. Mayhall, and many other people reportedly made valuable efforts in making the factory a reality in Belmont. In due time, the new factory building in Belmont was constructed; and about 300 employees were soon working. Belmont had entered into a new phase of living – industrialization!

Roy P. Allen replaced S. S. Strickland on the school board in early 1949. W. W. Heflin was named superintendent of the Fifth District Special Consolidated School for a second term in 1949-1950. In early 1950, the school board agreed to sell for $25 the old Cotton Springs School property of about two acres to B. Ellis Wright whose land joined the school property. The board passed a motion in March that the Allen Line School building when it ceased to be used for school purposes be deeded to a committee of three men and their successors for the community and cemetery for the neighborhood. The board of trustees consisted now of President Roy P. Allen, Secretary H. R. Davis, J. M. Wilson, L. K. Cain, and O. N. Searcy. W. W. Heflin was re-elected superintendent at Belmont for the 1950-1951 school term. In May, 1950, the board of trustees voted to launch on a bond issue of $65,000 for the erection of classrooms and repair of the existing building.

The Belmont mayor, N. C. (Noonan) Deaton, was a versatile person. He was a barber in partnership with Paul Moore in Moore-Deaton Barber Shop. He was also the undertaker in the only funeral home in Belmont – Deaton Funeral Home. Friends joked Mayor Deaton about being able to shave, bury, or marry people. He remarked that the first two were correct; but he left the marriage ceremonies to his barber associate, the likeable, sincere T. J. (Jeff) Cook, who was a Baptist minister. Additionally, N. C. Deaton was active in area singings and dedicated to church work.

In July, 1950, Dr. Jack M. Senter came to Belmont to begin his medical practice that continues to the present. In his medical tenure here, Dr. Senter was to deliver the Hastings triplets. Several years later, Belmont medical services and civic developments were to benefit again when Dr. Leon H. Ratliff and his family moved to Belmont in March, 1958. Most certainly, this place called Belmont has been blessed with capable, dedicated doctors who have a sincere concern for both the well-being of our people and the growth of our area. Dr. Senter, Dr. Ratliff, and Dr. Billy V. Stephens, our local dentist, presently continue this proud medical tradition. Recently, Dr. Don Ratliff, a son of Dr. Leon Ratliff, located in Belmont to further expand the very capable medical services of the Belmont area.

In 1950, anxiety and expansion were very prevalent in Belmont when Dr. Senter moved here. The town conducted a clean-up campaign. The town board had in June voted to declare their intent to exempt new factories and new enterprises of public utility from advalorem taxation. In August, the board passed a resolution exempting the Belmont Blue Bell plant from advalorem taxes that the town had levied to Blue Bell Mid-South Division, Inc. This exemption was to take effect November 29, 1947, and extend for a period of five years from that date. Things were looking up in Belmont in 1950. Industrialization in the form of the Blue Bell plant added new hope to our "beautiful mountain."

The 1950 census showed 15,544 people in Tishomingo County and 3,915 in the Fifth District. The Village of Dennis had disincorporated, and its area reverted to the Fifth District. Golden had 206 compared to 340 in 1940. However, the period of anxiety and expansion had bloomed out in Belmont where the population had risen from 594 to 814 in 1950.

In December, 1950, a devastating fire destroyed the First Baptist Church building on Main Street in Belmont. Despite this serious setback, the members of First Baptist Church and their pastor, L. C. Riley, in keeping with the enthusiasm of this period of growth and expansion soon began work on the new church building which still stands today. For sure, renewed determination and progress characterized Belmont as 1950 came to an end.

CHAPTER 17

GROWING WITH THE TIMES

Belmont in 1951 was growing and changing with the times. The Blue Bell factory was furnishing jobs and a new source of income for many. Expansion and industrialization led to a new enthusiasm among the Belmont area people in their daily "life, liberty and pursuit of happiness."

Mayor N. C. (Noonan) Deaton headed the new town administration in 1951. Aldermen were Etha Mann, Hobson Tiffin, Hershel Harris, Hoyt Griffin, and Henry Yarber. Henry Yarber served on as town clerk, and J. T. (Thomas) Ozbirn was marshal and tax collector. O. M. "Cotton" Cain was night watchman. Election commissioners were T. H. Dean, V. T. Griffin, and S. L. Sumners. In February, the town board voted to enter into contract with T. O. Mabry, Jr. for a study of the feasibility of constructing a natural gas system to serve the town. The board raised water rates from the existing rate of $1.75 for 3,000 gallons to $2.00 for 3,000 gallons and $2.75 for all business houses and commercial users due to increase in the cost of operation. The board agreed to look into extending some water mains after considering the feasibility.

At school the respected L. G. (Leonard) Phillips, whose ancestors were some of the first settlers in our area near Dennis, came from New Site to become superintendent for the 1951-1952 term. Mr. Phillips was to serve seven consecutive terms with very noteworthy educational leadership. His diplomacy, his keen insight to problems, his objectivity, his educational training, and his desire to strengthen the school enabled L. G. Phillips to be a successful, effective educational leader who was respected very much among students, parents, teachers, and school patrons.

In May, 1951, Mayor N. C. Deaton was authorized to contract with Texas Eastern Transmission Corporation for the purpose of getting natural gas in Belmont. A special election was held June 12, 1951, to determine a $150,000 bond issue for Gas System Revenue Bonds. The bond issue passed with 114 for and 34 against. In October, the town voters approved the issuance of $7,000 Special Revenue Bonds for the purpose of extending and improving the municipally owned waterworks and distribution system then serving Belmont.

In January, 1952, Brewer Moore was named an alderman replacing Hoyt Griffin who resigned earlier. In February, the board approved $20,500 Waterworks Revenue Bonds after calling in $13,500 outstanding bonds. In a special election set for April 21, 1952, for a $45,000 bond issue for extension and improvement of the waterworks system, 159 voted for the improvements; and 23 voted against. In March, E. Clay Wright, Paul Allen, and Dewey Reed were appointed to assist the town in planning the construction improvements of the water system in connection with the new Blue Bell building and other improvement. In May, the board took action necessary to issuance of the $45,000 General Obligation Bonds for waterworks improvement and extension in Belmont. At its meeting in October, 1952, the town board decided to install two traffic lights in Belmont on Highway 25. At a special November meeting, the board levied 10 mills to retire the $45,000 bonds for improvements of the waterworks.

The school board now was composed of President Roy Allen, Secretary Raymond Yarber, O. E. Sparks, L. K. Cain, and H. R. Davis. Veterans farm training and night programs continued. About 1953, the Golden high school students came to Belmont. Golden and South Tishomingo schools consolidated into Golden School in about 1954.

In March, 1953, the aging Belmont builder, J. E. Clement, and his wife, Emma, deeded property south of their home to S. S. Strickland, J. E. Stephens, J. C. Taylor, and H. C. Hughes, trustees of Belmont Methodist Church for a church site. The first worship service at the new Belmont Methodist Church building was held on January 16, 1955, with Rev. E. S. Furr as pastor. The Methodists still worship today at this church, which is located just south of where the old two-story school building once stood.

Mrs. Luna C. Davis retired as Belmont postmaster on October 31, 1952. Otha Ivy succeeded her as the postmaster and continued to furnish kind, capable postal service to the area patrons. In late 1954 Luther V. Taylor, Sr. became the Belmont postmaster. On March 15, 1955, Lealon Yarber began as Belmont postmaster and continues to serve ably in this position today.

A new Belmont town administration took office in July, 1953. D. F. Lambert, Jr. was the new mayor. Aldermen were Blake Moore, Paul Moore, Wallace Poole, B. E. Wright, Jr., and Lealon

Yarber. Marcus L. (Leon) Shook became town clerk. J. T. Ozbirn was marshal. Brooks Holcomb was night watchman about this time. Energetically, the town officials continued to make improvements whereby Belmont could grow with the times while furnishing more conveniences and opportunities for our people.

Alderman Wallace Poole gave the results of a survey concerning a paving project on Washington Street from 2nd Street to Front Street and on Front Street from Washington Street to Main Street. About $1,000 would be needed after Blue Bell had paved the street where their property touched. Fifth District supervisor, Walton Montgomery, who served the 1952-1956 term, helped make repairs on this, on the town square parking area, and on the turning area (dollhead) on Main Street.

Courtesy Howard Johnson

Masons at the 100th anniversary of Bay Springs F. and A. M. Lodge No. 167 in 1953.

In July, 1953, historic Bay Springs was the scene of a memorable gathering. The Masons of Bay Springs Masonic Lodge No. 167 celebrated their hundred year anniversary. The 1953 Masonic officers at Bay Springs were Hardie Moore, W.M.; Ray McKinney, S. W.; Herman Johnson, J. W.; Willie Gentry, treasurer; Noel Caveness, secretary; R. C. McCarver, senior deacon; Jim Moore, junior deacon; and Jim Calley, tyler. Two fifty year members, D. P. Goodwin and J. H. Denson, were on hand.

Nearly 200 persons jammed the lodge hall and surrounding grounds for the celebration. An old-fashioned fish fry and a fifty foot table loaded with food opened the festive event. Several speeches, including the featured speech of Tom Q. Ellis, supreme court clerk, were well-received. Still, the day involved even more. Old friends renewed acquaintances and talked over old times. Long after the last speech was made and after the last crumb was cleared off the big table, people were still standing around, talking, and shaking hands. Historic, picturesque Bay Springs once again resounded with the voices of happy people. Many of them were Belmont citizens whose ancestors had been a part of the lodge and Bay Springs heydays many, many years ago.

In September, 1953, Elwood Hallmark was elected Belmont night watchman. The valuable contributions of Elwood for several years in taking care of our youth at night around town and in protecting our town are definitely part of the proud Belmont heritage. His unique counsel to many youth at night on Main Street or at the depot waiting for the train steered them on the right path in a rapidly changing world.

The town officials were working on a zoning project, a project for a town garbage dumping area, and a volunteer fire department project. In September, 1953, Jack Howell was hired as a town policeman. A bond issue election on October 12, 1953, passed easily 162-13 for the issuance of $150,000 natural gas revenue bonds with which to acquire a natural gas transmission system and a natural gas distribution system for Belmont. This insured that the natural gas system could be installed, and Slade and McElroy got the contract. Furthermore, repairs were made on the town hall. Lines designating parking lanes were painted on the streets uptown. E. F. White was named head of the water and gas departments.

In February, 1954, Henry Holcomb was elected policeman. Like so many of his predecessors, he was to serve capably, fairly, and reasonably as a law enforcement officer protecting the people and property of our area. In fact, he today serves in his capable, reasonable way of enforcing the law as police chief of Belmont. The town decided to charge a fee of twenty-five dollars when the fire truck went out of town on calls; only adults were to ride the fire truck. In June, 1954, the town officials voted to add some land around Golden Road to the corporation limits of Belmont. The board also passed an ordinance making it unlawful for vehicles with "gutted" mufflers or similar noise-making devices to operate within the corporation limits of Belmont. In September, 1954, James Stephens was elected gas superintendent for the Town of Belmont. In October, Blake Moore resigned as alderman. S. S. Strickland took his place later through action of the board. New water rates were to be a $2.00 minimum up to 3,000 gallons and 50 cents per thousand over 3,000 gallons. The board also voted to hard-surface Main Street from the existing pavement to the Belmont Cemetery Road and to pave Madison Street, starting at 2nd Street and continuing to 5th Street. A special assessment was levied against affected property owners in a sum not to exceed 48 cents per cubic yard.

When I graduated from high school at Belmont in April, 1954, the school faculty consisted of the following educators: L. G. Phillips, superintendent; Curtis Duncan, high school principal; Clyne Harris, grammar school principal and coach; Mrs. Ruth Fulton; Orville Helton; Mrs. Yvlette Helton; Earl H. Alexander; Christeen Hankins; Mrs. Ruth Mann; Mrs. Genia Phillips; Mrs. Ila Trimm; D. Catherine Plumer; Lyman C. McAnally; Tom Duncan; Mrs. Byrd Moore; Mrs. Irene Harris; Nadine Searcy; Rada Ivy; Louise Northcutt; and Mrs. Arvis Clark. This faculty, like many other faculties past and present, taught, counseled, and supported students to become contributing citizens in the society. In fact, Belmont teachers down through the years with their exemplary lives and educational influence on students have greatly influenced the emergence and progress of a place called Belmont.

Around 1954, continuing growth at school in Belmont was noticeably evident under the diplomatic L. G. Phillips. The school board consisted of the following builders: Roy P. Allen, Raymond Yarber, Hoyt Griffin, O.E. Sparks, and H. R. Davis. A $79,000 bond issue was passed in 1954. The bond issue proceeds were used to erect new school buildings, equip the buildings, repair existing old buildings, equip the old buildings, convert one old building into an equipped lunch room, and install sanitary equipment in the old school buildings. A heating system was also installed. The school board also approved a paving project for the school streets.

Tennis had been a casual sport for several years in growing Belmont with scattered interest. In the mid-1950's increased interest became evident. Courts were graded off where the Belmont High School building is presently located on the east side of the street. Compared to our present, beautiful, well-surfaced tennis courts in the Belmont Blue Springs City Park, the tennis courts then were primitive indeed. Although no backstops were available and despite the problem of nearly ankle-deep dust, many youth and our adult friend and leader, Mrs. Merle Whitfield Strickland, enjoyed many summer days of well-contested tennis. Merle Strickland with her warm, enthusiastic personality contributed to the overall heritage in so many ways in the community, in church, and in business with her husband, Arlie Strickland. For sure, Merle W. Strickland has brightened the day for many people, including the youth at the dusty tennis courts with no backstops where the new school building was soon to be built on the east side of School Drive.

Courtesy Mr. and Mrs. Joe Vaughn

Site of the new high school-administration building on the east side of School Drive in Belmont. The building was completed and classes were held in the building in the 1955-56 term. On property in the vicinity of the lower left hand corner of the picture, the J. R. Cranford home, one of the first in Belmont, once stood.

In 1955, our area continued to prosper. Our public officials continued to initiate progressive improvements. In January, 1955, the town board voted to provide garbage disposal service for our citizens. The town sent a truck to pick up garage on the first three days of the month, beginning February 1, 1955.

Elna C. Shackelford was now town clerk. Street paving improvements and associated assessments took place in 1955. Refunding Paving and Street Improvement Bonds for $40,000 were approved. Instead of petitions protesting improvements, some citizens filed petitions for street paving improvements with assessments not to exceed 48 cents per cubic yard. Streets affected were Witt Road through the C. G. Harris property, Washington Street east to Moore's Mill Road through the Charles McAnally property, and Main Street south, beginning at Highway 25 through the Mollie Flynn property. In June, two more petitions were approved for street paving and assessment: Seago Street from Bay Springs Street to the Herbert Hollingsworth line and Bay Springs Street from Washington Street to Seago Street. Mayor Lambert was authorized to sign a lease between the Illinois Central Railroad and the Town of Belmont whereby the Illinois Central Railroad would pay ten dollars per year for using about 13,000 square feet of property along Front Street for use as a parking lot for the depot. In August, the town board authorized $25,000 in Special Street Improvement Notes.

In September, the price of cemetery lots was raised from ten dollars to twenty-five dollars. An ordinance was passed raising water bills from two dollars to three dollars inside the corporation limit and from $2.50 to three dollars outside the corporation. In November, Paul Moore resigned as alderman. In December, 1955, the town board passed a resolution authorizing the issuance of Refunding Special Street Improvement Bonds of the Town of Belmont for $25,000.

In January, 1955, the school trustees, no longer seeing a need for the Valley School property for school purposes, had recommended that that Tishomingo County Board of Supervisors sell the Valley School property of about one acre to L. K. Cain, whose property joined it, for $25. The new school buildings and improved facilities at Belmont were a definite source of pride to our people and our leadership. The lunch room was located in the building presently being used as the agriculture and shop building.

For sure, the early 1950's constituted a definite period of growth in Belmont. Belmont and the surrounding area assuredly grew with the economic opportunities of the times. Progressive leadership and good support from the people for progressive projects made the Belmont area a most enjoyable place in which to live and grow with the times.

CHAPTER 18

GROWING PAINS

Growth and new opportunities were prominent in Belmont in the mid-1950's. With the growth also came new problems and a serious strain on leadership. Our area encountered what many called "growing pains."

For business reasons, need for their time and effort elsewhere, and possibly some other varied reasons, Mayor D. F. Lambert, Jr. and aldermen Blake Moore, Lealon Yarber, Paul Moore, and Wallace Poole had resigned their positions when January, 1956, rolled around. D. F. Lambert, Jr. became an effective state senator from our area in 1956. Blake Moore and Paul Moore continued to serve Belmont locally as respected business men. Lealon Yarber became Belmont postmaster and serves ably in that capacity to the present. Wallace Poole moved from Belmont and became a bank leader in several cities in later years. To the credit of these men, many before them, and many after them, our people are indebted for their contributions to the growth and progressive heritage of a place called Belmont.

Thomas M. (Tom) Duncan, who had been county tax assessor several years earlier, was elected Tishomingo County state representative for the 1956-1960 term. His stepsister, Verna Wood, had served several terms as county circuit clerk in the late 1930's and 1940's. Tom Duncan, a long-time educator, had served as girls basketball coach at Belmont in the 1954-1955 school year. This powerful team lost only one game all year – an upset to stall-minded Algoma in the district tournament. Of further significance in 1956, J. S. South began his first of three consecutive, progressive terms as Fifth District supervisor. L. K. Cain, who had held the office of justice of the peace in earlier years, again became Fifth District justice of the peace in 1956.

In the Town of Belmont, S. S. Strickland agreed to serve as town clerk until a new mayor and board could be named. On January 24, 1956, a new town board and mayor took office to fill out the unexpired term. N. C. Deaton returned as mayor. Aldermen were L. C. McAnally, Hershel Harris, A. B. Campbell, B. E. Wright, Jr., and Robert Cross. Irene McAnally became town clerk. The new officials extended garbage collection, supported continuing the police job, and had several new street lights installed. They passed a resolution authorizing that traffic could turn right on red. In April, the board at the request of school officials passed a motion the Marshal J. T. Ozbirn and policeman Henry Holcomb police the school grounds to keep annoying drivers off the school campus during recess and the lunch period. Improvements were made to the town jail, and restroom facilities at town hall were improved. Furthermore, the town officials gave support to youth recreation programs in keeping with a Belmont tradition that is still carried on today. E. F. White was recognized as senior inspector of the gas system. The town and school officials worked to get a Pee Wee football program started. Despite "growing pains" all along, Belmont continued to furnish new conveniences and more opportunities.

At Belmont School, the likeable Coach Donald Johnson, a son-in-law of former Belmont coach, Bonner Arnold, guided the Belmont basketball girls to the state tournament in 1956. They lost a hard-fought overtime decision in the semi-finals to Agricola. Dot Crowe and Etta Rae Crowe earned All-State honors. The next year under Coach Johnson, the Belmont girls lost in the state tournament to powerful Forest Hill. Charlene Cox Rhodes earned All-State honors for Belmont.

The 1959-1960 Belmont school year under principal Windle C. (Clyne) Harris was very eventful. At this time the local school board consisted of Roy Allen, Raymond Yarber, Charles Bostick, Zeke Harrison, and O. E. Sparks. Belmont started a varsity football team after having organized Pee Wee football previously. T. D. (Dolan) Owens was head football coach, and E. H. Alexander served as assistant coach. Bob Russell, a young community leader, also helped coach football and along with Coach Owens and Coach Alexander made key contributions to the fundamental football development at Belmont. In the 1959 developmental football season the local team was called the Belmont Red Raiders. Thomas L. Ozbirn was captain of this Red Raider team. In later years, Belmont became the Belmont Cardinals.

A former Belmont basketball All-Stater and a successful coach, Coach Windle "Buster" Davis, brought Belmont boys basketball to new heights of success. The powerful 1959-1960 Belmont boys team that included Phillip McCreary, one of Belmont's finest, had the misfortune to be upset in a foul-plagued game at Greenwood in the North Half Tournament. Belmont now started play in a new gymnasium. The new gym with expanded seating facilities beyond the original plan was a definite tribute to the school board, Principal Clyne Harris, Coach Buster Davis, and the solid support of area backers like Anthony Yarber. Despite competing in the A-AA bracket that included many much larger city schools in the state, the Belmont basketball boys of Coach Buster Davis went to State in 1961. They lost a hard-fought 77-70 semi-final game to the Ocean Springs Greyhounds, who had two "jumping jacks" named Jones and Hughes. From this team that won fourth place, Hugh Welborn and James Wigginton made All-State. Coach Davis guided the Belmont boys to the state tournament again in 1962 in a stout-hearted effort. They lost to a tough Forest Hill team. In time, Coach Buster Davis followed his twin brother, Coach Bud Davis, as basketball coach at Itawamba Junior College in Fulton. Like Bud, Buster was very successful at I. J. C.

Belmont football continued to develop down through the years under Coach Jim Weatherly, Coach James Gray, Coach Kenneth McKinney, Coach Jimmy Mayfield, Coach Paul Prestage, Coach Roger Moore, Coach Johnny Buskirk, and Coach Roger Akers. It continues to progress today under Coach Jackie Senter.

Essentially, sports has been a part of the proud Belmont heritage. Despite growing pains and temporary setbacks, Belmont sports has formed a source of beaming pride for many Belmontians down through the years. In fact, Belmont in general, despite "growing pains" all along, continued to furnish new conveniences and programs. This growth was noticeable back in 1957.

In 1957, a new administration started at city hall in Belmont. The personable builder, N. C. Deaton, served on as mayor. Aldermen were B. E. Wright, Jr., H. R. Davis, Houston Ivy, Lyman C. McAnally, and Hershel Harris. Irene McAnally continued as town clerk; and J. T. Ozbirn, her father, continued as marshal. The town fathers had an official map made of the Town of Belmont. Extension of the city limits, a sanitation project, talk about a sewage system, and adjustments of taxes and assessments constituted some of the decisions of the town officials. In November, James Stephens became superintendent of the Gas and Water Department.

In 1957, O. E. (Orville) Bostick, a prominent area civic leader from Golden, received an appointment from Secretary of Agriculture, Orville Freeman, to serve on the State A. S. C. S. Committee. Later, in 1961, O. E. Bostick became chairman of the State A. S. C. S.

Committee. He served in this capacity until 1969 when he concluded 27 years of very effective service and leadership in the A. S. C. S. program.

Belmont election commissioners were S. S. Strickland, W. B. Shackelford, and Dave Whitfield. A special election was held on April 7, 1959, to determine two bond issues concerning sewer and water system construction and improvements. The voters approved Proposition One 157-49, allowing the Town to issue General Obligation Sewer Bonds in the maximum amount of $38,000 to raise money for the purpose of paying part of the cost of the estimated sewerage system in Belmont. The voters approved Proposition Two 159-46, allowing the Town to issue Combined Water and Sewer System Revenue Bonds in the maximum amount of $92,000 to raise money to pay part of the cost of establishing a sewerage system in Belmont. These bonds were to be paid solely from revenues derived from the operation of the combined water and sewer system. The town board agreed to refund some waterworks bonds and issued Combined Water and Sewer Bonds in the amount of $105,000. The town bought sewage lagoon property from Archie Mitchell in east Belmont near the old ball field site and bought lagoon property from J. T. Ozbirn in west Belmont. The board agreed in September, 1959, to accept the $10,825.80 grant from the government. In other action the town board declared a 15 mile per hour speed zone at school effective during school hours from 7 until 4 on school days. A motion was passed in December outlawing fireworks on the streets of Belmont.

More classrooms were added at school around 1960. Personable Clyne Harris continued as Belmont principal. J. R. (Julian) Long, a Golden native, was county superintendent of education at this time; and G. F. Harris was president of the county school board. Previously, the prominent educator and former Belmont superintendent, L. G. Phillips, served on the county school board. Travis Cain succeeded G. F. Harris later as school board member from the fifth district and served two terms. W. L. (Leon) Wilson became Belmont principal in the 1961-1962 school term and served three school terms.

Around 1960, the Town of Belmont constructed the sewerage system. Lots were bought from Mrs. Walton (Bonnie) Montgomery upon which to construct a health clinic. In May, 1960, the town board voted to transfer the clinic property to the county board of supervisors. A health clinic was constructed on the site, and it has served a valuable health function down through the years for our school children and for our area people. Sewer installing equipment was purchased in 1960, and Simon Sisk was hired to help James Stephens in installation and maintenance. A paving project was enacted on old Highway 25 north. In September, 1960, after a favorable election, the board adopted an ordinance to put on a ½ of 1 per cent sales tax in Belmont. In October, school authorities were given permission to erect gates and close the school drive as they saw fit.

The 1960 census revealed 13,889 people in Tishomingo County compared to 15,544 in 1950. The Fifth District had dropped to 3,356 compared to 3,915 in 1950. Golden had dropped from 206 in 1950 to 121 in 1960. Unlike the trend, Belmont showed a population increase with 901 people in 1960 compared to 814 in 1950. This is a tribute to our leadership and the faith in and pride for our community among the people of a place called Belmont.

In 1961, growing pains still were apparent as some citizens met the board to get their property assessment reduced. In other action, the town officials in June permitted the National Guard to use the rooms in city hall that the Health Department formerly occupied until an armory could be erected on the Legion Field property of Bear Creek Road. The town also agreed to furnish utilities.

In July, 1961, Fifth District supervisor, Steve South, serving in his second of three successive terms, swore in the town officials of the newly elected administration in Belmont. N. C. Deaton continued as mayor. Aldermen were B. E. Wright, Jr., Archie Mitchell, Dewey Reed, L. C. McAnally, and Houston Ivy. Irene McAnally was town clerk, and J. T. Ozbirn was marshal. The board adopted a resolution for Civil Defense, and Murray Adams was appointed as Civil Defense Director. The board of aldermen also agreed to get Mr. Smith from the University of Mississippi to draw up a zoning plan and survey for Belmont. In November and December, fires at city dump caused problems and justifiably disturbed nearby landowners. The town officials met the problem "head-on" and decided to maintain a fire lane, have someone check the dumping area at regular intervals, and keep accumulated rubbish burned.

Along about this time, M. P. Haynes of Belmont served with enthusiasm on the State Park Commission. His efforts on behalf of Tishomingo State Park, J. P. Coleman State Park, and other state recreation areas were most valuable. Prim Haynes was very instrumental in the expansion and lake construction at Tishomingo State Park. In fact, the lake at Tishomingo State Park is named in honor of M. P. Haynes of Belmont. Additionally, Mr. Haynes promoted the completion of the Natchez Trace project through Tishomingo State Park to Mingo. For sure, many of the efforts of M. P. Haynes deserve builder status and form a part of the proud progressive spirit of our area.

At Golden, Miss Lela Epps concluded her long tenure of capable postmaster service, retiring in March, 1962. C. Allan Montgomery then became postmaster at Golden. Hollis E. Long was the Golden postmaster in October, 1962. In August, 1963, Eupal G. Byram became the Golden postmaster and has this same position today.

In February, 1963, the following were appointed to a Planning Commission in Belmont: B. E. Wright, Jr., Jesse Comer, M. P. Haynes, Clay Wright, Lealon Yarber, J. S. South, and Etha Mann. In March, the Town of Belmont bought a police car and approved an ordinance that prevented the building of commercial chicken houses in the Belmont corporate limits and limited the number of chickens per place not to exceed one dozen. In September, the town agreed to cooperate with the Chamber of Commerce and supplement $100 toward purchase of street name signs for Belmont. In October, the town cooperated with the Chamber of Commerce in a Clean-Up, Paint-Up Campaign.

Monday, November 11, 1963, was Black Monday in Belmont. Three business houses burned on Main Street in a terrible fire. They were Belmont Dollar Store, Belmont Washeteria, and L. E. Deaton cotton classing office. Nearby damaged businesses were Sparks Grocery and Market, Griffin Home and Auto Supply, and C and P Auto Supply. Others in the block that were endangered were Warren Piano House, Murphy Shoe Shop, and Hobson Tiffin. Fire departments from Belmont, Red Bay, and Tishomingo along with young men from the Belmont Blue Bell plant subdued the blazing inferno.

The board voted in April, 1964, to place four-way street signs at the Hobson Tiffin Store intersection, O. L. Hunt intersection, and

Howell intersection. The old firehouse was torn down, and the fire truck was to be kept in a garage behind Deaton Funeral Home. The court yard was sodded. Alderman B. E. Wright, Jr. was appointed chairman of a special cemetery paving project. Several street segments were paved. Further improvements were made to the water and sewer system. The board thoroughly discussed a separate school district. In addition, a resolution was passed whereby the town would participate in a program authorized under the Urban Renewal Program and available under the Economic Opportunity Act of 1964.

Winfield Manufacturing Company opened at Golden in the old school building on August 17, 1964, with about 24 employees. Milton Weinsten was the owner, and Billy Martin was general manager. Transformation of the school building to a factory was made through work days of local area citizens. Many including several area contractors generously donated their labor. Once again, the people of our area had manifested their co-operative, progressive spirit in welcoming industry to our area. After six months of operation, the Winfield payroll was around $30,000; and those employed had risen to 145. By 1966, over 400 people were employed at Winfield Manufacturing Company in Golden.

Around 1965, the Belmont School Cafeteria was built. In a special election, the citizens of Belmont voted to make the office of marshal and tax collector elective in a 142-41 vote. Some telephone units were installed for volunteer firemen. In May, Sixty Yarber became an election commissioner to fill out an unexpired term.

W. E. Boggs, a most capable young educator, was principal at Belmont Schools for the 1964-1965 term; and our school progressed well under his solid, constructive leadership. In January, 1965, the Belmont Cardinals of Coach Conwell Coggins won the Highland Conference Basketball Championship on the strength of a hard-fought 87-85 victory over the Iuka Chieftains in seven exciting overtimes. A Roger Moore jump shot finally decided the contest with only a few seconds left in the seventh overtime. Gerald Henley led Belmont, pumping in 32 points. Steve Alexander had 15 points; Danny Brown, 13; and Ralph Cain, 10.

On January 31, 1965, Dr. Claude Cromeans was honored in a special ceremony at First Baptist Church marking his fiftieth anniversary in the medical profession. Dr. Jack M. Senter, a fellow practicing physician in Belmont, presented Dr. Cromeans a pin and certificate on behalf of the Northeast Mississippi Medical Society. Tribute was extended to the late Dr. D. D. Johnson, and a plaque in his memory was presented to Mrs. Johnson in memory of the 46 years of dedicated medical service of Dr. D. D. Johnson. Dr. Z. L. Weatherford of Red Bay, a member of the 1914 graduating class with Dr. Cromeans and Dr. Johnson, was given recognition at the impressive, well-deserved ceremony.

In February, approximately 127 people attended the Belmont-5th District Chamber of Commerce banquet. Joe Bullock, Director of the Mississippi A. & I. Board, was guest speaker. Chamber of Commerce officers were the following: Ralph Bowen, President; Dr. Leon H. Ratliff, 1st Vice-president; M. P. Haynes, 2nd Vice-president; and Dr. Billy V. Stephens, Secretary.

The Belmont basketball Cardinalettes of Coach Conwell Coggins won the Tishomingo County Tournament in 1965, defeating Iuka, 31-30. In March, the Belmont Rescue Squad was organized with Paul Spears as president. Down through the years, the Rescue Squad contributions to our area have been many. Members, most assuredly, have worked hard and faithfully in serving in sitting up at the funeral home, in rescue missions, in telethons and radiothons, in benevolent road blocks, in parking cars at large gatherings, and in many other missions of public service in the truest sense of the term.

On June 6, 1965, over 6,000 persons reportedly attended the dedication of the Fifth District Airport with former governor Ross Barnett as guest speaker. Dr. L. H. Ratliff was Chairman of the Airport Board Authority, and Harmon Davis was airport manager. Other members of the Airport Board Authority were Ralph Bowen, L. E. Griffin, J. C. McMurray, and Jack Mann.

In July, 1965, a new town administration in Belmont took office. Ralph Bowen was the new mayor. Aldermen were Robert Sparks, A. J. Waddle, L. C. McAnally, Hershel Harris, and J. P. Wilemon, Jr. Phillip Williams was the newly elected marshal and tax collector. Phillip Williams was also named town clerk. Election commissioners were Sixty Yarber, Leonard E. Griffin, and E. C. (Zeke) Clark.

The new Liberty Church of Christ building between Belmont and Dennis was completed, and the congregation held services there the first Sunday in August, 1965. Winfield Manufacturing Company expanded further through the passage of a $60,000 bond issue which the voters of the Fifth District overwhelmingly approved, 772-8. Winfield signed a lease whereby rent money they paid would retire the bonds. Down at Dennis, Hildred J. Tidwell became the postmaster when Mrs. Kate Campbell concluded over 37 years of postal service with her retirement around August, 1965. Charles E. Monroe was Dennis postmaster in 1966 and continues in this office today.

The Belmont football Cardinals of Coach Kenneth McKinney won the 1965 Highland Conference Championship in very impressive form. The Cardinals won ten games, lost none, and had only a scoreless tie in a nonconference game with archrival, Red Bay, for their rewarding season record. The Cardinals scored 357 points, while their opponents could manage only 12 points the entire season. In fact, the first team defense of Belmont was not scored upon the entire season.

In the 1965-1966 school year, a school band was formed. Pat Phillips was band director. Lealon Yarber was elected president of the Belmont Band Auxiliary. The dynamic, friendly school builder, Dexter Montgomery, was school principal at Belmont. Obviously, the band would progress along with the school when the leadership and faculty are considered.

In late 1965, the Town of Golden served its residents with Gene Moore as mayor. Erskine Payne was marshal, and Roy Bethune was town clerk. Aldermen were S. B. Hargett, Robert Deaton, Hollis D. Sparks, O. B. (Owen) Ginn, and Kyle Bostick.

J. W. (Bill) Davis of Belmont retired December 30, 1965, after 51 ½ years of service as a rural mail carrier and was honored with a surprise supper on January 14, 1966. He started at Belmont in 1921 and carried the mail by horse and buggy. J. W. Davis covered 26 ½ miles per day. He received a Safe Drivers Award for 31 years of safe driving. During his years at Belmont, he served under the following postmasters: T. C. Stanphill, Lumpkin Hallmark, Bertie Hallmark, W. W. Shook, Mrs. L. L. Davis, Otha Ivy, Luther Taylor, and Lealon Yarber. Upon retirement, J. W. Davis was serving approximately 400 families as rural mail carrier and covering 86 miles each day.

At Hamilton, the Belmont basketball Cardinals of Coach Hoyle Payne won the Highland Conference Championship, 54-48, over Randolph. Steve Alexander had 17 points; Gerald Henley, 14; and Larry Fancher, 11.

Growth in Belmont and the Belmont area was evident and had

been evident for several years. Both Blue Bell and Winfield Manufacturing Company expanded their plants. More jobs became available for our people.

In 1966, L. E. (Ellis) Deaton became president of the Chamber of Commerce. Later presidents were Dr. Billy V. Stephens, Dr. L. H. Ratliff, and Horace (Jack) Vaughn. In February, 1966, approximately 100 Blue Bell officials and salesmen toured the Blue Bell facilities in the area and were treated through the Chamber of Commerce to lunch at Tishomingo State Park.

The Belmont basketball boys defeated Nettleton, 57-38, for the District I, Class A championship. They won third place in the North Half. In the State Tournament, Belmont boys lost 73-60 to a tough West Lauderdale team. Gerald Henley was named to the All-State team.

Mayor Ralph Bowen appointed the following to a Buy Mississippi Products Committee: Dr. Billy V. Stephens, Chairman; Jack Yarber; K. E. Mayhall; B. E. Wright, Jr.; Jack Mann; Jesse Comer; and Dr. Leon H. Ratliff. At this time, officers of the Belmont Sportsmen Club were Sixty Yarber, President; L. E. Deaton, Vice-president; and Carlton Pounds, Secretary-Treasurer. Another civic organization, the Belmont Lions Club, functioned well in the community. In fact, the Belmont Lions Club down through the years has been one of the most effective civic organizations in Belmont.

A Mississippi Legislators Day was held at Tishomingo State Park and Coleman Park in April, 1966. United States Senator, James O. Eastland, was the principal speaker. One state senator commented that the legislators had never before been treated so royally. For sure, the day was excellent public relations for our area and county. It was a definite tribute to M. P. Haynes and countless others who worked very hard in planning, supporting and promoting the Legislators Day.

The city limits of Belmont were extended again in July, 1966. Around the first of September, 1966, Mrs. Ann Shook became town clerk. In November, 1966, Travis Cain was re-elected school board member.

In November, 1966, a howling, early morning storm "roaring like a freight train" came through the school area, damaging the auditorium roof and the band room. The Floyd Montgomery home west of the school was demolished. The John Stockton home was damaged, and the trees were badly damaged at the nearby Eddie James home.

Legal sale of alcoholic beverages, beer, and wine was defeated in Tishomingo County on December 3, 1966. Growing pains in the form of problems, adjustments to growth, and conflicting views surfaced more often as growth became more pronounced and complex.

In January, 1967, the Belmont basketball Cardinals won their third consecutive Highland Conference Championship, 69-45, over Ecru. Larry Fancher paced the Cardinals of Coach Hoyle Payne with 22 points, followed by Ralph Sexton with 16 and Phillip Reeves with 12 points.

Effective March 6, 1967, Mayor Ralph Bowen resigned his office to accept another position with North American Mogul Products Company. E. C. (Zeke) Clark, a retired highway patrolman descended from the pioneer Clark and Hallmark families of the Belmont area, was named mayor on March 14. The second mayor of Belmont, G. A. "Dick" Clark, was the grandfather of E. C. Clark. Paul Moore replaced E. C. Clark on the election commission.

A Belmont Merchants Association was organized on April 18, 1967, with Jesse Comer, President; Henry Yarber, Vice-president; and Lealon Yarber, Secretary-Treasurer. In a special election on May 9, 1967, the voters of Belmont with a 109-42 vote favored a ½ of 1 percent sales tax increase in Belmont to help the town get on sounder footing.

In the 1966-1967 school year, Belmont became an "A" accredited school for the first time. The following are among the improvements in curriculum that made the rating possible: physical education for all not in major sports, band, or chorus; public school music in elementary grades; band; guidance counselor; a foreign language, German, being taught in the school, and speech being taught in the school. Much deserved credit goes to Principal Dexter W. Montgomery and the faculty. Then, in July, Dexter Montgomery resigned to become Assistant Superintendent at Russellville, Alabama. Belmont Schools suffered a serious loss because dedicated, dynamic educators and school builders like Deck Montgomery are extremely hard to find. In a subsequent school development, W. W. Grisham was named Belmont principal for the 1967-1968 school term.

Improvements, repairs, and extensions on the natural gas

system in Belmont were made through the issuance of revenue bonds. In a special election on July 11, 1967, Mayor E. C. Clark was elected to fill the unexpired term of his office.

In 1967, the dreams and wishes of many in the Golden-Patterson Chapel area came true. The Golden Methodist Church and the Patterson Chapel Methodist Church joined together into the Golden Chapel United Methodist Church. On November 5, 1967, the first service of the Golden Chapel United Methodist Church was held in the beautiful new church building in Golden. The pastor, Rev. Ruth Wood, delivered the first message in the new church.

With the 1968-1972 term, Leon Cook of the New Bethel community began a progressive program of service as Fifth District supervisor that continues to the present. In addition, J. C. (Calvin) Long began his third consecutive term as Fifth District justice of the peace in 1968 and was re-elected to the post for the next term.

In January, 1968, the Belmont basketball Cardinals of Coach Hoyle Payne defeated New Site, 65-63, in three overtimes in the championship game of the Belmont Invitational Tournament. The thrilling game was finally decided when Ronnie Brown sank two free throws at the end of the third overtime. Phillip Reeves pumped in 30 points for Belmont.

The Cardinals won the Highland Conference Basketball Championship for the fourth year in a row with a 67-62 win over Hatley at Iuka. Phillip Reeves paced Belmont with 29 points, followed by Donnie Dill with 19. This marked the end of the Highland Conference after a five year existence.

The Belmont basketball Cardinalettes of Coach Hoyle Payne caught fire in 1968, winning the Tishomingo County Tournament; the District Tournament, 45-39 over Shannon; and the North Half, 26-24 over Calhoun City. In the well-balanced State Tournament, the Cardinalettes lost a heart-breaker 38-37 decision to Purvis in overtime. Ruth Cain and Barbara James were named to the All-State team.

In 1968, Kaydee Metal Company, Inc. located in north Belmont on the east side of the railroad. The Belmont people welcomed the Saul Rubin family to our area and solidly passed a $350,000 bond issue. The Fifth District bond issue was $190,000 and the Town of Belmont bond issue was $160,000. Groundbreaking ceremonies for the new Belmont industry were held in June, 1968.

In May, 1968, the Belmont area was stunned and saddened over the death of B. E. Wright, Jr. and Jackie Clingan in an airplane crash. Jackie Clingan was a likeable high school student who was from a pioneer family in the Valley community. B. E. Wright, Jr., a respected Belmont builder, was president of The Bank of Belmont. B. E. had vision, training, resources, and a burning desire to help Belmont grow. He had compassion and respect for people from different walks of life. The tragic death of B. E. Wright, Jr. in the prime of life left a certain void in the Belmont leadership that, in all probability, has not been filled to date. The plane crash in Belmont in 1968 deprived Belmont of one of its young people, deprived it of an outstanding builder, slowed down airport activity, and caused many to realize more fully, although too late, the value of the contributions of a builder like B. E. Wright, Jr.

Later in 1968, The Bank of Belmont and its Tishomingo branch combined with First Citizens National Bank of Tupelo. J. S. Bishop, a son-in-law of Dr. K. F. McRae, assumed the local leadership of the newly merged bank. His banking experience and insight proved very important to the bank along with the help and co-operation of the local bank employees in the transitional period. In early 1969, James S. Wall became Belmont Manager and Vice-president of First Citizens National Bank and continues today to serve capably with sincere leadership.

In the summer of 1968, Noble Keys became the Belmont Division Manager of Blue Bell, replacing the late Dewey Reed. The contributions of Dewey Reed, Noble Keys, Roy Rial, and other Blue Bell officials have been very valuable to the continuing progress of Belmont.

In September, 1968, women served on the grand jury reportedly for the first time in county history. Local women serving on the Tishomingo County Circuit Court Grand Jury were Rae Yarber, Lorene Byram, and Ruth Rester.

By and large, Belmontians had experienced a trying leadership year in 1968 involving several changes. Still, leadership arose; and progress continued. Belmont in 1968 with its growth, despite growing pains, seemed to be "on the verge."

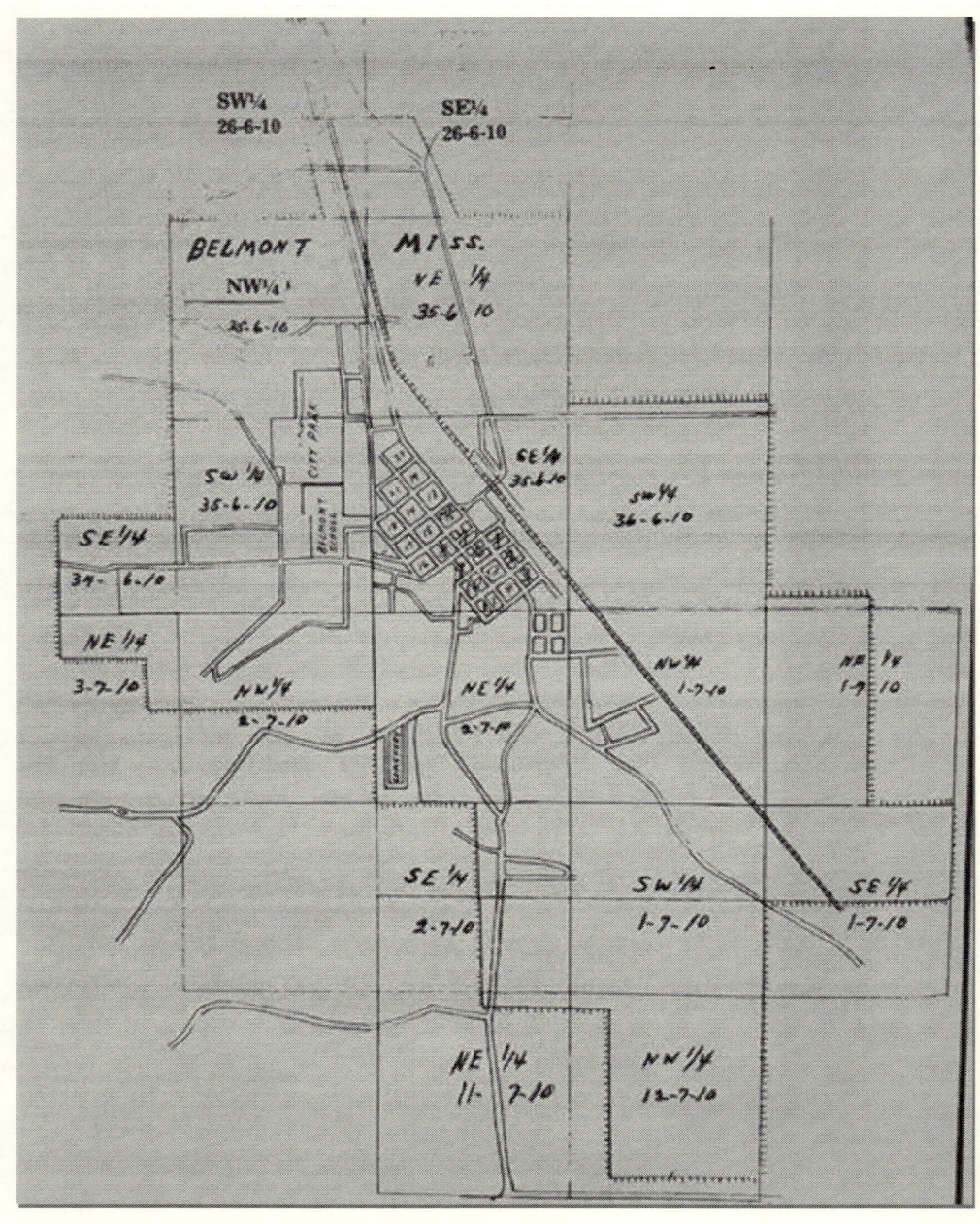

Courtesy Cecil L. Sumners

Map of Belmont in the early 1970's

CHAPTER 19

ON THE VERGE

Modern life on "the beautiful mountain" has seen much progress and accomplishment. Growing pains have stymied some growth at times. Overall, with the pride of our area people, the determined efforts of our leadership, and the backing of our people, the Belmont area seems on the verge of an era of growth and opportunities which our people richly deserve.

In 1969, the Belmont city limits were expanding. In fact, several were interested in their property becoming part of Belmont. In February, 1969, the office of marshal and tax collector was made appointive; and the two positions were separated, effective July 1969.

The Belmont basketball Cardinalettes won the Tishomingo County Tournament early in 1969, defeating Iuka, 55-47. The Cardinalettes of Coach Hoyle Payne placed third in the state tournament at Florence. Kathy Spencer and Larue Thorne were named to the All-State team. In the tournament action at Florence, Kathy Spencer pumped in 79 points in three games.

In May, 1969, First National Bank of Iuka opened its branch bank at Golden. Expanded banking facilities and more borrowing power became available for the people of our area.

Belmont election commissioners at this time were Sixty Yarber, Jean Ratliff, and Gladys Stephens. A new town administration took office in Belmont in July, 1969; and Fifth District supervisor, Leon Cook, swore the new officials into office. E. C. Clark continued as mayor. Aldermen were Lyman C. McAnally, Billy Martin, Hershel Harris, Hugh Nichols, and J. P. Wilemon, Jr. Ann Shook served on as town clerk. Henry Holcomb was Chief of Police.

A paving project was conducted. The town officials worked with housing authorities and local civic leaders to furnish low rent housing in the Jack Yarber Subdivision between Main Street and Second Street. To help cover the costs of new water line, a new well, and labor, the town board increased water rates fifty cents on the minimum rate. Additionally, working criteria for town employees and policemen were established to create better understanding. City hall was repaired with aluminum windows and brick veneer.

In June, 1969, Dr. Webster Cleveland, Sr. was honored at the University of Tennessee in Memphis for fifty years of service in the dental profession. Graduating with a D. D. S. in 1919, Dr. Cleveland came to Belmont. He became a town builder, respected dentist, and contributing leader in various areas of the town.

On August 18, 1969, the Belmont-Fifth District Jaycees held their Charter Night Banquet. Charter officers of the Jaycees were Jerry Martin, President; Pat Allen, Internal Vice-president; Jerry McAnally, External Vice-president; Harold C. Sparks, Secretary; J. C. Clement, Jr., Treasurer; Carroll Ivy, Director; Johnny B. Moore, Director; Jim Byram, Director; Glen Harrison, Director; and Billy H. Tidwell, Director. Later Jaycee presidents were Bob Yarber, J. C. Clement, Jr., Wayne White, Larry Don Taylor, and Larry Cromeans. The Jaycees gained leadership training through community service to our area before becoming inactive in 1975. The Jaycees became active again in late 1977 with Mike Kemp as president. With their community service projects, the Jaycees have helped Belmont in many ways.

The local Jaycettes had their charter night in September, 1969, at the Redmont Country Club. Gunita Cashion was Charter Jaycette President. Later Jaycette presidents were Margaret Byram, Quaye Yarber, Kathy Allen, Kathleen Tidwell, Jeannie Taylor, and Cathy Alexander. The Jaycette contributions to the Jaycee movement and to the Belmont area were most valuable.

In September, 1969, George Morris, Jr. bought the **Belmont Tri-County News and Vidette** in Iuka from the E. C. Holtsford family. The Holtsfords made many contributions to not only Tishomingo County but also the Belmont area with their newspaper. Community growth and development benefitted from their effective newspaper.

In early 1970, the Belmont basketball Cardinalettes were again county champs. At Kosciusko in the North Half, the Cardinalettes of Coach Hoyle Payne defeated the previously undefeated, talented Hernando girls in one of the great games in Belmont basketball history. Mary Hallmark will recall this game readily because her clutch rebound, goal, and free throw saved the day for an exciting overtime victory. In the state tournament at Florence, the Cardinalettes lost a heartbreaking decision in the championship game to Florence. Joan Nichols, Donna Pharr, and Barbara Pharr were All-State selections.

In 1970, the town officials agreed for the V. F. W. to have a recreation center in its building in north Belmont. Tom Thrasher had begun a new newspaper, **The Belmont-Tishomingo Journal**. This paper has made many contributions to our area under Tom Thrasher, under Delmus Harden, and under the M. W. Mitchell family, the present owners.

A Belmont Planning Commission was formed in April, 1970, with the following members: M. P. Haynes, Chairman; Jean Ratliff, Helen Yarber, Jerry Martin, Hugh Nichols, Sixty Yarber, and John Denson. Working with the town and governmental officials, this commission was instrumental in the purchase of about 27 acres of land by the Town of Belmont for a town park north of the school property which included the historic Gum Springs, Blue Springs, and log school site. The planning commission worked with T. V. A. planners in drawing up a blueprint for the town park. The town officials issued $40,000 in General Obligation Bonds for the park. Despite the park progress, the park reality was to be a few years later because of the human element, growing pains problems, and the need for a new source of federal money for the park effort.

In 1970, the Belmont football Cardinals of Coach Paul "Bear" Prestage won the Tippamingo Conference Championship, going undefeated in the conference. The only blemishes on their record were an 8-6 loss to Iuka and a scoreless stand-off with Red Bay. Hard-hitting, hustle, and overall team effort highlighted the Cardinal championship efforts.

The 1970 census showed the population of Tishomingo County to be 14,940 and the population of the Fifth District to be 3,697. Belmont showed a census report population of 968, but a local population survey showed Belmont with a population of around 1,300 people. Golden showed a census population of 115.

In 1971, the Belmont basketball Cardinalettes again went to the state tournament, losing a 31-30 struggle to the rangy Madison-Ridgeland team. With an excellent chance for a state championship in 1972, the Cardinalettes lost to North Pontotoc in the state semi-finals. All-State selections from Belmont were Tawanna Griffin, Donna Pharr, and Donna Strickland. One other consoling fact of this season was that the Belmont girls had defeated the eventual state champion, Hatley, in the North Half Championship, 43-41. In 1973, the Belmont girls of Coach Hoyle Payne again were in the state tournament, losing to Scott Central. Tawanna Griffin won All-State recognition that year.

The Belmont basketball Cardinals of Coach Glen Harrison also went to the State Tournament at Brookhaven that year, losing a hard-fought decision to Terry. Basketball fans will long remember the decisive jump shot of Andy Chumbley against Hatley in the District Tournament that really got the Cardinals winging. Obviously, sports are a proud part of the Belmont heritage. There is good reason to believe that this heritage will continue into future years, bringing the elusive basketball state championship to Belmont along with a conference championship in football.

In 1971, the town board of Belmont approved the purchase of the farm co-op building (the old Methodist Church building) on Third Street for $7,000 for town usage. In July, 1971, the board approved the purchase of the Higginbottom and Cooper property in north Belmont for industrial usage. In November the town officials approved an appreciation supper for the Rescue Squad members. They also donated $100 on the Jaycee project of Christmas baskets for the needy.

Aubrey Patterson became Belmont Chief of Police in January, 1972, replacing Henry Holcomb, who had become a deputy sheriff. The town sponsored Teacher Appreciation Night in May. State Superintendent of Education, Dr. Garvin Johnston, was the featured speaker at this well-received event honoring our teachers.

On November 23, 1972, Mack Sartain, a respected building contractor and area leader, was killed in a tractor accident while working on a house lot near his home. Mack Sartain was a dynamic leader of the Sunnybrook Children's Home and Church of Christ at Liberty. A builder in the truest sense of the word, Mack Sartain with his enthusiastic determination to succeed made many valuable contributions to the growth and development of our area before his tragic death.

Town election commissioners in Belmont about this time were reportedly Earl Pace, Flora Dobbs, and Gladys Stephens. A new town administration in Belmont took office in July, 1973. Mayor E. C. Clark was re-elected to serve another term. Aldermen were Robert H. (Bob) Yarber, James C. (Jim) Byram, Roy P. (Pat) Allen, Jr., J. P. Wilemon, Jr., and Jack R. Mann. Fifth District supervisor, Leon Cook, swore in the new town officials. Ann Shook continued as town clerk and tax collector.

Gary Deaton became principal of Belmont Schools in the 1973-1974 term. He replaced Carlton Abels, who had served four previous terms. Area school board members at this time were Claude Stacy and Charles Bostick. Present school board members from this area are Claude Stacy and Harold C. Sparks.

At Golden, Dr. Raymond Shook remained mayor. Aldermen were O. B. (Owen) Ginn, Hollis Long, Davy Ginn, Jimmy Timms, and Gene Moore. Roy Bethune was town clerk at Golden. Of further interest, Davy Ginn, who had just become 18 years old, was one of the youngest aldermen, if not the youngest, to ever serve in the state.

At Belmont, repairs were made on the courthouse. The interior was renovated in a very commendable manner. The town board passed an ordinance about keeping property clean. Garbage cans were purchased and put on the streets of town. In December, 1973, Henry Holcomb again became Chief of Police.

The town officials worked to bring a new group of low rent houses to Belmont. In June, 1974, a new public library board was formed as follows: Mary Fisher Wright, Chairman; Bobbie Jean Wall; Mae Bess Yarber; Vaudie Marshall; and Claire Griffin. Nadine Patton later was named a library board trustee to fill an unexpired vacancy. In other progressive developments, the town agreed to work with the Northeast Mississippi Planning and Development District. The town officials issued $350,000 in bonds for expanding, enlarging, and improving the water and sewer system.

In September, 1974, the town purchased the Adron Boyd property. In the summer of 1975, the town got an E. D. A. grant which insured that the long-awaited town park would become a reality. The town was to furnish $50,000 and the officials issued $32,000 in bonds to go with available park funds. The E. D. A. would put up $200,000 for the park. In November, Bob Lovelady was hired as gas system consultant. In March, 1976, a fire department was newly organized with Harold Holley as Fire Chief. Street paving continued, and important improvements were made on the sewerage system.

The Bicentennial Celebration – the Belmont Freedom Family Fun Festival – was well-received in Belmont and was a definite tribute to its planners. Betty Jo Dickinson was chairman of the committee. The beautiful new Belmont park was dedicated July 3, 1976, before a large gathering in the joyous day of food and festivity. Congressman Jamie Whitten was on hand to help dedicate the scenic park with its lighted baseball field, swimming pool, top-notch tennis courts, original playground equipment, and other recreational features. The old Belmont depot was restored on the park property to the appreciation and nostalgic remembrances of many Belmontians. A very colorful fireworks display and music concluded the Bicentennial Celebration. The park was officially named Belmont Blue Springs City Park and is a definite tribute to those who worked hard to make the park a reality. The Belmont Blue Springs City Park is, most assuredly, a radiant source of pride for Belmont and Belmontians!

In July, 1976, Moore Chevrolet Company, which began in April, 1949, under the ownership of Brewer Moore, became a father-son firm when Johnny B. Moore joined the firm. Brewer Moore installed the first electric gas pump in Belmont. The Chevrolets for his opening day in 1949 came on the train and consisted of the following: four trucks, four cars, and four pick-ups.

Another father-son involvement had existed in the Ford dealership. Anthony Yarber, a Ford dealer in early Belmont, had sold Fords for years in the Town of Belmont. In 1955, his son, Jack Yarber, took over the Ford dealership in a continuing, progressive manner. In addition, Helen Yarber, wife of Jack Yarber, worked with her husband, the P. T. A., and several other area groups in promoting safety programs. She won eight consecutive National Awards of Excellence in this field, including one National Grand Award in 1974. In the early 1970's, Helen Yarber spearheaded the establishment of the first Safety Bug Park in the nation on the Belmont School campus.

Jimmy Byram now owns the Ford dealership in Belmont, having bought the dealership from Jack Yarber a few years back. The annual Ford Punt, Pass, and Kick Contest is only one example of many community involvements from our car dealerships. With Byram Ford, Moore Chevrolet, and several used car dealers, the people of our area also can usually find the car they want at a reasonable price and know that they are trading with people who are interested in helping our area continue to grow.

The 1977 election commissioners in Belmont were Ruth Fulton, Chairman; Arah W. Ivy; and Gladys Stephens. The town officials worked to combat the energy problem and agreed to co-operate in the county landfill project. In the spring of 1977, a new honor came to Belmont. Ricky Wooten, a personable youth at Belmont Schools, climaxed his successful high school tennis career in fine fashion. Ricky Wooten won the Mississippi B-BB Singles Tennis Championship.

On May 1, 1977, the beautiful new Belmont Library, located on 3rd Street where the old telephone exchange building once stood, was dedicated. The new library is a valuable asset to Belmont and its value will be appreciated far into the future. Shara Sparks Holley served as librarian when the library was dedicated. Under her leadership and the leadership of Pam Pardue, the present librarian, the Belmont Library has grown and is bound to grow further to meet the needs of the area people.

A new administration took office at city hall in Belmont in 1977. E. H. (Earl) Alexander was the new mayor. Aldermen were Bob Yarber, A. J. Waddle, Pat Allen, J. P. Wilemon, Jr., and Jack Mann. Frances Byram became town clerk. Henry Holcomb continued as Chief of Police.

At Golden, Dr. Raymond Shook began his fourth term as mayor. Aldermen were Gene Moore, Hollis Long, Harold "Gabby" Ginn, Addis Stanphill, and Reman "Billy" James.

At the mid-term break of the 1977-1978 Belmont school year, Jerry Hughes became Belmont principal to fill out the term. Jack Robinson recently became Belmont principal for the 1978-1979 term. Boys sports at school are in the capable hands of Glen Harrison, boys basketball coach, and Jackie Senter, boys football and baseball coach. In 1978, Coach Hoyle Payne guided the Belmont basketball Cardinalettes to the State Tournament at Jackson. This young team lost in the semi-finals to South Pontotoc. Freshman Debbie Parker earned All-State honors. In his thirteen year tenure at Belmont, Coach Hoyle Payne has won 285 girls games while losing only 92. As the future unfolds, both boys and girls sports as in the past will surely have a strategic role in Belmont Schools and the community that is served.

In the spring of 1978, the town officials continued to work for improvements. Several streets were resurfaced in Belmont. The paving project on the drive through the Belmont Cemetery is a sure source of pride in present Belmont.

In 1978, the Belmont area in general is characterized with growth and a desire to progress. Inflation and energy shortages pose serious problems. More community involvement from a broader segment of our people combined with a revival of brotherly love and understanding are bound to insure that the

Belmont area will continue to prosper. Our area is truly on the verge.

In Belmont, so many people have done so many things down through the years to make "the beautiful mountain" a wonderful place in which to live. Then too, there is something about Belmont that draws "its children" back home. If you have never been to Belmont, Mississippi, you have missed a real treat of "down-to-earth" hospitality and Belmont enthusiasm. Actually, Belmont encompasses more than its city limits. It is in a sense Belmont and the surrounding area. Moreover, the Town of Belmont is the hub of a trade area in the old Fifth District of Tishomingo County and is the result of pioneer families from surrounding settlements blending into a working village when the railroad came through. You owe to yourself to visit Belmont, trade with our friendly merchants, talk with our people about the proud Belmont heritage, visit beautiful Belmont Blue Springs City Park, and enjoy "down-to-earth" living in a friendly, progressive little town. Yes, good people, there is a place called Belmont. I, like countless others, beam with pride to call it my home town!

Courtesy Bertie H. Taylor

The Belmont depot on the railroad in early Belmont.

Courtesy THE BELMONT AND TISHOMINGO JOURNAL

View in 1978 of the restored Belmont depot. Instead of facing the Illinois Central Railroad and welcoming train passengers, friends, and family as in bygone years, the historic old depot now faces in this view in 1978 young and adults at the swimming pool, tennis courts, and the Blue Springs area of the beautiful Belmont Blue Springs City Park.

Courtesy THE BELMONT AND TISHOMINGO JOURNAL

View in 1978 from Main Street of Highway 25 south (2nd Street) in Belmont. The Belmont post office is at the right down the hill.

Courtesy THE BELMONT AND TISHOMINGO JOURNAL

Eastward view toward the railroad of Main Street in downtown Belmont in 1978.

Courtesy THE BELMONT AND TISHOMINGO JOURNAL

1978 view of Main Street in downtown Belmont from Third Street.

Courtesy THE BELMONT AND TISHOMINGO JOURNAL

View of Belmont in 1978 eastward from the junction of Highway 25 (2nd Street) and Main Street.

Courtesy THE BELMONT AND TISHOMINGO JOURNAL

View of Belmont in 1978 from the corner of Main Street and Highway 25 (2nd Street).

Courtesy THE BELMONT AND TISHOMINGO JOURNAL

Westward view of Belmont Main Street in 1978 from the railroad and the old Belmont depot site.

Courtesy THE BELMONT AND TISHOMINGO JOURNAL

The restored Belmont depot in beautiful Belmont Blue Springs City Park.

Courtesy THE BELMONT AND TISHOMINGO JOURNAL

Belmont City Hall in 1978

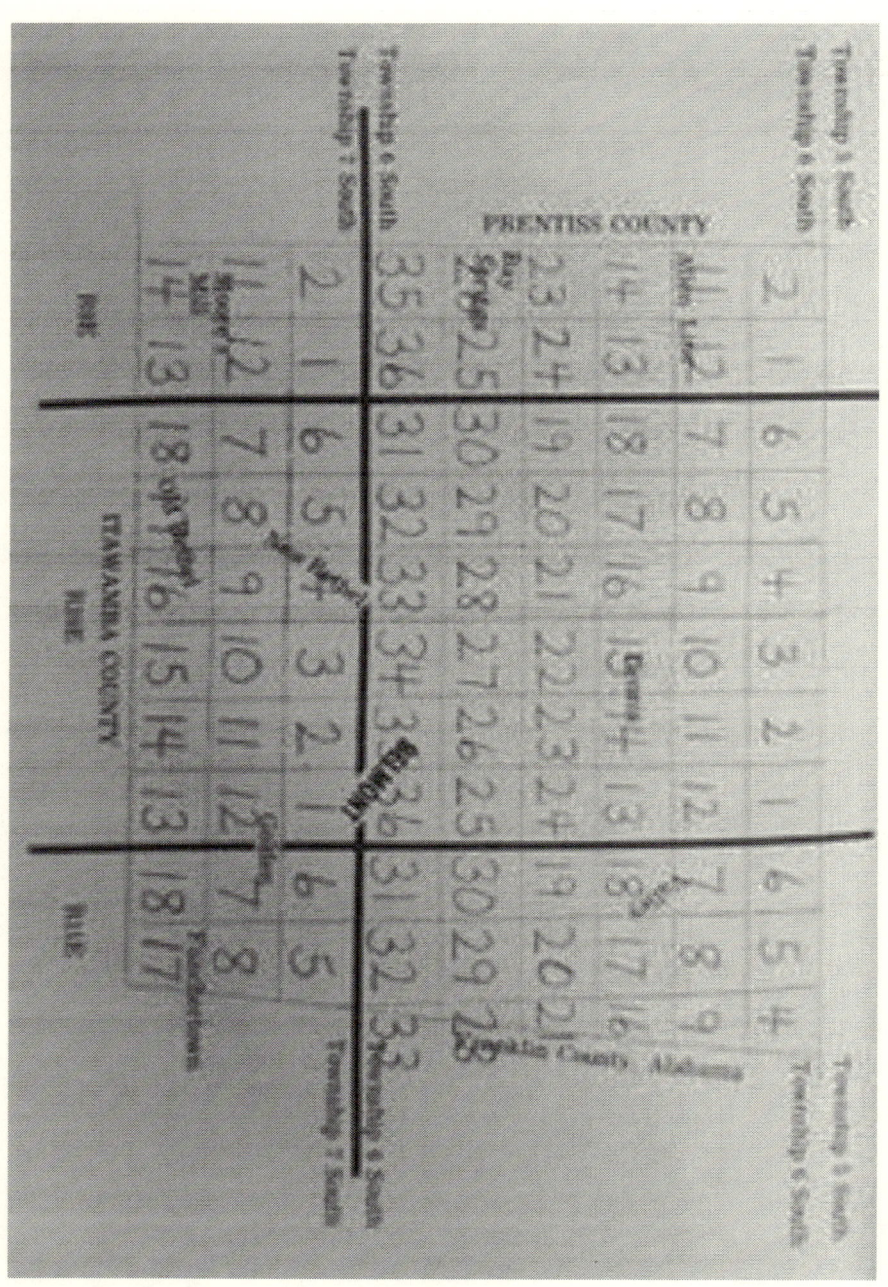

Section, Township, and Range location of land in the southern part of Tishomingo County. Present towns and communities are also located.

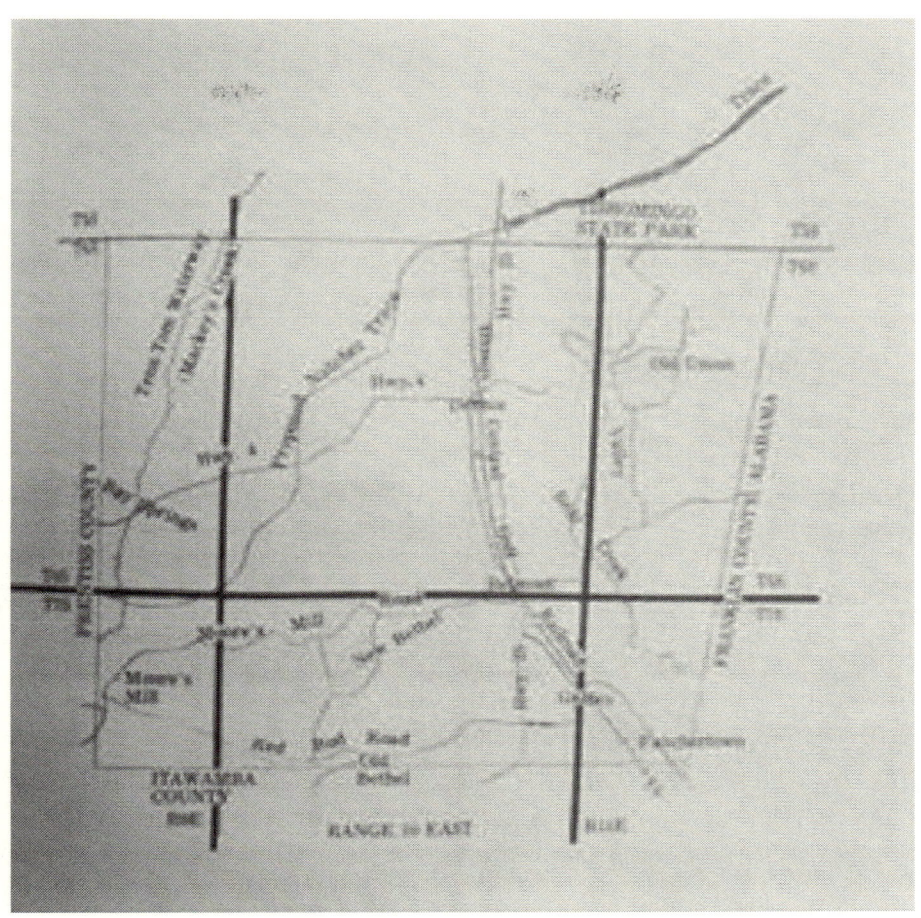

Sketch of the southern part of present Tishomingo County, including "A Place Called Belmont"

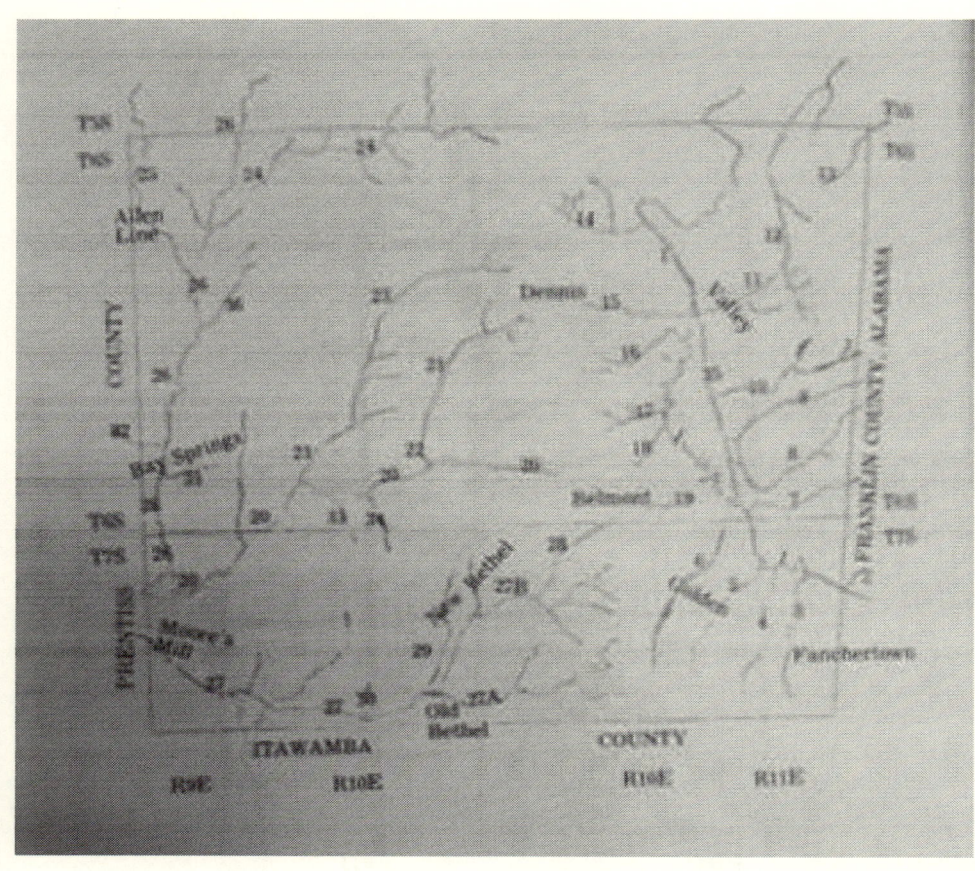

Streams of the Belmont area: 1. Bear Creek, 2. Gee Branch, 3. Prairie Branch, 4. Mink Branch, 5. Epps Branch, 6. Wofford Branch, 7. Brumley Branch, 8. Fowler Branch, 9. Harris Branch, 10. Mann Branch, 11. Bridges Branch, 12. Holly Branch, 13. Bloody Springs Branch, 14. Mauldin (Harrison) Branch, 15. McNutt Branch, 16. Campbell Branch, 17. Byram (Rob Epps) Branch, 18. Carr Branch, 19. Ab Wood Branch, 20.Rock Creek, 21. Perry Branch, 22. Fuller Branch, 23. Jourdan Creek, 24 McDougal Branch, 25. Riddle Creek, 26. Mackey's Creek, 27. Red Bud Creek, 27A. Red Bud Creek (South Fork) 27B. Red Bud Creek (North Fork), 28. Ben Martin Branch, 29. Lynn Branch, 30. Ivy Branch, 31. Burnt Mills Branch, 32. Gin Branch, 33. Lake Branch, 34. Betty Branch, 35. Bear Creek Channel, and 36. Moore Branch.

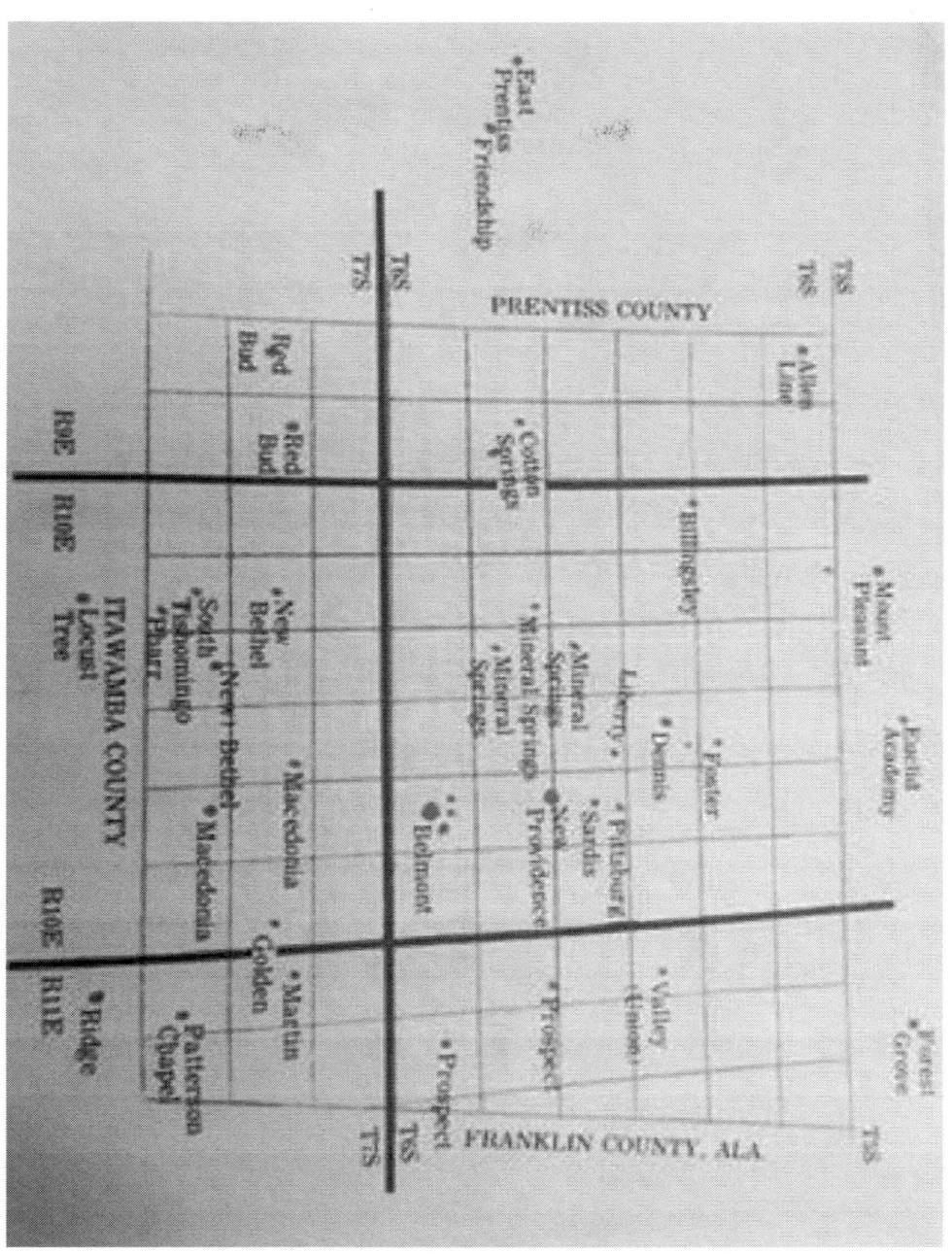

Schools of the Belmont area. Only one school, Belmont, presently exists.

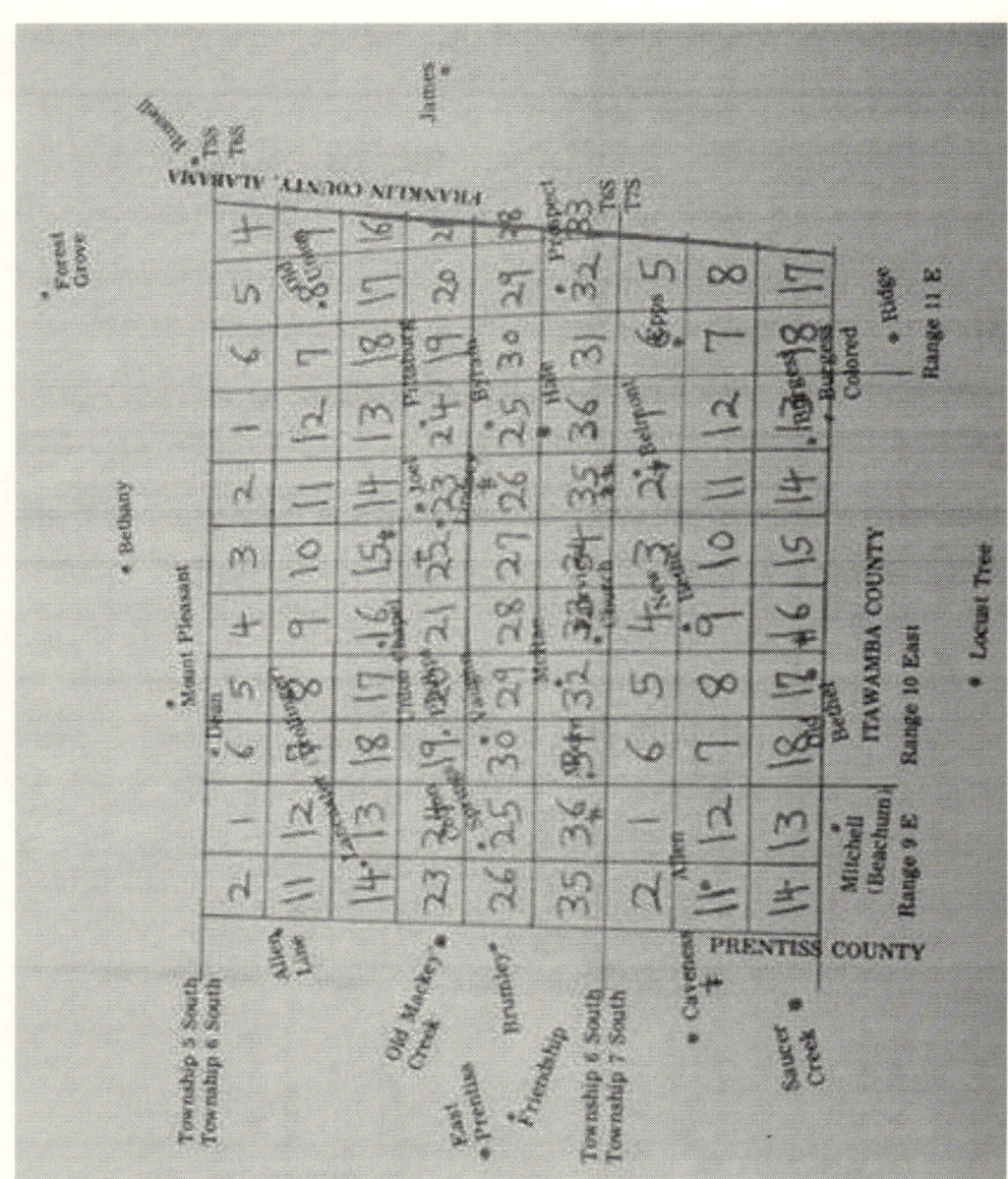

Cemeteries located in the Belmont area. Some other known grave sites are identified with a cross on the map.

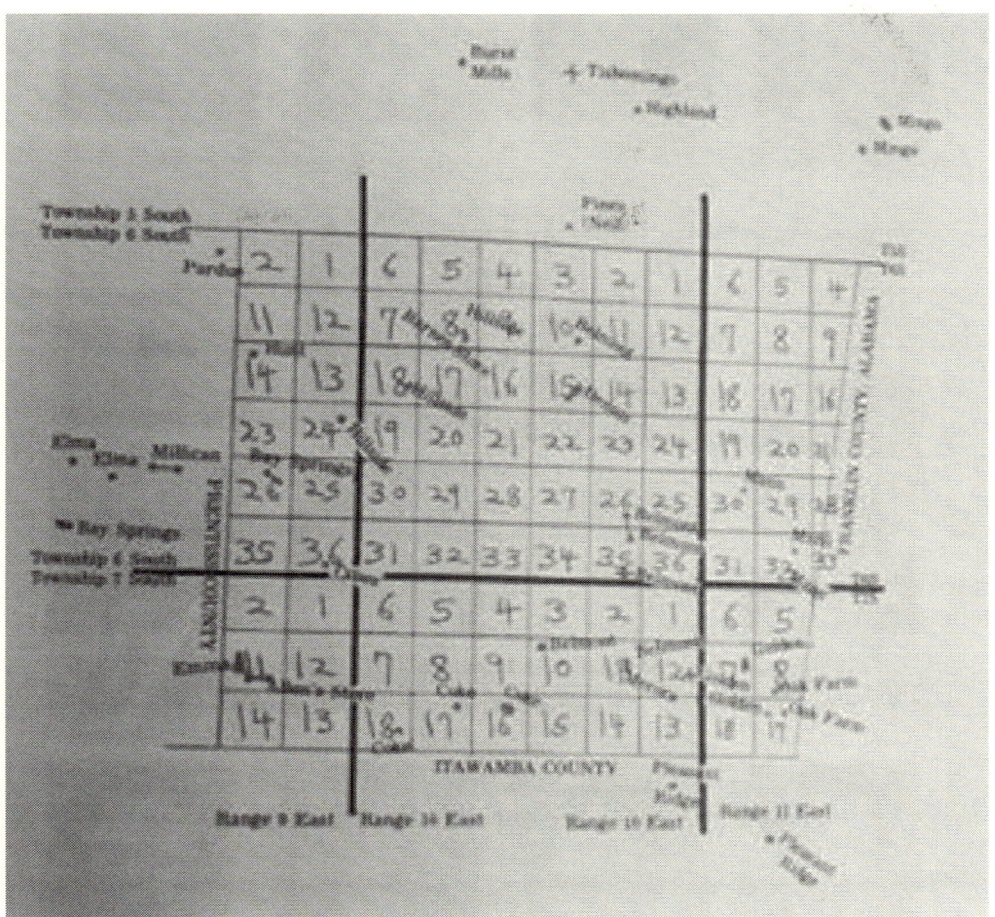

**Post offices of the Belmont area.
(Present post offices are marked with +)**

Mayors of Belmont, Mississippi. Top Row: C. C. Shook (1908-1913), G. A. Clark (1913-1915), Charles Googe (1915-1915), and T. W. Hunnicutt (1915-1917). 2nd row from top: S. L. Sumners (1917-1921), M. Arthur Shook (1921-1923), A. G. W. Byram (1923-1925, 1933-1937), and W. A. Jackson (1925-1927). 3rd row from the top: L. P. Allen (1927-1931, 1937-1945), M. P. Haynes (1931-1933), Roy P. Allen (1945-1947), and N. C. Deaton (1947-1953, 1956-1965). Bottom Row: D. F. Lambert, Jr. (1953-1956), Ralph Bowen (1965-1967), E. C. Clark (1967-1977), and Earl H. Alexander (1977-).

BIBLIOGRAPHY

I. Unpublished Manuscripts and Documents

Akers, W. R., Papers. Belmont, Mississippi.

Belmont, Town of. Minutes of meetings of Town Aldermen and Mayors, 1908-1978.

Epps, Annie, Scrapbook. Belmont, Mississippi.

Fifth District Special Consolidated School, Tishomingo County, Mississippi. Minutes of School Board, 1929-1956.

Itawamba County, Mississippi. Abstract Title Books, 1836-1870.

_____. Deed Books, 1836-1870.

Mann, Verd, Scrapbook. (In possession of Dexter Mann, Pleasant Grove, Alabama).

Mississippi. *Code*, 1906. Chapter 99, section 3299-3314.

_____. *Laws*, 1852-1884.

Mississippi Secretary of State. Records of Incorporations, 1899-1924, 1967.

_____. *Report*, 1908-1960.

Morse, William C. "The Highland Church Sandstone as a Building Stone." Mississippi State Geological Survey, *Bulletin 26*. Jackson, Miss., 1935.

National Archives Microfilm Publications. "Record of Appointment of Postmasters, 1832- September 30, 1971." Microfilm Publication M841, Rolls 67-69. Washington, D. C.: National Microfilm Publications, 1973.

Old Tishomingo County, Mississippi. Abstract Title Books, 1836-1870.

_____. Deed Record Books, 1836-1870.

_____. Records of Police Court, 1836-1862.

_____. School Fund Accounts Book, 1856-1858.

Prentiss County, Mississippi. Deed Books, 1870-1900.

Tishomingo County, Mississippi. Corporation Record Book 1.

_____. Deed Books, 1887-1945.

_____. Minutes of the Board of Supervisors, 1887-1936.

Tombigbee Baptist Association. Minutes of the Messengers, 1899, 1905.

U. S. Department of Agriculture. *Soil Survey of Tishomingo County, Mississippi*. A.C. Orvedal and Thomas Fowlkes. Series 1937, No. 10. Washington, D. C.: Government Printing Office, 1944.

U. S. Department of Commerce. *Census,* 1880-1970.

U. S. Postmaster General. Appointment Records in Itawamba, Prentiss, and Tishomingo Counties in Mississippi, 1867-1956. (Photocopies from record group 28 of the National Archives in Washington, D. C.)

_____. Topographer's Office. Relative Positions of Post Offices in Itawamba, Prentiss, and Tishomingo Counties in Mississippi, 1867-1945. (Photocopies from record group 28 of the National Archives in Washington, D. C.)

II. Books and Periodicals

Akers, W. R. *Our Kinsfolk.* Booneville, Miss.: Milwick Printing Company, 1957.

Biographical and Historical Memoirs of Mississippi. 2 volumes. Chicago: Goodspeed Publishing Company, 1891.

Booneville Centennial, 1861-1961. Booneville, Miss.: Milwick Printing Company, 1961.

Brown, Andrew. *History of Tippah County, Mississippi: The First Century.* Ripley, Miss.: The Tippah County Historical and Genealogical Society, Inc., 1976.

Cochran, Fan Alexander, comp. *History of Old Tishomingo County, Mississippi Territory.* Oklahoma City: Barnhart Letter Shop, 1969.

Evans, W. A. "Stagecoach Lines and Inns in Monroe County, Mississippi." *The Journal of Mississippi History*, IV (July, 1942), 162-167.

Federal Writers Project, W. P. A. *Mississippi A Guide to the Magnolia State.* New York, 1938.

Gilbert, Ida B. *History of Presbyterianism in Old Tishomingo County, Mississippi, 1836-1936.* Booneville, Miss., 1936.

Kirkham, E. Kay. *A Genealogical and Historical Atlas of the United States of America.* Logan, Utah, 1976.

Leftwich, Nina. *Two Hundred Years at Muscle Shoals.* Birmingham: Multigraphic Advertising Company, 1935.

Mississippi Historical Records Survey. Service Division, W. P. A. *Guide to Vital Statistics Records in Mississippi.* Volume II. Church Archives. Jackson, Miss.: The Mississippi Historical Records Survey, 1942.

_____. *Mississippi Newspapers, 1805-1940.* Jackson, Miss., 1942.

Nabors, S. M. *History of Old Tishomingo County.* Privately published by the author, 1940.

Stephens, Joe K. and Bryant, Stephen H. *Josiah Stephens and Other Heterogeneous Groups.* West Point, Miss., 1963.

Sumners, Cecil L. *The True Story of Chief Tishomingo.* Amory, Miss.: *Amory Advertiser*, 1974.

Sumners, Mary F. "Education in Ante-Bellum Tishomingo County." *The Journal of Mississippi History*, XX (October, 1958), 224-233.

Williams, Rosemary. *Cross City Chronicle.* Corinth, Miss., 1976.

Winston, E. T. *Story of Pontotoc.* Pontotoc, Miss.: Pontotoc Progress Print, 1931.

III. Newspapers

Belmont (Miss.) *Belmont and Tishomingo Journal*, 1976.

Belmont (Miss.) *Herald*, 1916-1921.

Belmont (Miss.) *Times*, 1925.

Belmont (Miss.) *Tri-County News*, 1932-1967.

Booneville (Miss.) *Independent*, 1937.

Corinth (Miss.) Daily Corinthian, 1929.

Iuka (Miss.) *Belmont Tri-County News and The Vidette*, 1967-1969.

Iuka (Miss.) *Tishomingo County News- The Vidette – Belmont News*, 1970-1971.

Iuka (Miss.) *Vidette*, 1913-1960.

Memphis *Commercial Appeal*, 1929, 1940.

Tupelo *Daily Journal*, 1953-1970.

A Place Called Belmont
1920

INDEX

A

Abel, 25
Abel, Joseph, 26
Abel, Mary, 26
Abel, William, 26
Abels, Carlton, 245
Aberdeen, 85
Aberdeen-Eastport stagecoach route, 33
Acklin, Bill, 68
Adams, M. D. L., 47
Adams, Mae, 89
Adams, Murray C., 216-217, 231
Agricola, 228
Agricultural Adjustment Act, 190
Airport Board Authority, 234
Akers, Columbus, 44
Akers, Jackson M., 44
Akers, Roger, 229
Akers, W. R., 44, 62
Akins, Will, 175
Alcorn County, 17, 48, 123, 142, 172
Alexander, Cathy, 242
Alexander, Earl H., 223, 228, 247, 260
Alexander, Steve, 233, 235
Algoma, 227
Allen, 25, 40, 139
Allen, Barcia Hood, 27
Allen, Charnel Hightower, 27, 52, 58
Allen, Conrad, 9
Allen, Cordelia, 27
Allen, Dave, 43
Allen, Guthrie, 45
Allen, Holland, 27, 29-30
Allen, J. H., 45
Allen, Jim, 87, 137
Allen, John, 30
Allen, Joseph, 26-27, 30
Allen, Kathy, 242
Allen, Kiever T., 27, 45
Allen, L. B. (Benona), 27
Allen, L.P., 58, 105, 106, 107, 119, 129, 133, 134, 137, 145, 146, 147, 152, 162, 169, 170, 173, 179, 181, 186, 198, 204, 205, 206, 208, 209, 260
Allen, Mrs. L. P. (Annie), 119, 181, 198
Allen, L. P., and Son (funeral home directors), 189
Allen Line, 3

Allen Line School, 193, 217
Allen, Pat (Roy P., Jr.) 242, 244, 247
Allen, Paul, 217, 220
Allen, Pete, Hill, 82
Allen, Roy P., 205-206, 209, 214, 217, 220, 223, 228, 260
Allen, Sarah, 26-27, 30
Allen, T. J., 42
Allen, Wister (C. W.), 27
Allen-Wright Hardware and Furniture Company, 116, 130, 133, 134, 138, 140, 147, 167, 168
Allen's Mill, 26-27
Allen's Store, 26-27, 42, 47, 50, 51, 52, 58
Allsboro, Ala., 21
Alton, Ill., 42
Amory, 10, 85
Anderson, James, 21
Anderson, Rollie (B. R.), 105, 141, 149, 150, 154, 176
Anglin, C. M., 67
Anglin, R. L., 64, 67
Apperson, D. C., 45
Appomattox Court House, 45, 46
Ardis, Dave 43, 62

Ardis, James D., 62
Armstrong, C. M., 87
Armstrong, C. W. (Wilson), 199
Arnold, Bonner, 208, 210, 228
A. S. C. S., 229-230
Ashley, George, 182
"Aunt Barb," 95
Avery, J.O., 207, 209
Ayres, 152

B

Bailey, 25, 26
Bailey, James B., 26
Bailey, Martin, 35
Baker, Frank, 115
Baker's Creek, Battle of, 42
Baldwyn, 41, 61, 162, 194
Baldwyn and Pleasant Site Road, 82
Baldwyn and Russellville Public Road (Red Bud Road), 182
Baley, C. W., 157-158
Baley, Mrs. C. W., 160
Baley, C. W., Jr., 157-158, 163, 168, 170
Bank of Belmont, 134, 147, 169, 171, 185-186, 207-208, 239
Banner, 34, 43

Barber camp, 95

Barber's Chapel 52

Barham, A. H., 174, 188, 199

Barham, Addie, 188

Barnes, G. W. (George), 195, 198, 204, 205, 208

Barnes, Samuel A., 33, 34, 43, 47

Barnes Store, 25, 33, 47, 51, 52, 53

Barnett, Ross, 234

Barnett Supply Company, 119

Barron, David, 42

Barron, W. W., 45

Barton, Armistead, 18

Bass, 55

Bass, Dave, 111

Bassfield, 210

Bates, 25

BAWI, 213

Bay Springs, 1, 3, 4, 7, 23, 27-33, 35, 36, 38, 40-41, 42, 46-47, 51, 52, 54-55, 59-62, 63, 85-86, 121-124, 125, 158, 163, 177, 221-222

Bay Springs F. & A. M. Lodge No. 167, 32, 55, 56, 59-60, 221-222

Bay Springs Union Factory, 31-33, 36, 38, 40, 46, 54-55, 59, 61

Beachum, Ann, 95

Beachum Cemetery, 27, 258

Beachum, Isabella Allen, 27

Beachum, John, 27

Beachum, John A., 27

Bear Creek, 1, 2, 3, 4, 5, 6, 9, 10, 12, 19, 21, 22, 33, 41, 52, 67-68, 72, 77, 87, 91, 93, 174, 184, 256

Bear Creek Channel, 2, 3, 5, 10, 256

Bear Creek Watershed Association, 5

Beard, Waldrep, 214

Beaty, Samuel Porter (Sam), 100, 110, 116, 118, 129

Bell, Isaac H., 18

Bellamy, W. J., 45

Belmont, climate, 5; incorporation, 110-111; location, 1; physical features, 1, 3-4; population, 71, 110-111, 120, 125, 152, 183, 205, 218, 231, 243;

Post offices and postmasters, 2, 53, 54, 55-56, 63, 71-72, 88, 100, 105, 116, 168, 172, 188, 220, 227, 235, 250, 259; Tax levies, 115, 117, 125, 151, 184, 189, 205, 207, 212, 214, 220

Belmont Band Auxiliary, 235

Belmont Blue Springs City Park, 3, 22, 54, 73, 120, 152, 224, 245-246, 248, 249, 253

Belmont Business Men's Club, 146

Belmont Cemetery, 144, 154-155, 181, 189, 204, 205-206, 225, 233, 247, 258

Belmont Chamber of Commerce, 213

Belmont Church of Christ, 115-116, 151, 152, 189, 199

Belmont Cleaners, 134

Belmont Colored First Baptist Church, 187

Belmont Concert Band, 121-123, 142

Belmont Consolidated School, 176, 182

Belmont Dollar Store, 232

Belmont Drug Company, 117, 140, 145, 198

Belmont F. & A. M. Lodge No. 237, 35, 119, 129, 149

Belmont Fabric Shop, 134

Belmont – 5th District Chamber of Commerce, 232, 234, 236

Belmont – 5th District Jaycees, 242, 244

Belmont – 5th District Jaycettes, 242

Belmont Freedom Family Fun Festival, 245-246

Belmont Hardware and Furniture Company, 115, 119

Belmont Herald, 135, 140, 145, 147-148, 156, 162

Belmont High School, Incorporation, 74

Belmont Hotel, 105, 116, 135, 169-170, 180, 181, 189

Belmont Library, 116, 154, 247

Belmont Lions Club, 236

Belmont Merchants Association, 237

Belmont Methodist Church, 115, 116, 142, 158, 189, 220

Belmont Planning Commission,

232, 243
Belmont and Pleasant Site Road, 140
Belmont Public Free School, see "Ebenezer school"
Belmont Public Park, 115, 120, 136, 164
Belmont Rescue Squad, 234, 244
Belmont Road District 142, 150
Belmont Safety Bug Park, 156, 246
Belmont Schools, 156, 228-229, 230, 233, 234, 235, 236, 237, 238, 241, 242, 243-245, 246-247, 257
Belmont Separate School, 113-114, 115, 116, 118, 125, 140, 149-150, 151, 154, 156-157, 158, 159, 160, 162-164, 169, 171, 173, 176, 207
Belmont Sportsmen Club, 236
Belmont Steak House, 148
Belmont Teacher Appreciation Night, 244
Belmont Telephone Company, 149, 199
Belmont Theatre, 210
Belmont Times, 162, 170, 174
Belmont and Tishomingo Journal, 243
Belmont Townsite Company, 96
Belmont Tri-County News, 174, 188-189, 199
Belmont Tri-County News and Vidette, 242
Belmont Washeteria, 232
Belmont Woman's Club, 180
Belmont Woodmen of the World Camp No. 518, 146, 149
Bennett, 25, 93
Bennett, A. R. (Ab), 182
Bennett, F., 50
Bennett, Francis M., 58, 76
Bennett, W. T., 119
Benson, William, 35
Bethany, 23-25, 46
Bethany Cemetery, 24, 258
Bethany Presbyterian Church, 23-25, 41
Bethany Protestant Methodist Church, 137, 182
Bethel Baptist Church, 70, 76, 91
Bethel School, 70
Bethesda Church, Battle of, 43
Bethune, Roy, 235, 245

Bible Belt, 7, 76

Bicentennial Celebration, 245-246

Big Creek, 214

Bilbo, Theodore G., 123

Billy Goat Hill, 86

Birmingham, Ala., 1, 109, 189, 195

Bishop, G. W., 127

Bishop, J. S., 239

Black Friday, 179

Black, Moman, 175

Black Monday, 232

Blanchard, John T., 100

Blue Bell, Inc., 6, 95, 116, 216-217, 218, 219, 220, 221, 232, 236, 239

Blue Hill, 208

Blue Springs, 3, 54, 152, 243, 249

Blythe, J. J., 18

Blythe's Chapel, 120

Boggs, T. C. (Billy), 209, 212, 215

Boggs, W. E., 233

Bolton Site, 10

Bond, W. F., 181

Boone, F. M., 38, 42-43

Boone, F. M., U. C. V. Camp No. 1694, 43, 109, 121, 142

Boone, Jordan M., 96

Booneville, 1, 57, 60, 77, 119, 131, 163, 169, 192, 194

Bostick, 69, 111

Bostick, A. E., 86, 98, 136-137, 147, 152, 165

Bostick, Mrs. A. E. (Mary), 136, 176

Bostick, Charles, 19, 228, 245

Bostick, Flora Belle (Mrs. Aderine), 109

Bostick, G. L., 188

Bostick, J. A., 187

Bostick, Kyle, 235

Bostick, M. A., 88

Bostick, O. E. (Orville), 229-230

Bostick theater, 161

Bostick, Tulon, 161, 173

Bostick, W. F., 69, 88, 136

Bottoms, Thomas E., 128

Bowen, Ralph, 234, 236, 237, 260

Boyd, Adron, 245

Boydson, William, 133

Brakefield, W. L., 82

Brandon, B. F., 192

Brazil, Harlon, 33
Brazil, Ruth, 62
Bridges, G. H., 87
Bridges, Mrs. J. A., 87
Bridges Mound, 10
Briggs and Gresham, 30
Briggs, Gresham, and Company, 31-32
Briggs, John, 30-32, 33
Brookhaven, 244
Brooks, H. S., 52, 53
Brown, Bud, 193
Brown, Danny, 233
Brown, John, Hill, 82
Brown, Ronnie, 238
Brown, T. J., 140, 150
Brown, Wayne, 175
Brumley, Ben, 114, 128
Brumley Branch, 2, 68, 256
Bruton, John A., 128
Bruton Mound, 9
Bullen, 2, 169
Bullen, Omer J., 169
Bullen, Robert, 34
Bullock, Joe, 234
Burgess, 25
Burgess Cemetery, 1, 6, 19, 258
Burleson, C. M., 65
Burleson, James M., 151
Burnsville, 131, 142, 194
Burnsville Good Roads District, 142
Burnt Mills, 25, 87
Burton, 199
Busby, Jeff, 89
Buskirk, Johnny, 229
Butler, James T., 43, 62
Buzzard Roost, Ala., 15
Byram, A. G. W. (Green), 65, 86, 107, 115, 116, 118, 121-122, 128, 129, 136, 137, 162, 163, 170, 173, 189, 191, 195, 196, 198, 260
Byram, Mrs. A. G. W. (Elizabeth) 116, 157, 160, 182
Byram, Alden, 21
Byram, Alford W., 43
Byram, Alfred, 21
Byram, Cavalier, 21, 45, 121
Byram Cemetery, 208, 258
Byram, Deck, 62
Byram, E. A., 195, 198
Byram, Erasmus, 21
Byram, Eupal G., 232

Byram Ford, 21, 68, 72; *see also* Rob Epps Ford
Byram Ford, Inc., 198, 246
Byram, Frances, 247
Byram, J. A., 98, 111
Byram, J. F., 66, 67
Byram, J. M., 45
Byram, Jenkins, 72
Byram, Jim (James C.), 242, 244, 246
Byram, John, 21, 46, 47, 50, 66, 94
Byram, Lorene, 239
Byram, Margaret, 242
Byram, Martha 21
Byram, Martha Blythe, 21
Byram, O. H., 203
Byram, Otis, 122
Byram, Quinn, 209
Byram, Ruby, 86
Byram, S. S. (Tinker), 65
Byram, Sarah, 86
Byram, Silas C., 18, 20, 21
Byram, William, 21

C
Cain, 67
Cain, E. L., 76, 87, 91
Cain, Faye, 210
Cai, Howard "Ram," 208-209
Cain, Kenneth, 209
Cain, L. A., 91
Cain, L. J., 43
Cain, L. K., 166, 191, 195, 204, 207, 216, 217, 220, 225, 227
Cain, Lex, 209
Cain, Margaret, 210
Cain, Marshall, 98, 166
Cain, O. M. (Cotton), 98, 219
Cain, Ralph, 233
Cain, Ruth, 238
Cain, Stella, 210
Cain, Steve, 68
Cain, Travis, 230, 236
Cain, Vaudie Mae, 215
Calhoun City, 238
Calley, Jim, 222
Calvary Baptist Church, 209
Calvert, 25
Campbell, 34
Campbell, A. B., 67, 161, 168, 209, 227
Campbell, Bill, 70
Campbell, Billy (William M.), 21, 22, 54, 65, 67, 85
Campbell Branch, 3, 67, 256

Campbell, Cora Byram, 65, 67
Campbell, Earl, 135, 143
Campbell, Guy, 209
Campbell, John, 71
Campbell, Kate, 151, 203, 235
Campbell, Lawrence L., 67
Campbell, O. G. (Olen), 176, 214
Campbell, Rachel Angeline, 22
Campbell, W. D., 67
Camp Chase, 39
Camp Morton, Indiana, 39
Camp Pike, 143
Candler, E. S., Sr., 62
Cape Fair, 33
Cape Horn, 23, 33
Cape Horn Grays, 38
Carmack, Cornelius, 24-25
Carmack, E. W., 24-25, 34, 46
Carr, Claude, 22
Carr, Luvenia, 65
Carrollville, 19, 29
Carter, 72
Carter, Kilpatrick, 15
Cashion, Gunita, 242
Caveness, Edwin (E. W.), 33, 120
Caveness, Emily, 58

Caveness, Eula Mae, 182
Caveness, Irene, 82
Caveness, James Henderson, 33
Caveness, John, 82, 182
Caveness, John, Jr., 194
Caveness, Noel, 222
Caveness School, 182
Celtics, 194
Champion's Hill, Battle of, 42
Chapel Hill Church of God, 208
Chapel Hill Church of God of Prophecy, 26
Cherokee, Ala., 161, 163, 194
Chickasaw Bluffs (Memphis), . 10, 12, 13
Chickasaw Cession, 17
Chickasaw Council House, 13, 14
Chickasaw County, 17
Chickasaws, decline, 15; duties of men, 11; duties of women, 11; legend of Lover's Leap, 28; location, 10; physical builds, 11; removal, 14, 15, 17, 19; size of nation, 11; trade policy, 12-13; treaties, 12-15; and village composition, 10-11

Chief Itawamba, *see* Levi Colbert

Chief Tishomingo, *see* Tishomingo, Chief

Chinnubby, King of Chickasaws, 13

Chinquapin Ridge, 10

Choate, Mart, 45

Choctaws, 12, 13, 14, 15

Christmas of 1836, 19

Christmas of 1918, 145

Christmas of 1929, 182-183

Christmas of 1938, 199-200

Christmas of 1945, 212

Chumbley, Andy, 244

Cincinnati, 18

City of Miami, 102

Civil Defense, 231

Civilian Conservation Corps (CCC), 190-191

Civil War (War Between the States), 25, 35, 37-46, 47, 109

Clark, 71, 72, 237

Clark, A. G., 50

Clark, Arvis, 223

Clark, E. C. (Zeke), 234, 237, 238, 241, 244, 260

Clark, G. A. (Dick), 47, 72, 74, 83, 86, 89, 107, 118, 119, 126, 129, 131-132, 136, 141, 144, 237, 260

Clark, Henry, 208

Clark, James A. (Jim), 107, 110, 115, 117, 118, 126, 129, 137, 141, 145, 146, 148, 149, 154, 171, 184, 189

Clark, Mrs. James M., 47

Clark, Jeanette, 210, 215

Clark, John Henry, 47, 54, 58, 71-72, 86, 98, 100, 101, 110, 113, 115, 140

Clark, Julia, 215

Clark, Julia Ann, 72

Clark, Julius Taylor, 43

Clark, Julius U., 71, 140, 171, 187, 195, 216

Clark, Leland, 214

Clark, Martha, 70

Clark, Mary L. D. (Mollie), 44, 72, 189

Clark, Sarah Ann, 47

Clark, T. A., 89, 119, 125, 132, 140, 143, 183

Clark, W. T., 41, 44, 47, 54, 58, 71-72, 74, 95, 107, 113, 115, 118, 189

Clark, W. T., and Son, 107, 126, 145
Clark, W. T., Store, 71
Clark, Will, 95
Clark's Gin, 56, 71
Claude's Dollar Store, 147
Clay community, 91
Clay, H. R., 195, 201
Clement, 25, 180
Clement, D. W., 137, 147
Clement, Emma, 220
Clement, J. C., Jr., 242
Clement, J. E., 113, 147, 150, 151, 164, 166, 170, 180, 210, 220
Clement, J. E., Lumber Co., 180
Clement, J. W., 21
Clement planer, 120, 166
"Clement school," 113, 115; *see also* Belmont Separate School
Clement, W. A., 164
Clement-Woodruff Lumber Co., 166
Cleveland, 215
Cleveland, Evie Harris, 92, 110
Cleveland, Webster, 93, 148, 154-155, 189, 191, 193, 195, 197, 198, 204, 205, 207, 208, 242
Cleveland, Webster, Jr., 215
Cliff, 152
Clingan, G. W., 39
Clingan, G. W., Jr., 45
Clingan, J. A., 86, 127
Clingan, Jackie, 239
Clingan, Laura Bridges, 86
Clingan, Mary, 23
Clingan, S. J., 52
Clingan, Sarah Elizabeth 52
Clingan, W. J., 52
Clingan, W. M., 52
Clingan, William, 23
Cobb, 25
Cobb, James H., 43, 44
Cobb, Martha, 44
Cobb, Mary Lou (Mollie), 44
Coffee, John, 14
Coffeeville, Battle of, 39
Coffin, Mrs. M. E., 137
Coggins, Conwell, 233, 234
Coke, 70, 87
Colbert, 14
Colbert, George, 13
Colbert, Levi, 13, 14, 15
Cole, 25
Cole, A. F., 70, 76

Cole, E. A., 82
Coleman, J. P., State Park, 232, 236
Collier, Henry, 32
Collier, Jack, 42
Collier, W. H., 165, 187, 195, 201
Collum, John E., 151
Colson, Roy C., 174, 181
Colson, Mrs. Roy C., 181
Comer, Jesse, 232, 236, 237
Commercial Appeal, 180-181, 199
Condry, Benjamin, 18, 21
Confederate Veterans Reunions, 60, 109, 121-124, 142
Conner, Martin S. (Mike), 190
Constitution of 1869, 49, 50
Continental Trailways, 6
Conwill, 66
Conwill, M. C., 70
Cook, Gene, 10
Cook, Henry, 18
Cook, Jeff (T. J.), 217
Cook, Leighvelia, 182
Cook, Leon, 7, 238, 241, 244
Cooper, 244
Cooper, Clyda, 135

Copeland, Alcanda (Dit), 51-52, 135-136, 143-144, 152
Copeland, Mrs. Alcanda (Mittie), 135, 164
Copeland, Alice, 51
Copeland, Fae, 135, 144
Copeland, Jim, 52
Copeland, Morton, 135
Copeland, Orlando, 51-52
Copeland, Oscar, 52, 133, 134, 154
Copeland Telephone Company, 149, 154
Copeland, Thomas E., 51
Copeland, Walter Kelley, 135
Copeland, Winona, 135
Corinth, 1, 37, 85, 102, 131, 135, 141, 142, 161, 194, 196, 206
Cornelius, E. C., 64
Cornelius, John C., 111
Cotton Gin Port, 10
Cotton Ridge, 26
Cotton Springs Missionary Baptist Church, 137
Cotton Springs School, 63, 137, 182, 188, 217
County Line Road, 110, 138
C and P Auto Supply, 122, 143,

Crabb, 203
Crabb, D. H., 209
Crabb, John, 203
Crabb, Kirk, 122, 202
Crabb, W. W., 165
Crane, Dennis W., 64, 66
Crane, J. W., 156, 165
Cranford, 73, 156, 224
Cranford, C. H., 76, 139, 165, 188
Cranford, J. R., 76, 88, 224
Cranford, M. D., 70
Cranford, Mary Almedia, 151, 156, 164, 176
Cranford, Nancy, 52
Cranford, S. J., 52
Cranford, W. L., 74, 113, 116, 118, 135, 152, 157
Credille, Andrew, 81
Credille, Arthur, 4
Credille, Charlene, 210
Credille, Dillard, 75
Credille, J. C. (Jack), 43
Credille, Margaret Stacy, 81
Credille, Tom, 157
Creel, 111
Creel, W. R., 187

Cromeans, Claude, 136, 152-153, 191, 195, 198-199, 204, 205, 208, 233-234
Cromeans, Larry, 242
Cross, Robert, 227
Crouch and Hellums, 138
Crouch, R. C. (Bob), 120-122, 138, 145
Crow, Verna Wood, 54
Crowe, Dot, 228
Crowe, Etta Rae, 228
"Cumberland lands," 12
Cumberland Presbyterian Church, 26
Cumberland Telephone and Telegraph Company, 127
Cummings, Levi M., 188, 191, 195
Cunningham, Andy, 45
Cunningham, Riley, 45
Curtis, R. L., 152
C. W. A., 193

D
Dailey, John, 45
Davis, 62
Davis, Audie, 175

Davis, Becky, 44
Davis, Belle, 94, 100, 101
Davis, Bud, 214, 229
Davis, Buster, 209, 214, 228-229
Davis, C. W., 113-114
Davis, Catherine R., 52, 62
Davis, E. C., 213
Davis, Ernie, 175
Davis, G. W., 59, 125
Davis, Garland, 69
Davis, Harmon, 234
Davis, Harold, 94
Davis, Harriet, 128
Davis, Hubert (H. R.), 59, 184, 188, 191, 204, 207, 208, 209, 214, 216, 217, 220, 223, 229
Davis, J. R., 98
Davis, J. W. (Bill), 235
Davis, Mrs. J. W. (Mrs. Bill), 157
Davis, Jane (Mrs. Matthew), 20
Davis, Jefferson, 37, 38, 46
Davis, Kindle, *see* Bud Davis
Davis, L. L., 148, 164, 171, 173
Davis, L. R., 54, 64, 93, 94, 96, 100, 101, 166
Davis, L. R., Store, 64, 96, 100
Davis, Luna C. (Mrs. L. L.), 171, 188, 220, 235
Davis, M. G. (Mack), 165
Davis, M. M. (Mid), 43-44, 47, 53, 54, 63-64, 78, 91, 92, 93, 96, 112
Davis, M. M., Jr., *see* Major Davis
Davis, M. M., and Son Store, 91, 92
Davis, Major, 91, 93, 112, 138
Davis, Mary, 93
Davis, Mary Jane, 92
Davis Mills, 64
Davis, N. S. (Pole), 64, 93, 96, 101, 165
Davis, Nancy, 93
Davis, Ransom, 47, 52, 55
Davis, Roy, 209
Davis, S. J., 182
Davis Store, 53
Davis, Vaudrie, 94
Davis, Vinnia, 93
Davis, Walter, 169
Davis, Willard Faye, 215
Davis, Willis M., 50, 58, 128
Davis, Windle, *see* Buster Davis
D Day (Normandy), 209
Dean, T. H., 127, 140, 144, 146,

216, 219
Deaton, 67
Deaton, Amy, 147
Deaton, Bobbie, 215
Deaton, Bonifaye, 215
Deaton, Ellis (L. E.), 157, 212, 215, 216, 232, 236
Deaton Funeral Home, 107, 110, 217, 233
Deaton, G. P., 128
Deaton, Gary, 244-245
Deaton, H. L., 166, 184, 209
Deaton, H. S., 64, 87
Deaton, Joe, 2
Deaton, L. A., 67
Deaton, L. H., 151
Deaton Lake, 196
Deaton, Lewis Jackson, 33
Deaton, N. C. (Noonan), 120, 141, 214, 216, 217, 219, 227, 229, 231, 260
Deaton, Robert, 235
Deaton, Verda Mae, 147
Deaton, Verona, 147
Demopolis, Ala., 42
Dennis, 1, 2, 3, 4, 6, 7, 19, 23, 25, 33, 39, 44, 53, 62, 63, 64, 66, 77, 83, 86, 87, 88, 91, 93, 96, 98, 100, 101, 102, 110-111, 120, 127, 128, 131, 133, 151, 152, 163, 165, 166, 183, 193, 195, 199, 201-203, 205, 208, 209, 218, 219, 234, 235
Dennis Methodist Church, 128
Dennis population, 111, 120, 152, 183, 205
Dennis School, 128
Denson, J. H., 222
Denson, John, 243
Denson Radio and TV, 148
Denson, Ray, 64
Depression, *see* Great Depression
Derma, 210
De Soto, 11
De Soto County, 17, 21
Dexter, Dixie, 160
Dickinson, Betty Jo, 245
Dickinson, W. B., 69
Dickinson, W. P., 87
Dill, Donnie, 238
Dixie Store, 180
Doaksville, Treaty of, 15
Dobbs, Flora, 244
Dobbs Grocery Store, 189
Dobbs, John, 189

Dodd, W. R., 82
Donelson and Martin Treaty, 12
"Doodlebug," 79, 102, 103, 109, 168
Doty, W. E., 213
Duckworth, 66
Duncan, Curtis, 223
Duncan, J. W., 45
Duncan, Thomas M. (Tom), 178, 223, 227

E
Eason, Cliff, 169
Eastland, James O., 236
Eastport, 2, 30, 33, 38, 208
Eastport and Aberdeen Public Road, 34
Eastport and Fulton Road, 63
Eastport and Pikeville Road, 69
East Prentiss, 35, 62, 119
East Prentiss School, 192, 193, 199
Eaton, John, 14
Eaton, John E., 73
Eaton, Lee, 193
Eaton, O. T., 204, 207
Ebenezer Baptist Church, 74, 75, 76, 82, 91, 109; *see also* First Baptist Church
Ebenezer Missionary Baptist Church (Washington Street), 209
"Ebenezer school," 74-75, 89, 90, 113, 150, 156
Economic Opportunity Act of 1964, 233
Ecru, 190, 237
E. D. A., 245
Edmondson, R. C., 131
Effie's Café, 128
Elledge, J. R., 164
Elledge, Walter, 74
Elledge, Willie, 89-91
Elledge, Wister, 136, 168
Ellis, Tom Q., 222
Elma, 35, 62, 119
Embrey, A. J., 45
Embrey, Kenneth, 67
Embrey, W., 34
Emma, 58, 82
Epps, 69, 111, 184-185
Epps, Annie, 185
Epps, Cleo, 172
Epps, Edgar, 145
Epps, Elbridge (W. E.), 43, 184-185

Epps, G. B., 39
Epps, J., 58
Epps, J. I. (Jim), 68, 98
Epps, J. I., Ford, 68
Epps, J. O. (Oscar), 165
Epps, Lela, 172, 232
Epps, Levi, 86, 135, 145
Epps, Levi (Civil War soldier), 43
Epps, Mrs. Levi, 145
Epps, Rob, Ford, 21, 68, 72
Epps, W. F., 187
Etheridge, W. S., 166
Euclid Academy, 24-25
Evans, Jesse, 21
Evergreen Baptist Church, 76
Ezzell, Bill, 22

F

Faircloth, James H., 127
Fairview, 75-76
Fancher, 69
Fancher, Alexander, 43, 50
Fancher, H. B. (Bud), 69
Fancher, Larry, 235, 237
Fanchertown, 10, 17, 35, 41, 50, 52, 68-69, 169
Farley, William, 26

Farmer, A. F., 45
Farmers Union, 68
Farmington, 194
Fayette, Ala., 147
Federal Emergency Administration, 196
Ferguson, Belle D., 82
Ferguson, Bob, 105
Ferguson, Dick, 105, 115
Ferguson, Mrs. Dick, 115
Ferguson, Frank, 105
Ferguson, Frank (Civil War soldier), 39
Ferguson, James, 45
Ferguson, W. T. (Willie), 105
Ferguson, Will, 82
Fifth District Airport, 234
Fifth District Special Consolidated School, 182, 184, 186-187, 188, 191-194, 195, 197-198, 199, 204, 207, 208-209, 210, 212, 214, 215, 216, 217, 219, 220, 223-224, 225, 228
Fifth District, Tishomingo County, population, 57, 77, 120, 152, 183, 205, 218, 231, 243

Files, Carl, 161-162
Files, I. C. (Clint), 131, 135
Files, W. H., 18, 28, 29
Finch, J. D., 169
First Baptist Church, 82, 115, 116, 119, 155, 189, 218, 233
First Baptist Church (Kossuth), 172
First Citizens National Bank, 239
First National Bank of Iuka, 241
Fish, Wallace, 175
Flashel Lumber Company, 193
Flat, 69
Flat Rock, 67
Fleemon, Roy, 182
Florence, Ala., 28
Florence, Miss., 241, 242
Flurry, Charlie, 64, 82, 88, 93-94, 100, 101, 151, 165
Flurry, J. T., 58
Flurry, James G., 128
Flurry, Jean, 215
Flurry, Lillie Cleo Davis, 65, 100, 101
Flurry, R. D., 65
Flurry, R. E., 195, 201, 209
Flurry, R. F., 72, 111, 128

Flynn, Mollie, 225
Flynt, Charlie, 89
Ford, John, 187
Forest Hill, 228, 229
Fort Benning, Georgia, 190
Fort Coffee, 15
Fort Donelson, Tennessee, 39
Fort Towson, Oklahoma, 15
Forty-second Mississippi, 44
Foster School, 64, 128
Fowler, Amelia, 86
Fowler Branch, 2, 68, 256
Fowler, Robert W., 62
Frankfort, Ala., 19
Frankfort- Carrollville Road, 19, 22
Franklin County, Ala., 22, 215
Franklin, Jesse, 13
Franklin, Mary (Mrs. David), 20
Franklin, Tennessee, 14
Franklin Treaty, 14
Franks, Pomp, 145
Frederick, N. H., 66
Freedman's Bureau, 49
Freedom Hills, 2, 6, 77, 175, 198
Freedom Hill Stock and Poultry Farm, 180
Freeman, Orville, 229

Free State of Tishomingo, 17, 23, 47; *see also* Old Tishomingo County
French, Fae Copeland, 144
Friendship Church, 35, 62
Friendship Grange No. 305, 55
Frost, W. A., 164
Fry, John B., 21, 22
Fugitt, Audie, 122
Fugitt, Eula, 133
Fugitt, Gladys, 133
Fugitt, Lucy, 132-133
Fuller Branch, 3, 4, 256
Fuller, C. L. (Calvin), 173, 208
Fuller, E. G., 87
Fulton, 1, 135, 194, 229
Fulton-Iuka Road, 40, 62, 82, 83, 120
Fulton, J. P., 212, 214, 215
Fulton, J. P., Jr., 110
Fulton, Ruth Stockton (Mrs. J. P., Jr.), 110, 223, 246
Furr, E. S., 220

G
Gable, James, 45
Gahagan, "Hoss," 196
Gaines, John Strother, 27, 38
Gamble, Luther (Peanut), 168, 169, 184
Gannaway, Edmond, 26
Gardner, Frank, 64, 175
Gardner, Mrs. Frank, 64
Garrett, Lalla, 215
Garth, Jesse W., 18
Gates, P. A., 73
Gatlin, Bud, 175
Gatlin, Shack, 175
Gee Ford, 68
Gentry, Willie, 222
George, J. C., 52
George, Lester, 120
Gettysburg, Battle of, 44
Gilbert, 73
Gilbert, Annie O., 107, 113, 164, 205
Gilbert, Carroll, 84
Gilbert, Charlie, 160, 164
Gilbert, Ed (W. E.), 72, 75, 76, 81, 164, 205
Gilbert, Mary Jane, 21, 75
Gilbert, W. W., 50, 75-76
Gillenwaters, E. C., 30
Gilley, 64
Gilley, C. B., 176

Gilley, Evelyn, 157
Gilley, Ruth, 164
Gilley, T. A. (Tom), 107, 113, 115, 125, 171, 173, 196, 204, 205, 208, 209, 214
Gilley, Mrs. T. A. (Carrie), 119
Gin Branch, 3, 28, 59, 124, 256
Ginn, Davy, 245
Ginn, Ed, 173
Ginn, Harold (Gabby), 247
Ginn, O. B. (Owen), 235, 245
Gipson, Frank E., 52
Gober, Era Mae, 183
Gober, "Lef," 168
Gober and Strickland, 164, 183
Gober, W. T. (Bill), 143, 147, 156, 169, 174, 179, 183, 186
Golden, 1, 2, 4, 6, 10, 17, 50, 68, 69, 77, 83, 87, 91, 94, 96, 98, 99, 100, 102, 110-112, 120, 131, 133, 136, 151, 152, 163, 165, 172, 174-176, 183, 187-188, 193, 195, 201, 205, 209, 218, 220, 229, 230, 231, 232, 233, 235, 238, 241, 243, 245, 247
Golden Chapel United Methodist Church, 169, 238
Golden Methodist Church, 111, 137, 189, 238
Golden population, 111, 120, 152, 183, 205, 218, 231, 243
Golden Saw Mill, 151-152, 174-176, 193, 205
Golden School, 94, 111, 189, 220, 233
Golden Townsite Company, 98
Goodhue, W. H., 173
Good Springs, 24
Goodwin, 56, 71
Goodwin, D. P., 222
Goodwin, Fred, 174
Goodwin, Sam, 140
Googe, Charles, 116, 137, 138, 260
Googe, Henry, 128
Gordon, Julia, 182
Goyer, Homer H., 135
Graham, S. J., 166
Grange, 54, 55
Grant, Ulysses, 46
Gray, A. A., 91
Gray, James, 229
Gray, John, 166
Great Depression, 179-201, 204
Green, Bill, 175

Green, W. G. 135
Greene, 191
Greene, Anna Wright, 119
Greene, Benton, 118, 127
Greene, J. C., 169
Greene, L. S., 107, 119, 134
Greenville, South Carolina, 23
Greenwood, 228
Greenwood, D. G., 21
Gresham, 35, 39
Gresham, G. N. G., 39
Gresham, George, 28-29, 32
Gresham, James Files, 29-33, 34, 35, 36, 38-39, 45, 46, 60
Gresham, Keziah Lacy, 30
Gresham, Savilla Tipton, 32
Gresham, W. G. C. (Billie), 30
Gresham's Mills, 28-29, 31
Griffin, Brooks, 135
Griffin, Claire, 245
Griffin Home and Auto Supply, 232
Griffin, Hoyt, 194, 216, 219, 220, 223
Griffin, John T., 96
Griffin, L. E. (Leonard), 234
Griffin, Tawanna, 243
Griffin, V. T., 208, 209, 216, 219

Grimsley, A. M., 147
Grisham, W. W. (Wesley Waters), 237
Grissom, D. N., 136
Grissom, Lucy, 143, 155
Grissom, Marion, 143, 155
Groover, Massey, 66
Gum Springs, 3, 54, 198, 243
"Gum Springs school," 22, 54, 73
Guntersville, Ala., 10
Guntown, 158
Gurley, J. M., 73
Gurley, W. H., 64, 72-73, 128

H

Hackleburg, Ala., 102, 163, 213
Hagins, Elizabeth, 160, 170
Hale, A. P., 172
Hale, Audie, 175
Hale, D. J., 98
Hale Ford, 68
Hale, Iva, 172
Hale, J. W., 58
Hale, Joab, 34, 43
Hale, Lillie, 98
Hale, M. J., 98, 111, 195
Hale, N. A., 98

Hale, Ozema Epps, 68
Hale, Tom, 172, 187
Hale, W. J., 69
Haley, Enoch, 69
Haleyville, Ala., 85, 102, 161, 163
Hall, A. G., 175
Hall, A. R., 147
Hall, L. E., 189
Hall, T., 98
Hallmark, 157, 237
Hallmark, Bertie, 70, 168, 172, 176, 235
Hallmark, Chester (G. C.), 70, 143, 146, 149, 151
Hallmark, Elwood, 222
Hallmark, G. W., 21
Hallmark, Jesse, 18, 21, 156
Hallmark, Mrs. Jesse (Mary), 21
Hallmark, Jesse Cummings, 58, 72, 74, 113, 151, 155-156
Hallmark, Mrs. Jesse Cummings (Elizabeth), 81
Hallmark, John C., 74, 113, 128, 129, 150, 151, 164
Hallmark, John Lumpkin, 122, 148, 153, 154, 155, 156, 162, 168, 172, 235

Hallmark, Kiziah, 21
Hallmark, Mary, 242
Hallmark, Wells (J. W.), 169, 170, 173, 174
Hamill, M. N., 210
Hamilton, 235
Hamilton, Bent, 65
Hamilton, Ella Sartain, 65
Hamilton, Sylvia, 215
Hamilton, W. H., 91
Hammett, 25
Hammett, Alton, 26
Hammett, C. C. (Columbus), 26, 83, 165
Hammett, P. E., 70
Hammett, R. J., 76
Hammett, Sarah, 26
Hampton, 34
Haney, James, 26
Haney, T. P., 198
Hankins, Christeen, 223
Harden, Delmus, 243
Hardy, A. W., 32
Hargett, Herbert, 214
Hargett, Lauree, 210
Hargett, P. T., 152
Hargett, Rob, 175
Hargett, S. B., 195, 235

Harris, 87
Harris, Anna 96
Harris, Basil, 93, 96
Harris, Bud, Pond, 2
Harris, Mrs. C. M., 93
Harris, C.P., 52
Harris, Charlie C., 45, 121
Harris, Clyne (Windle C.), 223, 228-229, 230
Harris, Cora L, 86-87
Harris Crossing, 86
Harris, F. L. (Finess), 63, 91, 96, 98
Harris, George (G. F.), 87, 184, 188, 195, 198, 204, 230
Harris, Guy, 225
Harris, Hershel, 216, 219, 227, 229, 234, 241
Harris, Ira O., 140, 176
Harris, Irene, 223
Harris, J. G. (Bud), 91
Harris, J. M., 52
Harris, James W., 151
Harris, John C., 52
Harris, Lee R., 195, 204, 205, 208
Harris, Loammi, 98, 100, 111, 137

Harris, M. L. (Fayette), 77, 92, 93, 96, 116, 138, 148
Harris, Mrs. M. L. (Parthenia), 77, 92, 93
Harris, Nim, 170, 180-181
Harris, Mrs. Nim, 180-181
Harris, Polly Ann, 93
Harris, Sarah, 210
Harris, Turner, 86
Harris, W. H., 52
Harris, William, 45
Harris, Windle C., *see* Clyne Harris
Harrison, 67
Harrison Branch, 3, 67, 256
Harrison, Glen, 242, 244, 247
Harrison, J. M., 64, 76, 91
Harrison, Zeke, 64, 228
Hart, William J., 38, 46, 54
Hartford Musical Institute, 167
Hartsell, William, 50
Hartsfield, W. W., 137
Hastings, 217
Hatley, 194, 238, 243, 244
Hattisburg, 173
Haynes, Bill, 161-162
Haynes Chevrolet, 184
Haynes, Dave, 188

Haynes, Ernest, 161
Haynes, James E., 128
Haynes, John W., Jr., 128
Haynes Lake (Three Hollows), 187
Haynes Lake (Tishomingo State Park), 232
Haynes, M. P. (Prim), 146, 147, 154, 161, 169, 170, 176, 186, 187, 189, 198, 232, 234, 236, 243, 260
Haynes, M. P., Lumber Co., 166
Hazeldell, 9
Heflin, W. W., 217
Hellums, John, 120, 121
Hellums, Raymond, 166
Hellums, Tom, 98
Helton, Orville, 223
Helton, Mrs. Orville (Yvlette), 223
Henley, 70
Henley, Elbert, 182
Henley, Gerald, 233, 235, 236
Henley, J. S., 91
Henry, W. D., 152
Hernando, 242
Herring, Edith, 160
Hester, C. H., 62
Hester, Mrs. C. H., 62
Hester, J. P., 67, 87
Hester, Will, 87
Hicks, 125, 166
Hicks, Aubrey, 2
Hicks, B. L. (Fayette), 113, 119, 128, 134, 143, 146, 147, 164, 166, 171
Hicks, C. L. (Lee), 70, 94, 118, 136, 148, 153, 155, 156, 162, 166, 169, 171
Hicks-Mann Lumber Company, 166
Higginbottom, 244
Highland, 25, 33, 53
Highland Baptist Church, 91
Highland Conference, 233, 235, 237, 238
Hill, 68
Hill County, Texas, 27, 58
Hill, Jake, 45
Hill, John, 45
Hill, Ransom, 21, 22
Hillside, 25, 52, 62, 86-87
Hillside-Rara Avis mail route, 69, 71
Hillside-Shottsville, Ala., mail route, 52

Hiroshima, 211
Hitler, Adolf, 201, 204, 210
Hodge, J. M., 21
Hodges, Bill, 86
Hodgkinson, Mrs. W. H., 189
Holcomb, Arthur, 173
Holcomb, Brooks, 221
Holcomb, G. W., 91
Holcomb, Henry, 222-223, 228, 241, 244, 245, 247
Holcomb, W. H., 70, 91
Holcut, 194
Holder, O. T., 18
Holley, Harold, 245
Holley, Shara Sparks, 247
Hollingsworth, Herbert, 225
Holly Branch, 3, 166, 256
Holly Springs, 39
Holmes, H. K., 165
Holt, John, 64
Holtsford, E. C., 242
Hood, John, 27
Hood, Maggie Lou, 187
Hood, S. H., 187
Hopewell, Treaty of, 12
Hopkins, 21, 34, 71, 73
Hopkins, Benjamin (Ben), 21-22, 34, 73, 156

Hopkins, Frank (B. F.), 21, 22, 43, 73, 121
Hopkins, H. B., 21
Hopkins, J. A., 21
Hopkins, J. B., 98
Hopkins, J. I. C., 21, 50, 54, 70-71, 98
Hopkins, John I. C., Store, 54, 70-71
Hopkins, Larkin C., 21
Hopkins, Lucinda A. (Bam), 21; *see also* Bam (L. A.) Vinson
Hopkins, M. J., 54
Hopkins, Margaret, 52
Hopkins, Mary Campbell, 22, 73
Hopkins, "Mary Frank," 73
Hopkins, R. S., 21
Hopkins, Sarah (Sallie), 73
Hopkins, W. A., 21
Hopper, T. J., 73
Horn Grocery, 6
Horn, Oco, 19, 67, 184
Houston, R. K., 208
Houston, S. L., 35
Howell, 233
Howell, Abe, 45
Howell, E. A., 45
Howell, Jack, 222

Hubbard, J. F., 191
Hughes, Charles, 73
Hughes, Goodlow, 65
Hughes, H. C., 220
Hughes, Jerry, 247
Hughes, Kermit, 175
Hundley, W. M., 73
Hunnicutt, T. W. (Tom), 138, 141, 146, 147, 149, 154, 156, 164, 173, 260
Hunt, 87
Hunt, David, 45
Hunt, Joseph, 21, 46, 47, 50
Hunt, O. L., 232
Hunt, William Henry, 87
Hutcheson, Tom, 176-177

I

Illinois Central Railroad, 1, 6, 85, 95, 97, 98, 99, 101, 102, 107, 109, 110, 112, 140, 168, 193, 213, 222, 225, 249, 252
Independent Utilities Corporation, 193
Inland Utilities Company, 173, 174, 188
Isbell, George, 120
Ishtehotopah, 14-15
Itawamba County, 2, 17, 19, 25, 27, 29, 34, 50-52, 91, 105, 119, 152, 175, 187, 193, 208, 215
Itawamba Junior College, 193, 229
Iuka, 1, 6, 33, 38, 39, 40-41, 57, 58, 62, 66, 77, 83, 89, 91, 119, 131, 143, 145, 183, 199, 233, 234, 238, 241, 242, 243
Iuka, Battle of, 40-41
Iuka-Fulton Road, 143, 171, 214
Iuka Hardware Company, 107, 119
Iuka-Pikeville, Ala., mail route, 53
Iuka-Pikeville, Ala., Road, 52, 66
Iuka-Ryan's Well mail route, 47
Ivey, Coolidge, 214
Ivy, 25
Ivy, Arah W., 173, 178, 216, 246
Ivy, Arnelia, 137
Ivy, C. L., 173, 182
Ivy, Carroll, 242
Ivy, Ella, 182
Ivy, Houston, 229, 231
Ivy, John, 70, 137

Ivy, Otha, 220, 235
Ivy, Rada, 223
Ivy, Rebecca, 182
Ivy, Sim, 137, 173

J
Jacaw Lumber Company, 148
Jacinto, 18, 25, 34, 38
Jacinto Courthouse, 18
Jacinto Foundation, Inc., 18
Jacinto-Russellville Road, 24
Jacks, W. G., 192
Jackson, 25, 72, 88, 89
Jackson, Amanda Millican, 72, 88, 120
Jackson, Andrew, 13, 14, 24
Jackson, Arthur (W. A.), 70, 84, 121-122, 171, 176, 260
Jackson, Belle, 72, 116; *see also* Mrs. B. N. Patterson
Jackson County, Ala., 23
Jackson, Ezekiel, 83
Jackson, George S., 72, 81, 83, 88, 89, 95, 113, 118, 127, 128, 134, 135, 137, 141, 144
Jackson, Jesse (J. C.), 70, 72, 116

Jackson, Luther A., 72, 74, 127, 158, 164, 191, 195
Jackson Meeting House, 83
Jackson, Miss., 1, 24, 39, 42, 60, 197, 247
Jackson, Ollie Kizer, 127
Jackson Purchase, 13
Jackson, Tommy, 83
James, Barbara, 238
James, Billy (Reman), 247
James, Claudius, 175
James, Eddie, 237
James, Rob, 175
James, T. E. (Tom), 165, 186
Jefferson, Thomas, 12-13
Jeffreys, Gainer, 29
Joel, 66
Joel Cemetery, 7, 66, 85, 87, 129, 258
Joel, Elizabeth (Mrs. John), 20
Joel, John, 18, 20
Johnson, 102
Johnson, Mrs. B. L. (Lera), 157
Johnson, D. D., 119, 136, 146, 147, 148, 149, 152, 153, 164, 170, 215, 234
Johnson, Mrs. D. D., 198, 234
Johnson, Donald, 228

Johnson, Durell, 87, 173
Johnson, Herman, 222
Johnson, J. C., 65
Johnson, J. P., 162, 170, 174
Johnson, Newt, 177
Johnson, T. J., 76
Johnson's Island, Ohio, 39, 43
Johnston, Garvin, 244
Johnston, Thomas H., Jr., 196
Jordan Creek, *see* Jourdan Creek
Jordan, Ed, 175
Jordan, Enoch, 50, 58
Jordan, J. H., 33
Josh Pond, 3
Joslin, Beatrice, 70
Jourdan Creek, 3, 33, 256
Jourdan Hill, 33, 211
Jourdan, J. C., 66
Jourdan, J. C., Drug Co., 145
Jourdan, J. M., 45
Jourdan, W. A., 45
Jowell, *see* Joel

K

Kay, Joe, 73
Kaydee Metal Company, Inc., . 238
Keith, Ernest, 105
Keller, W. M., 187
Kelly, J. George, 33
Kemp, J., 18
Kemp, Mike, 242
Kendrick, Carroll, 123
Kennedy, W. R., 165
Kennesaw Mountain, Battle of, 44
Keys, Noble, 239
Kinard, Luther, 215
Kirk, Ruth, 128
Kizer, Ben J., 38, 127
"Know Mississippi Better" Train, 172-173
Kosciusko, 242
Kossuth, 131, 142, 172
Ku Klux Klan, 49, 123

L

Lacenberry, Elmer, 182
Lacy, W. C., 30
Ladd, Thomas H., 55
Lafayette County, 17
Lambert, Bobby, 214
Lambert, D. F., Jr., 220, 225, 227, 260
Lambert, J. H. (Jim), 115, 135, 151, 173, 176

Lancaster, 86
Lancaster Cemetery, 3, 86, 258
Lane, Myrtle Mae, 182
Langston, J. D., 157, 163
Leatherwood, W. A., 76
Lee, George, 30
Lee, Robert E., 44, 45, 46
Leedy (Berea), 143, 166
Legion Field, 231
Lennon, Joseph, 96
Lentz, J. C., 199
Leslie, 42
Leslie, Jerry, 69
Liberty Christian Church, 64-65
Liberty Church of Christ, 65, 95, 115, 234, 244
Liberty Loans, 143
Liberty school, 65
Lindsey, A. L., 195
Lindsey, Bazzle L., 20
Lindsey, Caleb, 18
Lindsey, Carroll, 20
Lindsey Cemetery, 19, 39, 135, 258
Lindsey, Clabe (M. C.), 20, 39, 43, 121
Lindsey, Elisabeth, 20
Lindsey, Elizabeth McClurkin, 19, 20, 39
Lindsey Ford, 68
Lindsey, H. E., 201, 209
Lindsey, Holland, 20
Lindsey, J. P., 128
Lindsey, J. T., 64
Lindsey, James, 20, 29
Lindsey, M. W. (Mike), 20, 66
Lindsey, Martha Bullen, 39
Lindsey, Mary, 20
Lindsey, Micajah, 18, 19, 20, 21, 39
Lindsey, Myrtie, 86
Lindsey, T. B. (Tom), 20, 39, 43, 50, 58, 62, 64-66, 83, 113, 115- 116, 118, 121, 126, 129
Lindsey, Thomas Oscar, 94, 128, 203
Lindsey, W. H., 58, 63, 111, 127
Lindsey, William Carroll, 18, 19, 20, 21, 22, 34, 39
Lindsey, Willie B., 192, 199
Little, Henry, 40-41
Livingston, Verda Mae, 154
Livingston, W. A. (Blackie), 154, 199
Long, A. J., 98
Long, C. M., 91

Long, Hollis E., 232, 245, 247
Long, J. C. (Calvin), 238
Long, J. C. (John), 76, 82
Long, J. R. (Julian), 230
Long, Roxie Davis, 93
Looney, J. F., 72, 76
Looney, L. B., 63
Louis Werner Saw Mill Company, 152
Lovelady, Bob, 245
Loveless, Mary E., 82
Lover's Leap, 28
Lowrey, M. P., 142
Lowry, Robert, 29
Lowry, Robert, Jr., 29
Loyal Leagues, 49
Luck, 68
Luster, Adline, 94
Luster, Alrada, 94
Luster, Arvilla, 94
Luster, Dolphus, 94
Luster, G. M. (Mart), 94
Luster, Isom, 94
Luster, Jonah, 94
Luster, Len, 94
Luster, Viola, 94
Luster, Walker, 94
Lynch, Charles, 89
Lynn, 25

M

Mabry, T. O., Jr., 219
Macedonia, 210
Macedonia Missionary Baptist Church, 69
Macedonia Public Free School, 69
Macedonia School, 70
Mackey's Creek, 2, 3, 4, 5, 9, 28-29, 32, 41, 42, 47, 55, 61, 85, 86, 124, 256
Mackey's Creek Primitive Baptist Church, 27, 29-30, 47
Macon, 158
Madison-Ridgeland, 243
Malone, C. C., 34
Malone, C. E., 213-214
Malone, Mrs. C. E., 213-214
Malone, Lumis, 213-214
Malone, Wayne, 214
Malone, Winona, 214
Manley, Billy, 182
Mann, 68, 82, 87
Mann, A. V., 166
Mann, Amon, 68, 98
Mann, Brison, 209

Mann, Charlie, 68
Mann, Eber, 194
Mann, Emmett, 68, 82, 91
Mann, Etha, 8, 150, 219, 232
Mann, H., 198
Mann, Henry, 68
Mann, J. A., 191, 195, 196-197, 199
Mann, J. D. (John), 58, 68, 76, 86, 165, 187, 191, 195
Mann, J. R. (Rufus), 68, 76, 82, 87, 138
Mann, Jack, 209, 234, 236, 244, 247
Mann, John William, 166
Mann, Marion E., *See* Emmett Mann
Mann, Ruth, 223
Mann, Whitfield E., 68, 82, 98
Marietta, 9, 61, 120, 131, 135, 146, 163, 194
Mars Hill, Ala., 28
Marshall County, 17
Marshall, Vaudie, 245
Martin, Ben, Branch, 3, 75, 94, 256
Martin, Bill (G. W.), 116, 153, 184

Martin, Billy, 233, 241
Martin, Elizabeth, 30
Martin, Fred, 121-122
Martin, G. C. (George), 115, 162, 165, 180, 183
Martin, Jerry, 242, 243
Martin, John R., 23, 30, 32, 34
Martin School, 69, 94
Martin, W. A., 58
Martin, W. T., 69
Martin, William, 21
Matthews, D. N., 45
Matthews, David, 43
Matthews, H. L., 154
Matthews, J. P., 89
Matthews, V. L., 154
Maulden, Andrew, 26
Maulden, Hiram, 21-22
Maulden, Isaac, 21
Maulden, S. R., 39
Mauldin, 67
Mauldin Branch, 3, 67, 256
Mauldin, R. T., 91
Maxey, Burton, 182
Mayfield, Jimmy, 229
Mayfield, Kentucky, 162
Mayhall, Bill, 182
Mayhall, Bob (R. S.), 148, 183

Mayhall, Elijah, 69
Mayhall, Henry E., 17, 173, 184, 186, 188, 191, 195
Mayhall, Kenneth E., 110, 212, 217, 236
Mayhall, M. J., 125
Mayhall, Mrs. Sam, 193
Mayhall, Thomas, 86
Mayhall, Willie, 86
Mayhall's Store, 148, 158
Maynard's Cove, 23
Mayo, Ruth McCreary, 46
McAnally, Charles, 212, 214, 225
McAnally, Mrs. Charles (Irene), 212, 214, 227, 229, 231
McAnally, Claude, 94
McAnally, Jerry, 242
McAnally, Lyman C., 223, 227, 229, 231, 234, 241
McAnally, Marie, 210
McCants, Bob, 175
McCarver, R. C., 222
McClung, 34
McClung, David, 21, 22, 35, 47
McClung, W. T., 76
McClung, William, 34
McCollum, W. B., 58
McCormack, W. R. (Rady), 147-148, 149, 162, 171
McCormack, Mrs. W. R. (Edna), 147-148
McCoy, L. D., 160, 162-163, 164, 170
McCreary, Andrew, 30
McCreary, Andy, 43, 46
McCreary, Frances, 30
McCreary, Phillip, 228
McCreary, Sallie Harris, 40
McCulloch, E. L., 63, 66, 72
McCulloch, James W., 35
McDonald, F. M., 76
McDougal, J. W., 45
McDougal, James F., 24
McDougal, Mary, 25
McGavock, W. J., 55
McKinney, Jack, 66, 67
McKinney, Kenneth, 229, 235
McKinney, Ray, 222
McKinney, Rob, 29
McLane, Mildred, 187
McLaurin, A. J., 74
McMechan, Robert C., 55
McMurray, J. C., 234
McRae, 23, 33, 51
McRae, A. C., 87

McRae, Amanda, 19
McRae Cemetery, 19, 258
McRae, Edith, 157
McRae, Inez, 195
McRae, John, 4, 19, 34, 47, 50, 63, 70
McRae, John, water mill, 63
McRae, K. F., 63, 86, 107, 110, 113, 115, 116, 126, 129, 135, 146, 149, 152, 157, 171, 176, 191, 239
McRae, Kenneth, 33
McRae Lumber Company, 166
Medford, Harvey, 60-61
Melton, Willie D., 21
Memphis, 1, 13, 46, 199, 242; *see also* Chickasaw Bluffs
Memphis and Charleston Railroad, 40
Meridian, 42
Meriwether, David, 13
Mero District, 12
Merora, 71
Messer, 69
Messer, J. F., 69
Methodist Episcopal Church South (Belmont), 116
Methodist Episcopal Church South (Belmont Circuit), 136
Methodist Episcopal Church South (Golden), 137
Methodist Episcopal Church South (New Valley Grove Church), 72
Methodist Episcopal Church South (Old Bethel), 26
Methodist Episcopal Church South (Patterson Chapel), 88
Milam, A. N., 177
Miller, Albert, 175
Miller, J. C., 86
Miller, Richard (R. A.), 111, 175, 187, 195, 201
Millican, 121, 147, 148
Millican, C. A. (Dolphus), 120, 121-122, 135, 137, 140, 144, 146, 147, 148
Millican, Dora, 135, 147
Millican, G. T., 43
Millican theater, 148, 161
Millican, William, 45, 120
Mills, Sanders, 29
Mineral Springs School, 63, 87, 173
Mingo, 2, 9, 87, 232

Mink, 69, 111
Mink, N. B., 88, 98, 111, 136
Minute Men, Tishomingo County, 142
Mississippi A. & I. Board, 213, 214, 234
Mississippi and Alabama Railroad, *see* Illinois Central Railroad
Mississippi Code of 1906, 110-111
Mississippi Legislators Day, 236
Mississippi Power Company, 173, 183, 186, 188
Mississippi River campaign, 42
Mississippi Secession Convention, 35, 37
Mississippi Utilities Company, 193
Mitchell, Archie, 230, 231
Mitchell, Becky Davis, 93
Mitchell, C. O., 213
Mitchell, Jerome, 20
Mitchell, Jim, 70
Mitchell, M. W., 243
Mitchell, Margaret Hopkins, 21
Mobile, Alabama, 193
Monroe, Charles E., 235

Monroe, S. B., 52
Monroe, Wincy, 52
Montgomery, Ala., 37
Montgomery, Alexander Houston, 25, 26
Montgomery, Booker, 25, 70
Montgomery, C. Allan, 232
Montgomery, Dexter, 235, 237
Montgomery, Floyd, 236
Montgomery, G. C., 173
Montgomery, George Houston, 25, 43
Montgomery, J. T. (Jim Tom), 43, 44, 72, 107, 116
Montgomery, James G., 70
Montgomery, Lee (R. L.), 86, 105, 107, 110, 113, 126, 135
Montgomery, Martha, 44
Montgomery, Walton, 138, 221
Montgomery, Mrs. Walton (Bonnie), 230
Moody, Fayette, 45
Moody, J. C., 50
Moody, Jack, 64
Moody, Jeff, 45
Moody, Olivia, 210
Moore, 34, 51
Moore, Ben, 177

Moore, Blake, 220, 223, 227
Moore, Brewer, 220, 246
Moore, Buck, 193
Moore, Byrd, 223
Moore, C. L., 165
Moore, Callaway A., 23, 63
Moore, Callaway, water mill, 63, 147
Moore Chevrolet Company, 246
Moore-Deaton Barber Shop, 217
Moore, Emily A., 58
Moore, G. M. (Murph), 171, 176
Moore, Gene, 235, 245, 247
Moore, Hardie, 193, 201, 222
Moore, Hugh, 32
Moore, Jim 222
Moore, Johnny B., 242, 246
Moore, Lucy McDougal, 30
Moore, Paul, 217, 220, 225, 227, 237
Moore, R. J. (Will), 38, 42, 43, 45, 62
Moore, Robert, 23
Moore, Roger, 229, 233
Moore, Stephen R., 23, 30, 34, 42
Moore, Steve, 58, 120
Moore, Steve, Jr., 177
Moore, Tom (T. J.), 139, 165
Moore, W. C., 82
Moore, Willy Robert (Will), 58
Moore's Mill, 1, 3, 6, 17, 26, 27, 40, 47, 50, 58, 82, 83, 119, 120, 133, 176-177
Moreland, George, 180-181
Mormons, 54
Morris, George, Jr. 242
Morse, William C., 28
Mt. Pisgah Methodist Protestant Church, 66
Mt. Zion Methodist Church, 69
Murphree, Dennis, 172
Murphy Shoe Shop, 232
Murray, 162
Muscle Shoals, Ala., 143

N

Nabers, 69
Nabers Store, 52
Nabers, W. N., 52
Nagasaki, 211
Nash Store, 131
Nashville, Tenn., 1, 12
Natchez, 12
Natchez Trace, 9, 12, 15, 23, 232
National Guard, 231

Neil, 3, 4, 102, 128
Nelson, Charles, 180-181, 189
Nelson, Mrs. Charles, 189
Nelson, John M., 55, 59, 60
Nelson, John M., and Company, 55
Nelson, John M., Jr., 55, 59
Nelson, Marion E., 59
Nelson and McMechan, 55
Nelson, R. A., 137, 144
Nelson, Willie Mae, 140
Nettleton, 180, 236
New Baptist Church, 209
New Bethel, 1, 3, 6, 17, 50, 70, 83, 133, 238
New Bethel Baptist Church, 70; *see also* Bethel Baptist Church
New Bethel School, 70, 84, 182
New Deal, 190-191, 195
New Home Church, 91
New Providence Primitive Baptist Church, 6, 19, 20, 34, 53-54, 64, 79, 95, 100
New Site, 82, 123, 219, 238
New Valley Methodist Church, 72-73, 83, 88
Nichols, Hugh, 91, 202, 241, 243
Nichols, Joan, 242
Nix, A. M., 155
Nix, J. M., 98
Nobles, 175
Noel, Edmond F., 110, 119, 123, 126
Noel, H. M., 97, 98
Noel Survey (Belmont), 96, 97, 98, 100, 106, 205
Norman, John, 41
Norman, Phebe, 41
North American Mogul Products Company, 237
Northcutt, Louise, 223
Northeast Mississippi Medical Society, 234
Northeast Mississippi Planning and Development District, 245
Northington, Leon, 72
North Pontotoc, 243

O

Oak Farm, 35, 50, 51, 52, 53, 68
Oaks, Curg, 63, 64
Oaks, Grady, 64, 148
Oaks, J. F., 127
Oaks, Millard, 194
O'Brien, A. E., 170

Ocean Springs, 229
Old Bethel, 1, 3, 6, 17, 25-26, 27, 44, 50, 51, 70, 133, 137
Old Bethel Cemetery, 25, 258
Old Bethel Methodist Church, 26, 70
Old Mackey's Creek Church Cemetery, 30, 32, 258
Old Tishomingo County, 10, 17-18, 19, 20, 21, 23, 24, 25, 29, 30, 33, 34, 35, 37, 39, 42, 46, 47-48, 142
Old Union Baptist Church, 52, 208
O-nah-ho-chubby, 18, 19
O'Riley, Phillip, 18
Osbirn, Maudie Stacy, 43, 81
Overton, John, 13
Owens, Billy, 214
Owens, T. D. (Dolan), 228
Ozark community, 105
Ozbirn, Carl, 214
Ozbirn, Mrs. Carl, 214
Ozbirn, J. T. (Thomas), 214, 215, 216, 219, 221, 228, 229, 230, 231
Ozbirn, Mrs. J. T., 214
Ozbirn, Martha Jane Davis, 93
Ozbirn, Thomas L., 228

P

Pace, Earl, 244
Paden, 25, 87, 194
Paden, Alexander, 23, 25
Paden, Catherine, 24
Paden, D. D., 98
Paden, Daniel A., 23, 24
Paden, David, 23, 25
Paden, Elizabeth, 24
Paden, Jessie E., 59
Paden, Margaret, 24
Paden, Porter (H. P.), 24, 41
Paden, Ramsey, 59
Paden, Robert W., 23, 24
Paden, W. A., 46, 47, 58
Page, R. L., Jr., 135, 140, 141, 145, 146, 147-148
Page, R. L., Music Company, 140
Page, R. L., Quartet, 147
Palmer camp, 95
Panola County, 17
Pardue, C. G., 32
Pardue, D. G., 46
Pardue, K. H. (Bud), 74
Pardue, Maurine, 215

Pardue, Otis, 62
Pardue, P. G., 50
Pardue, Pam, 247
Pardue, W. P., 45, 47
Parker, Debbie, 247
Parker, J. E., 209
Parker, M. L., 91
Parker, Suzie, 192
Parnell, E. F., 128
Parrish, Rob, 10, 68
Pate, 25, 69
Pate, C. L., 69, 82
Pate, Ed, 116
Pate, Georgia, 176
Pate, H. D., 110, 126
Pate, H. L., 127
Pate, Lewis, 32
Pate, Troy, 116
Pate, W. L., 87
Patrick, 143
Patterson, 69, 111
Patterson, A. W., 69
Patterson, Aubrey, 215, 244
Patterson, B. F., 98
Patterson, B. N., 132, 137, 138, 141, 164, 186, 191, 193
Patterson, Mrs. B. N. (Belle), 116, 198

Patterson, Mrs. Ben, 72
Patterson Chapel Methodist Church, 69, 79, 88, 169, 238
Patterson Chapel Public Free School, 69, 84, 158
Patterson, Charlie Gaines, 214
Patterson, D. D., 209
Patterson Ford, 68
Patterson Gin, 120, 164, 189
Patterson, Hardin, 35, 42, 47, 50, 55, 69
Patterson, Mrs. J. C. (Louise), 157
Patterson, J. F., 52
Patterson, J. N. (John), 86, 91, 96, 97, 107, 116, 120, 129, 137, 138, 141, 144, 147, 148, 154
Patterson, P. W., 97, 99, 101
Patterson, Richard, 10
Patterson, W. H., 98, 111, 136-137, 152, 188, 195
Patton, Nadine, 245
Payne, Erskine, 235
Payne, Hoyle, 235, 237, 238, 241, 242, 243, 247
Pearl Harbor, 207
Peoples Bank and Trust Co., 169

Perry Branch, 3, 63, 256
Perry, G. M., 63, 87
Perry, R. M., 73
Perry, W. M. (Bill), 165
Perryville, Kentucky, 45
Petersburg, Battle of, 43, 44-45
Pharr, 26
Pharr, B. S. (Smith), 182
Pharr, Barbara, 242
Pharr, Bill, 70
Pharr, Donna, 242, 243
Pharr, Frank, 182
Pharr, Holland (J. H.), 43, 70, 87, 136, 137, 173
Pharr, Holland, water mill, 70, 87, 173
Pharr, J. M., 107
Pharr, J. N., 208
Pharr, James N. T., *see* Turner Pharr
Pharr, Jim, 70
Pharr, John Christian, 25
Pharr Mounds, 9
Pharr, "Red," 163
Pharr School, 137, 173, 182
Pharr, Thomas, 25
Pharr, Tom (T. C.), 165. 186
Pharr, Turner, 70, 87

Phillips, 2, 44, 53
Phillips, Ada, 65
Phillips, Bill, 192
Phillips, Dave, 65
Phillips, David, 23
Phillips, Dema Cornelius, 65
Phillips, Genia, 223
Phillips, L. G. (Leonard), 64, 219, 223, 230
Phillips, Lucy Davis, 93
Phillips, N. L., 89, 127, 169
Phillips, O. L., 43, 58, 63, 64, 82, 91, 93
Phillips, Pat, 235
Phillips, W. A. (Dolphus), 199
Pilley, J. E., 166
Pilley, Mrs. J. E., 180
Pilley, Nell Rose, 157
Pines, 128
Pittsburg, 1, 10, 20-21, 22, 39, 51, 66-67, 184, 199
Pittsburg Cemetery, 23, 67, 258
Pittsburg Ferry, 19-20, 22
Pittsburg Ford, 3, 10, 68
Pittsburg Public Free School, 67, 176
Pleasant Hill F. & A.M. Lodge No. 237, 35, 82, 119; *see also*

Belmont F. & A. M. Lodge No. 237
Pleasant Ridge, 52, 69, 82
Pleasant Valley, 9, 27, 38, 127
Plumer, D. Catherine, 223
Pogo, Ala., 72, 133, 166
Pontotoc, 13, 17, 19
Pontotoc County, 17
Pontotoc Creek, Treaty of, 14-15, 17
Poole, Wallace, 220, 221, 227
Pounders, A. S., 209
Pounders Department Store, 184
Pounders, Grover, 54, 71, 165
Pounds, Carlton, 236
Pounds, Samuel, 46
Pounds, Seth, 169, 171, 173, 176, 191
Powers, James W., 110
Prentiss County, 7, 17, 27, 38, 48, 70, 120, 121, 127, 165, 169, 208
Prestage, John "Bo," 208-209
Prestage, Paul, 229, 243
Price, Sterling, 41
Prospect, 2, 4, 68, 82, 87
Prospect Baptist Church, 68, 76, 82, 91
Prospect Cemetery, 68, 208, 258
Prospect School, 68
Providence, 51, 63, 83
Pruitt, M. P., 209
Pruitt, Sidney, 66
Public Works Administration, 195-196, 198
Purdy, Tom, 45
Purple Shell Springs, 61, 131
Purvis, 238

Q
Qualls, Henry, 175
Quinn, H. F., 152, 187

R
Ramsey, Tom, 69
Randolph, 235
Ratliff, Don, 218
Ratliff, Jean, 241, 243
Ratliff, Leon H., 3, 217-218, 234, 236
Reager, John, 18
Reagor, J. D., 35
Red Bay, Ala., 1, 6, 52, 102, 131, 133, 144-145, 169, 174, 183, 189, 194, 232, 234, 235, 243

Red Bud Baptist Church, 76, 91
Red Bud Creek, 3, 5, 10, 26, 27, 47, 56, 58, 70, 71, 87, 173, 256
Red Bud School, 82, 120, 182
Redden, John M., 47
Red Hill Church, 66
Reed, Dewey, 220, 231, 239
Reed, Lessie, 120
Reeves, 25
Reeves, Phillip, 25, 237, 238
Reid, Ephraim, 20
Regan, George, 50
Reno Crossing, 71
Reno, E. H., 55
Rester, Ruth, 239
Revised Code of 1871, 50-51
Reynolds, Arthur E., 38
Reynolds, Bluford, 21
Reynolds, C., 21
Reynolds, T. M., 18
Rhodes Barber Shop, 104
Rhodes, Charlene Cox, 228
Rial, Roy, 239
Rice Grant, 13
Richardson, Wiley, 187, 194
Richmond, Va., 38, 43, 44
Riddle, 161-162
Riddle, Charles, 29
Riddle, Elliot, 45
Riddle, James M., 30, 47
Riddle, William H., 30, 45
Ridge, 41, 43, 198
Riley, L. C., 218
Robbins, Verlia Dean, 211
Roberts, B. N., 136
Robertson, James, 12
Robins, Jephtha, 21
Robinson, Jack, 247
Robinson, John, 31, 32, 46
Rock Creek, 3, 4, 9, 19, 23, 59, 62, 63, 139, 147, 173, 256
Rogers, Hugh, 18, 40
Roosevelt, Franklin D., 190, 207, 210
Rubin, Saul, 238
Ruple, Hubert, 63
Rushing, William, 45
Russell, Atha Wayne, 9
Russell, Bob, 3, 228
Russell, George, 45
Russell, J. H., 45
Russell, James M., 45
Russell, Jane, 52
Russell, John A., 23
Russell, W. A., 34

Russellville, Ala., 237
Russellville, Kentucky, 39
Ryan, Charles, 35, 40, 62
Ryan's Well, 152

S
Salem, 175
Salem Baptist Church, 76, 91
Samples, 25
San Jacinto, Battle of, 18
Sardis School, 66, 67
Sartain, A. R., 192
Sartain, Billy P., Grocery, 71, 95
Sartain, Carl, 54, 70
Sartain, Jim, 72
Sartain, L. F. (Lee), 86, 111, 127, 138, 165
Sartain, Mack, 244
Sartain, Mary A., 171
Sartain Texaco, 134
Sartain, Tom (J. T.), 66, 125, 129, 132, 133, 137, 171
Sartain, W. A., 43, 66, 67, 87
Saucier, J. H. (John), 209
Savage, Alexander, 24
Savannah, Tennessee, 161, 193
Scott Central, 243
Scott's Mill, 33

Seago Annex, 151, 158
Seago, J. C. (John), 118, 146, . 147, 150, 151, 158
Searcy, Erwin, 45
Searcy, Jack, 59
Searcy, Nadine, 223
Searcy, Oscar, 215, 216, 217
Selby, 148
Selby, Elledge, 163
Selby, J. T., 165
Selby, T. J., 43, 82
Selby, T. L., 138, 146, 148, 164
Seminole, 102
Seneca Old Town, 12
Senter, E. G., 160
Senter, Jack M., 135, 217, 218, 233
Senter, Jackie, 229, 247
Senter, John, 135
Seviles, 25
Sexton, 150
Sexton, Ralph, 237
Shackelford, Elna C., 225
Shackelford, Stanley, 213
Shackelford, W. A. H., 23, 38, 44-45
Shackelford, W. B., 230
Shady Cove, 95, 154

Shannon, 238
Sheffield, Alabama, 161, 163
Shelton, Bud, 189, 191
Shelton, D. R., 113-114, 119, 136
Sherrill, Clyde, 209
Shewbart, Avie, 154
Shewbart, Ila, 154
Shewbart, Virgil A., 154
Shiloh, 37, 40
Shook, 22-23, 25, 34, 110, 142
Shook, Ann, 236, 241, 244
Shook, Arthur (M. A.), 109, 114, 119, 138, 140, 145, 153, 155, 156, 159, 161-162, 206-207, 260
Shook, Austin (W. A.), 146, 162, 163, 171
Shook, Billy, *see* W. W. Shook
Shook Brothers Supply Company, 159
Shook, C. C. (Lum), 22, 34, 45, 47, 58, 73, 74, 82, 83, 86, 91, 94, 95, 96, 97, 98, 104, 107-108, 109-110, 113, 115, 116, 118, 119, 121, 126, 128, 129-130, 131, 132, 134, 136, 159, 260
Shook, Carter (C. S.), 74, 85, 86, 113, 127, 139, 140, 149, 191, 195, 199, 204, 205
Shook, Claude, 121-122
Shook, Floyd, 199
Shook, Frances, 182
Shook, H. L. (Herbert), 118, 121-122, 182, 186-187, 191, 195, 199, 204
Shook, H. M. (Hatley), 76, 94, 109, 115, 118, 134, 135, 136, 141-142, 147, 159, 164, 169
Shook, H. M., Athletic Park, 191
Shook, Harold, 164
Shook, Henry, 39, 45
Shook, Howard, 204
Shook, Irby, 201
Shook, Jewell, 110
Shook, Jim (J. W.), 116, 118
Shook, John, 34
Shook, John Henry, 64-65, 67, 115, 140, 141
Shook, Lee, *see* R. L. Shook
Shook, Leon (Marcus L.), 194, 221
Shook, Lera, 164
Shook and Lindsey, 104, 113, 116, 130

Shook, M. M., 146

Shook, Mahala, 109

Shook, Mark (M. L.), 115, 116, 122, 123, 140, 149, 168

Shook, Mary A. (Ann), 74, 90, 98, 115-116, 198

Shook, Mary E., 73, 82, 97, 98, 109

Shook, "Mary Lum," 73

Shook, Michael (Mike), 23, 43, 59, 64, 87

Shook, Myrtle Clark, 73

Shook, Nina, 206

Shook, Noah, 22

Shook, Paratine Cole, 76

Shook, R. L., 73, 74, 83, 96, 98, 104, 109, 113, 115, 116, 118, 125, 129, 132, 133, 137, 140, 146, 150, 152, 166, 189, 191, 199

Shook, R. L., Lumber Co., 166

Shook, Raymond, 245, 247

Shook, S. T., 45

Shook, Solomon, 22, 109

Shook, T. O., 146

Shook, W. O., 195, 201, 209

Shook, W. R., 208

Shook, W. T., 73, 76, 94, 96, 104, 109, 140, 187, 209

Shook, W. T., General Merchandise, 94, 104, 106, 115

Shook, W. W., 59, 63, 86, 87, 107, 113, 115, 118, 119, 122, 126, 127, 129, 132, 146, 154, 162, 164, 171, 173, 179, 180, 181, 186, 188, 199, 235

Shook, Mrs. W. W. (Belle), 87, 115-116

Shook, William Wiley (Bill), 22, 109

Short, L. S., 120

Simmons, Frank, 18

Sims, G. W., 82

Sisk, Simon, 231

Skinner, G. G., 182

Skinner, Tom, 145

Slade and McElroy, 222

Slayton, L. A. (Louie), 213, 215

Small, W. E., 96

Smith, 201, 231

Smith, Alfred, 19

Smith, E. W. (Eddie), 201

Smith, G. B., 146

Smith-Hughes program, 191-192

Smith, Jeff, 131

Smith, John P., 20

Smith, P., 34
Smith, Pete, 45
Smith, T. S. (Sank), 168
Smith, Mrs. T. S. (Hattie V.), 198, 216
Smith, Tom, 9
Smith, V. B. (Vinson), 181-182, 186
Smith, W. A. (Tack), 187, 195, 201, 209
Smith, Willie, 3
Smithville, 194
Snodgrass, Homer, 204
Snow, 93
South, J. S. (Steve), 227, 231, 232
South Pontotoc, 247
South, R. Q. (Crit), 194
South Tishomingo Consolidated School, 3, 120, 178, 182, 220
Sparks, 4
Sparks, Bryan, 214
Sparks, Eugene, 210, 215
Sparks, Harold C., 242, 245
Sparks, Hollis D., 235
Sparks, James, 43
Sparks, Luther, 83
Sparks, O. E., 194, 220, 223, 228

Sparks, O. E., Grocery and Market, 119, 194, 232
Sparks, R. T., 148, 162
Sparks, Robert, 234
Sparks, Ross, 19, 23, 63
Spears, George, 69
Spears, Paul, 234
Spencer, J. E., 52
Spencer, Kathy, 241
Spigner, Ira (Hump), 175
Spring City, Tennessee, 193
Spring Creek Academy, 24
Stacy, Billy, 81
Stacy, Claude, 245
Stacy, J. W., 45
Stacy, T. F., 43, 45
Stacy, W. T., 113, 177, 182
Stafford, James B., 24
Stanphill, Addis, 247
Stanphill Ford, 68
Stanphill, J. P., 88, 98
Stanphill and Johnson, 149
Stanphill, Sarah, 94
Stanphill, T. A., 98
Stanphill, T. C. (Tommy), 116, 119, 149, 171, 235
Stanphill, T. M., 113
Stanphill, V. S. (Vince), 69, 86,

94, 96, 98
Stantonville Telephone Company, 127
Stapps Writing School, 89
State Line, 210
Stephens, Alfred, 26
Stephens, Billy V., 93, 120, 217, 234, 236
Stephens, C. W. (Carey), 163, 184, 193, 204, 207, 208, 209, 212, 215
Stephens, G. C., 187
Stephens, Gladys, 241, 244, 246
Stephens, J. E. (Joe), 162, 165-166, 171, 173, 179, 184, 220
Stephens, James, 91, 96, 120, 223, 229, 231
Stephens, Joe K., 18
Stephens, John William, 23
Stephens, William, 23
Stephens, William Alexander, 43
Stepp, Horace, 9, 70
Stevens, Joshua, 35
Steve's Surplus Sales, 161, 168
Stewart, 25
Stewart, John, 26
Stewart, Mary, 26
Stewart, O. W., 35

Stockton, Beulah, 160, 172, 199
Stockton, J. S. (Joe), 43, 52, 75, 76, 91, 113, 121
Stockton, John, 236
Stockton, Lottie, (Mrs. W. O.), 109
Stockton, W. O. (Oscar), 81, 127, 128, 129, 140, 141, 147, 149
Storment, W. T., 128
Storment, William, 46
Strickland, Arlie, 224
Strickland, Belle, 149-150
Strickland, Benjamin P., 142
Strickland, Donna, 243
Strickland, Ed, 142, 146, 147, 149, 165, 172, 182
Strickland, J. B., 149-150, 196
Strickland, Merle Whitfield, 224
Strickland, S. S., 147, 154, 169, 176, 182, 198, 204, 205, 208, 209, 214, 216, 217, 220, 223, 227, 230
Strickland, Spencer, 176, 196
Stricklin, George W., 181
Suggs, William, 18
Sumners, Cecil L., 216
Sumners, J. W. (Warren), 176,

181, 182
Sumners, S. L. (Bud), 131, 137, 141, 144, 148, 165, 168, 176, 179, 195, 199, 204, 205, 208, 216, 219, 260
Sunnybrook Children's Home, 244
Sunshine Mills, 169
Sweat, L. N., 71

T
Tankersley, G. J., 119
Tankersley, George, 32, 33, 46
Tankersley, W., 121
Tankersley, W. A., 39
Tate, Lizzie C., 55
Tate, Sam, Jr., 55
Tatum, 169
Taylor, Albert, 45
Taylor, Albert D., 176
Taylor, Mrs. Blanchard, 182
Taylor, J. C. (Jess), 220
Taylor, Jeannie, 242
Taylor, Larry Don, 242
Taylor, Luther, 73, 220, 235
Taylor, Mitch, 45
Taylor, W. P., 165, 182
Taylor, Wesley, 45

Ten Islands, 3
Tennessee River, 2, 10, 13
Tennessee-Tombigbee Waterway, 61
Terry, 244
Terry, J. C. (Carroll), 33, 38, 46
Tesseneer, J. H., 209
Tesseneer Texaco Station, 104, 134
Tesseneer, Wilbur, 75
Texas Eastern Transmission Corp., 219
Thanksgiving of 1945, 212
Thirty-second Mississippi, 38, 142
Thomas Drug Store, 168
Thomas, Shearer, 180
Thomas, Web, 94
Thomas, Willis, 69
Thompson, John M., 47
Thompson, William, 30
Thorn, Charlie S., 186, 189, 191, 195
Thorn, Hubert, 10
Thorn, Thomas, 20
Thorne, 10
Thorne, Larue, 241
Thornton, Clyde (Bill), 194

Thrasher, 194
Thrasher, Arial (Bib), 175
Thrasher, Floyd (Dock), 175
Thrasher, Tom, 243
Thrasher, Toy, 175, 187, 195, 201, 209
Threadgill, Daniel, 149, 173
Threadgill and Ozbirn, 164
Three Forks, 166
Three Hollows, 187
Tidwell, Billy H., 242
Tidwell, Hildred J., 235
Tidwell, J. W., 209
Tidwell, Kathleen, 242
Tiffin, 184-185
Tiffin, Hobson, 194, 219, 232
Tiffin, W. V. (Bud), 182, 184-185
Tilghman, Lloyd, 39
Timbes, James, 113
Timbs, Bob, 4
Timbs, Charlie, 68
Timms, Jimmy, 245
Tippah County, 17
Tippamingo Conference, 243
Tipton, 33
Tipton, J. H., 45
Tishomingo, 1, 4, 6, 25, 102, 131, 146, 161, 163, 164, 187, 192, 194, 232, 239
Tishomingo Banking Company, 116, 127
Tishomingo, Chief, 13, 14, 15, 16
Tishomingo County, 1, 2, 4, 10, 15, 16, 17-18, 19, 20, 21, 23, 24, 25, 29, 30, 33, 34, 35, 37, 39, 42, 46, 47-51, 52, 53, 57, 58, 60, 62, 66, 86, 119, 120, 127, 139, 142, 143, 152, 165, 169, 182, 183, 187, 195, 205, 207, 215, 216, 218, 225, 227, 230, 231, 234, 236, 237, 238, 239, 241, 242, 243, 248, 254, 255
Tishomingo County population, 49, 57, 77, 120, 152, 183, 205, 218, 231, 243
Tishomingo County Singing Convetion, 140-141
Tishomingo School, 131
Tishomingo State Park, 4, 190, 232, 236
Tittle, J. C., 58
Toland, Isaac, 20
Toland, J., 34

Toland, J. W., 39
Toland, Jake, 45
Toland, W. M., 87, 91
Tombigbee Baptist Association, 91
Tombigbee River, 2, 10, 85
Tomlinson, A. J., 208
Tories, 40, 41-42, 46
Tornado of 1913, 131, 146
Totten and Loving, 195
Treaty of 1805, 13
Treaty of 1816, 13
Treaty of 1818, 13
Treaty of Doaksville, 15
Treaty of Hopewell, 12
Treaty of Pontotoc Creek, 14, 15, 17
Treaty of Washington (1834), 15
Tremont, 194
Trentham, 187
Tri-County Singing Convention, 140
Trimm, Ila, 223
Trollinger, 86
Trollinger, A. J., 4, 115
Trollinger, Mrs. A. J., 115
Trollinger, A. J., water mill, 63, 147

Trollinger, Lemuel, 58
Truman, Harry, 211
Tunica County, 17
Tupelo, 1, 60, 61, 161, 169, 198, 239
Turner, George, 175
Turner, Roscoe, 141
Turvaville, Carl, 177
T. V. A., 196, 243
Twenty-sixth Mississippi Regiment, 38, 39, 42, 43, 44-45, 109
Twitchell, M. H., 189
Tynes, 59, 62, 63, 82
Tynes, Carl, 62, 122
Tynes, Henry, 62, 86
Tynes, Mollie, 136
Tyson, W. H. H., 32

U

Underwood, Hector, 168
Union Missionary Batist Church, 52, 76, 91, 208; *see also* Old Union Baptist Church
Union School, 87
Union Telephone Company, 132-133, 154
Upton, T. L., 125

Urban Renewal program, 233

Voyles, James, 42

V

Valley, 1, 3, 10, 52, 67, 82, 86, 87, 133, 166, 167, 188, 189, 195, 208, 215, 225, 239
Valley Methodist Church, 72
Valley School, 87, 167, 182, 188, 215, 225
Vandiver, J. S., 207
Vardaman, James K., 123
Vaughn, G. W., Jr., 50, 63
Vaughn, Horace (Jack), 68, 236
Vaughn, J. T., 58, 73, 111, 187, 191, 192
Vaughn, Joe, 190
Vaughn, Sam, 43
Vaughn, Tulon, 190
V. F. W., 243
Vicksburg, 39, 42, 215
Vina, Ala., 102, 194
Vicennes Bridge Company, 91
Vincent, J. A., 162
Vinson, 25, 34, 73
Vinson, Ambrose, 87, 173
Vinson, Bam (L. A.), 21, 156
Vinson, J. F., 58
V-J Day, 211

W

Waddell, Frank, 194
Waddle, 70
Waddle, A. J., 234, 247
Waddle, B. D. (Boss), 182, 195
Waddle, M. B., 91
Waddle, Marion, Sr., 70
Wade, Margaret, 215
Waldrep, 19
Waldrep, Dayton, 131
Wall, Bobbie Jean, 245
Wall, James S. (Jim), 74, 239
Wall Street crash, 179, 182
Wambi, 98
Wamsley, 98
Wamsley, R. E., 128
Ward, A. F., 186
Ward, Earl, 192, 194, 195
Ward, J. C. (Jess), 186, 187, 188, 191, 195
Ward, Price, 188
Warm Springs, Ga., 210
Warren, Benny, 70
Warren, E. R., 175, 193, 209
Warren, Isom J., 42
Warren, James, 69

Warren, N. B., 35, 40, 62
Warren Piano House, 232
Warren, Sid, 175
Warrior Water Company, 176
Washington, Treaty of, 15
Weatherford, G. W., 52
Weatherford, S. N., 52
Weatherford, Sarah, 52
Weatherford, Z. L., 136, 234
Weatherly, Jim, 229
Webber, F. R., 137
Weems, 25, 26
Weinsten, Milton, 233
Welborn, Hugh, 229
Weldon Railroad, Battle of, 43
Western Auto Store, 105
West Lauderdale, 236
West Point, 18
Wheeler, 194
White, 10
White, Andrew, 94, 121
White, Candler, 164
White, E. F., 222, 228
White, H. J., 34
White, John, 20
White, Mary, 52
White, Rachel, 30
White, S. T., 98

White, W. F., 52
White, Wayne, 242
Whitehead, 25, 87
Whitehead, Edgar, 173, 182
Whitehead, Helen, 183
Whitehead, Henry, 70
Whitehead, J. S., 154
Whitehead, J. S. (Sion), 70, 76
Whitehead, Joseph, 70
Whitehead, Kelvy, 183
Whitehead, M. R., 23
Whitehead, Mahala A., 70
Whitehead, Martha, 164, 183
Whitehead, Mary, 133-134
Whitehead, W. R., 76
Whitfield, 68
Whitfield, A. D. (Dave), 189, 195, 199, 204, 230
Whitfield, Blanche, 178
Whitten, Jamie, 245
Wicks, Moses J., 46, 55
Wicks, Sarah A., 55
Wicks, Wiggs, and Hart, 46
Wiggins, 111
Wiggins, Golden Patrie, 98
Wiggins, Jim, 98
Wiggins, Mrs. Jim, 98
Wigginton, 25

Wigginton, Dallas, 26, 70
Wigginton, E. A., 208
Wigginton, Elmer, 208
Wigginton, James, 229
Wigginton, P. A., 201
Wigginton, S. A., 208
Wigginton, Silas, 182
Wiggs, Alexander R., 46, 54
Wiginton, E. E., 111
Wilderness, Battle of the, 42
Wilemon, J. P., Jr., 234, 241, 244, 247
Williams, Billy Walker, *see* W. W. Williams
Williams, "Cowhide," 67
Williams, Elizabeth, 64, 91
Williams, Mrs. Fayette, 18
Williams, Glenn B., 215
Williams, James, 45
Williams, Pearl, 172
Williams, Phillip, 234
Williams, R. L., 76
Williams, Robert, 73
Williams, Vernon, 175
Williams, W. M. 45
Williams, W. W. (Billy Walker), 117, 118, 125, 127, 137, 140, 145, 147, 168

Williams, Mrs. W. W., 127
Wilson Dam, 143
Wilson, J. M., 45
Wilson, J. N., 47
Wilson, John, 50
Wilson, Mark (J.M.), 207, 208, 209, 212, 215, 216, 217
Wilson, W. L. (Leon), 230
Wilson, Woodrow, 128, 136, 141, 144
Winchester, Marcus, 13
Winchester, Rachel Epps, 185
Winegar, John, 44
Winfield Manufacturing Company, 233, 234-235, 236
Witt Lake, 196
Wofford, Charlie, 68
Wofford, Charlie, sorghum mill, 68, 112
Womack, 25, 26, 44
Womack, Andrew J., 25
Womack, Elizabeth, 25
Womack, George L., 43
Womack, Keturah Allen, 27
Womack, Louvicia, 25
Womack, Martha, 44
Womack, Nathan, 25, 26
Womack, William P. (Bill), 27,

Wood, A. J., 39, 43, 46
Wood, Ab, Branch, 2-3, 256
Wood, Bill (W. C.), 91, 113
Wood, Bill, Ford, 68
Wood, Bob (R. L.), 195
Wood, Mrs. Dalton, 72
Wood, Henry, 161
Wood, J. M., 74
Wood, Olivia, 173
Wood, Ruth, 238
Wood, Savilla, 132
Wood, Sid (S. J.), 113
Wood, Verna, 182, 227
Wood, W. J., 189
Wood, Will, 72
Woodall Mountain, 208
Woodley, Gertrude, 182
Woodruff, Fred, 45
Woodruff, Fred B., 172
Woodruff, J. M., 142, 146, 147, 154, 155, 156
Woodruff, S. C., 26
Woodruff, Thad, 45
Woodruff, W. H., 34
Woods, Bobby, 69, 94
Wooten, George, 216
Wooten, Ricky, 246-247
World War I, 128, 136, 141-142, 144-146, 147, 158
World War II, 200, 201, 204-205, 207, 209, 210-212, 213, 214
WPA (Works Progress Administration), 190, 195-196, 197, 198
Wren, Annie, 131
Wright, 116
Wright, A. J. B., 34
Wright, B. E. (Ellis), 119, 133, 137, 141, 146, 147, 148, 149, 154, 162, 169, 171, 186, 193, 195, 198, 204, 208, 217
Wright, B. E., Jr., 220, 227, 229, 231, 232, 233, 236, 239
Wright, B. F. (Ben), 62, 107, 119, 131, 133, 136, 147, 150, 152, 172
Wright, Ben, 209
Wright, C. B. (Ben), 70, 140, 141, 146, 149, 154, 171, 195, 199, 208
Wright, Clay, 114, 119, 133, 152, 169, 173, 179, 186, 199, 208, 217, 220, 232
Wright, Mrs. Clay, 198

Wright, Elizabeth, 47
Wright, Forest, 107
Wright, I. J., 147
Wright, Isaac W., 32, 34
Wright, J. K., 45
Wright, J. T., 33
Wright, Martha Ann, 119, 172
Wright, Mary Fisher, 245
Wright, Toy, 119, 162
Wright and Winsett, 111
Wygle, Ephraim H., 18, 28, 32
Wylie, Isabelle, 24

Y

Yancy, Thomas E., 72
Yarber, Anthony, 75, 121-122, 138, 143, 145, 149, 162, 164, 170, 191, 192, 229, 246
Yarber, Betty Jo, 173
Yarber, Bob (Robert H.), 242, 244, 247
Yarber, Carroll (C. W.), 122, 188, 191, 193, 195
Yarber, Charles H., 121-122, 129, 134, 136, 145, 148, 162, 164, 173, 179, 186, 195, 199, 204, 205, 208, 209
Yarber, Claude (C. E.), 122, 195, 198-199, 204, 205
Yarber, Clyde (Peg), 190
Yarber, Floyd, 194
Yarber, G. W., 91
Yarber, Hallie, 41, 91
Yarber, Helen, 243, 246
Yarber, Henry (W. H.), 161, 173, 209, 214, 216, 219, 237
Yarber Insurance Agency, 198
Yarber, J., 113
Yarber, J. L., 140, 157
Yarber, Jack, 236, 241, 246
Yarber, Joe, 128
Yarber, Laura (Mrs. Charles), 109
Yarber, Lealon, 220-221, 227, 232, 235, 237
Yarber, Mae Bess, 173, 182, 245
Yarber, Olen, 121-122, 171
Yarber Pond, 155, 196
Yarber, Preston, 125, 128, 164, 184
Yarber, Quaye, 242
Yarber, R. L. (Tobe), 209-210
Yarber, Rae, 154, 239
Yarber, Raymond, 194, 220, 223, 228
Yarber Rexall Drugs, 104

Yarber, Sixty (S. L.), 154, 168, 215-216, 233, 234, 236, 241, 243

Yarbrough, Rosie Lee, 210

Yoncopin Pond, 3

York, Irene, 182

Young, 63

Young, Hubert, 152

Young, Ransom, 111, 128

Young, T. B., 88

Young, T. H. (Tom), 180-181, 189

Young, Mrs. T. H., 181, 189, 198

Made in the USA
Columbia, SC
17 May 2018